Dictionary of
Perfect Spelling

Christine Maxwell

This edition published in Great Britain by Barrington Stoke Ltd,
18 Walker St, Edinburgh, EH3 7LP

www.barringtonstoke.co.uk

Reprinted 2007

ISBN 978-1-84299-281-4

Edited by Julia Rowlandson and Jenny Watson
Cover design by Kate MacPhee

Trademarks
Words in this dictionary which we believe to be trademarks
have been acknowledged as such. The presence or absence of
such acknowledgements should not be regarded as affecting the
legal status of any trademark or proprietary name.

Typeset by GreenGate Publishing Services, Tonbridge TN9 2RN
Printed in Great Britain by The Charlesworth Group, 2007

Acknowledgements

I never dreamed that 30 years would go by before I would be involved in a Dictionary update. Nor did I ever imagine that even with tremendous advances in technology, producing a revised version would prove to be as hard – if not harder – than creating the original work.

I would like to thank in particular my development team members, Ajay Sreekanth and Bridget Samuels, for their respective expertise, ingenuity, unfailing patience and fortitude in working on the development of the misspelling program – which proved to be a formidable task!

My editorial team, made up of Pandora Maxwell, Matilda Maxwell, Sheryl Hiatt, Aude Letter and Arana Greenberg, all worked incredibly hard to revise the formatting and assist in the updating of the wordlist. Rosa Rankin is to be thanked for her work on the updating of the Appendices. I would also like to pay tribute to my original Perfect Spelling writing partner, Oliver Gregory, whose work and ability to create tough spelling practice exercises never ceased to inspire my efforts to work on helping others to solve the mysteries of British English spelling.

I cannot speak highly enough of the work of the Barrington Stoke editorial team led by Julia Rowlandson, assisted by Kate MacPhee, Alexandra Farrell and Ruth Paris. Jenny Watson's lexicographical knowledge and perceptive editing skills made a huge difference to the accuracy of the work as a whole. My very special thanks go to Julia Rowlandson, who managed with unfailing good humour and strong editorial guidance and encouragement to keep the project moving while juggling a million 'spelling issues' that needed to be worked out as the manuscript progressed.

My last words of thanks go to my husband Roger and to my long-suffering children, Xavier, Yuri and Giselle, for their patience and for many helpful and sometimes totally outrageous misspelling suggestions!

Christine Maxwell

Development Team

Ajay Sreekanth: Electronic Misspelling Program Director
Bridget Samuels: Linguistics, Phonology Director

Editorial Team

Pandora Maxwell, Matilda Maxwell, Sheryl Hiatt, Aude Letter,
Arana Greenberg

Appendices

Rosa Rankin, Consultant

Lexicographer

Jenny Watson

Barrington Stoke Editorial Team

Julia Rowlandson, Kate MacPhee, Alexandra Farrell, Ruth Paris

Preface

This dictionary is a completely revised and updated version of the original Pergamon *Dictionary of Perfect Spelling*, first published in 1977.

This new version contains over 20,000 headwords. The fully modernised word list includes words carefully selected from the National Curriculum. It has retained the unique feature of finding common misspellings written in RED and the corresponding correct spellings written in **BLACK**. The format is much improved: text is written in Barrington Stoke's easy-to-read font and more attention has been paid to spacing.

The dictionary contains new features. There is a detailed KEY to Suffixes, Compounds and Spelling Rules at the bottom of each page so users can quickly access and use the information they need.

In the many years that have passed since the publication of the first *Dictionary of Perfect Spelling*, the author has received letters from around the world asking where copies of the dictionary could still be found. Particularly striking were the number of letters coming from parents of dyslexic children, who often made the comment that it was the first dictionary that their child had been able to use independently.

More than 80% of employers believe that the poor grammar and sloppy spelling of their employees spoil otherwise excellent work. However, the poor speller is often too embarrassed to ask for assistance. The *Dictionary of Perfect Spelling* provides instant self-help and can be a major factor in encouraging reluctant dictionary users to become more proficient and to improve their spelling as a consequence.

It is hoped that this modernised and significantly updated version will prove to be even more accessible and helpful to all those with spelling difficulties, including those whose first language is not English.

Christine Maxwell
May 2005

Introduction

This new *Dictionary of Perfect Spelling* has an expanded and fully modernised word list. It includes National Curriculum words as well as vocabulary for the workplace.

There are two appendices at the back of the dictionary:

1 Abbreviations / acronyms
2 Country / Capital City / Citizen / Language

Regular use of the *Dictionary of Perfect Spelling* boosts the confidence of the user by effectively improving their ability to locate words easily and quickly without having to ask for help.

How the Dictionary is Laid Out

Each page is divided in half with two columns in each half. Correctly spelled words are printed in **black** and wrong spellings are printed in red.

> **BLACK** is correct – RED is wrong

The misspellings are mainly phonetic but also include commonly found incorrect attempts which may be attributed to mispronunciation, visual confusion, or just plain forgetfulness.

For example, 'knee' can be found by its sound under the letter 'N'.

> nee   knee[+]

The + sign tells the user that there is additional information at the root word, in its correct alphabetical order under the letter 'K'.

For example:

> knee ~ing ~cap ~-deep
> knee ~-high ~-jerk ~-length

Some of the commonest spelling errors are made when adding suffixes and in forming derivatives from root words. In a conventional dictionary a user may be able to find the spellings of infinitives like 'picnic', 'abandon' and 'span', but may encounter difficulties spelling their present and past participles.

The *Dictionary of Perfect Spelling* includes difficult and irregular word derivatives. Runners at the bottom of each page tell the user how to form participles, plurals and related words, and how to add on the correct spellings of suffixes and plurals.

The *Dictionary of Perfect Spelling* also helps with similar sounding words that may be confused. They have a star and a short descriptor beside them so that there is no confusion about which is the correct word to use in a given context.

Left hand column   Right hand column

poor[1] *[needy] ~ly   paw[1] *[foot],
                          pore[2] *[skin, over],
                          pour[1] *[liquid]

Choice of Words and Spellings

In the 30 years since the first *Dictionary of Perfect Spelling* was published, there have been considerable changes to vocabulary in daily use. For example, there is much greater acceptance in the English language of words of foreign origin and words that are considered informal or colloquial.

Most names have been excluded from the wordlist – except where they could be confused with the same word beginning in lower case.

For example:

conservative ~ly ~ness
Conservatives [the]

Use of British versus American Spellings

The Dictionary gives one acceptable British English spelling but does not include American spellings.

For example:

behaviour ~al ~ism
centre[2+]
realise[2]

However, because there is greater acceptance today of many American English spellings, the Dictionary does **NOT** list American correct spellings as British English misspellings.

Word Endings

It has not been possible to put in every derivation and inflection. In some cases, there has been insufficient space for all the derivatives to be placed on one line. In those cases they appear on consecutive lines.

For example:

    last[1] ~ly ~-ditch ~-gasp
    last ~-minute ~| name ~| orders
    last ~| post ~| rites ~| straw

Common suffixes such as ~**ly** and ~**ness** are generally shown first. Note that for the most part, suffix spellings are covered by a number which is explained in the KEY at the bottom of each page.

    happy[4] ~-go-lucky

The 4 after 'happy' directs the user to change the final y to i before adding an ending, so they can spell happ**i**ly and happ**i**ness.

Trademark

TM indicates the word is used officially as a trademark to identify a product.

Additional Guidance in Finding the Correct Spelling

In order to speed up the word-finding process, additional guidance appears in boxes on some pages.

For example:

    Under **ge** you will find a box saying

> ☞ Can't find your word here? Look under <u>je</u>

How to Use this Spelling Dictionary

Correct spellings, and misspellings, are arranged in alphabetical order down the left-hand column of each half of the page. Each misspelling (printed in RED) has its correct spelling (printed in **BLACK**) alongside it in the right-hand column.

First Step

To make it easier to find the word, the quartiles (4 parts) of the dictionary, A–D, E–M, N–R and S–Z are highlighted by a coloured tint on the page edge.

Think of the first two letters or first syllable (chunk) of the word you are looking for and look for the correct part of the alphabet in the *Dictionary*.

Go down the left-hand columns until you find the word you are looking for.

If the word is written in red, then your spelling is wrong.

You need to look across to the right hand column to find the correct spelling of the word in **black**.

Second Step

If the word you are looking for has a number or a symbol after it, look down at the **KEYS** at the bottom of the pages so you can find out what the number or symbol stands for.

The numbers give you more help in spelling other forms of the word.

The stars * are used when there are two or more words that look or sound alike. After a * you will find a descriptor [brief meaning] so you can choose the correct spelling to use.

A plus sign + in the right hand column means that you will find more information about the word when you look it up in its correct place in the alphabet.

Third Step

Sometimes you need to add a word ending or another word.

When there is just a tilde (~) between the main word and the next part, you simply put the two parts together (without a space or hyphen).
For example: careful ~ly ~ness

Add **ly** to **careful** to spell **carefully**.

Add **ness** to **careful** to spell **carefulness**.

When there is a tilde and a hyphen (~-), you put a hyphen in between the two parts.
For example:

pay ~-off
semi ~-final
Add -off to **pay** to spell **pay-off**.
Add -final to **semi** to spell **semi-final**.

When there is a tilde and a vertical line (~|), you keep the two words separate.
For example:

hot ~| dog
false ~| alarm

Keep **hot** and **dog** as separate words to write **hot dog**.
Keep **false** and **alarm** as separate words to write **false alarm**.

Remember the Symbols Keys at the bottom of every page are there to refer to. They are also on the last page of the book.

Correct Spelling of Suffixes

The Numbers Key gives you the rules for adding suffixes (the letters on the ends of words which make new words).

~ing is used to form the present participle of regular verbs.
~ed is used to form the past tense or past participle of regular verbs.
~er and **~est** are used to form comparative and superlative adjectives.
~er is also used to form operators (e.g. report ~er = reporter).
~ly is used to form adverbs.
~ness is used to form nouns.

Correct Spelling of Plurals

You can add 's' to any noun to make a plural unless different information is given.
For example: octopus[5]

The 5 after the word means you must add **es** to make the correct plural of **octopuses**.
The only time the plural is given is when the plural of a word does not follow any of the rules given in the KEYS.
For example:

curriculum   curricula
crisis   crises

Words that Can be Confused with Others

People confuse some words because:

The words sound exactly the same.
For example:
there and **their**
"I saw him place the plank over **there**."
"We gave them **their** money back."

The words sound similar.
For example:
beside meaning **at the side of**
besides meaning **as well as**

By spelling a word wrongly, you may accidentally write another word that sounds the same but has a quite different meaning.
For example:
byte for **bite**
brood for **brewed**

Use of * and Descriptors

When two words could be confused, you will find them next to each other, with a star and a simple descriptor. The descriptor gives you a pointer to help you pick the word you want to use.
For example:

bite *[teeth]   byte *[data]
brood[1] *[think, kids]   brewed *[beer, coffee]

Becoming a Successful Dictionary User

The *Dictionary of Perfect Spelling* has proved in the past that it can motivate poor spellers to check words independently. You can improve your spelling by using whatever basic knowledge you have. As you become used to following the Keys, you will soon learn the rules. Learning to spell correctly often means the difference between passing or failing an exam, getting a higher grade, or getting your job application to the top of the pile! Just remember, this special spelling dictionary is much easier to use on your own than a normal dictionary. Not only do you have many special features to help you get word endings correct, but you also have several chances of finding what you are looking for instead of only one!

Keys

KEY TO SPELLING RULES

Red words are wrong. **Black** words are correct.

~ Add the suffix or word directly to the main word, without a space or hyphen
e.g. ash ~en ~tray ashen ashtray

~- Add a hyphen to the main word before adding the next word
e.g. blow ~-dry blow-dry

~| Leave a space between the main word and the next word
e.g. decimal ~| place decimal place

+ By finding this word in its **correct** alphabetical order, you can find related words
e.g. about+ about-face about-turn

* Draws attention to words that may be confused

TM Means the word is a trademark

KEY TO SUFFIXES AND COMPOUNDS

These rules are explained on pages ix to x.

1 Keep the word the same before adding **ed, er, est, ing**
e.g. cool[1] cooled, cooler, coolest, cooling

2 Take off final **e** before adding **ed, er, est, ing**
e.g. fine[2] fined, finer, finest, fining

3 Double final consonant before adding **ed, er, est, ing**
e.g. thin[3] thinned, thinner, thinnest, thinning

4 Change final **y** to **i** before adding **ed, er, es, est, ly, ness**
e.g. tidy[4] tidied, tidier, tidies, tidiest, tidily, tidiness
Keep final **y** before adding **ing**
e.g. tidying

5 Add **es** instead of **s** to the end of the word
e.g. bunch[5] bunches

6 Change final **f** to **ve** before adding **s**
e.g. calf[6] calves

A ~-bomb ~-frame

A ~| Level ~| list ~-road

aardvark

aback

abacus

abait   abate²

abak   aback

abakus   abacus

abandon¹ ~ment

abashed

abate² ~ment

abattoir

abawd   aboard

abawshun   abortion⁺

abawt   abort¹⁺

abayunse   abeyance

abbey

abbot *[religious]   abet³ *[help]

abbreviate² abbreviation

abcent   absent⁺

abcentee   absentee⁺

abdamen   abdomen

abdicate² abdication

abdomen

abdominal ~ly

abduct¹ ~ion ~or

abee   abbey

abel   able²⁺

aberrant

abet³ *[help]   abbot *[religious]

abeyance

abgect   abject

abhor³

abhorrence abhorrent

abide²

ability⁴

abismal   abysmal⁺

abiss   abyss

abject ~ly

ablative

ablaze

able² ~-bodied   ably

abnormal ~ly

abnormality⁴

aboard *[on board]

abode *[dwelling]

abolish¹ ~ment

abolishun   abolition⁺

abolition ~ist

abominable abominably

abominate² abomination

abor   abhor³

aborant   abhorrent⁺

abord   aboard

Aboriginal   Aborigine

aborshun   abortion⁺

abort¹ ~ive

abortion ~ist

abot   abbot

abound¹

about ~-face ~-turn

above ~| board

abownd   abound¹

abowt   about⁺

abracadabra

abraciv   abrasive⁺

abrashun   abrasion⁺

abrasion

abrasive ~ly

abrawd   abroad

abreast

abrest   abreast

abreviate   abbreviate²⁺

abridge²

abroad

abrupt ~ly ~ness

KEY TO SUFFIXES AND COMPOUNDS

These rules are explained on pages ix to x.

1 Keep the word the same before adding **ed, er, est, ing**
e.g. cool¹ → cooled, cooler, coolest, cooling
2 Take off final **e** before adding **ed, er, est, ing**
e.g. fine² → fined, finer, finest, fining
3 Double final consonant before adding **ed, er, est, ing**
e.g. thin³ → thinned, thinner, thinnest, thinning

4 Change final **y** to **i** before adding **ed, er, es, est, ly, ness**
e.g. tidy⁴ → tidied, tidier, tidies, tidiest, tidily, tidiness
Keep final **y** before adding **ing** e.g. tidying
5 Add **es** instead of **s** to the end of the word
e.g. bunch⁵ → bunches
6 Change final **f** to **ve** before adding **s**
e.g. calf⁶ → calves

1

absail	abseil[1]
absalushun	absolution
absalute	absolute[+]
absant	absent[+]
absawb	absorb[1+]
absawpshun	absorption
abscent	absent[+]
abscess[5]	
abscond[1]	
abseil[1]	
absence	
absent ~ly	
absentee ~ism	
absent-minded ~ly ~ness	
abserd	absurd[+]
abserdity	absurdity[4]
absess	abscess[5]
abskond	abscond[1]
absolushun	absolution
absolute ~ly ~l value ~l zero	
absolution	
absolutism	
absolve[2]	
absorb[1] ~able ~ency ~ent	
absorption ~l lines	
abssess	abscess[5]
abstain[1]	
abstenshun	abstention
abstention	
abstinence abstinent	
abstract[1] ~ion	
absurd ~ly absurdity[4]	
abundance	
abundant ~ly	
abundens	abundance
abuse[2]	
abusive ~ly ~ness	
abuv	above[+]

abyde	abide[2]
abysmal ~ly	
abyss	
abyus	abuse[2]
abyusiv	abusive[+]
acacia	
academic ~ally ~ian	
academy[4]	
acasha	acacia
acawn	acorn
accede[2]	
accelerate[2] accelerator	
acceleration	
accent[1] *[speech]	ascent *[journey up]
accentuate[2]	
accept[1] [take] ~ance	except[1] *[other than]
acceptable acceptably	
accersed	accursed[+]
access ~ibility ~ible	
accessary[4] *[legal]	accessory[4] *[extra]
accession	
accessory[4] *[extra]	accessary[4] *[legal]
accident ~al ~ally ~-prone	
acclaim[1]	
acclimatise[2]	
accolade	
accommodate[2] accommodation	
accompaniment	
accompany[4] accompanist	
accomplice *[crime]	
accomplish[1] *[do] ~ment	
accompniment	accompaniment
accord[1] ~ance ~ingly	
accordion	
accost[1]	
account[1] ~ancy ~ant	
accountable accountability	
accoutrements	

KEY TO SPELLING RULES

Red words are wrong. **Black words are correct.**

~   Add the suffix or word directly to the main word, without a space or hyphen
    e.g. ash ~en ~tray → **ashen ashtray**

~- Add a hyphen to the main word before adding the next word
    e.g. blow ~-dry → **blow-dry**

~l Leave a space between the main word and the next word
    e.g. decimal ~l place → **decimal place**

+   By finding this word in its **correct** alphabetical order, you can find related words
    e.g. about[+] → **about-face about-turn**

*   Draws attention to words that may be confused

TM Means the word is a trademark

accredit[1] ~ation

accremony — acrimony

accross — across

accrue[2] accrual

accumulate[2] accumulator

accumulation

accupuncher — acupuncture

accuracy

accurate ~ly

accusative

accusatory

accuse[2] accusation

accustom[1]

ace

acelerate — accelerate[2+]

acent — accent[1+]

acepsis — asepsis[+]

acept — accept[1+]

acesion — accession

acetate

acetic *[acid] — ascetic *[simple life][+]

acetone

acetylene

ache[2] achy

acheivabul — achievable

acheive — achieve[2+]

achievable

achieve[2] ~ment

Achilles' ~| heel ~| tendon

achord — accord[1+]

achordian — accordion

acid ~ic ~ity ~| rain

acident — accident[+]

Acileys — Achilles

acknowledge[2] ~ment

acksel — axel *[jump], axil *[leaf], axle *[wheel]

ackses — axes *[lines, tools], axis *[line]

acksess — access[+]

acksiom — axiom[+]

ackwaint — acquaint[1+]

ackwire — acquire[2]

ackwit — acquit[3+]

aclaim — acclaim[1]

aclimatise — acclimatise[2]

acme *[highest achievement]

acne *[skin condition]

acnoledge — acknowledge[2+]

acolade — accolade

acolite — acolyte

acolyte

☞ Can't find your word here? Look under **acc**

acomodate — accommodate[2+]

acompaniment — accompaniment

acompliss — accomplice *[crime], accomplish[1] *[do][+]

acompny — accompany[4+]

acord — accord[1+]

acordion — accordion

acorn

acost — accost[1]

acount — account[1+]

acountabul — accountable[+]

acoustic ~ally ~s ~| coupler

acoutrements — accoutrements

acowntabel — accountable[+]

acquaint[1] ~ance

acquiesce[2]

acquiescence acquiescent

acquire[2]

acquisishun — acquisition[+]

acquisition acquisitive

acquit[3] acquittal

KEY TO SUFFIXES AND COMPOUNDS

These rules are explained on pages ix to x.

1 Keep the word the same before adding **ed, er, est, ing**
e.g. cool[1] → cooled, cooler, coolest, cooling

2 Take off final **e** before adding **ed, er, est, ing**
e.g. fine[2] → fined, finer, finest, fining

3 Double final consonant before adding **ed, er, est, ing**
e.g. thin[3] → thinned, thinner, thinnest, thinning

4 Change final **y** to **i** before adding **ed, er, es, est, ly, ness**
e.g. tidy[4] → tidied, tidier, tidies, tidiest, tidily, tidiness
Keep final **y** before adding **ing** e.g. tidying

5 Add **es** instead of **s** to the end of the word
e.g. bunch[5] → bunches

6 Change final **f** to **ve** before adding **s**
e.g. calf[6] → calves

acqusativ	accusative
acre ~age	
acredit	accredit[1+]
acrew	accrue[2+]
acrid	
acrilic	acrylic
acrimonious ~ly	
acrimony	
acrobat ~ic ~ically	
acrofobia	acrophobia
acronym	
acrophobia *	agrophobia *
[heights]	[open spaces]
acropolis	
across	
acrue	accrue[2+]
acryd	acrid
acrylic ~l acid	
acsede	accede[2]

☞ Can't find your word here? Look under **acc**

acselerate	accelerate[2+]
acsenshun	ascension
acsent	accent[1+]
acsentuate	accentuate[2]
acsept	accept[1+]
acseptabul	acceptable[+]
acseshun	accession
acsess	access[+]
acsessary	accessary[4] *[legal], accessory[4] *[extra]
acsetic	ascetic *[simple life][+], acetic *[acid][+]
acshun	action[+]
acsident	accident[+]
act[1] ~or	
acter	actor[+]
actinium	

action[1] ~able ~~-packed	
activate[2] activator	
activation	
active ~ly ~ness	
activism activist	
activity[4]	
actor actress[5]	
actual ~ly	
actuality[4]	
actuary[4]	
actyvate	activate[2+]
actyvisum	activism[+]
acumen	

☞ Can't find your word here? Look under **acc**

acumpaniment	accompaniment
acumpany	accompany[4+]
acumplish	accomplish[1] *[do][+]
acumpliss	accomplice *[crime]
acumpny	accompany[4+]
acumulate	accumulate[2+]
acumulator	accumulator
acupuncture acupuncturist	
acuracy	accuracy
acurate	accurate[+]
acursed	accursed[+]
acusative	accusative
acusatory	accusatory
acuse	accuse[2+]
acustics	acoustics
acustom	accustom[1]
acute ~ly	
acutrements	accoutrements
acwiescence	acquiescence[+]
acwiess	acquiesce[2]
acyd	acid[+]
ad *[advert]	add[1] *[sum]
adage	

KEY TO SPELLING RULES

Red words are wrong. **Black** words are correct.

~   Add the suffix or word directly to the main word, without a space or hyphen
     e.g. ash ~en ~tray → **ashen ashtray**

~-   Add a hyphen to the main word before adding the next word
     e.g. blow ~-dry → **blow-dry**

~l   Leave a space between the main word and the next word
     e.g. decimal ~l place → **decimal place**

+   By finding this word in its **correct** alphabetical order, you can find related words
     e.g. about[+] → **about-face about-turn**

*   Draws attention to words that may be confused

TM   Means the word is a trademark

adagio
adajo   adagio
adamant ~ly
Adam's apple
adapt[1] ~able ~ability ~ation
adapter *[person]   adaptor *[electric]
adaptive
adaptor *[electric]   adapter *[person]
adawn   adorn[1+]
add[1] *[sum]   ad *[advert]
addament   adamant[+]
addapt   adapt[+]
addaptor   adapter *[person],
              adaptor *[electric]
addendum   addenda
addenoyds   adenoids
addept   adept[+]
addequate   adequate[+]
adder
addhock   ad hoc
addict ~ed ~ion ~ive
addinfinitum   ad infinitum
addition *[sum] ~al ~ally   edition *[version]
additive
addle[2]
addministrativ   administrative[+]
addmisibul   admissible[+]
addmisshun   admission[+]
addolesense   adolescence[+]
addoor   adore[2+]
addorashun   adoration
addrenalin   adrenalin
address[1] ~ee ~es ~| book
addrift   adrift
addroit   adroit[+]
addulashun   adulation
ade   aid[1] *[help][+],
              aide *[helper]

adekwate   adequate[+]
adel   addle[2]
adendum   addendum[+]
adenoids
adept ~ly ~ness
adequate ~ly   adequacy
ader   adder
adhere[2]
adherence   adherent
adhesion   adhesive
ad hoc
adieu *[goodbye]   ado *[fuss]
adige   adage
ad infinitum
adishun   addition[+]
adjacent
adjective   adjectival
adjoin[1]
adjourn[1] ~ment
adjudicate[2]   adjudicator
adjudication
adjunct
adjust[1] ~able ~ment
ad-lib[3]
admeral   admiral[+]
admier   admire[2+]
administer[1]
administrate[2]   administrator
administration
administrative ~ly
admirable   admirably
admiral ~ty
admire[2]   admiration
admishun   admission[+]
admissible   admissibility
admission
admit[3] ~tedly
admitedly   admittedly

KEY TO SUFFIXES AND COMPOUNDS

These rules are explained on pages ix to x.

1 Keep the word the same before adding **ed, er, est, ing**
   e.g. cool[1] → cooled, cooler, coolest, cooling
2 Take off final **e** before adding **ed, er, est, ing**
   e.g. fine[2] → fined, finer, finest, fining
3 Double final consonant before adding **ed, er, est, ing**
   e.g. thin[3] → thinned, thinner, thinnest, thinning

4 Change final **y** to **i** before adding **ed, er, es, est, ly, ness**
   e.g. tidy[4] → tidied, tidier, tidies, tidiest, tidily, tidiness
   Keep final **y** before adding **ing** e.g. tidying
5 Add **es** instead of **s** to the end of the word
   e.g. bunch[5] → bunches
6 Change final **f** to **ve** before adding **s**
   e.g. calf[6] → calves

admittance

admonish[1] ~ment

admyrabul   admirable[+]

admyral   admiral[+]

admyre   admire[2+]

admyt   admit[3+]

adobe

adobi   adobe

adolescence   adolescent

Adonis

adopt[1] ~ion ~ive

adorable   adorably

adore[2]   adoration

adorn[1] ~ment

adrenal ~| gland

adrenalin

adress   address[1+]

adrift

adrinal   adrenal[+]

adroit ~ly

adsorb[1] *[science]   absorb[1] *[take in][+]

adsorb ~able ~ent

adsorbshun   adsorption

adsorption

adulation

adult ~hood

adulterous ~ly

adultery   adulterer

advance[2] ~ment

advant   advent

advantage ~ous ~ously

advecate   advocate[2+]

advencher   adventure[+]

advent *[arrival]

Advent *[before Christmas]

adventure ~some

adventurous ~ly ~ness

adverb ~ial

adversary[4]

adverse ~ly ~| reaction

adversity[4]

advertise[2] ~ment

advice *[suggestion]   advise[2] *[suggest][+]

advisable   advisability

advise[2] *[suggest]   advice *[suggestion]

advisedly

advisory

advocacy

advocate[2]

advunt   advent

advurb   adverb[+]

advursary   adversary[4]

advurse   adverse[+]

advursity   adversity[4]

advurtise   advertise[2+]

adynfynitum   ad infinitum

aegis

ael   ale

aer   air[+]

☞ Can't find your word here? Look under **air**

aerate[2]   aeration   aerator

aerial ~ly

aerobatics

aerobic ~ally ~s ~| exercise

aerodrome

aerodynamic ~s

aerofoil

aeronaut ~ical ~ics

aeroplane

aerosol

aerospace

aery   airy[4]

aesthetic ~ism ~s

afabul   affable[+]

afadavit   affidavit

KEY TO SPELLING RULES

Red words are wrong. **Black** words are correct.

~   Add the suffix or word directly to the main word, without a space or hyphen
    e.g. ash ~en ~tray → ashen ashtray

~-   Add a hyphen to the main word before adding the next word
    e.g. blow ~-dry → blow-dry

~| Leave a space between the main word and the next word
    e.g. decimal ~| place → decimal place

+   By finding this word in its **correct** alphabetical order, you can find related words
    e.g. about[+] → about-face about-turn

*   Draws attention to words that may be confused

TM   Means the word is a trademark

afar *[distant]   affair *[event]

afect   affect¹ *[influence],
                                effect¹ *[result]

afectashun   affectation

afectiv   affective *[emotions],
                                effective *[producing
                                                results]⁺

afeeld   afield⁺

affable   affability   affably

affair

affect¹ *[influence]   effect¹ *[result]

affectation

affection ~ate ~ately

affective *[emotions]   effective *[producing
                                                results]⁺

affekshun   affection⁺

affekshunayt   affectionate

afferm   affirm¹⁺

affermativ   affirmative⁺

affidavit

affiliate²   affiliation

affinity⁴

affirm¹ ~ation

affirmative ~ly

affix¹ ~es

afflict¹ ~ion

affluence *[wealth]   effluence *[waste]

affluent *[wealthy]   effluent *[waste]

afford¹ ~able ~ability

affraede   afraid

affray

Affro   Afro

affront¹

aficionado

afid   aphid

afidavit   affidavit

afield

afier   afire

afiliate   affiliate²⁺

afinity   affinity⁴

afirm   affirm¹⁺

afirmativ   affirmative⁺

afishenado   aficionado

afix   affix¹⁺

aflame

aflict   afflict¹

afloat

afluence   affluence⁺

afoot

aford   afford¹⁺

afore ~mentioned ~said

aforisum   aphorism

afraid

afray   affray

afresh

Afro

afrodisiac   aphrodisiac

afront   affront¹

after ~birth ~burner ~care

after ~-effect ~-hours ~image

after ~life ~math ~noon

after ~-school ~shave ~shock

after ~taste ~thought ~wards

afyliate   affiliate²⁺

again ~st

agane   again⁺

agarst   aghast

agate

agayn   again⁺

age² ~| group ~less

agectiv   adjective

agen   again

agency⁴

agenda

agent

agglomerate²   agglomeration

KEY TO SUFFIXES AND COMPOUNDS

These rules are explained on pages ix to x.

1 Keep the word the same before adding ed, er, est, ing
  e.g. cool¹ → cooled, cooler, coolest, cooling

2 Take off final e before adding ed, er, est, ing
  e.g. fine² → fined, finer, finest, fining

3 Double final consonant before adding ed, er, est, ing
  e.g. thin³ → thinned, thinner, thinnest, thinning

4 Change final y to i before adding ed, er, es, est,
  ly, ness
  e.g. tidy⁴ → tidied, tidier, tidies, tidiest, tidily,
  tidiness
  Keep final y before adding ing e.g. tidying

5 Add es instead of s to the end of the word
  e.g. bunch⁵ → bunches

6 Change final f to ve before adding s
  e.g. calf⁶ → calves

aggrandisement	
aggrarian	agrarian
aggravate² aggravation	
aggregate² aggregation	
aggression aggressor	
aggressive ~ly ~ness	
aggrieved	
aghast	
agile agility	
agitate² agitator	
agitation	
aglomerate	agglomerate²⁺
agnostic ~ism	
ago	
agog	
agonie	agony⁴
agonise² agonisingly	
agony⁴	
agonyse	agonise²⁺
agoraphobia	
agrafobia	agoraphobia
agragate	aggregate²⁺
agrarian	
agravate	aggravate²⁺
agre	agree⁺
agree ~d ~ing ~ment	
agreeable agreeably	
agregate	aggregate²⁺
agreived	aggrieved
agreshun	aggression⁺
agresiv	aggressive⁺
agribusiness	
agriculcher	agriculture
agricultural ~ly ~| revolution	
agriculture	
agronomy agronomist	
aground	
agytate	agitate²⁺

ahead	
ahoy	
aid¹ *[help]	
aide *[helper]	
AIDS *[illness]	
aigys	aegis
ailing ailment	
aim¹ ~less ~lessly	
aimen	amen
ainel	anal
aipex	apex⁵

☞ Can't find your word here? Take off **air** and look again

air¹ *[gas] ~bag ~borne	heir *[inheritor]⁺
air ~| brake ~brush	
air ~-conditioned ~-conditioning	
air ~crew ~drop	
air ~fare ~field ~flow ~| force	
air ~gun ~lift ~line	
air ~lock ~mail ~| mass ~| miles	
air ~| passage ~| pocket ~port ~| power	
air ~| raid ~| resistance ~| sac ~ship ~stream	
air ~strip ~tight ~waves	
airate	aerate²⁺
aircraft ~| carrier	
airea	area *[surface], aria *[song]
airial	aerial⁺
airobatics	aerobatics
airobic	aerobic⁺
airodrome	aerodrome
airodynamics	aerodynamic⁺
airofoil	aerofoil
aironaut	aeronaut⁺
aironort	aeronaut⁺
airoplane	aeroplane
airosol	aerosol

KEY TO SPELLING RULES

Red words are wrong. **Black** words are correct.

~ Add the suffix or word directly to the main word, without a space or hyphen
   e.g. ash ~en ~tray → **ashen ashtray**

~- Add a hyphen to the main word before adding the next word
   e.g. blow ~-dry → **blow-dry**

~| Leave a space between the main word and the next word
   e.g. decimal ~| place → **decimal place**

+ By finding this word in its **correct** alphabetical order, you can find related words
   e.g. about⁺ → **about-face about-turn**

* Draws attention to words that may be confused

TM Means the word is a trademark

airy⁴	
ais	ace
aisle *[passage]	isle *[island]

> ☞ Can't find your word here? Look under <u>adj</u>

ajacent	adjacent⁺
ajar	
ajasent	adjacent⁺
ajective	adjective
ajency	agency⁴
ajenda	agenda
ajent	agent
ajile	agile⁺
ajitate	agitate²⁺
ajoin	adjoin¹
ajourn	adjourn¹⁺
ajudicate	adjudicate²⁺
ajulashun	adulation
ajunct	adjunct
ajurn	adjourn¹⁺
ajust	adjust¹⁺
akacia	acacia
akademik	academic⁺
akademy	academy⁴
ake	ache²
akin	
aknolidge	acknowledge²⁺
akolyte	acolyte
akselerayt	accelerate²⁺

> ☞ Can't find your word here? Look under <u>ac</u>

akshun	action⁺
aksident	accident⁺
aksiom	axiom⁺
akt	act⁺
aktivate	activate²⁺
aktiv	active⁺
aktor	actor⁺

akweous	aqueous
akwiline	aquiline
akyn	akin
alabaster	
alabye	alibi
à la carte	
alack	
alacrity	
Alah	Allah
alakrity	alacrity⁴
alarm¹ ~| clock ~ist	
alas	
alay	allay¹ *[fears], alley *[path]
albatross⁵	
albeeno	albino
albeit	
albem	album
albetross	albatross⁵
albiet	albeit
albino	
album	
albumen *[egg]	
albumin *[protein]	
alchemy alchemist	
alcohol ~ic ~ism	
alcove	
aldehyde	
alderman	
ale	

> ☞ Can't find your word here? Look under <u>all</u>

alebaster	alabaster
alebye	alibi
aledge	allege²⁺
alegashun	allegation
alein	alien
aleinate	alienate²⁺

KEY TO SUFFIXES AND COMPOUNDS

These rules are explained on pages ix to x.

1 Keep the word the same before adding **ed, er, est, ing**
e.g. cool¹ → cooled, cooler, coolest, cooling

2 Take off final **e** before adding **ed, er, est, ing**
e.g. fine² → fined, finer, finest, fining

3 Double final consonant before adding **ed, er, est, ing**
e.g. thin³ → thinned, thinner, thinnest, thinning

4 Change final **y** to **i** before adding **ed, er, es, est, ly, ness**
e.g. tidy⁴ → tidied, tidier, tidies, tidiest, tidily, tidiness
Keep final **y** before adding **ing** e.g. tidying

5 Add **es** instead of **s** to the end of the word
e.g. bunch⁵ → bunches

6 Change final **f** to **ve** before adding **s**
e.g. calf⁶ → calves

alejans	allegiance	alkove	alcove
alement	ailment	all *[every]	awl *[tool]
alementary	alimentary+	all ~-clear ~-day ~-in	
alemony	alimony	all ~l right ~-purpose	
alert[1] ~ness		all ~-rounder ~-terrain ~-time	
aleviate	alleviate[2+]	Allah	
alfa	alpha+	allaie	allay[1] *[fears],
alfabet	alphabet+		alley *[path]
alfresco			

☞ Can't find your word here? Look under al

algae		allarm	alarm[1+]
algebra		allas	alas
algebraic ~l expression		allay[1] *[fears]	alley *[path]
algee	algae	allegation	
algorithm		allege[2] ~dly	
alian	alien	allegiance	
aliance	alliance	allegorical ~ly	
alias[5]		allegory[4]	
alibi		allegro	
alien		alleluia	
alienate[2] alienation		allergen	
aligator	alligator	allergic ~l reaction	
alight[1]		allergy[4]	
align[1] ~ment		allert	alert[1+]
aligorical	allegorical+	alleviate[2]	
alike		alley *[path]	ally[4] *[friend]
alimentary ~l canal		alliance	
alimony		allied ~l forces	
alinement	align[1+]	allienate	alienate[2+]
aling	ailing	alligator	
alite	alight[1]	alliteration alliterative	
aliterashun	alliteration+	allive	alive
alive		alliviate	alleviate[2+]
aljebra	algebra	allkali	alkali+
alkali ~l metal		allmighty	almighty
alkaline alkalinity		allmost	almost
alkaly	alkali+	allocate[2] allocation	
alkemey	alchemy+	allot[3] *[give] ~ment	a lot *[many]
alkohol	alcohol+		

<u>KEY TO SPELLING RULES</u>

Red words are wrong. **Black** words are correct.

~	Add the suffix or word directly to the main word, without a space or hyphen	
	e.g. ash ~en ~tray → **ashen ashtray**	
~-	Add a hyphen to the main word before adding the next word	
	e.g. blow ~-dry → **blow-dry**	

~l Leave a space between the main word and the next word
e.g. decimal ~l place → **decimal place**

+ By finding this word in its **correct** alphabetical order, you can find related words
e.g. about+ → **about-face about-turn**

* Draws attention to words that may be confused

TM Means the word is a trademark

allow¹ ~able ~ance		alpaca	
allowed *[permitted]	aloud *[out loud]	alpha ~l decay ~numeric ~l particle	
alloy *[metal]	aloe *[plant]⁺	alphabet ~ical ~ically	
alltho	although	Alps alpine	
alltogether	altogether	already	
allude² *[refer to]	elude² *[avoid]	Alsation	
allum	alum	also ~-ran	
allure alluring		altar *[church] ~piece	
allurgic	allergic	alter¹ *[change] ~able ~ation	
allusion *[hint]	elusion *[escape],	alter ego	
	illusion *[false idea]	altercation	
allusive *[suggestive]	elusive *[hard to find]	alternate ~ly ~l angles	
alluvial ~l deposit		alternate² alternator	
alluvium		alternating ~l current	
allways	always	alternative ~ly ~l medicine	
ally⁴ *[friend]	alley *[path]⁺	although	
almanac		althow	although
almighty		altimeter	
almond		altitude	
almoner		alto	
almost		altogether	
alms *[charity]	arms *[limbs, weapons]	altrooisum	altruism
		altruism	
alo	aloe⁺	altruist ~ic ~ically	
aloan	alone	alturnate	alternate⁺
alocate	allocate²⁺	alturnativ	alternative⁺
aloe *[plant] ~l vera	alloy *[metal]	alude	allude² *[refer to], elude² *[avoid]
aloft			
alokate	allocate²⁺	alum	
alone		aluminium ~l foil	
along ~side		alure	allure⁺
aloof ~ness		alurgy	allergy⁴
a lot *[many]	allot³ *[give]⁺	alurt	alert¹⁺
aloud *[out loud]	allowed *[permitted]	alushun	allusion *[hint], elusion *[escape]
alowed	allowed *[permitted], aloud *[out loud]	alusiv	allusive *[suggestive], elusive *[hard to find]
aloy	alloy *[metal], aloe *[plant]	aluvial	alluvial⁺

---

always	
aly	ally[4] *[friend], alley *[path]
alyas	alias[5]
alybi	alibi
alygn	align[1+]
alyke	alike
alyt	alight[1]
alyve	alive
Alzheimer's ~l disease	
am	
amalgam	
amalgamate[2] amalgamation	
amass[1]	
amateur ~ish ~ism	
amaze[2] ~ment	
Amazon ~ian	
ambassador ~ial	
ambel	amble[2]
amber	
ambidextrous	
ambience ambient	
ambiguity[4]	
ambiguous ~ly ~ness	
ambishun	ambition
ambishus	ambitious[+]
ambit	
ambition	
ambitious ~ly	
ambivalence ambivalent	
amble[2]	
ambletory	ambulatory
amboosh	ambush[1]
ambor	amber
ambrosia	
ambulance	
ambush[1] ~es	
ambyance	ambience[+]

ambydextrous	ambidextrous
ame	aim[1+]
ameeba	amoeba
ameliorate[2] amelioration	
amen	
amenable amenably	
amend[1] ~ment	
amenity[4]	
ameoba	amoeba
Americanise[2]	
ameter	ammeter
amethyst	
amfetamine	amphetamine
amfibian	amphibian
amfibious	amphibious[+]
amfitheearter	amphitheatre
amiable amiability amiably	
amicable amicably	
amid ~st	
amiebul	amiable[+]
amiliorate	ameliorate[2+]
aminabul	amenable[+]
amino ~l acid	
amiss	

☞ Can't find your word here? Look under <u>am</u>

ammalgam	amalgam
ammalgammate	amalgamate[2+]
ammaze	amaze[2+]
ammeter	
ammonia	
ammoral	amoral[+]
ammunition	
ammuse	amuse[2+]
amnesty[4]	
amoeba	
among ~st	
amonya	ammonia

<u>KEY TO SPELLING RULES</u>

Red words are wrong. **Black** words are correct.

~   Add the suffix or word directly to the main word, without a space or hyphen
     e.g. ash ~en ~tray → **ashen ashtray**

~-   Add a hyphen to the main word before adding the next word
     e.g. blow ~-dry → **blow-dry**

~l   Leave a space between the main word and the next word
     e.g. decimal ~l place → **decimal place**

+   By finding this word in its **correct** alphabetical order, you can find related words
     e.g. about[+] → **about-face about-turn**

*   Draws attention to words that may be confused

TM   Means the word is a trademark

amoral ~ity ~ly
amorfus   amorphous+
amorous ~ly
amorphous ~ly
amorus   amorous+
amount[1]
amownt   amount[1]
amp
ampair   ampere+
ampel   ample+
ampere   amperage
ampersand
amphetamine
amphibian
amphibious
amphitheatre
ample   amply
amplify[4]   amplification
amplitude
amplytude   amplitude
ampursand   ampersand
amputate[2]   amputation
amulet
amung   among+
amunishun   ammunition
amunition   ammunition
amuse[2] ~ment
amycabul   amicable+
amyd   amid+
amyno   amino+
amyss   amiss
amythist   amethyst
amyulet   amulet
an
anabolic ~l steroid
anachronism
anachronistic ~ally
anaconda

anacronisum   anachronism
anacronistic   anachronistic+
anaemia   anaemic
anaesthesia   anaesthetic
anaesthetise[2]   anaesthetist
anagram
anakonda   anaconda
anal *[anus]   annul[3] *[not legal]
analgesic
analise   analyse[2+]
analisis   analysis+
analogous ~ly
analogue ~l computer ~l signal
analogy[4]
analyse[2]
analysis   analyses
analyst
analytic ~al ~ally
anarchism   anarchist
anarchy   anarchic
anarkisum   anarchism+
anarky   anarchy+
anastehsia   anaesthesia+
anathema
anatomical ~ly
anatomy   anatomist
anceint   ancient+
ancestor   ancestral   ancestry
anchor[1] ~age ~man ~woman
anchovee   anchovy[4]
anchovy[4]
ancient ~ness
ancillary[4]
ancor   anchor[1+]
and
andante
androginous   androgynous+
androgynous

---

anealing	annealing
anecdotal	
anecdote *[story]	antidote *[poison]
aneemia	anaemia[+]
anel	anal
anemone	
anemosity	animosity[4]
anenimity	anonymity
anestetise	anaesthetise[2+]
anestheisia	anaesthesia[+]
anetomical	anatomical[+]
aneurysm	
aneversary	anniversary[4]
anew	
anex	annex[1] *[control][+], annexe *[building]
aney	any[+]
angel *[heavenly]	angle[2] *[turn, maths]
angel ~l dust	
angelic ~ally	
anger	
angina	
angish	anguish[+]
anglar	angular[+]
angle[2] *[turn, maths]	angel *[heavenly]
angler	
Anglican ~ism	
anglicise[2]	
Anglophile	
Anglophone	
Anglo-Saxon	
anglur	angler
angora	
angree	angry[4]
angry[4]	
angst	
anguish ~ed	
angular ~ity	

angur	anger
angwish	anguish[+]
angyna	angina
anhydrous	
anihilate	annihilate[2+]
animal ~ism ~istic	
animate[2] ~dly animator	
animation	
animel	animal[+]
animia	anaemia[+]
animosity[4]	
aniseed	
aniversary	anniversary[4]
aniyelate	annihilate[2+]
anjel	angel[+]
anjelic	angelic[+]
anjina	angina
ankel	ankle[+]
ankle ~l bone anklet	
ankor	anchor[1+]
ankshus	anxious[+]
anksiety	anxiety[4]
anmils	animals
annachronysm	anachronism
annalogy	analogy[4]
annals	

☞ Can't find your word here? Look under **an**

annalyse	analyse[2+]
annalysis	analysis[+]
anneal[1]	
annex[1] *[control] ~ation ~es	
annexe *[building]	
annihilate[2] annihilation	
annimosity	animosity[4]
annisede	aniseed
anniversary[4]	
Anno Domini	

KEY TO SPELLING RULES

Red words are wrong. **Black** words are correct.

~ Add the suffix or word directly to the main word, without a space or hyphen
e.g. ash ~en ~tray → **ashen ashtray**

~- Add a hyphen to the main word before adding the next word
e.g. blow ~-dry → **blow-dry**

~l Leave a space between the main word and the next word
e.g. decimal ~l place → **decimal place**

+ By finding this word in its **correct** alphabetical order, you can find related words
e.g. about[+] → **about-face about-turn**

* Draws attention to words that may be confused

TM Means the word is a trademark

14

annoint   anoint[1+]
annonymous   anonymous[+]
annorak   anorak
annotate[2]   annotation
annother   another
announce[2] ~ment
annoy[1] ~ance ~ingly
annual ~ly ~l percentage rate
Annual ~l Report ~l General Meeting
annuity[4]
annul[3] *[not legal]   anal *[anus]
annul ~ment
annular
annunciate[2] *[say]   enunciate[2] *[clearly]
annunciation *   enunciation *
        [announcement]   [clarity]
anode
anodyne
anoint[1] ~ment
anomalous ~l results
anomaly[4]
anomelus   anomalous[+]
anon
anonymity
anonymous ~ly
anorak
anorexia   anorexic
anotate   annotate[2+]
another
anounce   announce[2+]
anourak   anorak
anownce   announce[2+]
anoy   annoy[1+]
anoynt   anoint[1+]
anser   answer[1+]
ansestor   ancestor[+]
anshent   ancient[+]
ansient   ancient[+]

ansillaree   ancillary[4]
answer[1] ~able
ant *[insect] ~eater ~hill   aunt *[relative][+]
antacid
antagonise[2]   antagonism
antagonist ~ic ~ically
Antarctic ~l Circle
antasid   antacid
antchovy   anchovy[4]
antebyotic   antibiotic
antecedence   antecedent
antechamber
Antechrist   Antichrist
anteclimax   anticlimax[+]
antecyclone   anticyclone[+]
antediluvian

☞ Can't find your word here? Take off **ante** and look again or look under **anti**

antedote   antidote *[poison],
                anecdote *[story][+]
anteek   antique
ante-freeze   anti-freeze
antehistamine   antihistamine
ante-inflammatory   anti-inflammatory
antelope
antenatal
antenna   antennae
anterior
anteroom
antesemitisum   anti-Semitism
antesoshall   antisocial[+]
antesyclone   anticyclone[+]
anthem
anther
anthology[4]
anthracite
anthrax

KEY TO SUFFIXES AND COMPOUNDS

These rules are explained on pages ix to x.

1 Keep the word the same before adding ed, er, est, ing
   e.g. cool[1] → cooled, cooler, coolest, cooling
2 Take off final e before adding ed, er, est, ing
   e.g. fine[2] → fined, finer, finest, fining
3 Double final consonant before adding ed, er, est, ing
   e.g. thin[3] → thinned, thinner, thinnest, thinning

4 Change final y to i before adding ed, er, es, est, ly, ness
   e.g. tidy[4] → tidied, tidier, tidies, tidiest, tidily, tidiness
   Keep final y before adding ing e.g. tidying
5 Add es instead of s to the end of the word
   e.g. bunch[5] → bunches
6 Change final f to ve before adding s
   e.g. calf[6] → calves

anthresite	anthracite
anthropoid	
anthropologist	
anthropology	anthropological
anthum	anthem
anthur	anther

> ☞ Can't find your word here? Take off **anti** and look again

anti-aircraft	
antibiotic	
antibody[4]	
antic *[prank]	antique *[old][+]
anticedence	antecedence[+]
anticemite	anti-Semite[+]
anticemitisum	anti-Semitism
anticeptic	antiseptic
antichamber	antechamber
Antichrist	
anticipate[2] anticipation	
anticlimax anticlimatic	
anticlockwise	
anticyclone anticyclonic	
antidepressant	
antidiluvian	antediluvian
antidote *[poison]	anecdote *[story][+]
antifreeze	
antigen	
anti-hero	
antihistamine	
anti-inflammatory	
antiklimax	anticlimax[+]
antiklockwise	anticlockwise
antikwarian	antiquarian
antikwated	antiquated
antikwity	antiquity[4]
antilope	antelope
antimatter	

antinatal	antenatal
antipathy[4]	
antipersonnel	
antiperspirant	
antipodes	
antiquarian	
antiquary[4]	
antiquated	
antique *[old]	antic *[prank]
antiquity[4]	
antirior	anterior
antiroom	anteroom
antisedence	antecedence[+]
anti-Semite anti-Semitic	
anti-Semitism	
antiseptic	
antisipate	anticipate[2+]
antisocial ~ly	
antithesis antitheses	
antler	
antonym	

> ☞ Can't find your word here? Look under **anti**

antybiotic	antibiotic
antybody	antibody[4]
anual	annual[+]
anue	anew
anuity	annuity[4]
anul	anal *[anus], annul[3] *[not legal]
anular	annular
anunsiate	annunciate[2] * [say], enunciate[2] *[clearly]
anurisum	aneurysm
anuroid	aneroid
anus	
anuther	another
anuver	another

KEY TO SPELLING RULES

Red words are wrong. **Black** words are correct.

~	Add the suffix or word directly to the main word, without a space or hyphen e.g. ash ~en ~tray → ashen ashtray
~-	Add a hyphen to the main word before adding the next word e.g. blow ~-dry → blow-dry

~|	Leave a space between the main word and the next word e.g. decimal ~| place → decimal place
+	By finding this word in its **correct** alphabetical order, you can find related words e.g. about+ → about-face about-turn
*	Draws attention to words that may be confused
TM	Means the word is a trademark

anvil
anxiety[4]
anxious ~ly
any ~body ~how ~one
any ~| more ~| place ~| time
any ~thing ~way ~where
anymal   animal[+]
anymate   animate[2+]
aorta
Apache

☞ Can't find your word here? Look under **app**

apal   appal[3]
aparant   apparent[+]
apart
apartheid
apartide   apartheid
apartment
Apatchy   Apache
apathetic   apathy
ape[2]
apeal   appeal[1+]
apear   appear[1+]
apel   apple[+]
aperitif
apertain   appertain[1]
aperture
apetight   appetite
apex[5]
aphid
aphorism
aphrodisiac
apiary[4]
apiece
aplaud   applaud[1]
aplie   apply[4+]
aplikashun   application
aplom   aplomb

aplomb
aplord   applaud[1]
aply   apply[4+]
apocalypse   apocalyptic
apocryphal
apoint   appoint[1+]
apolagise   apologise[2]
apolitical
apologetic ~ally
apologise[2]
apology[4]   apologist
apoplectic
apoplexy
aporshun   apportion[1+]
apostle
apostrofee   apostrophe
apostrophe
apothecary[4]
apoynt   appoint[1+]
apoynty   appointee
appal[3]
appalling ~ly
apparatus
apparel
apparent ~ly
apparition
appart   apart
appartied   apartheid
appartment   apartment
appeal[1] ~ingly
appear[1] ~ance
appease[2] ~ment
appellation
append[1] ~age
appendicitis
appendix   appendices
apperchure   aperture
apperitif   aperitif

KEY TO SUFFIXES AND COMPOUNDS

These rules are explained on pages ix to x.

1 Keep the word the same before adding **ed, er, est, ing**
   e.g. **cool**[1] → **cooled, cooler, coolest, cooling**
2 Take off final **e** before adding **ed, er, est, ing**
   e.g. **fine**[2] → **fined, finer, finest, fining**
3 Double final consonant before adding **ed, er, est, ing**
   e.g. **thin**[3] → **thinned, thinner, thinnest, thinning**

4 Change final **y** to **i** before adding **ed, er, es, est, ly, ness**
   e.g. **tidy**[4] → **tidied, tidier, tidies, tidiest, tidily, tidiness**
   Keep final **y** before adding **ing** e.g. **tidying**
5 Add **es** instead of **s** to the end of the word
   e.g. **bunch**[5] → **bunches**
6 Change final **f** to **ve** before adding **s**
   e.g. **calf**[6] → **calves**

appertain[1]
appetiser
appetising ~ly
appetite
applaud[1]
applause
apple ~cart ~| pie ~| sauce
appliance
applicable   applicability
applicant
applicator
apply[4]   application

☞ Can't find your word here? Look under **ap**

appocalips   apocalypse[+]
appoint[1] ~ee ~ment
appolagise   apologise[2]
appologetic   apologetic[+]
apportion[1] ~ment
appossel   apostle
appraisal
appraise[2] *[assess]   apprise[2] *[inform]
appreciable   appreciably
appreciate[2]   appreciation
appreciative ~ly
apprehend[1]
apprehension
apprehensive ~ly ~ness
apprentice ~d ~ship
apprise[2] *[inform]   appraise[2] *[assess]
approach[1] ~able
approbation
approcksimate   approximate[2+]
approksimately   approximately
appropriashun   appropriation
appropriate[2] ~ly ~ness
appropriation
approve[2]   approval

approximate[2]   approximation
approximately
aprapo   apropos
aprayski   après-ski
aprechabul   appreciable[+]
Aprel   April[+]
apren   apron[+]
après-ski
apricot
aprikot   apricot
April ~| Fool's Day
aprise   apprise[2] *[inform],
                              appraise[2] *[assess]
aproach   approach[1+]
aprobashun   approbation
aproche   approach[1+]
apron ~| strings
apropos
apropriashun   appropriation
apropriate   appropriate[2+]
aprove   approve[2+]
aproximate   approximate[2+]
aproximately   approximately
apruve   approve[2+]
apt ~ly ~ness
aptitude
aptytude   aptitude
apurtain   appertain[1]
apyary   apiary[4]
aqewus   aqueous
aqua ~lung ~marine
aquaplane[2]
aquarium
Aquarius
aquatic
aqueduct
aqueline   aquiline
aqueous ~| solution

---

aquiline		archor	archer[+]	
aqusatory	accusatory	archway		
Arab ~ian ~ic		Arctic ~l Circle		
arabesque		ardent ~ly		
arable ~l farming		arder	ardour	
arachnid		ardour		
araign	arraign[1+]	arduous ~ly		
araknid	arachnid	arduus	arduous[+]	
Aramaic		ardvark	aardvark	
arange	arrange[2+]	are *[we are]	our *[belonging]	
aray	array[1]	area *[surface]	aria *[song]	
arbeter	arbiter	areal	aerial[+]	
arbetrary	arbitrary[4]	arears	arrears	
arbiter		arebul	arable	
arbitrait	arbitrate[2+]	Aremaic	Aramaic	
arbitrary[4]		arena		
arbitrate[2] arbitrator		aren't *[are not]	aunt *[relative][+]	
arbitration		arest	arrest[1]	
arboretum		argew	argue[2+]	
arbytrate	arbitrate[2+]	argue[2] arguable arguably		
arc[1] *[curve, power]	ark *[boat]	argument ~ative		
arc ~l light		aria *[song]	area *[surface]	
arcade		arial	aerial[+]	
arcane		arid ~l region aridity		
arch[1] ~ly ~ness ~bishop		arie	awry	
arch ~deacon ~-enemy ~way		Arien	Aryan[+]	
archaeological		arise arising arisen		
archaeology archaeologist		aristocracy[4]		
archaic		aristocrat ~ic		
archangel		arithmetic ~al ~ian		
archeology	archaeology[+]	arithmetic ~l mean ~l progression		
archer ~y		arithmia	arrhythmia	
archetype		arival	arrival	
Archimedes' principle		arive	arrive[2]	
archiology	archaeology[+]	arjuous	arduous[+]	
archipelago		ark *[boat]	arc[1] *[curve, power][+]	
architect ~ure ~ural ~urally		arkade	arcade	
archive[2] archivist		arkaic	archaic	

KEY TO SUFFIXES AND COMPOUNDS

These rules are explained on pages ix to x.

1 Keep the word the same before adding ed, er, est, ing
   e.g. cool[1] → cooled, cooler, coolest, cooling
2 Take off final e before adding ed, er, est, ing
   e.g. fine[2] → fined, finer, finest, fining
3 Double final consonant before adding ed, er, est, ing
   e.g. thin[3] → thinned, thinner, thinnest, thinning

4 Change final y to i before adding ed, er, es, est, ly, ness
   e.g. tidy[4] → tidied, tidier, tidies, tidiest, tidily, tidiness
   Keep final y before adding ing e.g. tidying
5 Add es instead of s to the end of the word
   e.g. bunch[5] → bunches
6 Change final f to ve before adding s
   e.g. calf[6] → calves

arkane	arcane	aronaut	aeronaut⁺
arkangel	archangel	aroplane	aeroplane
arkayic	archaic	arora	aurora⁺
arketipe	archetype	arose	
Arkimides	Archimedes	arosol	aerosol
arkiology	archaeology⁺	around ~-the-clock	
arkipelago	archipelago	arouse² arousal	
arkipeligo	archipelago	arow	arrow⁺
arkitect	architect⁺	arownd	around⁺
arkive	archive⁺	arowse	arouse²⁺
Arktik	Arctic	arpeggio	
arm¹ armed forces		arraign¹ ~ment	
arm ~band ~chair ~ful ~pit		arrain	arraign¹⁺
arma	armour¹⁺	arrange² ~ment	
armada		array¹	
armadillo		arrears	
Armageddon		arrest¹	
armament		arrhythmia	
armie	army⁴	arria	aria *[song],
armistice			area *[surface]
armmament	armament	arrid	arid
armond	almond	arrise	arise⁺
armoner	almoner	aristocracy	aristocracy⁴
armour¹ ~-plated		arristocrat	aristocrat⁺
armoury⁴		arrithmatic	arithmetic⁺
arms *[limbs, weapons]	alms *[charity]	arrival	
army⁴		arrive²	
armystis	armistice	arrogance	
arnt	aren't *[are not],	arrogant ~ly	
	aunt *[relative]⁺	arrow ~-head ~root	
aroas	arose	arse ~hole	
arobatics	aerobatics	arsen	arson⁺
arobic	aerobic⁺	arsenal	
arodrome	aerodrome	arsenic	
arofoil	aerofoil	arsk	ask¹
arogance	arrogance	arsnal	arsenal
arogant	arrogant⁺	arsnick	arsenic
aroma ~tic ~therapy		arson ~ist	

---

art ~l form ~l gallery ~work	
artcher	archer[+]
artefact	
arterie	artery[4]
arteriosclerosis	
artery[4]	
artesian ~l well	
artful ~ly ~ness	
arthritic arthritis	
arthropod	
artichoke	
article ~d	
articulate[2] articulation	
artifice	
artificial ~ly ~l intelligence ~l limb	
artifishall	artificial[+]
artifiss	artifice
artillery[4]	
artirisclerosis	arteriosclerosis
artisan	
artist *[painter][+] ~ry	
artiste *[performer]	
artistic *[skill] ~ally	autistic *[condition]
artless ~ly ~ness	
artrey	artery[4]
artychoke	artichoke
artycle	article[+]
artyculate	articulate[2+]
artyfiss	artifice
artysan	artisan
artyst	artist *[painter][+],
	artiste *[performer]
Aryan ~l race	
aryd	arid
arye	awry
arystocrasy	aristocracy[4]
arystocrat	aristocrat[+]
as *[comparing, referring] ass[5] *[animal]	

asail	assail[1+]
asap	
asassin	assassin
asassinate	assassinate[2+]
asault	assault[1]
asbestos ~is	
asc	ask[1]
ascance	askance
ascend[1] ~ancy ~ant	
ascension	
ascent *[incline]	accent[1] *[speech],
	assent[1] *[agree]
ascertain[1] ~able	
ascertane	ascertain[1+]
ascetic *[simple life]	acetic *[acid]
ascetically	
ASCII ~l code	
ascorbic ~l acid	
ascorbick	ascorbic[+]
ascribe[2] ascribable	

☞ Can't find your word here? Look under <u>ace</u> or <u>ass</u>

ase	ace
aseksual	asexual[+]
asembul	assemble[2+]
asembly	assembly[4+]
asenshun	ascension
asent	assent[1] *[agree],
	accent[1] *[speech],
	ascent *[incline]
asepsis aseptic	
asert	assert[1+]
asess	assess[1+]
aset	asset[+]
asetate	acetate
asetic	acetic *[acid][+],
	ascetic *[simple life][+]
asetone	acetone

---

asetylene	acetylene
asexual ~ly ~l reproduction	
asfixia	asphyxia
asfyxia	asphyxia
asfyxiate	asphyxiate [2+]
ash[5] ~en ~tray	
ashamed	
ashore *[on beach]	assure[2] *[convince]

> ☞ Can't find your word here? Look under **ass**

ashram	
Ashun	Asian
Ash Wednesday	
Asian	
aside	
asiduous	assiduous[+]
asign	assign[1+]
asignee	assignee
asilum	asylum
asimilate	assimilate[2+]
asimmetry	asymmetry[+]
asimptomatic	asymptomatic
asine	assign[1+]
asinine	
asist	assist[1+]
ask[1]	
askance	
askew	
Aski	ASCII[+]
askribe	ascribe[2+]
askue	askew
asleep	
asma	asthma
asociate	associate[2+]
asonance	assonance
asorbic	ascorbic[+]
asorlt	assault[1+]
asortid	assorted

asparagus	
aspartame	
aspect	
aspershun	aspersion
aspersion	
asphalt	
asphyxia	
asphyxiate[2] asphyxiation	
aspic	
aspidistra	
aspik	aspic
aspire[2] aspiration	
aspirin	
aspon	aspen
asprin	aspirin
aspurshun	aspersion
aspydistra	aspidistra
aspyre	aspire[2+]
ass[5] *[animal]	as * [comparing, referring]
assail[1] ~able ~ant	
assassin	
assassinate[2] assassination	
assault[1]	
assemble[2] assemblage	
assembly[4] ~l language ~l line	
assend	ascend[1+]
assent[1] *[agree]	accent[1] *[speech], ascent *[incline]
assert[1] ~ion ~ive	
assertain	ascertain[1+]
assess[1] ~ment ~or	
asset ~-stripping	
assetic	ascetic[+]
assexual	asexual[+]
assfalt	asphalt
assiduous ~ly	
assign[1] ~able ~ation ~ment	

KEY TO SPELLING RULES

Red words are wrong. **Black** words are correct.

~ Add the suffix or word directly to the main word, without a space or hyphen
   e.g. ash ~en ~tray → **ashen ashtray**

~- Add a hyphen to the main word before adding the next word
   e.g. blow ~-dry → **blow-dry**

~l Leave a space between the main word and the next word
   e.g. decimal ~l place → **decimal place**

+ By finding this word in its **correct** alphabetical order, you can find related words
   e.g. about[+] → **about-face about-turn**

* Draws attention to words that may be confused

TM Means the word is a trademark

assignee
assimilate[2] assimilation
assist[1] ~ance ~ant
associate[2] association
associative
assonance
assorted assortment
assuage[2] ~ment
assume[2]
assumption
assurance
assure[2] *[convince]   ashore *[on beach]
assymilate   assimilate[2+]
Astec   Aztec
asterisk
astern
asteroid
asthma ~tic
astigmatic astigmatism
astonish[1] ~ingly ~ment
astound[1] ~ingly
astownd   astound[1+]
astral
astray
astreisk   asterisk
astrel   astral
astreoid   asteroid
astride
astringency astringent
astrofysics   astrophysics
astrologer astrologist
astrology astrological
astronaut
astronomy astromoner
astronomical
astronort   astronaut
astrophysics
Astroturf™

astryde   astride
asturn   astern
astute ~ly ~ness
astygmatyc   astigmatic[+]
astyut   astute[+]
asuage   assuage[2+]
asume   assume[2+]
asumpshun   assumption
asumshun   assumption
asunder
asurance   assurance
asure   ashore *[on beach],
            assure[2] *[convince]
asure   azure
aswage   assuage[2+]
asyde   aside
asylum ~| seeker
asymmetric ~al assymetry
asymptomatic
asynine   asinine[+]
at ~| rest ~-risk

☞ Can't find your word here? Look under att

atach   attach[1+]
ate *[food]   eight *[number]
atempt   attempt[1+]
atheist ~ic atheism
athlete
athlete's foot
athletic ~ism ~s
atic   attic
atire   attire[+]
atishoo
atitude   attitude
Atlantic
atlas
atmosfere   atmosphere
atmosphere

Key to Suffixes and Compounds

These rules are explained on pages ix to x.

1 Keep the word the same before adding ed, er, est, ing
e.g. cool[1] → cooled, cooler, coolest, cooling
2 Take off final e before adding ed, er, est, ing
e.g. fine[2] → fined, finer, finest, fining
3 Double final consonant before adding ed, er, est, ing
e.g. thin[3] → thinned, thinner, thinnest, thinning

4 Change final y to i before adding ed, er, es, est, ly, ness
e.g. tidy[4] → tidied, tidier, tidies, tidiest, tidily, tidiness
Keep final y before adding ing e.g. tidying
5 Add es instead of s to the end of the word
e.g. bunch[5] → bunches
6 Change final f to ve before adding s
e.g. calf[6] → calves

atmospheric ~| pollution

atmospheric ~| pressure

atoan · · · · · · · · · · · · · · atone²⁺

atoll

atom ~| bomb

atomic ~| clock ~| energy ~| mass

atomiser

atone² ~ment

atract · · · · · · · · · · · · · · attract¹⁺

atractiv · · · · · · · · · · · · · attractive⁺

atrium

atrocious ~ly

atrocity⁴

atrofee · · · · · · · · · · · · · · atrophy⁴⁺

atrophy⁴   atrophic

atroshus · · · · · · · · · · · · · atrocious⁺

atrosity · · · · · · · · · · · · · atrocity⁴

attach¹ ~able

attaché ~| case

attachment

attack¹

attain¹ ~able ~ment

attempt¹

attend¹ ~ance ~ant

attention ~-deficit ~-seeker ~span

attentive ~ly ~ness

attenuate² attenuation

attest¹ ~ation

attic

attire ~d

attitude

attorney

attract¹ ~ion

attractive ~ly ~ness

attributable

attribute   attribution

attrition

attune²

aturney · · · · · · · · · · · · · attorney

atypical ~ly

atyshoo · · · · · · · · · · · · · atishoo

aubergine

auburn

auction¹ ~eer

audacious ~ly   audacity

audashus · · · · · · · · · · · · audacious⁺

audeince · · · · · · · · · · · · audience

audible   audibly   audibility

audience

audio ~| cassette recorder

audio ~tape ~-visual

audishun · · · · · · · · · · · · audition¹

audit¹ ~or

audition¹

auditorium

auditory ~| canal

auful · · · · · · · · · · · · · · · awful *[terrible]⁺,
offal *[meat]

aught *[anything]   ought *[should]

augment¹ ~ation

augur¹

augury⁴

August

aukshun · · · · · · · · · · · · auction¹⁺

auksiliary · · · · · · · · · · · auxiliary⁴

☞ Can't find your word here? Look under **or**

aukward · · · · · · · · · · · · awkward⁺

auld lang syne

auning · · · · · · · · · · · · · · awning

aunt *[relative] ~ie   ant *[insect]⁺,
aren't *[are not]

au pair

aura

aural *[ear] ~ly   oral *[mouth]⁺

au revoir

KEY TO SPELLING RULES

Red words are wrong. **Black** words are correct.

~   Add the suffix or word directly to the main word, without a space or hyphen
e.g. ash ~en ~tray → ashen ashtray

~- Add a hyphen to the main word before adding the next word
e.g. blow ~-dry → blow-dry

~| Leave a space between the main word and the next word
e.g. decimal ~| place → decimal place

+   By finding this word in its **correct** alphabetical order, you can find related words
e.g. about⁺ → about-face about-turn

*   Draws attention to words that may be confused

TM Means the word is a trademark

☞ Can't find your word here? Look under **or**

auricle
aurora ~l borealis
auspices
auspicious ~ly ~ness
austere ~ly austerity
authentic ~ally authenticity
authenticate² authentication
author
authorise² authorisation
authoritarian ~ism
authoritative ~ly
authority⁴
autistic *[condition]   artistic *[skill]⁺
autism
autobiographical ~ly
autobiography⁴
autocrat ~ic ~ically
autograph¹
automate² automation
automatic ~ally ~l pilot
automatism
automaton
automobile
autonomous ~ly
autonomy
autopilot
autopsy⁴
autumn ~al
auxiliary⁴
avacado   avocado
avail¹
available availability
avalanche
avale   avail¹
avaleabul   available⁺
avant-garde

avarice avaricious
avaris   avarice⁺
avary   aviary⁴
avelanch   avalanche
avencherous   adventurous⁺
avenew   avenue
avenge²
aventure   adventure⁺
avenue
average²
averige   average²
averse aversion
avert¹
aviary⁴
aviashun   aviation⁺
aviation aviator
avid ~ly
avionics
avlanch   avalanche
avocado
avoid¹ ~able ~ably ~ance
avongar   avant-garde
avoyd   avoid¹⁺
avrage   average²
avurse   averse⁺
avurt   avert¹⁺
avyd   avid⁺
awaiken   awaken¹
awair   aware⁺
await¹
awake
awaken¹
award¹ ~able ~-winning
aware ~ness
awash
awate   await¹
away
awayk   awake

KEY TO SUFFIXES AND COMPOUNDS

These rules are explained on pages ix to x.

1 Keep the word the same before adding ed, er, est, ing
e.g. cool¹ → cooled, cooler, coolest, cooling

2 Take off final e before adding ed, er, est, ing
e.g. fine² → fined, finer, finest, fining

3 Double final consonant before adding ed, er, est, ing
e.g. thin³ → thinned, thinner, thinnest, thinning

4 Change final y to i before adding ed, er, es, est, ly, ness
e.g. tidy⁴ → tidied, tidier, tidies, tidiest, tidily, tidiness
Keep final y before adding ing e.g. tidying

5 Add es instead of s to the end of the word
e.g. bunch⁵ → bunches

6 Change final f to ve before adding s
e.g. calf⁶ → calves

awayken	awaken[1]
awayt	await[1]

☞ Can't find your word here? Look under **au**

awdience	audience
awdio	audio[+]
awe[2] ~-inspiring	
awe ~some ~struck	
awful *[terrible]	offal *[meat]
awful ~ly ~ness	
awght	aught *[anything], ought *[should]
Awgust	August
awhile	
awile	awhile
awkward ~ly ~ness	
awl *[tool]	all *[every][+]
awlmost	almost
awning	
awoke ~n	
awra	aura
awral	aural *[ear][+], oral *[mouth][+]
awry	

☞ Can't find your word here? Look under **au**

awspices	auspices
awspishus	auspicious[+]

awstere	austere[+]
awt	aught *[anything], ought *[should]
awtumn	autumn[+]
axe[2]	
axel *[jump]	axle *[wheel]
axil *[leaf]	
axiom ~atic	
axis axes	
axle *[wheel]	axel *[jump], axil *[leaf]
ayatollah	
ayce	ace
ayd	aid[1] *[help], aide *[helper]
AYDS	AIDS
aye *[yes]	eye *[sight], I *[me]
ayerveda	Ayurveda
ayl	ale
ayling	ailing
aylment	ailment
aym	aim[1+]
ayt	ate *[food], eight *[number]
Ayurveda	
azalea	
Aztec	
azure	

26

B ~-list ~-movie ~-road
baa¹
babble²
babe
babey   baby⁴⁺
babminton   badminton
baboon
babul   babble²
baby⁴ ~ish ~l boomer
babysit³
bac   back¹⁺
baccalaureate
bace   base² *[bottom],
                               bass *[music, fish]⁺
bacen   bacon
bach   batch⁵
bachelor ~hood
bacilika   basilica
bacillus bacilli

> ☞ Can't find your word here? Take off **back** and look
> again

back¹ ~ache
back ~-bench ~bencher
back ~bone ~breaking ~l burner
back ~-date ~l door ~drop
back ~fire ~gammon ~ground
back ~l issue ~lash ~list ~log
back ~pack ~l pain ~pay ~pedal
back ~rest ~scratch ~seat ~side ~space
back ~stage ~stitch ~stroke
back ~ward ~wards ~wash ~water ~woods
backhand ~ed ~er
backup ~l system
bacon ~l and eggs
bacteria bacterial bacterium
bacteriology bacteriologist
bacyllus   bacillus⁺

bad ~ly ~ness
bad ~l blood ~l debt
bad ~l faith
bad ~mouth ~-tempered
baddy⁴
bade *[said]   bayed *[howled]
badge
badger¹
badminton
baffle²
bag³ ~pipes
bagage   baggage
bagatelle
bage   badge *[pin],
                               beige *[colour]
bagel
bager   badger¹
bagett   baguette
baggage
baggie   baggy⁴
baggy⁴
baguette
baib   babe
baige   beige
baik   bake²⁺
bail¹ *[out, pay, cricket]   bale² *[bundle]
baileful   baleful⁺
bailey
bailiff
bain   bane⁺
bair   bare² *[naked]⁺,
                               bear *[carry, animal]⁺
bairn
bais   base² *[bottom],
                               bias *[favouritism]⁺
bait¹
baited *[trap, teased]   bated *[breath]
bak   back¹⁺

---

bakaloriate	baccalaureate
bake²	
baked beans	
bakery⁴	
baking ~l powder ~l sheet	
bakon	bacon
bakry	bakery⁴
baksheesh	
bakteriology	bacteriology⁺
bakteria	bacteria⁺
bal	ball *[sport, dance],
	bale² *[bundle]
balaclava	
balad	ballad
balalaika	
balance² ~l of trade ~l sheet	
balarst	ballast
balay	ballet
balcony⁴	
bald¹ *[no hair] ~ing	bawled *[cried],
	bold¹ *[strong]
balderdash	
bale² *[bundle]	bail¹ *[out, pay,
	cricket]
baleful ~ly	
balelieka	balalaika
balense	balance²⁺
balerina	ballerina
balet	ballet *[dance],
	ballot¹ *[vote]⁺
baligerence	belligerence⁺
balistic	ballistic⁺
balkony	balcony⁴
ball *[sport, dance]	bawl¹ *[cry]
ball ~l bearing ~point	
ballad	
ballast	
ballay	ballet

ballerina	
ballet *[dance]	ballot¹ *[vote]⁺
ballistic ~l missile	
ballony	baloney
balloon¹ ~ist	
ballot¹ *[vote]	ballet *[dance]
ballot ~l box ~l paper	
ballroom ~l dancing	
ballsa	balsa
ballsum	balsam
ballsumic	balsamic⁺
balm *[comfort]	barm *[froth]
balmy *[mild]	barmy⁴ *[mad]
baloney	
baloon	balloon¹⁺
balot	ballot¹⁺
balroom	ballroom⁺
balsa ~l wood	
balsam	
balsamic ~l vinegar	
balune	balloon¹⁺
baluster balustrade	
balystik	ballistic⁺
bamboo ~l shoot	
bamboozle²	
bambu	bamboo⁺
ban³	
banal banality⁴	
banana ~l skin ~l split	
band¹ *[group, stripe]	banned *[stopped]
bands *[groups, stripes]	banns *[marriage]
band ~stand ~wagon ~width	
bandage²	
bandana	
bandie	bandy⁴⁺
bandige	bandage²
bandit ~ry	
bandy⁴ ~l around ~-legged	

bandyt	bandit⁺
bane	
baned	band[1] *[group, stripe], banned *[stopped]
banel	banal⁺
baner	banner⁺
bang[1]	
bangle	
banish[1] ~ment	
banister	
banjo	
bank[1] ~| account ~| card	
bank ~| holiday ~note ~roll	
banker's ~| draft ~| note	
bankrupt[1] bankruptcy[4]	
bankwet	banquet[1]
bannana	banana⁺
banned *[stopped]	band[1] *[group, stripe]
banner ~| headline	
bannish	banish[1+]
bannister	banister
banns *[marriage]	bands *[groups, stripes]
banquet[1]	
bantam ~-weight	
banter[1]	
bantumwait	bantam-weight
banysh	banish[1+]
baonnet	bayonet[1]
baptise[2]	
baptism Baptist	
bar[3] *[stop, line, pub]	bare[2] *[naked]⁺
bar ~| chart ~| code	
bar ~| graph ~maid ~man	
bar ~| staff ~stool ~tender	
barack	barrack[1]
barage	barrage
barak	barrack[1]

barb	
barbarian	
barbaric barbarism barbarous	
barbarity[4]	
barbecue[2]	
barbed ~| wire	
barber ~-shop	
barberian	barbarian
barbican	
Barbie™ ~| doll	
barbikan	barbican
barbiturate	
bard *[poet]	bared *[showed], barred *[stopped]
bare[2] *[naked]	bear *[carry, cub]⁺
bare ~ly ~back ~faced	
bare ~foot ~headed ~legged	
barehug	bear hug
barekaid	barricade[2]
barel	barrel[3+]
barelief	bas-relief
baren	baron *[noble]⁺, barren *[empty]⁺
bareskin	bearskin
bargain[1] ~-basement	
bargaining ~| chip ~| position	
barge[2] ~-pole	
bargen	bargain[1+]
bargin	bargain[1+]
bariam	barium⁺
baricade	barricade[2]
bariem	barium⁺
barier	barrier
barister	barrister
baritone	
barium ~| meal	
barje	barge[2+]
bark[1]	

KEY TO SUFFIXES AND COMPOUNDS

These rules are explained on pages ix to x.

1 Keep the word the same before adding **ed, er, est, ing**
   e.g. cool[1] → cooled, cooler, coolest, cooling

2 Take off final **e** before adding **ed, er, est, ing**
   e.g. fine[2] → fined, finer, finest, fining

3 Double final consonant before adding **ed, er, est, ing**
   e.g. thin[3] → thinned, thinner, thinnest, thinning

4 Change final **y** to **i** before adding **ed, er, es, est, ly, ness**
   e.g. tidy[4] → tidied, tidier, tidies, tidiest, tidily, tidiness
   Keep final **y** before adding **ing** e.g. tidying

5 Add **es** instead of **s** to the end of the word
   e.g. bunch[5] → bunches

6 Change final **f** to **ve** before adding **s**
   e.g. calf[6] → calves

barley ~l sugar ~l water	
barm *[froth]	balm *[comfort]
bar mitzvah	
barmy⁴ *[mad]	balmy *[mild]
barn *[building] ~l dance	
barn ~l owl ~l yard	
barnacle	
barock	baroque
barometer barometric	
baron *[noble]	barren *[empty]⁺
baron ~ess ~et ~ial	
baroque	
barow	barrow
barrack¹	
barrage	
barrel³ ~ful ~l organ	
barren *[empty] ~ness	baron *[noble]⁺
barricade²	
barrier ~l reef	
barrister	
barrometer	barometer⁺
barrow	
barscit	basket
barter¹	
barth	bath¹⁺
barytone	baritone
bas	base² *[bottom]⁺,
	bass *[music, fish]⁺
basalt	
basc	bask¹ *[soak up],
	basque *[clothing]
bascet	basket⁺
base² *[bottom]	bass *[music, fish]⁺
base ~angle ~ball ~less	
base ~line ~l metal ~l rate	
basement	
bash¹ ~es	
bashful ~ly ~ness	

basic *[simple] ~ally	
Basic *[program]	
basil	
basilica	
basillus	bacillus⁺
basin ~ful	
basis bases	
bask¹ *[soak up]	basque *[clothing]
basket ~ful ~ry ~ball ~work	
basooka	bazooka
basoon	bassoon⁺
basque *[clothing]	bask¹ *[soak up]
bas-relief	
bass *[music, fish]	base² *[bottom]⁺
bass ~l clef ~l drum	
bass ~-guitar ~-guitarist	
basset ~l hound	
bassilus	bacillus⁺
bassoon ~ist	
bastard	
bastardise² bastardisation	
baste²	
bastion	
bastjun	bastion
basune	bassoon⁺
basyl	basil
basylica	basilica
basyn	basin⁺
bat³ ~sman	
batalion	battalion
batch⁵ ~l processing	
batcheler	bachelor⁺
bated *[breath]	baited *[trap, teased]
baten	baton *[carried],
	batten¹ *[fixed]
bater	barter¹ *[buy],
	batter¹ *[food, hit]
batery	battery⁴⁺

KEY TO SPELLING RULES

Red words are wrong. **Black** words are correct.

~   Add the suffix or word directly to the main word, without a space or hyphen
    e.g. ash ~en ~tray → ashen ashtray

~--   Add a hyphen to the main word before adding the next word
    e.g. blow ~-dry → blow-dry

~l   Leave a space between the main word and the next word
    e.g. decimal ~l place → decimal place

+   By finding this word in its **correct** alphabetical order, you can find related words
    e.g. about⁺ → about-face about-turn

*   Draws attention to words that may be confused

TM   Means the word is a trademark

bath¹ *[tub, wash]	bathe² *[wash, swim]
bath ~mat ~l oil	
bath ~robe ~room	
bathe² *[wash, swim]	bath¹ *[tub, wash]
bathing ~l costume ~l suit	
batik	
batle	battle²⁺
baton *[carried]	batten¹ *[fixed]
batrie	battery⁴⁺
battalion	
battel	battle²⁺
batten¹ *[fixed]	baton *[carried]
batter¹	
battery⁴ ~l acid ~l pack	
battle² ~-axe ~-cry	
battle ~dress ~field ~ground	
battle ~ments ~-ram ~ship	
batton	baton *[carried],
	batten¹ *[fixed]
battrey	battery⁴⁺
batty⁴	
batyk	batik
bauble	
baud *[data]	bored *[dull],
	board¹ *[get on,
	panel]⁺
baudy	bawdy⁴
baujolais	Beaujolais
baul	ball *[sport, dance]⁺,
	bawl¹ *[cry]
baulk¹	
bauxite	
bawbul	bauble
bawdy⁴	
bawk	balk¹
bawl¹ *[cry]	ball *[sport, dance]
bawlderdash	balderdash
bawlk	baulk¹

bawn	born⁺
bawt	bought
bawxite	bauxite
bay¹ ~l window	
bayl	bale²*[bundle],
	bail¹ *[out, pay,
	cricket]⁺
bayley	bailey
baylful	baleful⁺
bayliff	bailiff
bayonet¹	
bayt	bait¹
baything	bathing⁺
bazaar *[sale]	bizarre *[strange]⁺
bazooka	
be *[I will be] ~ing	bee *[insect]⁺
beach¹ *[shore] ~es	beech⁵ *[tree]
beach ~l ball	
beach ~comber	
beach ~combing ~head	
beacon *[light]	bacon *[meat]
bead¹ ~y	
beaf	beef¹⁺
beagle beagling	
beak ~er	
beakeeper	beekeeper⁺
be-all and end-all	
Bealzebub	Beelzebub
beam¹	
bean ~l counter ~l curd	
bean *[vegetable] ~pole	been *[past of to be]
bean ~sprouts ~stalk	
beanie	
beap	beep¹
bear *[carry, cub]	bare² *[naked]⁺,
	beer *[drink],
	bier *[funeral]
bear ~hug ~l market ~skin	

KEY TO SUFFIXES AND COMPOUNDS

These rules are explained on pages ix to x.

1 Keep the word the same before adding **ed, er, est, ing**
  e.g. cool¹ → cooled, cooler, coolest, cooling
2 Take off final **e** before adding **ed, er, est, ing**
  e.g. fine² → fined, finer, finest, fining
3 Double final consonant before adding **ed, er, est, ing**
  e.g. thin³ → thinned, thinner, thinnest, thinning

4 Change final **y** to **i** before adding **ed, er, es, est, ly, ness**
  e.g. tidy⁴ → tidied, tidier, tidies, tidiest, tidily, tidiness
  Keep final **y** before adding **ing** e.g. tidying
5 Add **es** instead of **s** to the end of the word
  e.g. bunch⁵ → bunches
6 Change final **f** to **ve** before adding **s**
  e.g. calf⁶ → calves

bearable
beard ~ed
bearing *[point, carrying]   baring *[showing]
beast   beastly⁴
beat *[strike] ~en ~ing   beet *[food]⁺
beatific ~ation
beatify⁴ *[saint]   beautify⁴ *[pretty]
beatroot   beetroot
beatul   beetle
beau
Beaufort Scale
Beaujolais
beauteous
beautician
beautiful ~ly
beautify⁴ *[pretty]   beatify⁴ *[saint]
beauty⁴ *[lovely]   booty *[treasure]
beauty ~| queen ~| salon
beaver¹ ~| away
becalmed
became
because
beck ~| and call
beckon¹ ~ingly
become   becoming
becon   beacon *[light],
                 beckon¹ *[call]⁺
becos   because
becum   become
bed³ ~bugs ~clothes ~fellow
bed ~-linen ~ridden ~rock
bed ~-roll ~room ~side
bed ~-sit ~sore ~spread
bed ~stead ~time ~wetting
beday   bidet
bedazzled
bedevil³
bedlam

Bedouin
bedraggled
bedwin   Bedouin
bee *[insect] ~hive   be *[I will be]⁺
bee ~keeper ~line ~swax
beech⁵ *[tree]   beach¹ *[shore]⁺
beed   bead¹
beef¹ ~y ~burger
beef ~eater ~steak ~| up
beegul   beagle⁺
beek   beak⁺
Beelzebub
beem   beam¹⁺
been *[was]   bean *[vegetable]⁺
beep¹
beer *[drink]   bier *[funeral]
beerd   beard¹⁺
beest   beast⁺
beestro   bistro⁺
beet *[food] ~root   beat *[strike]⁺
beetle
beever   beaver¹⁺
befall ~en
befell
befit³
before ~hand
befrend   befriend¹
befriend¹
befuddle²
befyt   befit³
beg³
began
beggar¹
begile   beguile²
begin ~ner ~ning
begone
begonia
begrudge²

beguile[2]
begun
behalf
behave[2]
behaviour ~al ~ism
behead[1]
behed   behead[1]
beheld
behest
behind
behold ~en ~er ~ing
beige
being
bejewelled
bek   beck[+]
bekalmed   becalmed
bekame   became
bekause   because
bekome   become[+]
bekon   beacon *[light],
                               beckon[1] *[call][+]
bekweath   bequeath[1]
bekwest   bequest
belated ~ly
belch[1] ~es
beleaguered
belei   belie[+]
beleif   belief
beleive   believe[2]
belfry[4]
belicose   bellicose[+]
belie ~d belying
belief
believable believably
believe[2]
beligerent   belligerent[+]
Belisha beacon
belittle[2]

bell *[rings] ~-ringing   belle *[beauty]
belladonna
belle *[beauty]   bell *[rings][+]
bellicose bellicosity
belligerent ~ly belligerence
bellow[1] *[yell]   below *[under]
bellows
belly[4] ~ache ~-button
belly ~dance ~-flop ~ful ~-up
belong[1] ~ings
beloved
below *[under]   bellow[1] *[yell]
belt[1]
Belysha bekon   Belisha beacon
bemoan[1]
bemuse[2]
bench ~es ~-mark
bend ~able ~ing
beneath
benedicshun   benediction
Benedictine ~I monk
benediction
beneeth   beneath
benefactor
beneficial ~ly
beneficiary[4]
benefishal   beneficial[+]
benefisiary   beneficiary[4]
benefit[1]
benevolent benevolence
benidicshun   benediction
Benidictine   Benedictine[+]
benign ~ly
benine   benign[+]
bent
benzene *[single compound]
benzine *[mixture]
bequeath[1]

---

bequest

> ☞ Can't find your word here? Look under **bur**

ber	burr
berate[2]	
beray	beret
berbul	burble[2]
berch	birch[1+]
berd	bird[+]
berden	burden[1+]
bereave[2] ~ment	
bereft	
beret *[hat]	berry[4] *[fruit], bury[4] *[cover]
bereve	bereave[2+]
berger	burger
bergeun	burgeon[1]
berglar	burglar
berglary	burglary[4]
bergul	burgle[2]
berial	burial[+]
beriberi	
berlap	burlap
berlesk	burlesque
berly	burly[4]
bern	burn[1+]
bernish	burnish[1]
berray	beret
berry[4] *[fruit]	beret *[hat], bury[4] *[cover]
bersar	bursar[+]
berserk	
berst	burst
berth[1] *[moor, bunk]	birth *[born][+]
bery	beret *[hat], berry[4] *[fruit], bury[4] *[cover]
beryberi	beriberi

beseech[1]	
beseige	besiege[2]
beset[3]	
beside *[at the side]	
besides *[as well as]	
besiege[2]	
besmirch[1]	
besotted	
bespectacled	
bespoke	
best ~| man ~| practice ~-seller	
bestial ~ity	
bestow[1] ~al	
bet[3]	
beta ~-blocker ~| particle ~| test	
betray[1] ~al	
betroth[1] ~al	
better[1] ~ment	
between	
betwixt	
beuteful	beautiful[+]
beutifull	beautiful[+]
beutishun	beautician
beverage	
bevrige	beverage
bevvy[4] *[drink]	
bevy[4] *[group]	
beware	
bewich	bewitch[1]
bewilder[1] ~ment	
bewitch[1]	
beyond	
bhaji	
bi ~polar ~sexual	
biannual *[twice a year]	biennial *[every two years]
bias ~ed ~es	
biatify	beatify[4]

KEY TO SPELLING RULES

Red words are wrong. **Black** words are correct.

~ Add the suffix or word directly to the main word, without a space or hyphen
  e.g. ash ~en ~tray → **ashen ashtray**

~- Add a hyphen to the main word before adding the next word
  e.g. blow ~-dry → **blow-dry**

~| Leave a space between the main word and the next word
  e.g. decimal ~| place → **decimal place**

+ By finding this word in its **correct** alphabetical order, you can find related words
  e.g. about[+] → **about-face about-turn**

* Draws attention to words that may be confused

TM Means the word is a trademark

bib

Bible ~| belt

biblical ~ly

bibliographic ~al

bibliography[4]   bibliographer

bicarbonate ~| of soda

bicentennial   bicentenary[4]

biceps

bich   bitch[1+]

bicker[1]

bicycle[2]

bid *[say] ~den ~ding   bide[2] *[wait]

bidazled   bedazzled

biddy[4]

bide[2]

bidet

bidevil   bedevil[3]

bie   by *[near][+],
                                  buy *[shop][+],
                                  bye *[farewell][+]

bief   beef[+]

☞ Can't find your word here? Look under **be**

biege   beige

Bielzebub   Beelzebub

biennial *[every two   biannual *[twice a
          years]   year]

biep   beep[1]

bier *[funeral]   beer *[drink][+],
                                  buyer *[shop]

biet   beat *[strike][+],
                                  beet *[food][+]

bietle   beetle

bifocal ~s

bifour   before[+]

bifriend   befriend[1]

bifuddul   befuddle[2]

bifurcate[2]   bifurcation

big[3] ~| business ~| game

big ~head ~-mouth

big ~-shot ~| top ~wig

Big ~| Bang ~| Ben ~| Dipper

bigamist   bigamous   bigamy

bigan   began

bigon   begone

bigonia   begonia

bigot ~ed ~ry

bigruge   begrudge[2]

bigun   begun

bihalf   behalf

bihave   behave[2]

bihavior   behaviour[+]

bihed   behead[1]

biheld   beheld

bihind   behind

bihold   behold[+]

bijwelled   bejewelled

bike[2]

biker *[motorcyclist]   bicker[1] *[squabble]

bikini

bil   bill[1] *[invoice][+],
                                  bile *[body, feeling][+]

bilabong   billabong

bilated   belated[+]

bilateral ~ism ~ly

bilberry[4]

bild   billed *[invoiced],
                                  build *[construct][+]

bilding   building[+]

bile ~| duct

bileagered   beleaguered

bilet   billet[1]

bilevabul   believable[+]

bilge

bilingual ~ism ~ly

bilion   billion[+]

KEY TO SUFFIXES AND COMPOUNDS

These rules are explained on pages ix to x.

1 Keep the word the same before adding **ed, er, est, ing**
e.g. cool[1] → cooled, cooler, coolest, cooling

2 Take off final **e** before adding **ed, er, est, ing**
e.g. fine[2] → fined, finer, finest, fining

3 Double final consonant before adding **ed, er, est, ing**
e.g. thin[3] → thinned, thinner, thinnest, thinning

4 Change final **y** to **i** before adding **ed, er, es, est, ly, ness**
e.g. tidy[4] → tidied, tidier, tidies, tidiest, tidily, tidiness
Keep final **y** before adding **ing** e.g. tidying

5 Add **es** instead of **s** to the end of the word
e.g. bunch[5] → bunches

6 Change final **f** to **ve** before adding **s**
e.g. calf[6] → calves

bilittul	belittle[2]
bill[1] ~board	
billabong	
billed *[invoiced]	build *[construct][+]
billet[1]	
billiards	
billion ~aire ~th	
billow[1] *[wave] ~y	below *[under]
billy goat	
biloved	beloved
bilow	below *[under], billow[1] *[wave][+]
bilt	built[+]
Bilzebub	Beelzebub
bimone	bemoan[1]
bimonthly	
bimuse	bemuse[2]
bin[3] *[box] ~liner	been *[was]
binacle	binnacle
binary ~l number	
binary ~l system ~l star	
bind ~er ~ing	
bineath	beneath
binge[2]	
bingo	
binnacle	
binoculars	
binomial ~l system	
biochemical ~ly	
biochemist ~ry	
biodegradable	
bio-feedback	
bio-fuel	
biofysics	biophysics[+]
biografer	biographer
biografy	biography[4+]
biographer	
biography[4] biographical	

biokemical	biochemical[+]
biological ~ly ~l clock	
biological ~l warfare	
biologist biology	
biomass	
biomedicine biomedical	
bionic	
biophysics	
biopsy[4]	
biosphere	
biotechnology	
bipartisan	
bipass	bypass[1]
biped	
biplane	
bipolar ~l disorder	

☞ Can't find your word here? Look under **by**

biqueath	bequeath[1]
biquest	bequest
birbel	burble[2]
birch[1] ~es	
bird ~l bath ~-brained ~cage	
bird ~like ~seed	
bird ~l table ~-watching	
birden	burden[1+]
birdie	
bird's-eye view	
birgen	burgeon[1]
birger	burger
birgler	burglar
birgul	burgle[2]
biriani	
birlap	burlap
birlesk	burlesque
birnt	burnt
birth *[born]	berth[1] *[moor, bunk]

KEY TO SPELLING RULES

Red words are wrong. **Black** words are correct.

~   Add the suffix or word directly to the main word, without a space or hyphen
     e.g. ash ~en ~tray → **ashen ashtray**

~-   Add a hyphen to the main word before adding the next word
     e.g. blow ~-dry → **blow-dry**

~l   Leave a space between the main word and the next word
     e.g. decimal ~l place → **decimal place**

+   By finding this word in its **correct** alphabetical order, you can find related words
     e.g. about[+] → **about-face about-turn**

*   Draws attention to words that may be confused

TM   Means the word is a trademark

birth ~day ~| certificate ~| control
birth ~mark ~place ~| rate ~right
biscit   biscuit
biscuit

☞ Can't find your word here? Look under **be**

biseach   beseech[1]
bisect[1] ~ion ~or
biseige   besiege[2]
bisen   bison
bisentennial   bicentennial+
biseps   biceps
bisexual ~ity ~ly
bishop
biside   beside+
bisk   bisque
biskit   biscuit
bison
bisoted   besotted
bispoke   bespoke
bisque
bistro
bisycul   bicycle[2]
bit ~ten
bitch[1] ~es ~y
bitchumen   bitumen
bite *[teeth]   biting   byte *[data]
bite-size ~d
bitray   betray[1+]
bitter ~ly ~ness ~| end
bitter ~| lemon ~-sweet
bitumen
bitween   between
bitwixt   betwixt
bivouac
bivouacked   bivouacking
biware   beware
biway   byway

bi-weekly
biwich   bewitch[1]
biwilder   bewilder[1+]
biword   byword
biyond   beyond
Bizantine   Byzantine
bizarre *[strange] ~ly   bazaar *[sale]
bizness   business+
bizy   busy[4+]
blab[3] ~bermouth

☞ Can't find your word here? Take off **black** and look again

black[1] ~| and blue ~| and white
black ~| ball ~| belt ~bird
black ~board ~box ~currant
black ~| eye ~head ~| hole
black ~| ice ~jack ~leg ~list
black ~magic ~mail ~| mark
black ~| market ~out
black ~| sheep ~smith ~| tie ~| widow
Black Death
blackberry[4]
blacken[1]
blackguard
bladder
blade ~-runner
blader *[skater]   bladder *[urine]
blading
blag[3]
blaggard   blackguard
blah
blaid   blade+
blaim   blame[2+]
blair   blare[2]
blak   black[1+]
blamange   blancmange
blame[2] ~able ~less ~lessly

KEY TO SUFFIXES AND COMPOUNDS

These rules are explained on pages ix to x.

1 Keep the word the same before adding **ed, er, est, ing**
e.g. cool[1] → cooled, cooler, coolest, cooling
2 Take off final **e** before adding **ed, er, est, ing**
e.g. fine[2] → fined, finer, finest, fining
3 Double final consonant before adding **ed, er, est, ing**
e.g. thin[3] → thinned, thinner, thinnest, thinning

4 Change final **y** to **i** before adding **ed, er, es, est, ly, ness**
e.g. tidy[4] → tidied, tidier, tidies, tidiest, tidily, tidiness
Keep final **y** before adding **ing** e.g. tidying
5 Add **es** instead of **s** to the end of the word
e.g. bunch[5] → bunches
6 Change final **f** to **ve** before adding **s**
e.g. calf[6] → calves

blameworthy
blanch[1] ~es
blancmange
bland ~ly ~ness
blandishments
blank[1] ~ly ~ness ~| cartridge ~| verse
blanket[1]
blare[2]
blarney ~| stone
blarst   blast[1+]
blarzay   blasé
blasé
blasfeme   blaspheme[2+]
blasfemy   blasphemy[4]
blaspheme[2]   blasphemous
blasphemy[4]
blast[1] ~-furnace ~-off
blatancy
blatant ~ly
blazé   blasé
blaze[2]
blazer
bleach[1] ~es
bleak[1] ~ly ~ness
bleary ~-eyed
bleat[1]
bleech   bleach[1+]
bleed ~ing
bleek   bleak[+]
bleep[1]
bleery   bleary[4+]
bleet   bleat[1]
blemish[1]
blench[1]
blend[1]
bler   blur[3+]
blert   blurt[1+]
bless[1]

blest
blet   bleat[1]
blew *[wind]   blue *[colour][+]
blight[1]
blimey
blimp
blind[1] ~ly ~ness ~| alley
blind ~| date ~fold ~-man's-buff
blind ~| side ~| spot
blini
blink[1]
blinkered   blinkers
blip[3]
bliss ~ful ~fully ~fulness
blister[1]
blite   blight[1]
blithe ~ly ~ness
blithering
blitz[1] *[attack]
Blitz *[World War II]
blizzard
blo   blow [+]
bloat[1] ~edness
blob[3]
bloc *[political]   block[1] *[stop][+]
bloch   blotch[1+]
blochy   blotchy[4]
block[1] *[stop] ~age   bloc *[group]
block *[chunk] ~-booking
block ~buster ~| grant ~head ~| vote
blockade[2]
blod   blood[+]
blog[3]
bloke
blond
blood ~| bank ~bath ~| cell ~| clot
blood ~| count ~curdling ~| donor
blood ~| flow ~| group ~hound

☞ Can't find your word here? Take off **blood** and look again

blood ~less ~lust ~| money
blood ~| poisoning ~| pressure
blood ~shed ~shot ~stain ~| stream ~| sugar
blood ~| test ~thirsty ~| transfusion
blood ~| type ~| vessel
bloody[4]
Bloody Mary
bloody-minded ~ly ~ness
bloom[1]
blossom[1]
blot[3]
blotting paper
blotch[1] ~es   blotchy[4]
blote   bloat[1+]
blotto
blouse
blow ~er ~ing ~n
blow ~fly ~hole ~lamp
blow ~out ~pipe ~torch
blubber[1]
blud   blood[+]
bluddy   bloody[4+]
blue *[colour]   blew *[wind]
blue ~-berry ~bell
blue ~-bird ~bottle ~-collar
blue ~grass ~print ~| ribbon
blue ~-rinse ~tooth
blues ~y
bluff[1]
bluish
blume   bloom[1+]
blunder[1]
blunt[1] ~ly ~ness
blur[3] ~ry
blurb

blurt[1] ~| out
blush[1]
bluster[1] ~y

☞ Can't find your word here? Look under **bli**

blymp   blimp
blynd   blind[1+]
blyzzard   blizzard
bo   beau *[boyfriend],
                             bow[1] *[arrow, knot][+]

boa ~| constrictor
boagy   bogey
boahmian   bohemian
boan   bone[2+]
boar *[pig]   bore[2] *[drill, dull][+]
board[1] *[get on, panel]   baud *[data],
board ~game ~room   bored *[dull][+]
boarding ~| card
boarding ~| house ~| school
boast[1] ~ful ~fully ~fulness
boat ~ing ~yard   bot *[computer]
bob[3] ~sleigh
bobbin
bobble[2]
bobin   bobbin
bobul   bobble[2]
boch   botch[1+]
bocks   box[1+]
bodice
bodie   body[4+]
bodily ~| harm
bodiss   bodice
body[4] ~| bag ~| builder
body ~| building ~| clock
body ~| count ~guard ~| shop
body ~-snatcher ~-suit
bog[3]
bogel   boggle[2]

KEY TO SUFFIXES AND COMPOUNDS

These rules are explained on pages ix to x.

1 Keep the word the same before adding **ed, er, est, ing**
e.g. cool[1] → cooled, cooler, coolest, cooling
2 Take off final **e** before adding **ed, er, est, ing**
e.g. fine[2] → fined, finer, finest, fining
3 Double final consonant before adding **ed, er, est, ing**
e.g. thin[3] → thinned, thinner, thinnest, thinning

4 Change final **y** to **i** before adding **ed, er, es, est, ly, ness**
e.g. tidy[4] → tidied, tidier, tidies, tidiest, tidily, tidiness
Keep final **y** before adding **ing** e.g. tidying
5 Add **es** instead of **s** to the end of the word
e.g. bunch[5] → bunches
6 Change final **f** to **ve** before adding **s**
e.g. calf[6] → calves

bogey *[golf, mucus]

boggle²

boggy⁴ *[ground]

bogus

bohemian

boiant   buoyant⁺

boil¹ ~| down ~| over

boiled ~| sweet

boiler ~room ~| suit

boisterous ~ly ~ness

bok   book¹⁺

bolard   bollard

Bolchevic   Bolshevik

bold¹ *[strong] ~ly ~face   bald *[no hair]⁺,
                 bowled *[sport]

boler   bowler⁺

bolero

Boliwood   Bollywood

bolk   baulk¹

bollard

bollderise   bowdlerise²

bolled   bald *[no hair]⁺,
                 bold¹ *[strong]⁺,
                 bowled *[sport]

bollock¹

Bollywood

Bolshevik

bolshy⁴

bolster¹ ~| up

bolt¹ ~-hole

bom   bomb¹⁺

bomb¹ ~-disposal ~-proof

bomb ~shell ~| shelter ~site

bombard¹ ~-ment

bombastic ~ally

bomber ~| jacket

bommer   bomber⁺

bon appétit

bon vivant

bon voyage

bona fide   bona fides

bonanza

bonbon

bond¹ ~age ~-holder

bone² ~| china ~-dry ~-mass

bone ~-meal ~| marrow ~| structure

bonfire   Bonfire Night

bongo ~| drums

bonhomie

bonk¹ ~ers

bonnafidy   bona fide⁺

bonnansa   bonanza

bonnet

bonomie   bonhomie

bonus⁵ ~| track

bony⁴

boo¹ ~-hoo

booby ~-prize ~-trap

boofant   bouffant

boogie ~| board ~-woogie

book¹ ~able ~binder ~case

book ~-club ~-end ~keeping

book ~let ~maker ~mark

book ~rest ~seller ~shelf

book ~shop ~worm

bookay   bouquet⁺

Boolean ~| logic ~| search

booles   boules

boolevard   boulevard

boom¹ ~| box ~| town

boomerang

boorish

boose   booze²⁺

boost¹

booster ~| seat

boot¹ *[shoe] ~| camp

---

boot ~leg ~strap		botanical ~l garden	
bootee *[shoe]	booty *[treasure]	botanist botany	
booth		botch¹ ~es	
booty *[treasure]	bootee *[shoe]	bote	boat⁺
booze² ~-up		both	
borax boracic		bother¹ ~some	
borbul	bauble	botle	bottle²⁺
Bordeaux		botocks	botox
bordello		botom	bottom¹⁺
border¹ ~line		botox	
bording	boarding⁺	bottanical	botanical⁺
bordom	boredom	bottle² ~l bank ~-feed	
bordor	border⁺	bottle ~neck ~-opener	
bordow	Bordeaux	bottom¹ ~l drawer ~less	
bore² *[drill, dull] ~hole	boar *[pig]	bottom ~l line ~l out	
bored *[dull] ~l stiff	baud *[data],	botul	bottle²⁺
	board¹ *[get on,	botulism	
	panel]⁺	botum	bottom¹⁺
boreding	boarding⁺	bouffant	
boredom		bougainvillea	
borganvilla	bougainvillea	bough *[branch]	bow¹ *[bend]
borjwa	bourgeois⁺	bought *[shop]	brought *[bring]
boric ~l acid		bouillon *[soup] ~l cube	bullion *[gold]
born *[birth] ~-again		boukay	bouquet⁺
borne *[carried]		boulder	
borough *[place]	burrow¹ *[dig, hole]	boules	
borrow¹ *[loan] ~ings		boulevard	
borstal		bounce² bouncy⁴	
borte	bought	bound¹ ~less	
boso	bozo	boundary⁴	
bosom ~y		bounse	bounce²⁺
boss¹		bounteous ~ly	
bossa nova		bountiful ~ly	
bossen	bosun	bounty⁴ ~l hunter	
bossy⁴ ~-boots		bouquet ~l garni	
bost	boast¹⁺	bourax	borax⁺
bosun		bourdello	bordello
bot *[computer]	boat *[water]⁺	bourder	border¹⁺

KEY TO SUFFIXES AND COMPOUNDS

These rules are explained on pages ix to x.

1 Keep the word the same before adding **ed, er, est, ing**
e.g. cool¹ → cooled, cooler, coolest, cooling
2 Take off final **e** before adding **ed, er, est, ing**
e.g. fine² → fined, finer, finest, fining
3 Double final consonant before adding **ed, er, est, ing**
e.g. thin³ → thinned, thinner, thinnest, thinning

4 Change final **y** to **i** before adding **ed, er, es, est, ly, ness**
e.g. tidy⁴ → tidied, tidier, tidies, tidiest, tidily, tidiness
Keep final **y** before adding **ing** e.g. tidying
5 Add **es** instead of **s** to the end of the word
e.g. bunch⁵ → bunches
6 Change final **f** to **ve** before adding **s**
e.g. calf⁶ → calves

bourdom	boredom
bourgeois ~ie	
bourn	born[+]
bourstal	borstal
bout	
boutick	boutique
boutique	
bovine	
bow[1] *[bend]	bough *[branch]
bow *[arrow, knot]	beau *[boyfriend]
bow ~-legged ~l tie ~l window	
bowdlerise[2]	
bowel *[tummy]	bowl[1] *[food, sport][+]
bower	
Bowfort skale	Beaufort scale
Bowjolais	Beaujolais
bowl[1] *[food, sport] ~ful	bowel *[tummy]
bowler ~l hat	
bowling ~l alley ~l ball	
bownd	bound[+]
bowndry	boundary[4]
bownse	bounce[2+]
bowntiful	bountiful[+]
bownty	bounty[4+]
bowt	bout
bowur	bower
bow-wow	
box[1] ~es ~l office ~l spring ~wood	
boxer ~l shorts	
Boxing Day	
boxite	bauxite
boxsight	bauxite
boy *[male] ~friend	buoy[1] *[float]
boy ~hood	
boyant	buoyant[+]
boycott[1]	
boyish ~ly ~ness	
boyl	boil[1]
boyled	boiled

boyler	boiler[+]
Boy Scout	
boystrous	boisterous[+]
bozo	
bra	
brace[2]	
bracelet	
bracken	
bracket[1]	
brackish	
brag[3]	
Brahmin	
braid[1] *[cloth, hair]	brayed *[donkey]
braille	
brain[1] ~l cell ~child	
brain ~l damage ~-dead	
brain ~less ~power	
brain ~-stem ~storm ~-teaser	
brain ~l tumour ~wash ~wave	
brainy[4]	
braise[2] *[food]	brace[2] *[hold, teeth]
braiselet	bracelet
brake[2] *[slow] ~l fluid	break *[snap, stop][+]
brake ~l light ~l pad	
braket	bracket[1]
brakish	brackish
bramble	
bran *[cereal]	brain *[mind][+]
branch[1] ~es ~l line ~l office	
brand[1] ~l loyalty	
brand ~l name ~-new	
branding ~l iron	
brandish[1] ~es	
brandy ~l butter ~l snap	
brane	brain[2+]
brar	bra
bras *[underwear]	brass *[metal]
brase	braise[2] *[food]

	brace² *[support, teeth]		breathe² *[in, out]
braselet	bracelet	breathable	
brasen	brazen⁺	breathalyse²	
brash		breathe² *[in, out]	breath *[air]⁺
brass ~y ~| band ~| rubbing		breathless ~ly ~ness	
brasserie *[restaurant]		breathtaking ~ly	
brassière *[bra]		breaze	breeze²⁺
brat ~tish ~| pack		bred *[created]	bread *[food]⁺,
braul	brawl¹		breed [create, type]⁺
brauny	brawny⁴	bredth	breadth *[width]
bravado		breech *[back] ~| birth	breach¹ *[break]
brave² bravery		breeches	
bravo		breed ~ing	
bravura		breeder ~| reactor	
brawd	broad⁺	breef	brief¹⁺
brawl¹		breethe	breathe²
brawn brawny⁴		breeze² ~| block ~| in	
brawt	brought	breezy⁴	
bray¹		breif	brief¹⁺
brayed *[donkey]	braid¹ *[cloth, hair]	brekfast	breakfast¹⁺
brayny	brainy⁴	brest	breast⁺
brazen ~ly ~ness		breth	breath *[air]⁺,
brazier			breathe² *[in, out]
breach¹ *[break]	breech *[back]⁺	brethalise	breathalyse²⁺
bread *[food] ~ed	breed *[create, type]⁺	brethren	
bread ~-and-butter ~| basket		brethtaking	breathtaking⁺
bread ~crumbs ~winner		brevity	
breadth *[width]	breath *[air]⁺	brew¹ brewery⁴	
break *[snap, stop]	brake² *[slow]	brewed *[beer, coffee]	brood¹ *[think, kids]⁺
break ~able ~ing ~down		bribe² bribery⁴	
break ~in ~neck ~point		bric-à-brac	
break ~through ~-up ~water		brick¹ ~layer ~work	
breakage		bridal *[wedding]	bridle² *[horse]⁺
breakfast¹ ~| television		bridal ~| party ~| suite	
breast ~bone ~feed ~plate		bride ~groom ~smaid	
breast ~| pocket ~stroke		bride ~-to-be	
breath *[air] ~| test	breadth *[width],	bridge² ~-building ~head	
		bridle² *[horse] ~-way	bridal *[wedding]⁺

---

brief[1] ~ly ~s ~case		broch	broach[1] *[subject][+],
brieze	breeze[2+]		brooch[5] *[jewellery]
brigade		brocher	brochure
brigadier ~l general		brochure	
brige	bridge[2+]	brocoli	broccoli
brigedier	brigadier[+]	brogue	
bright[1] ~-eyed		brokade	brocade
brighten[1]		broke ~n	
brik	brick[1+]	broker[1] ~age	
brik-a-brak	bric-à-brac	brokn	broken
brikette	briquette	brolly[4]	
brilliant ~ly brilliance		bromide	
brim[3] ~ful ~stone		bromine	
brine		bronchial ~l tube	
bring ~er ~ing		bronchitis	
brink ~manship		bronco	
brioche		bronkial	bronchial[+]
briquette		bronkitus	bronchitis
brisk[1] ~ly ~ness		bronse	bronze[2+]
brisket		brontosaurus	
bristle bristly		bronze[2] ~l medal	
Britain *[country]	Briton *[person]	Bronze Age	
Britannia		brooch[5] *[jewellery]	broach[1] *[subject]
brite	bright[1+]	brood[1] *[think, kids]	brewed *[beer,
British ~l Empire ~l Isles			coffee]
Briton *[person]	Britain *[country]	broody[4]	
britten	Britain	brook[1]	
brittle ~ness		broom ~stick	
broach[1] *[subject] ~es	brooch[5] *[jewellery]	broose	bruise[2]
broad[1] ~ly ~band ~l bean		broot	brute[+]
broad ~-brush ~cast ~minded		brorde	broad[1+]
broad ~sheet ~side		brort	brought
broad ~-spectrum		broth	
broaden[1]		brothel	
Broadway		brother ~hood ~-in-law	
broak	broke	brought *[bring]	bought *[shop]
brocade		brouhaha	
broccoli		brow ~beat	

KEY TO SPELLING RULES

Red words are wrong. **Black** words are correct.

~   Add the suffix or word directly to the main word, without a space or hyphen
    e.g. ash ~en ~tray → **ashen ashtray**

~- Add a hyphen to the main word before adding the next word
    e.g. blow ~-dry → **blow-dry**

~l   Leave a space between the main word and the next word
    e.g. decimal ~l place → **decimal place**

+   By finding this word in its **correct** alphabetical order, you can find related words
    e.g. about[+] → **about-face about-turn**

*   Draws attention to words that may be confused

TM Means the word is a trademark

brown¹ ~| dwarf
brownie *[cake]
Brownie *[club]
brownie points
browse²
browser
bruch   brush¹⁺
bruck   brook¹
brud   brood¹⁺
brue   brew¹⁺
bruhaha   brouhaha
bruise²
brume   broom⁺
brunch⁵
brunette
brunt
brusck   brusque⁺
brush¹ ~es ~-off
brush ~wood ~work
brusque ~ly ~ness
Brussels ~| sprouts
brutal ~ly   brutality
brutalise²   brutalisation
brute ~| force ~| strength
bruther   brother⁺
brutish ~ly ~ness
brutle   brutal⁺

| ☞ Can't find your word here? Look under bri |

brydal   bridal *[wedding]⁺,
                               bridle² *[horse]
bryde   bride⁺
bu   boo¹⁺
bubble² bubbly⁴
buby   booby⁺
buccaneer
buch   butch
bucher   butcher¹⁺

buck¹ ~| up
bucket¹ ~ful
Buckingham Palace
buckle²
bucksom   buxom⁺
bud³
Buddha
Buddhism   Buddhist
buddy⁴
budge²
budgerigar   budgie
budget¹ ~ary
Budha   Buddha
bufalo   buffalo⁵
bufer   buffer¹⁺
buff¹
buffalo⁵
buffay   buffet
buffer¹ ~| state ~| zone
buffet *[food]
buffet¹ *[wind]
buffoon
bug³ ~bear
bugel   bugle² *[music],
                               burgle² *[steal]
bugerigar   budgerigar⁺
buget   budget¹⁺
bugger¹
buggy⁴
bugie   boogie⁺
bugle² *[music]   burgle² *[steal]
build *[construct] ~er   billed *[invoiced]
building ~| site ~| society
buillon   bouillon *[soup]⁺,
                               bullion *[gold]
built ~-in ~-up
bujet   budget¹⁺
buk   buck¹⁺

KEY TO SUFFIXES AND COMPOUNDS

These rules are explained on pages ix to x.

1 Keep the word the same before adding ed, er, est, ing
   e.g. cool¹ → cooled, cooler, coolest, cooling
2 Take off final e before adding ed, er, est, ing
   e.g. fine² → fined, finer, finest, fining
3 Double final consonant before adding ed, er, est, ing
   e.g. thin³ → thinned, thinner, thinnest, thinning

4 Change final y to i before adding ed, er, es, est, ly, ness
   e.g. tidy⁴ → tidied, tidier, tidies, tidiest, tidily, tidiness
   Keep final y before adding ing e.g. tidying
5 Add es instead of s to the end of the word
   e.g. bunch⁵ → bunches
6 Change final f to ve before adding s
   e.g. calf⁶ → calves

bul	bull+
bulb ~ous	
bulee	bully4
Buleean Logic	Boolean Logic
bules	boules
bulet	bullet+
buletin	bulletin
bulevard	boulevard
bulge2	
bulimia	
bulion	bouillon *[soup]+,
	bullion *[gold]
bulit	bullet+
bulitin	bulletin+
bulj	bulge2
bulk ~y ~| buy	
bulk ~| head ~| order	
bull ~ock ~dog ~fight ~finch ~frog	
bulldoze2 bulldozer	
bullet ~| point ~proof ~| train	
bulletin ~| board	
bullion	
bullshit	
bully4	
bulrush5	
bulshit	bullshit
bulwark	
bulwork	bulwark
buly	bully4
bulymia	bulimia
bum3	
bumble2 ~bee	
bumerang	boomerang
bumf	
bumkin	bumpkin
bump1 bumpy4	
bumpkin	
bumshus	bumptious+

bun ~fight	
bunch5	
bundle2 ~| up	
bung1 ~hole	
bungalow	
bungee ~| jumping	
bungel	bungle2
bungie	bungee+
bungle2	
bunie	bunny4+
bunion	
bunjie	bungee+
bunk ~| bed ~house	
bunker1	
bunkum	
bunny4	
Bunsen ~| burner	
bunsh	bunch5
bunyan	bunion
buoy1 *[float]	boy *[male]+
buoyant buoyancy	
burate	berate2

☞ Can't find your word here? Look under **ber**

burau	bureau+
buraucracy	bureaucracy4
buraucrat	bureaucrat+
burble2	
burch	birch1+
burd	bird+
burden1 ~some	
burdy	birdie
bureau ~|de change	
bureaucracy4	
bureaucrat ~ic ~ically	
bureave	bereave2+
bureft	bereft
buret	beret

KEY TO SPELLING RULES

Red words are wrong. **Black** words are correct.

~   Add the suffix or word directly to the main word, without a space or hyphen
     e.g. ash ~en ~tray → ashen ashtray

~-   Add a hyphen to the main word before adding the next word
     e.g. blow ~-dry → blow-dry

~\| Leave a space between the main word and the next word
     e.g. decimal ~\| place → decimal place

+   By finding this word in its **correct** alphabetical order, you can find related words
     e.g. about+ → about-face about-turn

*   Draws attention to words that may be confused

TM   Means the word is a trademark

burgeon ~ing	
burger	
burglar ~l alarm	
burglary⁴	
burgle² *[steal]	bugle² *[music]
burgundy	
burial ~l ground	
burito	burrito
burlesque	
burly⁴	
burn¹ ~able	
burnish¹	
burnt	
burocracy	bureaucracy⁴
burocrat	bureaucrat⁺
burp¹	
burr¹	
burrito	
burrow¹ *[dig, hole]	borough *[place], borrow¹ *[loan]⁺, bureau *[desk]⁺
bursar ~y	
bursitis	
burst *[open, in, out] ~ing	bust¹ *[break, art]
bursurk	berserk
burth	berth¹ *[moor, bunk], birth *[born]⁺
bury⁴ *[cover]	berry⁴ *[fruit]
bus⁵ ~es ~l station ~l stop	
busby⁴	
busel	bustle²
busem	bosom⁺
bush ~ed ~y ~man ~whacker	
bushel	
business ~l card ~l class ~like	
business ~man ~l plan ~woman	
busker	
bussel	bustle²

bust¹ *[break, sculpture]	burst *[open, in, out]
bustle²	
busy⁴ ~l bee ~body	
but *[however]	butt¹ *[end, hit]⁺
butane ~l gas	
butcher¹ ~y	
buten	button¹⁺
buteous	beauteous
buter	butter¹⁺
butician	beautician
butie	beauty⁴ *[lovely]⁺, booty *[treasure]
butiful	beautiful⁺
butify	beautify⁴
butique	boutique
butler	
buton	button¹⁺
butt¹	
butter¹ ~y ~cup ~fingers	
butter ~fly ~milk ~nut ~scotch	
buttock	
button¹ ~hole	
buttress¹	
buty	beauty⁴ *[lovely]⁺, booty *[treasure]
buxom ~ly ~ness	
buy *[shop] ~er ~ing	by *[near], bye *[farewell, sport]⁺
buzz¹ ~es ~word	
buzzard	
buzzby	busby⁴
by *[near]	buy *[shop]⁺, bye *[farewell, sport]⁺
bycarbonate	bicarbonate⁺

☞ Can't find your word here? Look under **bi**

byceps	biceps
bycicul	bicycle²

KEY TO SUFFIXES AND COMPOUNDS

These rules are explained on pages ix to x.

1 Keep the word the same before adding **ed, er, est, ing**
e.g. cool¹ → cooled, cooler, coolest, cooling
2 Take off final **e** before adding **ed, er, est, ing**
e.g. fine² → fined, finer, finest, fining
3 Double final consonant before adding **ed, er, est, ing**
e.g. thin³ → thinned, thinner, thinnest, thinning

4 Change final **y** to **i** before adding **ed, er, es, est, ly, ness**
e.g. tidy⁴ → tidied, tidier, tidies, tidiest, tidily, tidiness
Keep final **y** before adding **ing** e.g. tidying
5 Add **es** instead of **s** to the end of the word
e.g. bunch⁵ → bunches
6 Change final **f** to **ve** before adding **s**
e.g. calf⁶ → calves

bye *[farewell, sport]	buy *[shop]+, by [near]	
		beer *[drink]+, buyer *[shop]
bye ~-bye		
by-election		byroad
byer		bystander
	buyer *[shop], bier *[funeral]	bystro · bistro
byfocal	bifocal+	byte *[data] · bite *[teeth]+
bygone ~s		bytumen · bitumen
bylaw		byvouac · bivouac+
byline		byway
byngo	bingo	byweekly · bi-weekly
bynoculars	binoculars	byword
byofeedback	bio-feedback	byzarre · bizarre+
bypass[1]		
by-product		
byre *[cowhouse]	bier *[funeral],	

C ~| section
cab ~bie

cabage   cabbage
cabal *[plotters]   cable² *[wire]
cabaray   cabaret
cabaret
cabbage
cabin ~| boy ~| crew ~| cruiser ~| fever
cabinet ~-maker
cable² ~| car ~| stitch
cable ~| television ~| TV
cabriolet
cacao *[seed, tree]   cocoa *[chocolate]
cache² *[hide]   cash¹ *[money]+
cachet
cackle²
cacofony   cacophony+
cacophony cacophonous
cactus cacti
cad *[coward]
CAD *[computer-aided design]
cadaver
caddie *[carries golf clubs]
caddy⁴ *[tea, act as caddie]
cadence
cadenza
cadet ~| corps
cadge²
cadmium
Caesarian
café *[restaurant]   coffee *[drink]+
cafeteria
caffeine
cage² cagey⁴
cagoule
cahoots
caik   cake²
caim   came

cain   cane²
caiper   caper¹
cair   care²+
caireful   careful+
caireless   careless+
cairetaiker   caretaker
cajole² ~ry
cake²
calamine
calamity⁴   calamitous
calcify⁴   calcification
calcium
calculable
calculate²   calculator
calculation
calculus
calendar *[time]   colander *[food]
Caler Gas   Calor Gas™
calf⁶ *[baby cow]   calve² *[give birth]
calibrate²   calibrator
calibration
calibre
calico⁵
caligrapher   calligrapher+
caling   calling+
caliph
calisthenics   callisthenics
call¹ ~| back
call ~| by ~| girl ~| off
caller ~| ID
calliber   calibre
calligrapher   calligraphy
calling ~| card
callipers
callisthenics
callous *[unfeeling]   callus *[hard skin]
calloused ~| skin
callow

KEY TO SUFFIXES AND COMPOUNDS

These rules are explained on pages ix to x.

1 Keep the word the same before adding **ed, er, est, ing**
  e.g. cool¹ → cooled, cooler, coolest, cooling
2 Take off final **e** before adding **ed, er, est, ing**
  e.g. fine² → fined, finer, finest, fining
3 Double final consonant before adding **ed, er, est, ing**
  e.g. thin³ → thinned, thinner, thinnest, thinning

4 Change final **y** to **i** before adding **ed, er, es, est, ly, ness**
  e.g. tidy⁴ → tidied, tidier, tidies, tidiest, tidily, tidiness
  Keep final **y** before adding **ing** e.g. tidying
5 Add **es** instead of **s** to the end of the word
  e.g. bunch⁵ → bunches
6 Change final **f** to **ve** before adding **s**
  e.g. calf⁶ → calves

callus *[hard skin]   callous *[unfeeling]+
calm[1] *[quiet] ~ly   cam *[wheel]+
Calor Gas™
calorie   calorific
calow   callow
calqulable   calculable
calqulashun   calculation
calqulate   calculate[2+]
calqulator   calculator
calqulus   calculus
calsify   calcify[4+]
calsium   calcium
calumny[4]
Calvary *[hill]   cavalry[4] *[army]
calve[2] *[give birth]   carve[2] *[cut]
Calvinist ~ic   Calvinism
calypers   callipers
calyph   caliph
calypso
cam *[wheel] ~shaft   came *[arrived]
camaflage   camouflage[2]
camaraderie
camcorder
came *[arrived]   cam *[wheel]+
camel ~l hair
camelion   chameleon
Camelot
Camembert
cameo
camera ~man ~-shy
camfor   camphor
camio   cameo
camisole
camoflage   camouflage[2]
camomile
Camonber   Camembert
camouflage[2]
camp[1] ~fire ~ground ~site

campaign[1]
camphor
campus[5]
camra   camera+
camraderee   camaraderie
can[3] *[able, tin]   cane[2] *[stick]+
can ~-do ~not
canabis   cannabis
canal
canapé *[food]   canopy[4] *[covering]
canary[4]
canasta *[game]   canister *[box]
cancan
cancel[3] ~lation
cancer *[illness] ~ous
Cancer *[zodiac]
candee   candy[4+]
candel   candle+
candelabra
cander   candour
candid *[frank]   candied *[sugared]
candidacy[4]
candidasy   candidacy[4]
candidate   candidature
candied *[sugared]   candid *[frank]+
candle ~light ~lit ~stick
candour
candy[4] ~floss
cane[2] *[stick]   can[3] *[able, tin]
canery   cannery[4]
canibal   cannibal+
canine
canister *[box]   canasta *[game]
canker
cannabis
cannery[4]
cannibal ~ism ~istic
cannibalise[2]

---

cannon[1] *[gun]   canon *[writings]+

cannon ~ball ~l fodder

cannonade

cannot

canny[4]

canoe ~d ~ing ~ist

canon *[writings]   cannon[1] *[gun]

canonical

canonise[2]

canopy[4] *[covering] canapé *[food]

canquer   canker

cansel   cancel[3+]

canser   cancer *[illness]+,
          Cancer *[zodiac]

cant[1] *[slant, hypocrisy]

can't *[cannot]

cantaloupe

cantankerous ~ly ~ness

cantata

canteen

canter[1] *[horse]   cantor *[church]

cantilever[1]

canton

cantor *[singer]   canter[1] *[horse]

canue   canoe+

canvas[5] *[cloth]

canvass[1] *[opinion] ~es

cany   canny[4]

canyon

cap[3] *[hat, covering] cape *[cloak, land]

capability[4]

capable   capably

capacious ~ness

capacitor

capacity[4]

capashus   capacious+

capasiter   capacitor

capasity   capacity[4]

capcher   capture[2]

cape *[cloak, land]   cap[3] *[hat, covering]

caper[1]

capichulate   capitulate[2+]

capillary[4]

capital ~l asset ~l city

capital ~l gain ~l letter ~l punishment

capitalise[2]

capitalist ~ic capitalism

capitulate[2] capitulation

cappuccino

capreece   caprice

caprice

capricious ~ly ~ness

Capricorn

caprishus   capricious+

capshun   caption[1]

capsize[2]

capsule[2]

captain[1] ~cy

capten   captain[1+]

capter   captor

caption[1]

captivate[2]

captive captivity

captor *[one who captures]

capture[2] *[catch]

capucheeno   cappuccino

car ~l bomb ~jack

car ~l park ~l pool

car ~port ~l sharing

car ~sick ~l wash

caracter   character+

caracteristic   characteristic+

carafe

caramba

caramel ~ise

carat *[gold]   carrot *[food]

---

caravan ~ning ~| site
caraway ~| seed
carben   carbon[+]
carbenise   carbonise[2]
carbine
carbohydrate
carbolic ~| acid
carbon ~| copy ~| dating
carbon ~| dioxide ~| monoxide
carbonates
carbonise[2]
carbord   cardboard
carbuncle
carburettor
carcass[5]
carcinogen ~ic
carcinoma ~| index
card[1] ~-carrying ~holder ~phone
card ~| sharp ~| table
cardboard
cardiac ~| arrest
cardigan
cardinal ~| number ~sin
cardiogram
cardiology   cardiologist
cardiovascular
cardygan   cardigan
care[2] ~free ~worn
caree   carry[4]
careen[1]
career *[job]   carrier *[carries][+]
careful ~ly ~ness
careless ~ly ~ness
caress[1] ~es
caretaker
cargo[5]
Caribbean
caribou

caricature
carier   career *[job],
       carrier *[carries][+]
carisma   charisma
carm   calm
carnage
carnal ~ly
carnashun   carnation
carnation
carnel   carnal[+]
carnige   carnage
carnival
carnivore   carnivorous
carol[3] ~-singing
carot   carat *[gold],
       carrot *[food]
carotene *[carrots]   keratin *[protein]
carotid ~| artery
carouse[2]
carousel
carowse   carouse[2]
carp[1]
carpenter
carpentry
carpet[1] ~bagger ~-bomb
carriage ~| clock ~way
carrie   carry[4+]
carrier *[carries]   career *[job]
carrier ~| bag ~| pigeon
carrige   carriage[+]
carrion
carrot *[food]   carat *[gold]
carry[4] ~all ~cot
carsel   castle[2]
carsinogen   carcinogen
carsinoma   carcinoma
cart[1] *[transport]   kart *[go-kart]
cart ~horse ~load ~wheel

---

cart-blonsh   carte-blanche
carte-blanche
cartel
carten   carton
cartilage
cartography   cartographer
carton *[box]
cartoon *[comic strip] ~ist
cartoosh   cartouche
cartouche
cartridge ~l paper
cartune   cartoon⁺
carve² *[cut]   calve² *[give birth]
carving ~fork ~l knife
caryon   carrion
Casanova
cascade²
case² ~l history ~load ~l study
casel   castle²
caserole   casserole²
caset   cassette⁺
cash¹ *[money]   cache² *[hide],
               catch *[ball]⁺
cash ~l cow ~l crop
cash ~l flow ~point ~register
cashay   cachet
cashelty   casualty⁴
cashew
cashier
cashmere
cashoe   cashew
casino
cask *[container]   casque *[helmet]
casket
casock   cassock
casque *[helmet]   cask *[container]
casserole²
cassette ~l deck ~l player ~l recorder

cassock
cast *[select, throw]   caste *[social class]
cast ~ing ~l iron
castanets
castaway
caste *[social class]   cast *[select, throw]⁺
caster *[sugar, bait]   castor *[oil, wheel]
castigate²   castigator
castigation
castle²
cast-off
castor *[oil, wheel]   caster *[sugar, bait]
castrait   castrate²⁺
castrate²   castration
casual ~ly ~ness
casualty⁴
casum   chasm
CAT ~l scan
cat ~call ~kin ~l litter
cat ~nip ~walk
cataclysm *[catastrophe]   catechism *[religion]
cataclysmic ~ally
catacomb
catagoric   categoric⁺
catagorise   categorise²
cataleptic
catalogue²
catalyse²   catalyst
catalytic ~l converter
catamaran
catapult¹
cataract
catar   catarrh
catarrh
catastrofee   catastrophe
catastrofic   catastrophic⁺
catastrophe
catastrophic ~ally

KEY TO SUFFIXES AND COMPOUNDS

These rules are explained on pages ix to x.

1 Keep the word the same before adding ed, er, est, ing
   e.g. cool¹ → cooled, cooler, coolest, cooling
2 Take off final e before adding ed, er, est, ing
   e.g. fine² → fined, finer, finest, fining
3 Double final consonant before adding ed, er, est, ing
   e.g. thin³ → thinned, thinner, thinnest, thinning

4 Change final y to i before adding ed, er, es, est, ly, ness
   e.g. tidy⁴ → tidied, tidier, tidies, tidiest, tidily, tidiness
   Keep final y before adding ing e.g. tidying
5 Add es instead of s to the end of the word
   e.g. bunch⁵ → bunches
6 Change final f to ve before adding s
   e.g. calf⁶ → calves

catatonic
catawall   caterwaul[1]
catch *[ball] ~ing   cache[2] *[hide]
catch ~y ~-all ~phrase
catchment ~| area
catechism *[religion] cataclysm *[catastrophe]
cateclysum   cataclysm
categoric ~al ~ally
categorise[2]
category[4]
catekisum   catechism
catekoom   catacomb
catel   cattle[+]
cateleptic   cataleptic
catelog   catalogue[2]
catemaran   catamaran
catepolt   catapult[1]
cater[1]
cateract   cataract
caterpillar
catetonic   catatonic
catgut
catharsis
cathartic ~ally
cathedral
Catherine wheel
catheter
cathode
catholic *[varied]
Catholic *[religion] ~ism
Cathrin wheel   Catherine wheel
catkin
catnap[3]
cat-o'-nine-tails
cat's cradle
CAT scan
Catseyes™
cattle ~| grid ~| prod

catty[4]
caturpillar   caterpillar
Caucasian
caucious   cautious[+]
caucus[5]
caught *[ball]   court[1] *[law][+]
cauldron
cauliflower
caulk[1] *[seal] cork[1] *[stopper][+]
causal
cause[2] ~| célèbre ~way
caushun   caution[1][+]
caushus   cautious[+]
caustic ~ally
cauterise[2]
caution[1] ~ary
cautious ~ly ~ness
cauturise   cauterise[2]
cavalcade
cavalier *[off-hand] Cavalier *[Civil War]
cavalry[4] *[army]   Calvary *[hill]
cave[2] ~man
caveat
cavern ~ous
caviare
caviat   caveat
cavity[4]
cavort[1]
cavurn   cavern[+]
caw[1] *[crow]   core *[centre],
                  corps *[army, ballet]
cawling   calling[+]
cawps   corpse *[body],
                  corps *[army, ballet]
cawpulense   corpulence[+]
cawstic   caustic[+]
caydnce   cadence
cayenne ~| pepper

---

cayge	cage[2+]
caym	came
caynine	canine
CB Radio	
CD ~| burner ~| player ~-Rom	

☞ Can't find your word here? Look under <u>se</u>

cease[2] *[stop] ~fire	seize[2] *[grab hold]
ceaseless ~ly	
cedar *[tree]	Seder *[Jewish meal]
cedate	sedate[2+]
cede[2] *[give up]	seed[1] *[plant, number][+]
cedilla	
ceeje	siege[+]
ceffalitis	cephalitis
ceiling *[roof]	sealing *[fastening]
celary	celery
celebrate[2] *[party]	celibate *[no sex][+]
celebration	
celebrity[4]	
celenium	selenium
celery	
celestial ~| body ~| object	
celibacy	
celibate *[no sex]	celebrate[2] *[party][+]
cell *[prison, unit]	sell *[goods]
cell ~| division	
cellar *[room]	seller *[sales person]
cellfone	cellphone
cello cellist	
cellofane	cellophane
cellophane	
cellphone	
cellular	
cellule	
cellulite	
celluloid	
cellulose	

celry	celery
Celsius	
Celt	
Celtic ~| cross ~| fringe	
celule	cellule
celulite	cellulite
celuloid	celluloid
celulose	cellulose[+]
cemen	seaman *[sailor],
	semen *[sperm]
cement[1] ~| mixer	
cemetery[4]	
cene	scene *[theatre][+],
	seen *[eyes]
cenile	senile[+]
cenior	senior[+]
cenotaph	
censer *[incense holder]	
censor[1] *[restrict]	sensor *[detector]
censor ~ship	
censure[2] *[disapprove of]	
census	
censuus	sensuous[+]
cent *[money]	scent *[perfume],
	sent *[away]
centaur	
centenarian	
centenary[4]	
centennial	
centigrade	
centigram	
centilitre	
centimetre	
centipede	
centir	centre[2+]
central ~ity ~ly ~| heating	
central ~| nervous system	
central ~| processing unit	

<u>KEY TO SUFFIXES AND COMPOUNDS</u>

These rules are explained on pages ix to x.

1 Keep the word the same before adding **ed, er, est, ing**
e.g. cool[1] → cooled, cooler, coolest, cooling
2 Take off final **e** before adding **ed, er, est, ing**
e.g. fine[2] → fined, finer, finest, fining
3 Double final consonant before adding **ed, er, est, ing**
e.g. thin[3] → thinned, thinner, thinnest, thinning

4 Change final **y** to **i** before adding **ed, er, es, est, ly, ness**
e.g. tidy[4] → tidied, tidier, tidies, tidiest, tidily, tidiness
Keep final **y** before adding **ing** e.g. tidying
5 Add **es** instead of **s** to the end of the word
e.g. bunch[5] → bunches
6 Change final **f** to **ve** before adding **s**
e.g. calf[6] → calves

centre[2] ~fold ~l forward ~piece	
centre ~l stage	
centrifugal ~l force	
centrifuge	
centrist	
centrosphere	
centry	sentry[4+]
centuple[2]	
centurion	
century[4]	
cephalitis	
ceramic	
cerb	curb[1] *[stop],
	kerb *[edge][+],
	Serb [from Serbia]
cerca	circa
cercul	circle[2]
cercus	circus[5]
cerd	curd[+]
cerdul	curdle[2]
cereal *[grain]	serial *[sequence][+]
cerebellum	
cerebral ~l palsy	
cerebrum	
ceremonial ~ly	
ceremonious ~ly	
ceremony[4]	
cerf	serf *[slave][+],
	surf[1] *[sea][+]
cerfew	curfew
cerial	cereal *[grain],
	serial *[one after another][+]
cerialise	serialise[2+]
ceries	series
cerif	serif[+]

☞ Can't find your word here? Look under **cir**

cerkit	circuit[1+]

cerl	curl[1+]
cerlew	curlew
cername	surname
cernel	colonel *[officer],
	kernel *[seed]
cerse	curse[2]
cersive	cursive
cersor	cursor
cersory	cursory
cert *[definite]	curt *[rude][+]
certail	curtail[1+]
certain *[sure] ~ly	curtain *[screen][+]
certainty[4]	
certale	curtail[1+]
certen	certain *[sure][+],
	curtain *[screen][+]
certifiable certifiably	
certificate	
certify[4] certification	
certitude .	
certsy	curtsy[4]
cervashus	curvaceous[+]
cerve	curve[2+]
cervical ~l cancer ~l smear	
cervix	
cessation *[halt]	
cesspit cesspool	
cew	cue[2] *[billiards][+],
	queue *[line][+]
cha-cha-cha	
chador	
chafe[2] *[rub]	
chaff *[grain husks]	
chaffinch[5]	

☞ Can't find your word here? Look under **sh**

chagrin ~ed
chain[1] ~l gang ~l letter ~-link

KEY TO SPELLING RULES

Red words are wrong. **Black** words are correct.

~ Add the suffix or word directly to the main word, without a space or hyphen
e.g. ash ~en ~tray → ashen ashtray

~- Add a hyphen to the main word before adding the next word
e.g. blow ~-dry → blow-dry

~l Leave a space between the main word and the next word
e.g. decimal ~l place → decimal place

+ By finding this word in its **correct** alphabetical order, you can find related words
e.g. about[+] → about-face about-turn

* Draws attention to words that may be confused

TM Means the word is a trademark

chain ~| mail ~| reaction ~saw ~| store
chain-smoke[2]
chair[1] ~lift ~man
chair ~person ~woman
chaised   chased *[pursued],
            chaste *[pure]
chalet
chalice
chalinge   challenge[2]
chalk[1] ~y ~board
challenge[2]
chamber ~maid ~| music ~| pot
Chamber of Commerce
chamberlain
chameleon
chamois
chamomile
champ[1]
champagne *[wine] campaign[1] *[activity]
champion[1] ~ship
chance[2] chancy
chancel
chancellery[4] *[money]
Chancellor ~| of the Exchequer
Chancery[4] *[court]
chandelier *[light]
chandler *[ships]
chane   chain[+]
chane-smoke   chain-smoke[2]
change[2] ~able ~ling ~over
changing ~| room
chanj   change[2+]
channel[3]
Channel *[the English]
chanse   chance[2+]
chansellery   chancellery[4]
Chansellor   Chancellor[+]
Chansery   Chancery[4]

chant[1]
chaos ~| theory
chaotic ~ally
chap
chapati
chapel
chaperone[1]
chaplain chaplaincy[4]
chaplin   chaplain[+]
chapped ~| lips
chaps
chapter
chapul   chapel
char[3] ~woman
character ~| actor
character ~| assassination
characterise[2] characterisation
characteristic ~ally
charade
charcoal
chard *[beet]   charred *[burned]
chare   chair[1+]
chared   chard *[beet],
            charred *[burned]
charge[2] ~able
charge ~| account ~| card
chargé-d'affaires
chargrill[1]
chariot ~eer
charisma
charitable charitably
charity[4] ~| shop
charlatan
Charleston
charlie
charm[1] ~| offensive
charnce   chance[2+]
charnt   chant[1]

KEY TO SUFFIXES AND COMPOUNDS

These rules are explained on pages ix to x.

1 Keep the word the same before adding ed, er, est, ing
e.g. cool[1] → cooled, cooler, coolest, cooling
2 Take off final e before adding ed, er, est, ing
e.g. fine[2] → fined, finer, finest, fining
3 Double final consonant before adding ed, er, est, ing
e.g. thin[3] → thinned, thinner, thinnest, thinning

4 Change final y to i before adding ed, er, es, est, ly, ness
e.g. tidy[4] → tidied, tidier, tidies, tidiest, tidily, tidiness
Keep final y before adding ing e.g. tidying
5 Add es instead of s to the end of the word
e.g. bunch[5] → bunches
6 Change final f to ve before adding s
e.g. calf[6] → calves

charred *[burned]   chard *[beet]
chart[1]
charter ~l flight
chartism   chartist
charysma   charisma
chase[2]
chased *[pursued]   chaste *[pure]
chasen   chasten[1]
chasm
chassee   chassis
chassis
chaste *[pure]   chased *[pursued]
chasten[1]
chastise[2] ~ment
chastity ~l belt
chastize   chastise[2]+
chat[3] ~line ~l room ~l show
chateau   chateaux
chattels
chatter[1] ~box
chattuls   chattels
chatty[4]
chauffeur ~-driven
chauvinism
chauvinist ~ic ~ically
chaw   chore
cheap[1] *[money]   cheep[1] *[bird]
cheap ~ly ~ness ~skate
cheapen[1]
cheat[1]
check[1] *[control]   cheque *[money]+
check ~l box ~list ~out
check ~point ~l up
checkmate[2]
Cheddar ~l cheese
cheef   chief
cheeften   chieftain
cheek[1] ~bones

cheeky[4]
cheep[1] *[bird]   cheap *[money]+
cheepen   cheapen[1]
cheer[1] ~less ~s
cheerful ~ly ~ness
cheerio
cheery[4]
cheese ~board ~burger ~cake
cheesed off
cheesy[4]
cheetah
chef *[cook]   chief *[leader]+
chef-d'oeuvre
chellist   cellist
chello   cello
chemeez   chemise
chemical ~ly
chemical ~l engineer ~l engineering
chemical ~l warfare ~l weapons
chemise
chemist ~ry
chemotherapy
cheque *[money]   check[1] *[control]+
cheque ~book
chequered
cherch   church+
cheree   cherry[4]
cherish[1]
cherlish   churlish+
chern   churn[1]
cheroot
cherry[4] [fruit]   sherry *[drink]
cherrypick[1]
cherub ~ic
Cheshire ~l cat
chess ~board ~l piece
chest ~l of drawers
chestnut

---

chevalier
chew[1]
chewing ~I gum
chews *[food]   choose *[pick][+]
chewy[4]
chiabarta   ciabatta
Chianti
chic *[elegant]   chick *[bird]
chicanery
chi-chi
chick *[bird]   chic *[elegant]
chicken ~-and-egg ~feed ~pox
chickpea
chickweed
chicory
chide[2]
chief ~ly
chief ~I constable ~I inspector
chieftain
chier   cheer[1+]
chierful   cheerful[+]
chierio   cheerio
chiery   cheery[4]
chiese   cheese[+]
chiesy   cheesy[4]
chietah   cheetah
chiffon
chignon
chihuahua
chiite   Shiite
chilblain
child ~ish   children
child ~I abuse ~bearing ~birth
child ~care ~hood
child ~less ~like ~minder ~proof
chill[1] ~-out
chilli[5] *[food] ~I con carne ~I powder
chilly[4] *[cold]

chime[2]
chimera
chimney ~I pot ~I stack ~I sweep
chimp ~anzee
chin ~less
china ~I clay
Chinatown
chinchilla
Chinese ~I lantern ~I whispers
chink[1]
chintz ~y
chinwag[3]
chip[3] ~board
chipmunk
chipolata
Chippendale
chiropodist   chiropody
chiropractor   chiropractic
chirp[1]   chirpy[4]
chisel[3]
chit
chit-chat[3]
chivalry   chivalrous
chives
chivvy[4]
chiwawa   chihuahua
chlorate
chloride
chlorinate[2]
chlorine
chloroform[1]
chlorophyll
chloroplast
choc *[chocolate] ~oholic ~I ice
chock *[holds in place] ~-a-block
chocolate ~-box ~I cake ~-chip cookie
choffeur   chauffeur[+]
choice

---

choir *[singers]	coir *[coconut fibre]
choir ~boy ~girl	
choir ~master	
choke² ~l chain	
choler *[rage]	collar¹ *[seize, neckband]
cholera *[disease]	
cholesterol	
choose *[pick]	chews *[food]
choosing choosy	
chop³ ~sticks ~-suey	
chopping ~l board ~l block	
choppy⁴	
choral *[singing]	
chorale *[hymn]	
chord *[music]	cord *[rope]⁺
chore	
choreographer choreography	
chorister	
chork	chalk¹⁺
chortel	chortle²
chortle²	
chorus⁵	
chose *[chosen]	choose *[pick]
chovinist	chauvinist⁺
chow *[food]	ciao *[greeting]
chow ~mein	
chowder	
choys	choice
Christ Christendom	
christal	crystal⁺
christen¹	
Christian ~l name Christianity	
Christmas ~l card ~l carol ~l cracker	
Christmas ~l Day ~l Eve	
Christmas ~-time ~l tree	
chromate chromatography	
chromatic	
chrome	

chromium	
chromosome	
chronic ~ally ~l fatigue	
chronicle²	
chronograph	
chronological ~ly	
chronology⁴	
chronometer	
chrysalis⁵	
chrysanthemum	
chrystaline	crystalline
chrystallise	crystallise²⁺
chub	
chubby⁴	
chuck¹	
chucka	chukka
chuckle²	
chue	chew¹⁺
chug³	
chukka	
chum ~my	
chunk chunky⁴	
church⁵ ~goer ~warden ~yard	
Church ~l of England ~l of Scotland	
churlish ~ly	
churn¹	
churp	chirp¹⁺
chuse	choose *[pick]⁺
chute *[slide]	shoot *[weapon, goal]⁺
chutney	
chutzpah	
chyli	chilli⁵ *[food]⁺,
	chilly⁴ *[cold]
chyme	chime²
chyna	china⁺
Chynatown	Chinatown
Chynese	Chinese⁺
chyntz	chintz⁺

---

chyves	chives
ciabatta	
cianide	cyanide
ciantee	Chianti
ciao *[greeting]	chow *[food]+
ciatic	sciatic
ciatica	sciatica+
cibernetics	cybernetics
cicada	
ciclamate	cyclamate
ciclamen	cyclamen
cicle	cycle²
ciclick	cyclic+
ciclist	cyclist
ciclone	cyclone
Ciclops	Cyclops
ciclotron	cyclotron
cider	
cience	science+
cientific	scientific+
cifer	cipher¹
cigar	
cigarette ~| butt	
cigarette ~| holder ~| lighter	
cigarette ~| paper	
cignet	cygnet *[swan], signet *[ring]
cilia	
cilinder	cylinder
cilindrical	cylindrical+
cimbal	cymbal *[music], symbol *[sing]+
cinch¹ ~es	
cinder ~block	
Cinderella	
cine ~| camera ~| film	
cinema ~tic ~tically	
cinematographer	cinematography

cinic	cynic+
cinical	cynical+
cinnamon	
cinosure	cynosure
cintillating	scintillating
cinus	sinus⁵
cipher	
cipress	cypress *[tree], Cyprus *[country]
circa	
circadian ~| rhythm	
circit	circuit+
circle²	
circuit¹ ~| board ~| breaker	
circuit ~| judge ~| switch ~| training	
circuitous ~ly	
circuitry	
circular	
circulate² circulation	
circumcise² circumcision	
circumference	
circumflex	
circumlocution	
circumnavigate²	
circumscribe²	
circumscription	
circumspect ~ly ~ion ~ive	
circumstance	
circumstantial ~ly	
circumvent¹ ~ion	
circus⁵	
Cirillic	Cyrillic
cirogenics	cryogenics
cirrhosis	
cirrocumulus	
cirrostratus	
cirrus	
cissors	scissors

cissy⁴

cist   cyst⁺

cistern

citadel

citation

cite² *[quote]   sight *[seeing]⁺,
                        site² *[place]

citee   city⁴⁺

citizen ~ship

citizen's arrest

Citizen's Band

citric ~| acid

citrus ~| fruit

city⁴ ~| centre ~| council ~| hall

civet

civic ~| centre

civies   civvies

civil ~| defence

civil ~| disobedience ~| engineer

civil ~| engineering ~| law ~| liberties

civil ~| rights ~| service ~| war

civilian

civilisation

civilise²

civility⁴

civvies

clacissisum   classicism⁺

clad

claim¹ ~ant

clairvoyant clairvoyance

clam³ ~| up

clamber¹

clame   claim¹⁺

clammer   clamour⁺

clammy⁴

clamour clamorous

clamp¹ ~down

clan ~nish

clandestine ~ly

clang¹

clank¹

clans ~man ~woman

clap³ ~board ~trap

claret

clarify⁴ clarification

clarinet ~tist

clarion ~| call

clarity

clark   clerk

clarss   class¹⁺

clash¹

clasic   classic⁺

clasified   classified⁺

clasp¹

class¹ ~| action

class ~| consciousness ~mate

class ~room ~work

classic ~al ~ally ~s

classicism classicist

classified ~| ad ~| directory

classify⁴ classification

clatter¹

clause *[sentence]   claws *[animal]

claustrophobia claustrophobic

clavichord

clavicle

claw¹

claws *[animal]   clause *[sentence]

clay ~| pigeon shooting

clean¹ ~ly ~able ~liness

clean ~-cut ~-living ~-shaven

cleanse²

clear¹ ~ance ~ly

clear ~-headed ~-sighted

clearing ~| bank ~| house

cleave²

---

cleavage
cleaver
cleek   clique[+]
cleen   clean[+]
cleeontel   clientele
cleer   clear[+]
cleering   clearing[+]
cleeshay   cliché
cleeve   cleave[2]
cleever   cleaver
clef
cleft ~l palate
clemency   clement
clementine
clench[1]
clense   cleanse[2]
clergy[4]
cleric ~al
clerk
clever[1] ~ly ~l ness ~l dick
clew   clue[+]
cliché
click[1] *[sound]   clique *[group][+]
client ~-server
clientele
cliff ~hanger
clik   click[1] *[sound],
                 clique *[group]
clim   climb[1] *[up, down],
                 clime *[climate]
climactic ~ally
climate ~l change climatic
climax[1] ~es
climb[1] *[up, down]   clime *[climate]
climbdown
climbing ~l frame ~l wall
clime *[climate]   climb[1] *[up, down]
climing   climbing

clinch[1] ~es
cling ~ing ~film
clinic ~al ~ally ~ian
clink[1]
clip[3] ~l art ~board ~-clop ~-on
clipper
clique   cliquish
clitoris
cloak[1] ~-and-dagger ~room
clobber[1]
cloche
clock[1] ~wise ~work
clockwatch[1]
clod ~hopper
clog[3]
cloister ~ed
cloke   cloak[1+]
clone
clorafill   chlorophyll
clorate   chlorate
clore   claw[1+]
cloride   chloride
clorinate   chlorinate[2]
clorine   chlorine
cloroform   chloroform[1]
clorophyll   chlorophyll
cloroplast   chloroplast
clors   clause *[sentence],
                 claws *[animal]
clorstrophobia   claustrophobia[+]
close[2] ~ly ~ness
close ~l call ~-fitting ~-knit ~l quarters
close ~-run ~-set ~-up ~l shave
closet[1]
closh   cloche
closher   closure
closure
clot[3]

---

cloth *[piece of fabric]
clothe² *[put clothes on]
clothes ~| horse ~| line ~| peg
clothing
clotted cream
cloud¹ ~burst ~less   cloudy⁴
clout¹
clove
clover ~| leaf
~~clowd~~   cloud¹⁺
clown¹ ~ish
~~clowt~~   clout¹
~~cloyster~~   cloister¹
~~clozher~~   closure
club³ ~| foot ~house
club ~| sandwich ~| soda
~~cluch~~   clutch¹⁺
cluck¹
clue ~less
clump¹   clumpy⁴
clumsy⁴
clung
clunk¹   clunky⁴
~~clurgy~~   clergy⁴
~~clurk~~   clerk⁺
cluster¹ ~| bomb
clutch¹ ~es
clutter¹
~~clyent~~   client⁺
~~clyme~~   climb *[up, down],
                         clime *[climate]
~~clynic~~   clinic⁺
coach¹ ~load
coagulate² coagulant
~~coak~~   coke² *[drug, fuel],
                         Coke™ *[cola]
coal ~field ~mine
coal ~| scuttle

coalesce²
coalescence   coalescent
coalition
coarse² *[rough]   course² *[order, path]⁺
coarse ~ly ~ness
coarsen¹
coast¹ ~al ~guard ~line
coat *[clothing]   cote *[doves]
coat ~| hanger ~| of arms
coat ~stand ~-tails
coax¹ ~es
coaxial ~| cable
cob ~nut
cobalt ~| blue
cobble² ~stone
cobra
cobweb
coca
Coca Cola™
cocaine
coccyx
~~coch~~   coach¹⁺
cochineal
cock¹ ~-a-doodle-doo ~-a-hoop
cock ~crow ~-up
cockatoo
cockchafer
cocker ~| spaniel
cockerel
cock-eyed
cockfight ~ing
cockle ~| shell
cockney
cockpit
cockroach
cockscomb
cocksure
cocktail ~| dress ~| party ~| stick

cocky⁴		cogitate²	
cocoa		cognac	
cocoe	cocoa	cognisance	
coconut		cognishun	cognition
cocoon¹		cognition	
cocsyx	coccyx	cognitive ~ly	
cocune	cocoon¹	cohabit¹ ~ation	
cod ~ling ~l liver oil		coherence	
coda		coherent ~ly	
coddle²		cohesion	
code² *[information] coda *[music]		cohesive ~ly ~ness	
code ~l breaking		cohort	
code ~l name ~l red		coie	coy⁺
codeine		coiffed	
codex codices		coiffure	
codger		coil¹	
codicil		coin¹ ~age	
codify⁴		coincide²	
codine	codeine	coincidence	
codisil	codicil	coincident ~ally	
codswallop		coir *[coconut fibre] choir *[singers]⁺	
co-ed		coitus	
co-education ~al		cojency	cogency
coefficient		cojent	cogent⁺
coegsist	coexist¹⁺	cojitate	cogitate²
coequal ~ly ~ity		cokatoo	cockatoo
coerce² coercible		cokchafer	cockchafer
coercion coercive		coke² *[drug, fuel]	
coexist¹ ~ence ~ent		Coke™ *[cola]	
cofer	coffer	coker	cocker⁺
coff	cough¹⁺	cokette	coquette⁺
coffee *[drink] café *[restaurant]		cok-eyed	cock-eyed
coffee ~l break ~l machine ~l pot ~l table		cola *[drink]	collar¹ *[seize, neckband]
coffer		colaborate	collaborate²⁺
coffin		colaborativ	collaborative⁺
cog cogged		colage	collage
cogent ~ly cogency		colagen	collagen
coger	codger	colander *[food]	calendar *[time]

KEY TO SUFFIXES AND COMPOUNDS

These rules are explained on pages ix to x.

1 Keep the word the same before adding **ed, er, est, ing**
   e.g. cool¹ → cooled, cooler, coolest, cooling
2 Take off final **e** before adding **ed, er, est, ing**
   e.g. fine² → fined, finer, finest, fining
3 Double final consonant before adding **ed, er, est, ing**
   e.g. thin³ → thinned, thinner, thinnest, thinning

4 Change final **y** to **i** before adding **ed, er, es, est, ly, ness**
   e.g. tidy⁴ → tidied, tidier, tidies, tidiest, tidily, tidiness
   Keep final **y** before adding **ing** e.g. tidying
5 Add **es** instead of **s** to the end of the word
   e.g. bunch⁵ → bunches
6 Change final **f** to **ve** before adding **s**
   e.g. calf⁶ → calves

colaps	collapse[2]	collecshun	collection
collarj	collage	collect[1] ~able ~or	
colate	collate[2]	collection	
colatteral	collateral[+]	collective ~ly ~I bargaining ~I noun	
cold[1] ~ly ~ness		collectivism	
cold ~-blood ~-blooded ~-call ~I cream		college collegiate	
cold ~-hearted ~-shoulder		collide[2]	
cold ~I snap ~I sore		collie	
cold ~I spell ~I storage		collier	
cold ~I sweat ~I turkey		colliery[4]	
cole	coal[+]	colliflower	cauliflower
colectiv	collective[+]	collision ~I course	
coleeg	colleague	collision ~I damage waiver	
colege	college[+]	collocate[2] collocation	
colen	colon	colloquial ~ism ~ly	
coler	choler *[rage],	colloquy[4]	
	collar[1] *[seize, neckband],	collude[2] collusion	
	colour[1] *[red, blue][+]	collum	column[+]
colera	cholera	colocate	collocate[2+]
colerbone	collarbone	cologne *[perfume]	
colerful	colourful[+]	colon *[body part]	
coleslaw		colonel *[officer] kernel *[seed]	
colesterol	cholesterol	colonial ~ism ~ist	
colic ~ky		colonie	colony[4+]
colide	collide[2]	coloniel	colonial[+]
colige	college	colonise[2] colonisation	
colitis		colonnade	
collaborate[2] collaborator		colony[4] colonist	
collaborative ~ly collaboration		colonyse	colonise[2+]
collage		colood	collude[2+]
collagen		coloquee	colloquy[4]
collapse[2] collapsible		coloquial	colloquial[+]
collar[1] *[seize, choler *[rage]		colossal ~ly	
neckband]		colossus	
collarbone		colour[1] ~-blind ~I change	
collate[2]		colour ~-code ~fast ~less	
collateral ~I damage		colour ~I scheme ~I supplement	
colleague		colourful ~ly	

KEY TO SPELLING RULES

Red words are wrong. **Black** words are correct.

~   Add the suffix or word directly to the main word, without a space or hyphen
     e.g. ash ~en ~tray → **ashen ashtray**

~-   Add a hyphen to the main word before adding the next word
     e.g. blow ~-dry → **blow-dry**

~I   Leave a space between the main word and the next word
     e.g. decimal ~I place → **decimal place**

+   By finding this word in its **correct** alphabetical order, you can find related words
     e.g. about[+] → **about-face about-turn**

*   Draws attention to words that may be confused

TM   Means the word is a trademark

colt ~ish

colude   collude[2+]

columbine

column ~ist

colyc   colic[+]

colyer   collier

colyery   colliery[4]

.com

coma *[unconscious]   comma *[text]

comando   commando

comb[1]

combat[1] ~ant ~ive ~l fatigue

combine[2] combination

combo

combustion combustible

come coming

come ~l back ~-uppance

comedian comedienne

comedy[4]

☞ Can't find your word here? Look under __comm__

---

comemorate   commemorate[2+]

comen   common[+]

comend   commend[1+]

comendabul   commendable[+]

comenplace   commonplace

comense   commence[2+]

comensurate   commensurate

coment   comment[1+]

comentry   commentary[4]

comerse   commerce

comershal   commercial[+]

comershalise   commercialise[2+]

comet *[in the sky]   commit[3] *[to do][+]

comfort[1]

comfortable comfortably

comfy

comic ~al ~ally ~-strip

comidian   comedian[+]

coming

comings-and-goings

comiserate   commiserate[2+]

comishion   commission[1]

comit   comet *[in the sky],

              commit[3] *[to do][+]

comitee   committee

comma *[text]   coma *[unconscious]

command[1] ~ant ~ment

commandeer[1] *[take over]

commander *[in charge] ~-in-chief

commando

commemorate[2] commemoration

commence[2] ~ment

commend[1] ~ation

commendable commendably

commensurate

comment[1] ~ator

commentary[4]

commer   comma

commerce

commercial ~ism ~ly

commercialise[2] commercialisation

commic   comic[+]

commiserate[2] commiseration

commissar ~iat

commission[1]

commit[3] *[to do]   comet *[in the sky]

commit ~ment ~tal

committee

commity   committee

commode

commodity[4]

common[1] ~ly

common ~l cold ~l denominator

common ~l factor ~l ground ~l law

common ~-place ~l room

Commons [the]
Commonwealth ~| Games
commotion
communal ~ly
commune[2]
communicable
communicashuns communications[+]
communicate[2] communication
communications ~| satellite
communicative ~ly
communion
communiqué
communism communist
community[4] ~| service
commutative
commute[2]
comodity   commodity[4]
comon   common[+]
comoshun   commotion
compact ~| disc
compair   compare[2]
companion ~able ~ship
company[4] ~| car ~| law
companyon   companion[+]
comparable comparably
comparative ~ly
compare[2]* [judge] compère *[show]
comparison
compartment
compartmentalise[2]
compashun   compassion[+]
compass[5]
compassion ~ate ~ately
compatebul   compatible[+]
compatible compatibility
compatriot
compeet   compete[2]
compel[3]

compendium
compensate[2] compensation
compère *[show] compare[2] *[judge]
compete[2]
competence
competent ~ly
competishun   competition
competition
competitive ~ly ~ness
competitor
compile[2] compilation
compitishun   competition
complacency
complacent ~ly
complain[1]
complaint
complasensy   complacency
complasent   complacent[+]
compleks   complex[+]
complekshun   complexion
complement[1] *   compliment[1] *
         [suit]   [praise][+]
complementary ~| angle ~| medicine
compleshun   completion
complete[2] ~ly ~ness
completion
complex
complexion
complexity[4]
compliance compliant
complicate[2] complication
complicity
complie   comply[4]
compliment[1] *   complement[1] *[suit]
         [praise]
complimentary
complisity   complicity
comply[4]

KEY TO SPELLING RULES

Red words are wrong. **Black** words are correct.

~   Add the suffix or word directly to the main word, without a space or hyphen
     e.g. ash ~en ~tray → **ashen ashtray**

~--   Add a hyphen to the main word before adding the next word
     e.g. blow ~-dry → **blow-dry**

~| Leave a space between the main word and the next word
     e.g. decimal ~| place → **decimal place**

+   By finding this word in its **correct** alphabetical order, you can find related words
     e.g. about[+] → **about-face about-turn**

*   Draws attention to words that may be confused

TM   Means the word is a trademark

component	
compose[2]	
composishun	composition
composite	
composition	
compositor	
compost	
composure	
compote	
compound[1] ~| fracture ~| interest	
comprabul	comparable[+]
comprehend[1]	
comprehensible	
comprehension	
comprehensive ~ly ~| school	
compress[1] ~ible ~ion ~or	
comprihenshun	comprehension
comprise[2]	
compromise[2]	
compulsion compulsive	
compulsory[4]	
compunction	
compute[2] computation	
computer ~~-aided-design ~| game	
computer ~| graphics ~~-literate	
computer ~| programme ~| science	
computerise[2]	
comrade ~ly ~ship	
comunal	communal[+]
comune	commune[2]
comunicabul	communicable
comunicate	communicate[2+]
comunications	communications[+]
comunicative	communicative[+]
comunikay	communiqué
comunion	communion
comunism	communism[+]
comunity	community[4+]

comunyon	communion
comutative	commutative
comute	commute[2]
con[3] ~| artist ~| man	
concave	
conceal[1] ~ment	
concede[2]	
conceit ~ed ~edly ~edness	
conceivable conceivably	
conceive[2]	
concensus	consensus
concentrate[2]	
concentration ~| camp	
concentric	
concepshun	conception
concept ~ual ~ually	
conception	
conceptualise[2]	
concequense	consequence
concequenshal	consequential[+]
concequent	consequent[+]
concern[1]	
concert ~| hall	
concertina[1]	
concerto	
concession ~ary	
conch	
conchertoe	concerto
conchusion	contusion
concienshus	conscientious[+]
conciliation	
conciliatory	
concious	conscious[+]
concise ~ly ~ness	
concist	consist[1]
concistency	consistency
conclave	
conclewd	conclude[2+]

KEY TO SUFFIXES AND COMPOUNDS

These rules are explained on pages ix to x.

1 Keep the word the same before adding **ed, er, est, ing**
e.g. cool[1] → cooled, cooler, coolest, cooling

2 Take off final **e** before adding **ed, er, est, ing**
e.g. fine[2] → fined, finer, finest, fining

3 Double final consonant before adding **ed, er, est, ing**
e.g. thin[3] → thinned, thinner, thinnest, thinning

4 Change final **y** to **i** before adding **ed, er, es, est, ly, ness**
e.g. tidy[4] → tidied, tidier, tidies, tidiest, tidily, tidiness
Keep final **y** before adding **ing** e.g. tidying

5 Add **es** instead of **s** to the end of the word
e.g. bunch[5] → bunches

6 Change final **f** to **ve** before adding **s**
e.g. calf[6] → calves

conclewsiv   conclusive[+]
conclude[2]   conclusion
conclusive ~ly
concoct[1] ~ion
concomitant
concord ~ance ~ant
concourse
concrete ~ly ~ness
concubine
concur[3] ~rence
concurrent ~ly
concussed   concussion
condem   condemn[+]
condemn[1] ~ation
condense[2]   condensation
condescend[1]
condescension
condiment
condisend   condescend[1+]
condishun   condition[1+]
condition[1] ~al ~ally
condolences
condom
condominium
condone[2]
conducive
conduct[1] ~ion ~or
conductive   conductivity
conduit
condwit   conduit
cone[2]
conerbashun   conurbation
confab
confecshun   confection[+]
confection ~er ~ery
confederacy[4]
confederate[2]
confederation

confer[3] *[give, talk]   conifer *[tree][+]
conference[2] ~call
conferm   confirm[1+]
confess[1] ~or
confession ~al
confetti
confidant [male]   confident *[can do][+]
confidante *[trusted female]
confide[2]
confidence ~l trick ~l trickster
confident *[can do]   confidant *[trusted male]
confident ~ly
confidential ~ity ~ly
configure[2]   configuration
confine[2] ~ment
confirm[1] ~ation ~ative
confiscate[2]   confiscation
conflagration
conflict[1]
conform[1] ~ation
conformist   conformity
confound[1]
confourm   conform[1+]
confourmist   conformist[+]
confownd   confound[1]
confront[1]
confrontation ~al
Confucius   Confucianism
confur   confer[3] *[give, talk],
              conifer *[tree][+]
confuse[2]
Confushus   Confucius[+]
confusion
confyde   confide[2]
congeal[1]
congenial ~ity ~ly
congenital ~ly
conger ~l eel

KEY TO SPELLING RULES

Red words are wrong. **Black** words are correct.

~   Add the suffix or word directly to the main word,
     without a space or hyphen
     e.g. ash ~en ~tray → ashen ashtray
~--   Add a hyphen to the main word before adding the
     next word
     e.g. blow ~-dry → blow-dry

~l   Leave a space between the main word and the next
    word
    e.g. decimal ~l place → decimal place
+   By finding this word in its **correct** alphabetical
    order, you can find related words
    e.g. about[+] → about-face about-turn
*   Draws attention to words that may be confused
TM   Means the word is a trademark

congest[1] ~ion ~ive
conglomerate[2]
conglomeration
congrachulate congratulate[2+]
congrachulatory congratulatory
congrats
congratulate[2] congratulations
congratulatory
congregate[2] congregation
congress ~ional
congruence
congruent
congugal conjugal
congur conger[+]
conical
conifer *[tree] ~ous confer[3] *[give, talk]
conive connive[2+]
conjeal congeal[1]
conjecture[2] conjectural
conjenial congenial[+]
conjenital congenital[+]
conjer conjure[2]
conjest congest[1+]
conjestiv congestive
conjoin[1]
conjugal
conjugate[2] conjugation
conjunction
conjunctivitis
conjure[2] conjuror
conkave concave
conker *[chestnut] conquer[1] *[defeat][+]
conkord concord[+]
conkrete concrete[+]
conkussed concussed
conkwest conquest
connect[1] ~ion
connective ~l tissue

connectivity
connive[2] connivance
connoisseur
connotation
conossir connoisseur
conqubine concubine
conquer[1] *[defeat] conker *[chestnut],
       concur[3] *[agree]
conqueror
conquest
conquistador
conscience ~-stricken
conscientious ~ly ~ness ~l objector
conscious ~ly ~ness
conscript[1] ~ion
conseal conceal[1+]
consecrate[2] consecration
consecutive ~ly
conseed concede[2]
conseit conceit[+]
conseivabul conceivable[+]
conseive conceive[2]
consensus
consent[1]
consentrate concentrate[2+]
consentrashun concentration[+]
consentric concentric
consept concept[+]
conseptualise conceptualise[2]
consequence
consequent ~ly
consequential ~ly
consern concern[1]
consert concert[+]
conservation
conservative ~ly ~ness
Conservatives [the]
conservatoire

KEY TO SUFFIXES AND COMPOUNDS

These rules are explained on pages ix to x.

1 Keep the word the same before adding ed, er, est, ing
e.g. cool[1] → cooled, cooler, coolest, cooling
2 Take off final e before adding ed, er, est, ing
e.g. fine[2] → fined, finer, finest, fining
3 Double final consonant before adding ed, er, est, ing
e.g. thin[3] → thinned, thinner, thinnest, thinning

4 Change final y to i before adding ed, er, es, est, ly, ness
e.g. tidy[4] → tidied, tidier, tidies, tidiest, tidily, tidiness
Keep final y before adding ing e.g. tidying
5 Add es instead of s to the end of the word
e.g. bunch[5] → bunches
6 Change final f to ve before adding s
e.g. calf[6] → calves

conservatory⁴
conserve²
conseshon · concession⁺
conshence · conscience⁺
conshienshus · conscientious⁺
conshus · conscious⁺
consicrate · consecrate²⁺
consider¹ ~able ~ably ~ately
considerate · consideration
consign¹ ~ment
consiliashun · conciliation
consiliatory · conciliatory
consine · consign¹⁺
consise · concise⁺
consist¹
consistency⁴
consistent ~ly
consolable
consolation ~l prize
console² *[comfort] consul *[official]
console *[controls]
consolidate² consolidation
consommé
consonant
consort¹
consortium consortia
conspicuous ~ly ~ness
conspiracy⁴
conspirator ~ial ~ially
conspire²
constable
constabulary⁴
constant ~ly constancy
constellation
consternation
constichuent · constituent
constipate² constipation
constituency⁴

constituent
constitute²
constitution ~al ~ally
constrain¹
constraint
constrew · construe²
constrict¹ ~ion
construcshun · construction⁺
construct¹
construction ~l line
constructive ~ly
construe²
consul ~ar ~ate
consult¹ ~ant ~ation
consultancy⁴
consumate · consummate²⁺
consume² consumable
consumer ~ism ~l goods ~l price index
consummate² ~ly
consumpshun · consumption
consumption
consurvashun · conservation
consurvativ · conservative⁺
Consurvatives · Conservatives [the]
consurvatory · conservatory⁴
consurvatwa · conservatoire
consurve · conserve²
consyoum · consume²⁺
contact¹ ~l lens
contagion
contagious ~ly ~ness
contain¹ ~ment
contajion · contagion
contajus · contagious⁺
contaminate² contamination
contane · contain¹⁺
contemplate² contemplation
contemplative ~ly

---

contemporaneous ~ly ~ness
contemporary[4]
contempt ~ible
contemptuous ~ly
contend[1]
contenshun   contention[+]
content[1] ~ment
contention   contentious
contest[1] ~ant
context   contextual
contiguous ~ly
continence
continent *[land mass]
Continent *[the]
continental ~l drift ~l shelf
contingency[4]   contingent
continual ~ly
continuance   continuation
continue[2]   continuity
continuous ~ly ~ness
continuum
contorshun   contortion
contort[1]
contortion ~ist
contour
contraband
contraception   contraceptive
contract[1] ~or
contraction
contractual ~ly
contradict[1] ~ion ~ory
contraflow
contralto
contraption
contrary[4]
contrast[1]
contratom   contretemps
contravene[2]   contravention

contreband   contraband
contrecepshun   contraception[+]
contredict   contradict[1+]
contredictree   contradictory
contrery   contrary[4]
contretemps
contreveen   contravene[2+]
contribute[2]   contributor
contribution   contributory
contrishun   contrition
contrite ~ly ~ness
contrition
contrive[2]   contrivance
control[3] ~l group
control ~l loop ~l room ~l tower
controllable
controlled ~l experiment ~l substance
controlling ~l variables
controversial ~ly
controversy[4]
controvurshal   controversial[+]
contryte   contrite[+]
contusion
conundrum
conurbation
convalesce[2]
convalescence   convalescent
convay   convey[1]
convayance   conveyance[+]
convayer belt   conveyor belt
convecshun   convection[+]
convection   convector
conveks   convex
convene[2]
convenience ~l food
convenient ~ly
convenshun   convention[+]
convent

---

convention ~al ~ly
converge²
convergent
conversant
conversation ~al ~alist
converse² ~ly
conversion
convert¹ ~ible
convex
convey¹ ~or
conveyance   conveyancing
conveyor belt
convict¹ ~ion
convince²   convincingly
convine   convene²
convinience   convenience
convinient   convenient⁺
convinse   convince²⁺
convivial ~ity ~ly
convocation
convoie   convoy¹
convoke²
convoluted
convoy¹
convulse²   convulsion
convurge   converge²⁺
convursant   conversant
convursashun   conversation⁺
convurse   converse²⁺
convurshun   conversion
convurt   convert¹⁺
conyak   cognac
coo¹ *[sound]   cue *[signal, card]
cook¹ ~book ~ware
cookery ~l book
cool¹ ~ant ~ly ~ness
co-op *[co-operative]
coop¹ *[not free] ~l up

co-operate²   co-operation
co-operative ~ly ~ness
co-opt¹
co-ordinashun   co-ordination
co-ordinate² *[arrange]   co-ordinator
co-ordinate *[number] ~l pair ~l point
co-ordination
coot
cop³
cope²
Copernican ~l system
copie   copy⁴⁺
co-pilot¹
copious ~ly
copiss   coppice
copius   copious⁺
copper ~plate ~sulphate
coppice
copse
copulate²
Copurnican   Copernican⁺
copy ~book ~cat ~l editor
copy⁴
copyright *[ownership]
copywrite² *[edit]
copywriter
coq au vin
coque   cock⁺
coquette   coquettish   coquetry
corage   courage
coral *[sea] ~l reef   choral *[singing],
                        chorale *[hymn],
                        corral³ *[animals]
Coran   Koran
Corcasian   Caucasian
corcus   caucus⁺
cord *[rope] ~age   chord *[music]
cordeal   cordial⁺

corden	cordon[1]
cordial ~ity ~ly	
cordite	
cordon[1]	
cordon ~l bleu ~l off	
corduroy	
core *[centre]	caw[1] *[crow],
	corps *[army, ballet]
corel	choral *[singing],
	coral *[sea][+]
corelate	correlate[2+]
corespond	correspond[1+]
corespondence	correspondence[+]
co-respondent	correspondent *[reporter]
*[divorce]	
coresponding	corresponding[+]
corgette	courgette
corght	caught *[ball],
	court[1] *[law][+]
corgi	
corida	corrida *[bull fight],
	corridor *[passage]
corigibul	corrigible
Corinthian	
coriographer	choreographer[+]
corister	chorister
corjet	courgette
cork[1] *[stopper]	caulk[1] *[seal]
cork ~screw	
corldron	cauldron
corlk	caulk[1] *[seal]
cormorant	
corn ~field ~flakes ~~on-the-cob	
cornea *[eye]	corner *[point]
corned ~l beef	
corner[1] ~stone	
cornet	
cornflour *[cooking]	

cornflower *[flower]	
cornice	
cornucopia	
corny	
coroborate	corroborate[2]
corode	corrode[2]
corollary	
corom	quorum
corona *[sun]	coroner *[law]
coronary	
coronashun	coronation
coronation	
coroner *[law]	corona *[sun]
coroshun	corrosion[+]
corporal ~l punishment	
corporashun	corporation
corporate ~ly ~l image	
corporation	
corprel	corporal[+]
corps *[army, ballet]	
corpse *[body]	
corpulence corpulent	
corpus	
corpuscle	
corral[3] *[animals]	choral *[singing],
	chorale *[hymn],
	coral *[sea][+]
correct[1] ~ion ~ive ~ness	
correlate[2] correlation	
correspond[1]	
correspondence ~l course	
correspondent * co-respondent *[divorce]	
[reporter]	
corresponding ~l angle	
corrida *[bull fight]	
corridor *[passage]	
corroad	corrode[2]
corroborate[2]	

KEY TO SUFFIXES AND COMPOUNDS

These rules are explained on pages ix to x.

1 Keep the word the same before adding ed, er, est, ing
 e.g. cool[1] → cooled, cooler, coolest, cooling
2 Take off final e before adding ed, er, est, ing
 e.g. fine[2] → fined, finer, finest, fining
3 Double final consonant before adding ed, er, est, ing
 e.g. thin[3] → thinned, thinner, thinnest, thinning

4 Change final y to i before adding ed, er, es, est, ly, ness
 e.g. tidy[4] → tidied, tidier, tidies, tidiest, tidily, tidiness
 Keep final y before adding ing e.g. tidying
5 Add es instead of s to the end of the word
 e.g. bunch[5] → bunches
6 Change final f to ve before adding s
 e.g. calf[6] → calves

corroborative ~ly
corrode[2]
corrosion   corrosive
corrugated ~| iron
corrupt[1] ~ible ~ion ~ly ~ness
corruptible
cors   cause[2] *[reason][+],
                              course *[order, path]
                              caws *[crow],
                              corps *[army, ballet]
corsage
corsal   causal
corse   cause[2] *[reason][+],
                              coarse[2] *[rough][+],
                              course[2] *[order, path][+]
corsen   coarsen[1]
corset ~ed
corshun   caution[1+]
corstic   caustic[+]
cort   caught *[ball],
                              court[1] *[law][+]
cortège
corteks   cortex
corterise   cauterise[2]
cortesan   courtesan
cortesy   courtesy[4]
cortex
cortier   courtier
cortion   caution[1+]
cortisone
cortmarshall   court-martial[3]
corugated   corrugated[+]
corupt   corrupt[1+]
coruptibul   corruptible
Cosack   Cossack
coschume   costume[+]
cosecant
cosee   cosy[4]

coset   cosset[1]
cosh[1]
cosie   cosy[4]
co-signatory[4]
cosine
cosmetic ~| surgery
cosmic ~ally ~| ray
cosmography
cosmology   cosmologist
cosmonaut
cosmopolitan ~ism
cosmos
co-sponsor
Cossack
cosset[1]
cost[1] *[value] ~ly   coast[1+] *[sea]
cost ~-benefit analysis
cost ~-cutting ~-efficient
cost ~-of living ~| price
costal *[ribs]   coastal *[sea]
co-star[3]
coste   coast[1+]
cost-effective ~ly ~ness
costly[4]
costume ~| jewellery
cosy[4]
cot *[bed]   coat *[clothing],
                       cote *[doves]
cotangent
cote *[doves]   coat *[clothing][+]
coterie
coton   cotton[+]
cottage ~| cheese ~| pie
cotton ~| reel ~tail ~| wool
couch[1] ~es ~| potato
cougar
cough[1] ~| mixture ~| sweet
could   couldn't [could not]

---

council *[assembly]   consul *[representative],
                       counsel³ *[advise]
councillor *
counsel³ *[advise]   counsellor *[adviser]
                       consul *[representative],
                       council *[assembly]
counsellor *   councillor *[member]
count¹ ~able ~down ~less
countenance

☞ Can't find your word here? Take off **counter** and
  look again

counter¹ ~act ~-attack
counter ~balance ~charge
counter ~-claim ~-espionage
counter ~foil ~mand
counter ~mine ~l offer ~pane
counter ~part ~point
counter ~productive ~sign
counter ~-weigh ~-weight
counterfeit¹
counterfit   counterfeit¹
countess
countrified
country⁴ ~l dancing ~l house ~men ~side
county⁴
coupay   coupé
coup d'état
coupé
couple²
couplet
coupling
coupon
courage
courageous ~ly
courd   cord *[rope]⁺,
                      chord *[music]
courduroy   corduroy
courgette

courier
courk   cork¹ *[stopper]⁺,
                      caulk¹ *[seal]
courny   corny
coursarge   corsage
course² *[order,   coarse² *[rough]⁺
         path]
course ~l book ~work
courset   corset⁺
court¹ *[law] ~ly   caught *[ball]
court ~l order ~ship ~yard
courtayzh   cortège
courteous ~ly
courtesan
courtesy⁴ *[polite]   curtsy⁴ *[bow]
courtier
court-martial³
cousin
cove
covenant ~l letter
cover¹ ~age
covert
covurt   covert
cow ~boy ~girl ~slip
coward *[runaway]   cowered *[cringed]
cowardly⁴ cowardice
cowch   couch¹⁺
cower¹
cowered *[cringed]   coward *[runaway]
cowl ~ing
cownsel   council *[assembly]
counsel³ *[advise]

☞ Can't find your word here? Look under **cou**

cownseller   councillor *[member]
                     counsellor *[adviser]
cownt   count¹⁺
cox¹ ~comb ~swain

KEY TO SUFFIXES AND COMPOUNDS

These rules are explained on pages ix to x.

1 Keep the word the same before adding ed, er, est, ing
e.g. cool¹ → cooled, cooler, coolest, cooling
2 Take off final e before adding ed, er, est, ing
e.g. fine² → fined, finer, finest, fining
3 Double final consonant before adding ed, er, est, ing
e.g. thin³ → thinned, thinner, thinnest, thinning

4 Change final y to i before adding ed, er, es, est,
ly, ness
e.g. tidy⁴ → tidied, tidier, tidies, tidiest, tidily,
tidiness
Keep final y before adding ing e.g. tidying
5 Add es instead of s to the end of the word
e.g. bunch⁵ → bunches
6 Change final f to ve before adding s
e.g. calf⁶ → calves

coxe	coax[1]
coy ~ly ~ness	
coyn	coin[1+]
coyote	
coyt	quoit
coytus	coitus
cozmetic	cosmetic[+]
cozmic	cosmic[+]
cozmografee	cosmography
cozmology	cosmology[+]
cozmonort	cosmonaut
cozmopolitan	cosmopolitan[+]
cozmos	cosmos
crab ~-apple ~meat	
crack[1] ~l cocaine ~down	
crack ~ers ~shot ~up	
crackle[2]	
cracknel	
cradle[2]	
craft	
crafts ~man ~manship ~woman	
crafty[4]	
crag ~gy	
craifish	crayfish
craip	crepe *[paper], crêpe [pancake]
crait	crate[2]
craiv	crave[2]
craiz	craze[2]
craizee	crazy[4]
crak	crack[+]
craknel	cracknel
crakul	crackle[2]
cram[3]	
cramp[1] ~on	
cranberry[4]	
crane[2]	
cranium	

crank[1] ~case ~shaft	
cranky[4]	
cranny[4]	
crap[3]	
cras	crass[+]
crash[1] *[accident]	crush[1] *[press hard][+]
crash ~l barrier	
crash ~l helmet ~-land	
crass ~ly ~ness	
crate[2] *[box]	
crater *[large hole]	
craul	crawl[1]
cravat	
crave[2] cravings	
craw ~fish	
crawl[1]	
crayfish	
crayon	
craze[2]	
crazy[4] ~l paving	
creacher	creature
cread	creed
creak[1] *[noise] ~y	creek *[stream]
cream[1] ~l cheese ~l cracker	
cream ~l soda ~l tea	
creamy[4]	
creap	creep[+]
crease[2]	
create[2] creator	
creation ~ism	
creative ~l accounting ~l writing	
creative ~ly ~ness	
creativity[4]	
creature	
crèche	
crecher	creature
credence	
credense	credence

---

credenshals   credential
credentials
credible   credibility
credit[1] ~able ~or ~| card
credit ~| limit ~| rating
creditworthy[4]
credo
credulity[2]   credulous
creed
creek *[stream]   creak[1] *[noise][+]
creem   cream[1+]
creep ~er ~ing
creepy[4]
creese   crease[2]
crejulity   credulity[+]
cremate[2]   cremation
crematorium
crème caramel   crème fraiche
cremetoriam   crematorium
crenellated
creole
creosote
crepe *[paper]
crêpe *[pancake]
crept
crepuscular
crescendo
crescent ~| moon
creshendo   crescendo
cress
cressent   crescent
crest[1] ~fallen
Cresus   Croesus
Creutzfeldt-Jakob Disease
crevasse *[ice]   crevice *[small]
crevat   cravat
crevice *[small]   crevasse *[ice]
crew[1] ~| cut ~| neck

crews *[teams]   cruise[2] *[trip]
crewdity   crudity *[coarseness],
             crudités *[food]
crewit   cruet
criashun   creation[+]
criate   create[2+]
criativ   creative[+]
crib[3]
cribbage
crick[1]
cricket ~er ~ing ~| captain
crido   credo
crie   cry[4+]
cried
crik   crick[1]
crikit   cricket[+]
crimate   cremate[2+]
crime ~wave
criminal ~ly
criminalise[2]   criminality
criminologist   criminology
crimp[1]
Crimplene™
crimsen   crimson
crimson
cringe[2]
crinj   cringe[2]
crinkle[2] crinkly
crinoline
criogenics   cryogenics
criole   creole
cripple[2]
cript   crypt[+]
cripul   cripple[2]
crisis   crises
crisp[1] crispy[4]
criss-cross[1]
crissen   christen[1]

KEY TO SUFFIXES AND COMPOUNDS

These rules are explained on pages ix to x.

1 Keep the word the same before adding ed, er, est, ing
e.g. cool[1] → cooled, cooler, coolest, cooling
2 Take off final e before adding ed, er, est, ing
e.g. fine[2] → fined, finer, finest, fining
3 Double final consonant before adding ed, er, est, ing
e.g. thin[3] → thinned, thinner, thinnest, thinning

4 Change final y to i before adding ed, er, es, est, ly, ness
e.g. tidy[4] → tidied, tidier, tidies, tidiest, tidily, tidiness
Keep final y before adding ing e.g. tidying
5 Add es instead of s to the end of the word
e.g. bunch[5] → bunches
6 Change final f to ve before adding s
e.g. calf[6] → calves

Crist   Christ[+]
cristal   crystal[+]
cristaline   crystalline
cristallise   crystallise[2+]
cristallografee   crystallography
Cristian   Christian[+]
Cristmas   Christmas[+]
criteek   critique *[criticism],
       critic *[evaluator]
criteria   criterion
critic *[evaluator]   critique *[criticism]
critical ~ly
criticise[2]
criticism
critique *[criticism]   critic *[evaluator]
critisize   criticise[2]
croak[1]
croch   crotch
crochet[1]
crock ~ery
crocodile ~| tears
crocus[5]
Croesus
croft ~er ~ing
croissant
Croitsfeld-Jacob   Creutzfeldt-Jakob
       Disease   Disease
crokay   croquet

☞ Can't find your word here? Look under **chro**

croke   croak[1]
crokodile   crocodile
crokus   crocus[5]
crome   chrome
crone *[old woman]   krone *[money][+]
crony[4] ~ism
crood   crude *[rough][+]
crook[1]

crooked ~edly ~edness
croon[1]
croop   croup
croopiay   croupier
crop[3] ~| circle ~| rotation
croquet *[game]
croquette *[food]
crore   craw[+]
croshay   crochet[1]

☞ Can't find your word here? Take off **cross** and look again

cross[1] ~ly ~ness ~bar ~bencher ~bones
cross ~bow ~bred ~breed ~check
cross ~-country ~-cultural ~-current
cross ~cut ~cutting ~-dress ~-examine
cross ~-examination ~-eyed ~-fertilise
cross ~fire ~-hatch ~-legged ~-match ~over
cross ~patch ~-purposes ~-question
cross ~-reference ~roads ~-section
cross ~wind ~wise ~word
crotch
crotchet
crotchety[4]
crouch[1]
croud   crowd
croup
croupier
crow[1] ~bar
crowch   crouch[1]
crowd *[people]
crowed *[cock]
crowkay   croquet *[game]
crowket   croquette *[food]
crown[1] ~| agent ~| jewels
crown ~| prince ~| princess
Crown [the]
cruch   crutch[5]

KEY TO SPELLING RULES

Red words are wrong. **Black** words are correct.

~   Add the suffix or word directly to the main word, without a space or hyphen
    e.g. ash ~en ~tray → **ashen ashtray**
~--   Add a hyphen to the main word before adding the next word
    e.g. blow ~-dry → **blow-dry**

~| Leave a space between the main word and the next word
    e.g. decimal ~| place → **decimal place**
+   By finding this word in its **correct** alphabetical order, you can find related words
    e.g. about[+] → **about-face about-turn**
*   Draws attention to words that may be confused
TM   Means the word is a trademark

crucial ~ly
crucible
crucifix
crucify⁴   crucifixion
crucks   crux
crud *[dirt]
crude² *[rough] ~ly ~ness
crudités *[food]
crudity *[coarseness]
crue   crew¹⁺
cruel³ ~ly ~ty
cruet
cruise² *[trip]   crews *[teams]
cruise ~ control
cruise ~ liner ~ missile
cruk   crook¹
crule   cruel³⁺
crum   crumb
crumb
crumble² *[break]   crumple² *[crease]
crumbly⁴
crummy⁴
crumpet
crumple² *[crease]   crumble² *[break]
crunch¹   crunchy⁴
crune   croon¹⁺
crusade²
crush¹ *[press hard] crash¹ *[accident]⁺
crushal   crucial⁺
crusibul   crucible
crusify   crucify⁴⁺
crust   crusty⁴
crustacean
crutch⁵
crux⁵
cry⁴ ~baby
crymp   crimp¹
crymplene   Crimplene™

crynolyne   crinoline
cryogenics
crypt ~ic ~ography

☞ Can't find your word here? Look under **chri** or **cri**

crysalis   chrysalis
crysanthemum   chrysanthemum
crystal ~ ball ~ clear
crystalline
crystallise²   crystallisation
crystallography
cryticyse   criticise²⁺
cryticysum   criticism
CT-scan
cu   coo¹
cub
Cub Scout
cubbyhole
cube² ~ number ~ root
cubeehole   cubbyhole
cubical *[cube-shaped]
cubicle *[small room]
cubism   cubist
cuboid
cubord   cupboard
cuckold¹
cuckoo ~ clock
cucoo   cuckoo⁺
cucumber
cud
cuddle²   cuddly⁴
cudgel³
cudjel   cudgel³
cue² *[billiards]   queue² *[line]⁺
cuff¹ ~link
cuger   cougar
Cuisenaire ~ rods
cuisine

---

culcher culture²⁺
cul-de-sac
cule cool¹⁺
culinary
cull¹
culla colour⁺
culminate² culmination
culottes
culpable culpability
culprit
cult
cultivate² cultivator
cultivation
cultural ~ly ~l norms
culture² ~ly
culvert
cum laude
cumbersome ~ly ~ness

☞ Can't find your word here? Look under **com**

cume come⁺
cumemorate commemorate²⁺
cumfertable comfortable⁺
cumfort comfort¹
cumfy comfy
cumlawday cum laude
cummand command¹⁺
cumpany company⁴
cumparison comparison
cumpass compass⁵
cumulative
cumulus
cuneiform
cunning ~ly
cuntree country⁺
cuntrified countrified
cup³ ~cake ~ful ~l tie
cuppa

cupboard
Cupid
cuple couple²
cupola
cupon coupon
cuppling coupling
curable
curate *[priest]
curate² [museum] curator
curb¹ *[stop] kerb¹ *[edge]
curd
curdle²
cure² ~-all curative
curensy currency⁴
curent currant *[fruit],
 current *[flow, now]⁺
curfew
curgette courgette
curiculum curriculum
curier courier
curio
curiosity⁴
curious ~ly ~ness
curl¹ curly⁴
curlew
currage courage
currageous courageous⁺
currant *[fruit] current *[flow, now]⁺
currency⁴
current *[flow, now] currant *[fruit]
current ~ly
current ~l account ~l affairs
curriculum ~l vitae curricula
curry⁴ ~l powder
curse² *[bad spell]
cursive
cursor
cursory⁴

---

curt ~ly ~ness
curtail[1] ~ment
curtain *[screen]   certain *[sure][+]
curtain ~| call ~| rail
curtifiable   certifiable[+]
curtificate   certificate
curtify   certify[4+]
curtitude   certitude
curtsy[4] *[bow]   courtesy[4] *[polite]
curvaceous ~ness
curve[2] curvature
curvical   cervical[+]
curvix   cervix
cury   curry[4+]
cushion[1]
cusin   cousin
cusp
cuss[1]
custard ~| pie
custody custodial custodian
custom ~er ~-made
customary[4]
customise
cut *[with a knife] ~ter ~ting
cut ~-and-paste ~back
cut ~-out ~-price ~-throat
cute[2] *[sweet] ~ly ~ness
cuticle
cutlass[5]
cutlery
cutlet
cuttlefish
cuvenant   covenant
cuver   cover[1+]
cyanide
cybernetics

☞ Can't find your word here? Look under <u>sy</u>

cyberspace
cyclamate
cyclamen
cycle[2]
cyclic ~al
cyclist
cyclone   cyclonic
Cyclops
cyclotron
cygnet *[swan]   signet *[ring]
cylinder
cylindrical ~ly
cymbal *[music]   symbol *[sign][+]
cymbolic   symbolic[+]
cymbolise   symbolise[2+]
cynch   cinch[5]
cynder   cinder[+]
Cynderella   Cinderella
cyne   cine[+]
cynema   cinema[+]
cynic ~ism
cynical ~ly
cynonim   synonym[+]
cynosure
cypress *[tree]   Cyprus *[country]
Cyrillic
cyringe   syringe
cyrup   syrup[+]
cyst
cystem   system[+]
cystitis
cyte   cite[2] *[quote],
                       sight *[seeing][+], site *[place]
czar ~ina

KEY TO SUFFIXES AND COMPOUNDS

These rules are explained on pages ix to x.

1 Keep the word the same before adding ed, er, est, ing
   e.g. cool[1] → cooled, cooler, coolest, cooling
2 Take off final e before adding ed, er, est, ing
   e.g. fine[2] → fined, finer, finest, fining
3 Double final consonant before adding ed, er, est, ing
   e.g. thin[3] → thinned, thinner, thinnest, thinning

4 Change final y to i before adding ed, er, es, est, ly, ness
   e.g. tidy[4] → tidied, tidier, tidies, tidiest, tidily, tidiness
   Keep final y before adding ing e.g. tidying
5 Add es instead of s to the end of the word
   e.g. bunch[5] → bunches
6 Change final f to ve before adding s
   e.g. calf[6] → calves

D ~-Day	
dab[4]	
dabble[2]	
dabel	dabble[2]
dachshund	
dad	
daddy ~-long-legs	
dael	dale
daffodil	
daft[1]	
dagger	
dahlia	
daily[4]	
daim	dame
dain	Dane *[Denmark, dog], deign[1] *[bother]
dainty[4]	
dair	dare[2+]
dairy[4] *[milk]	diary[4] *[journal]
daisy[4] ~l chain	
dakshund	dachshund
dale	
dally[4] *[be slow]	daily[4] *[every day]
Dalmashun	Dalmatian
Dalmation	
dam[3] *[water]	dame *[lady], damn[1] *[curse][+]
damage[2] ~l control	
dame *[lady]	dam[3] *[water]
damige	damage[2]
damn[1] *[curse] ~ation	dam[3] *[water]
damp[1] ~ness	
dampen[1]	
damson	
damzen	damson
dance[2] ~l floor ~l music	
dandelion	
dandruff	

dandy[4]	
dandylion	dandelion
Dane *[Denmark, dog]	deign[1] *[bother]
danety	dainty[4]
danger ~ous ~ously	
dangle[2]	
danjer	danger[+]
dank	
dans	dance[2+]
dapper	
dapple[2]	
dare[2] ~devil	
darey	dairy[4]
dark[1] ~ly ~ness ~room	
darken[1]	
darling	
darn[1]	
dart[1] ~board	
dash[1] ~board	
dashund	dachshund
dastardly	
data ~bank ~base ~l capture	
data ~l collection ~l entry ~l logger	
data ~l processing ~l search	
date[2] ~l line ~l of birth	
date ~l rape ~-stamp	
daub[1]	
daudle	dawdle[2]
daughter ~-in-law	
daun	dawn[1+]
daunt[1] ~ingly ~less	
dauphin	
dauter	daughter[+]
dawb	daub[1]
dawdle[2]	
dawn[1] ~l chorus ~l raid	
dawnt	daunt[1+]
daxhound	dachshund

☞ Can't find your word here? Take off **day** and look
again

---

day ~break ~dream ~light
day ~| nursery ~| release
day ~time ~~-to-day ~| trip

daybacle	débâcle
daybri	debris
daybue	début
daycor	décor
dayfacto	de facto

Day-Glo™

dayism	deism[+]
dayity	deity[4]
dayjarvoo	déjà vu
daylia	dahlia
dayly	daily[4]
daynooment	dénouement
days *[dates]	daze[2] *[stun]
dayt	date[+]
daytont	détente
daze[2] *[stun]	days *[dates]

dazzle[2]
de facto

☞ Can't find your word here? Take off **dead** and look
again

---

dead[1] *[not alive]	deed *[action][+]

dead ~beat ~| bolt ~| duck ~| end
dead ~head ~| heat ~line ~lock ~| loss
dead ~pan ~| weight ~| wood
deaden[1]
deadly[4]

deaf *[hearing] ~ness	deft *[nimble][+]

deaf ~~-and-dumb ~~-mute
deafen[1] ~ingly
deal ~ing
dealer ~ship

dealt
dean ~ship

dear[1] *[loved] ~ly	deer *[animal]

dearth *[not enough]
death *[being dead] ~ly ~bed
death ~| penalty ~| rate
death ~| sentence ~| toll
death ~| trap ~| warrant ~| wish

☞ Can't find your word here? Take off **death** and
look again

---

débâcle
debar[3]
debase[2]
debate[2] debatable
debauched debauchery
debilitate[2]
debit[1]
debonair
Debrett's
debrief[1]
debris
debt ~or ~| collector ~| relief
debug[3]
debunk[1]
début

débutant *[man]
débutante *[woman]

decade *[10 years]	decayed *[rotted]

decadence decadent
decaffeinated
decamp[1]
decant[1]
decapitate[2] decapitation
decathlon
decay[1]

decayed *[rotted]	decade *[10 years]
deceased *[dead]	diseased *[ill]

KEY TO SUFFIXES AND COMPOUNDS

These rules are explained on pages ix to x.

Keep the word the same before adding **ed, er, est, ing**
e.g. cool[1] → cooled, cooler, coolest, cooling
Take off final **e** before adding **ed, er, est, ing**
e.g. fine[2] → fined, finer, finest, fining
Double final consonant before adding **ed, er, est, ing**
e.g. thin[3] → thinned, thinner, thinnest, thinning

4 Change final **y** to **i** before adding **ed, er, es, est,
ly, ness**
e.g. tidy[4] → tidied, tidier, tidies, tidiest, tidily,
tidiness
Keep final **y** before adding **ing** e.g. tidying
5 Add **es** instead of **s** to the end of the word
e.g. bunch[5] → bunches
6 Change final **f** to **ve** before adding **s**
e.g. calf[6] → calves

deceit ~ful ~fully ~fulness

☞ Can't find your word here? Look under **di**

deceive[2]

December

decency

decent *[good] ~ly   descent *[down],
                       dissent *[argument]

decentralise[2]   decentralisation

deception

deceptive ~ly ~ness

decibel

decide[2] ~dly

deciduous

decigram   decilitre   decimetre

decimal ~| fraction ~| number

decimal ~| place ~| point

decimalise[2]   decimalisation

decimate[2]   decimation

decipher[1] ~able

decision ~-maker ~-making

decisive ~ly ~ness

deck[1] ~chair ~hand

declaration   declaratory

declare[2]

declassify[4]

declension

decline[2]

decode[2]

décolleté

decompose[2]   decomposition

decompress[1] ~ion ~or

decongestant

deconstruct[1]

decontaminate[2]   decontamination

décor

decorate[2]   decoration   decorator

decorative ~ly

decorous ~ly   decorum

decoy[1]

decrativ   decorative[+]

decrease[2]   decreasingly

decree *[legal] ~d ~ing   degree *[amount,
                                     study]

decrepit ~ude

decriminalise[2]   decrimilisation

decry[4]

ded   dead *[not alive][+],
                          deed *[action][+]

deden   deaden[1]

dedicate[2]   dedication

deduce[2]

deduct[1] ~ible ~ion

deed *[action] ~| poll   dead *[not alive][+]

deel   deal[+]

deeler   dealer[+]

deem[1]

deen   dean[+]

deep[1] ~ly ~freeze ~-frozen

deep ~-fry ~-rooted ~-seated ~-set

deepen[1]

deer *[animal]   dear *[loved][+]

de-escalate[2]

deezel   diesel

def   deaf[+]

deface[2] ~ment

defamation   defamatory

default[1]

defeat[1] ~ism ~ist

defecate[2]   defecation

defect[1] ~ion ~ive

defence ~less

defend[1] ~able ~ant

defens   defence[+]

defensible

defensive ~ly ~ness

---

defer³ *[put off] ~ment   differ¹ *[disagree]
deference
deferenshal   deferential⁺
deferential ~ly
defermashun   defamation⁺
deffen   deafen¹⁺
defiance defiant defiantly
deficiency⁴
deficient ~ly
deficit
defile²
define² definable
definishun   definition
definite ~ly ~l article
definition
definitive ~ly
defir   defer³ *[put off],
                            differ¹ *[disagree]
defisit   deficit
defishensy   deficiency⁴
deflate² deflation
deflationary⁴
deflect¹ ~ion ~or
deforest¹ ~ation
deform¹ ~ation
deformity⁴
defraud¹
defray¹ ~able
defrost¹
deft ~ly ~ness
defunct
defuse² *[calm, bomb]   diffuse² *[spread]⁺
defusion
defy⁴
degeneracy
degenerate² degeneration
degrade² degradation
degree *[amount, study]   decree *[legal]⁺

dehumanise² dehumanisation
dehydrate² dehydration
de-ice²
deign¹ *[bother]   Dane *[Denmark, dog]
deism deist
deity⁴
déjà vu
deject¹ ~ion
dek   deck¹⁺
dekonstrukt   deconstruct¹
dekorate   decorate²⁺
dekorum   decorum
dekorus   decorous⁺
deksterity   dexterity
dekstroze   dextrose
dekstrus   dexterous
delay¹
delectable
delegate² delegation
delete² deletion
deliberate² ~ly deliberation
delicacy⁴
delicate ~ly ~ness
delicatessen
delicious ~ly ~ness
delight¹ ~ful ~fully
delikatessen   delicatessen
delinquent delinquency⁴
delirious ~ly
delirium
delishus   delicious⁺
deliver¹ ~ance delivery⁴
dell
delouse²
delt   dealt
delta
delude² delusion delusional
deluge²

KEY TO SUFFIXES AND COMPOUNDS

These rules are explained on pages ix to x.

1 Keep the word the same before adding ed, er, est, ing
  e.g. cool¹ → cooled, cooler, coolest, cooling
2 Take off final e before adding ed, er, est, ing
  e.g. fine² → fined, finer, finest, fining
3 Double final consonant before adding ed, er, est, ing
  e.g. thin³ → thinned, thinner, thinnest, thinning

4 Change final y to i before adding ed, er, es, est,
  ly, ness
  e.g. tidy⁴ → tidied, tidier, tidies, tidiest, tidily,
  tidiness
  Keep final y before adding ing e.g. tidying
5 Add es instead of s to the end of the word
  e.g. bunch⁵ → bunches
6 Change final f to ve before adding s
  e.g. calf⁶ → calves

delusory
deluxe
delve[2]
demagogue   demagogic
demand[1]
demarcate[2]   demarcation
demean[1] ~our
demented
dementia
demer   demur[3] *[refuse],
                                    demure *[shy][+]
demerara
demilitarise[2]   demilitarisation
demise
demist[1]
demo
demobilise[2]   demobilisation
democracy[4]
democrat ~ic ~ically
democratise[2]   democratisation
demographic ~s   demography
demolish[1]
demolition
demon ~ic
demonstrable   demonstrably
demonstrate[2]   demonstrator
demonstration
demonstrative ~ly
demoralise[2]
demote[2]   demotion
demur[3] *[refuse]
demure *[shy] ~ly
demygod   demigod
demystify[4]
den
dence   dense[2]
dencher   denture
dencity   density[4]

denial
denigrate[2]   denigration
denim
denizen
denominate[2]   denominator
denomination ~al
denote[2]
denouement
denounce[2]
denowns   denounce[2]
dense[2] *[thick] ~ly   dents *[bangs]
density[4]
dent[1]
dental ~l hygeine
dentine
dentist ~ry
denture
dentyne   dentine
dentyst   dentist[+]
denude[2]
denunciate[2]   denunciation
deny[4]
denyal   denial
denygreat   denigrate[2+]
deodorant
deodorise[2]
depart[1] ~ure
department ~al ~ally ~l store
departmentalise[2]
depend[1] ~able ~ant
dependants *[people]
dependence *[reliance]
dependency[4]
dependent *[needy]   dependant *[person]
dependent ~l variable
depersonalise[2]
depict[1] ~ion
depilate[2]   depilation

---

deplete² depletion	derty	dirty⁴

deplete² depletion

deploma   diploma⁺

deplore² deplorable deplorably

deploy¹ ~ment

depo   depot

depopulate² depopulation

deport¹ ~ation

deportment

depose²

deposit

deposition

depository⁴

depot

depraved² depravity

deprecate² *[disapprove]

depreciate² *[value] depreciation

depress¹ ~ant ~ion ~ive

depressurise²

deprishiate   depreciate² *[value]⁺

deprive² deprivation

depth ~l charge

depute² deputation

deputie   deputy⁴

deputise²

deputy⁴

derail¹ ~ment

derange² ~ment

derby⁴

derelict ~ion

deride² derisive derisory

derision

derivative

derive² derivation

dermatitis

dermatology dermatologist

derogatory

derrick

dert   dirt⁺

derty   dirty⁴

dervish

desalinate² desalination

descant

descend¹ ~ant

descent *[down]   decent *[good]⁺, dissent *[argue]

descrete   discreet *[careful]⁺, discrete *[separate]

describe²

description descriptive

descurchus   discourteous⁺

desdain   disdain¹⁺

desecrate² desecration

deseet   deceit⁺

desegregate² desegregation

Desember   December

desend   descend¹⁺

desensitise²

desent   decent *[good]⁺, dissent *[argue]

desentralise   decentralise²⁺

desershun   desertion

desert *[sand]   dessert *[food]

desert¹ *[leave] ~ion

deserve² ~dly

desibell   decibel

desicated   desiccated

deside   decide²⁺

desifer   decipher¹⁺

design¹

designate² designation

desimal   decimal⁺

desimate   decimate²⁺

desirable desirability

desire² desirous

desisive   decisive⁺

desist¹

KEY TO SUFFIXES AND COMPOUNDS

These rules are explained on pages ix to x.

1 Keep the word the same before adding ed, er, est, ing
e.g. cool¹ → cooled, cooler, coolest, cooling

2 Take off final e before adding ed, er, est, ing
e.g. fine² → fined, finer, finest, fining

3 Double final consonant before adding ed, er, est, ing
e.g. thin³ → thinned, thinner, thinnest, thinning

4 Change final y to i before adding ed, er, es, est, ly, ness
e.g. tidy⁴ → tidied, tidier, tidies, tidiest, tidily, tidiness
Keep final y before adding ing e.g. tidying

5 Add es instead of s to the end of the word
e.g. bunch⁵ → bunches

6 Change final f to ve before adding s
e.g. calf⁶ → calves

desk ~| job ~top
desolate   desolation
despair¹ ~ingly
desperado⁵
desperashun   desperation
desperate *[need] ~ly   disparate *[unequal]⁺
desperation
despicable   despicably
despise²
despite
despondent
deposit¹
despot ~ic ~ically ~ism
despute   dispute²
dessend   descend¹⁺
dessent   decent *[good]⁺,
                               descent *[down],
                               dissent *[argue]
dessert *[food] ~spoon   desert *[sand],
                               desert¹ *[leave]⁺
dessicated
destichute   destitute⁺
destination
destiny⁴   destined
destitute   destitution
destroy¹
destruction   destructible
destructive ~ly
det   debt⁺
detach¹ ~able ~ment
detail¹
detain ~ee
detect¹ ~able ~ion ~or
detective ~| agency
détente
detention ~| centre
deter³
deterant   deterrent

detergent
deteriorate² deterioration
determinant
determination
determine² determinism
deterrent   deterrence
detest¹ ~able
deth   death
dethrone²
detonate² detonation detonator
detour
detriment ~al
deuce
Deurex   Durex™
devalue² devaluation
devastate² devastation
develop¹ ~ment
deviance   deviant
deviate² deviation
device *[thing]   devise² *[invent]
devide   divide²⁺
devil ~ment ~ry ~'s advocate
devilish ~ly
devious ~ly ~ness
devise² *[invent]   device *[thing]
devolution
devorse   divorce²⁺
devoshun   devotion⁺
devote² ~dly   devotee
devotion ~al
devour¹
devout ~ly
devulge   divulge²
devyce   device *[thing],
                       devise² *[invent]
dew *[drops] ~y   Jew *[religion]⁺,
                  due *[owing,
                          expected]⁺

---

dewet

dewp

dewplicate

dewplisity

dewrable

dewration

dewress

dexterity

dexterous *[skilful] ~ly

dextrose *[sugar]

diabetes   diabetic

diabolic ~al ~ally

diafram

diafunus

diagnose²

diagnosis   diagnoses

diagnostic ~ally ~ian ~s

diagonal ~ly

diagram ~matic ~matically

dial³ ~-up

dialing ~l code ~tone

dialect

dialogue

dialysis

diameter

diametrically

diamond ~l jubilee ~l wedding

diaphanous

diaphragm

diar

diarrhoea

diarria

diary⁴ *[journal]

diatribe

dibate

dice²

duet

dupe²

duplicate²⁺

duplicity⁺

durable⁺

duration

duress

diaphragm

diaphanous

dire *[bad],
dear *[loved]⁺,
deer *[animal]

diarrhoea

dairy⁴ *[milk]

debate²⁺

☞ Can't find your word here? Look under **de**

diceive

dicent

dichotomy⁴

dicky ~l bird ~l bow

dicree

dicshun

dicshunry

dictaphone

dictate²   dictation

dictator ~ial ~ship

diction

dictionary⁴

dictum

did *[past of do]

didactic ~ally

diddle²

didgeridoo

didn't [did not]

diduct

die *[death, dice]

die ~l away ~l down

die ~-hard ~l off ~l out

died *[past of die]

diek

diernal

diesel

diet¹ ~ary ~ician

dietetic ~s

difamatry

difase

difault

difend

difensiv

deceive²

decent *[good]⁺,
descent *[down],
dissent *[argue]

decree⁺

diction

dictionary⁴

died *[past of die]

deduct¹⁺

dye *[change colour]⁺

did *[past of do],
dyed *[changed colour]

dyke

diurnal

defamatory

deface²⁺

default¹

defend⁺

defensive⁺

KEY TO SUFFIXES AND COMPOUNDS

These rules are explained on pages ix to x.

1 Keep the word the same before adding **ed, er, est, ing**
e.g. cool¹ → cooled, cooler, coolest, cooling

2 Take off final **e** before adding **ed, er, est, ing**
e.g. fine² → fined, finer, finest, fining

3 Double final consonant before adding **ed, er, est, ing**
e.g. thin³ → thinned, thinner, thinnest, thinning

4 Change final **y** to **i** before adding **ed, er, es, est, ly, ness**
e.g. tidy⁴ → tidied, tidier, tidies, tidiest, tidily, tidiness
Keep final **y** before adding **ing** e.g. tidying

5 Add **es** instead of **s** to the end of the word
e.g. bunch⁵ → bunches

6 Change final **f** to **ve** before adding **s**
e.g. calf⁶ → calves

differ[1] *[disagree]	defer[3] *[put off]	dijest	digest[1+]
difference *[unlike]	deference *[respect]	dijestshun	digestion
different ~ly		dijit	digit[+]
differential *[difference]	deferential * [respectful][+]	dijital	digital[+]
		dikshun	diction
differentiate[2] differentiation		dikshunrey	dictionary[4]
difficult difficulty[4]		diktate	dictate[2+]
diffidence diffident		diktater	dictator[+]
diffurenshal	deferential * [respectful][+], differential * [difference]	diktum	dictum
		dilait	dilate[2+]
		dilapidated dilapidation	
		dilate[2] dilation	
diffurenshiate	differentiate[2+]	dilay	delay[1]
diffuse[2] *[spread]	defuse[2] *[calm, bomb][+]	dilaytantay	dilettante
		dilect	dialect
diffusion		dilemma	
difianse	defiance[+]	dilete	delete[2+]
difine	define[2+]	dilettante	
difrens	difference	diligence diligent diligently	
difunct	defunct	diling	dialing[+]
difuse	diffuse[2] *[spread][+] defuse[2] [calm, bomb][+]	dilinquent	delinquent[+]
		dilishus	delicious[+]
		dilude	delude[2+]
dify	defy[4]	dilute[2] dilution	
dig[3] ~l in ~l out ~l up		dim[3] ~ly ~ness	
digenerate	degenerate[2+]	dimand	demand[1]
digest[1] ~ible ~ion ~ive		dime	
digit ~alis ~ally		dimean	demean[1+]
digital ~l camera ~l divide ~l signature		dimensha	dementia
dignify[4]		dimension	
dignitary[4]		dimentid	demented
dignity[4]		diminish[1]	
digrade	degrade[2+]	diminution	
digraph		diminutive	
digree	degree	dimise	demise
digress[1] ~ion		dimple[2]	
diing	dyeing *[colour], dying *[about to die]	dimur	demur[3] *[refuse], demure *[shy][+]

☞ Can't find your word here? Look under **dy**

din

dinamic	dynamic[+]
dinamo	dynamo
dinasty	dynasty[4+]
dine[2] *[eat]	dyne *[force]

ding ~-dong ~bat

dinghy[4] *[boat]	dingy[4] *[shabby]

dingo[5]

dingy[4] *[shabby]	dinghy[4] *[boat]
dinial	denial

dining ~| car ~| room ~| table

dinner ~| jacket ~| table ~time

dinosaur

diocese diocesan

diodarise	deodorise[2]

diode

diodorant	deodorant
diosees	diocese[+]

dioxide dioxin

dip[3] ~stick

dipacher	departure
dipart	depart[+]

diphtheria

diphthong

dipict	depict[1+]
diplete	deplete[2+]

diploma

diplomacy[4]

diplomat ~ic ~ically

diplore	deplore[2+]
diposzit	deposit[1]
dipreshiate	depreciate[2]
diptheria	diphtheria
dipthong	diphthong
dirby	Derby[4]

dire[2]

direct[1] ~ly ~ness ~| debit ~| deposit ~| mail

direct ~| object ~| proportion ~| speech

direction directive

director ~ate ~ship

directory[4] ~| enquiries

dirijun	derision[+]
dirive	derive[2+]
dirmatitis	dermatitis
dirmatology	dermatology[+]

dirt ~-cheap ~| road ~| track

dirth	dearth

dirty[4]

dirvish	dervish

disability[4]

disable[2] ~ment

disabuse[2]

disadvantage

disaffected disaffection

disagree ~able ~ably ~ment

disagreed

disalinate	desalinate[2+]

disallow[1]

disappear[1] ~ance

disappoint[1] ~ment

disapproval

disapprove[2] *[bad]	disprove[2] *[false]

disarm[1] ~ament

disassemble[2]

disassociate[2] disassociation

disaster disastrous disastrously

disavow[1] ~al

disband[1] ~ment

disbar[3]

disbelief

disbelieve[2]

disburse[2] *[pay out]	disperse[2] *[scatter][+]
disc *[circle, music]	disk *[computer]

disc ~| brake ~| jockey

KEY TO SUFFIXES AND COMPOUNDS

These rules are explained on pages ix to x.

1 Keep the word the same before adding **ed, er, est, ing**
   e.g. cool[1] → cooled, cooler, coolest, cooling
2 Take off final **e** before adding **ed, er, est, ing**
   e.g. fine[2] → fined, finer, finest, fining
3 Double final consonant before adding **ed, er, est, ing**
   e.g. thin[3] → thinned, thinner, thinnest, thinning

4 Change final **y** to **i** before adding **ed, er, es, est, ly, ness**
   e.g. tidy[4] → tidied, tidier, tidies, tidiest, tidily, tidiness
   Keep final **y** before adding **ing** e.g. tidying
5 Add **es** instead of **s** to the end of the word
   e.g. bunch[5] → bunches
6 Change final **f** to **ve** before adding **s**
   e.g. calf[6] → calves

93

discard[1]
discend   descend[1+]
discern[1] ~ible ~ment
discharge[2]
disciple
discipline[2]   disciplinary
disclaim[1] ~er
disclose[2]   disclosure
disco ~theque
discolour[1]   discolouration
discomfort
disconcerted   disconcerting
disconnect[1]
disconsolate ~ly
discontent ~ed
discontinue[2]
discord
discotech   discotheque
discount[1] ~| card ~| rate
discourage[2] ~ment
discourse[2]
discourteous ~ly ~ness
discourtesy[4]
discover[1]   discovery[4]
discredit[1] ~able
discreet *[careful] ~ly   discrete *[separate]
discrepancy[4]
discrete *[separate]   discreet *[careful][+]
discretion ~ary
discribe   describe[2+]
discriminate[2]   discrimination
discripshun   description[+]
discurige   discourage[2+]
discursion   discursive
discurtesy   discourtesy[4]
discus[5] *[heavy disc]
discuss[1] *[debate] ~es ~ion
disdain[1] ~ful ~fully

disease
diseased *[ill]   deceased *[dead]
disect   dissect[1+]
disembark[1] ~ation
disembody[4]   disembodiment
disembowel[3]
disenchanted   disenchantment
disenfranchise[2] ~ment
disengage[2] ~ment
disenshun   dissension
disent   decent *[good][+],
              descent *[down],
              dissent *[argue]
disentangle[2] ~ment
disepshun   deception
diseptiv   deceptive[+]
disert   desert[1] *[leave],
              dessert *[food]
diserve   deserve[2+]
diseve   deceive[2]
disfavour[1]
disfigure[2] ~ment
disgorge[2]
disgrace[2] ~ful ~fully
disgruntled
disguise[2]
disgust[1]
dish[1] ~cloth ~washer ~water
disharmony
dishearten[1]
dishevelled
dishonest ~ly   dishonesty
dishonour[1] ~able ~ably
diside   decide[2+]
disiduus   deciduous
disign   design[1]
disillusion[1] ~ment
disincentive   disincentivised

---

disinclined
disine   design¹
disinfect¹ ~ant
disingenuous ~ly ~ness
disinherit¹ ~ance
disintegrate²   disintegration
disinter³ ~ment
disinterest ~d
disirabul   desirable⁺
disire   desire²⁺
disist   desist¹
disjointed
disk *[computer] ~| drive   disc *[circle, music]
diskomfort   discomfort¹
dislexsia   dyslexia⁺

> ☞ Can't find your word here? Take off **dis** and look
> again

dislike²
dislocate²   dislocation
dislodge²
disloyal ~ty⁴
dismal ~ly
dismantle²
dismay¹
dismember¹ ~ment
dismiss¹ ~al
dismount¹
Disney ~land
disobedience   disobedient
disobey¹
disorder¹ ~ly
disorganise²   disorganisation
disorientate²   disorientation
disown¹
dispair   despair¹⁺
disparage² ~ment
disparate *[unequal] ~ly   desperate *[need]⁺

dispare   despair⁺
disparity⁴
dispassionate ~ly
dispatch¹ ~es
dispear   despair¹
dispel³
dispensary⁴
dispense²   dispensation
dispersal
disperse² *[scatter]   disburse² *[pay out]
dispikabul   despicable⁺
dispirited   dispiriting
dispise   despise²
dispite   despite
displace² ~ment
display¹
displease²   displeasure
dispondunt   despondent
dispose²   disposable   disposal
disposition
dispossess¹ ~ion
dispraxia   dyspraxia⁺
disproportion ~ate ~ately
disprove² *[false]   disapprove² *[bad]
dispurse   disperse²
dispute²
disqualify⁴   disqualification
disquiet¹
disregard¹
disrepair
disreputable   disreputably
disrepute
disrespect ~ful ~fully
disrobe²
disrupt¹ ~ion
disruptive ~ly ~ness
dissability   disability⁴
dissapear   disappear¹⁺

KEY TO SUFFIXES AND COMPOUNDS

These rules are explained on pages ix to x.

1 Keep the word the same before adding **ed, er, est, ing**
  e.g. cool¹ → cooled, cooler, coolest, cooling
2 Take off final **e** before adding **ed, er, est, ing**
  e.g. fine² → fined, finer, finest, fining
3 Double final consonant before adding **ed, er, est, ing**
  e.g. thin³ → thinned, thinner, thinnest, thinning

4 Change final **y** to **i** before adding **ed, er, es, est, ly, ness**
  e.g. tidy⁴ → tidied, tidier, tidies, tidiest, tidily, tidiness
  Keep final **y** before adding **ing** e.g. tidying
5 Add **es** instead of **s** to the end of the word
  e.g. bunch⁵ → bunches
6 Change final **f** to **ve** before adding **s**
  e.g. calf⁶ → calves

dissapoint	disappoint[1+]
dissatisfy[4] dissatisfaction	
disscurrage	discourage[2]
dissect[1] dissection	
dissemble[2] dissemblance	
disseminate[2] dissemination	
dissendent	descendant
dissension	
dissent[1] *[argue]	decent *[good][+],
	descent *[down]
dissern	discern[1+]
dissert	desert[1] *[leave][+]
	dessert *[food]
dissertation	
disservice	
dissidence dissident	
dissimilar ~ity	
dissipate[2] dissipation	
dissiplin	discipline[2+]
dissolute ~ly dissolution	
dissolve[2]	
dissonance dissonant	
dissproov	disprove[2]
dissuade[2] dissuasion dissuasive	
dissypul	disciple
distance ~l time graph	
distant ~ly	
distaste ~ful ~fully	
distemper ~ed	
distend[1]	
distil[3] ~lation	
distillery[4]	
distinct ~ly distinction	
distinctive ~ly ~ness	
distinguish[1] ~able	
distort[1] ~ion	
distract[1] ~edly ~ion	
distraught	

distress[1] ~ingly	
distribute[2] distribution distributor	
district ~l council ~l nurse	
distrofee	dystrophy
distrort	distraught
distroy	destroy[1+]
distruction	destruction[+]
distructiv	destructive[+]
distrust[1] ~ful	
disturb[1] ~ance	
disunited disunity	
disurtashun	dissertation
disused	
diswade	dissuade[2]
disypher	decipher[1+]
ditain	detain[1+]
ditach	detach[1+]
ditch[1]	
ditect	detect[1+]
ditectiv	detective[+]
ditenshun	detention[+]
diter	deter[3]
diterent	deterrent
ditergent	detergent
diteriorate	deteriorate[2+]
diterminant	determinant
ditermination	determination
ditermine	determine[2+]
ditest	detest[1+]
dither[1]	
ditto	
ditty[4]	
diuretic	
diurnal ~ly	
diva	
divan	
dive[2] ~-bomb ~-bomber	
divelop	develop[1+]

diverge[2]
divergence   divergent
diverse ~ly
diversify[4]   diversification
diversion ~ary
diversity[4]
divert[1]
divest[1] ~iture
diviance   deviance[+]
diviate   deviate[2+]
divice   device
divide[2]
dividend
dividing ~I line
divine[2] ~ly   divination
diving ~I bell ~I board
divinity[4]
divisible
division   divisor
divisive ~ly ~ness
diviss   device *[thing],
                                  devise[2] *[invent]
divorce[2]
divorcé *[man]
divorcée *[woman]
divulge[2]   divulgence
divurge   diverge[2]
divurgence   divergence[+]
divurt   divert[1]
Divali
dizease   disease
dizzy[4]
DJ
DNA ~I profiling ~I testing
do *[get done] ~able   doe *[deer],
do ~er ~ing   dough *[bread]
Dobermann ~I pinscher
docile

dock[1] ~lands ~side ~yard
docket[1]
docking ~I station
doctor[1] ~al
doctorate
doctrine   doctrinaire
doctrinal
docudrama
document[1] ~ation
documentary[4]
doddering   dodderer   doddery
dodge[2]   dodgy[4]
dodgem ~I car
dodo
doe *[deer]   dough *[bread][+]
doefan   dauphin
does   doesn't [does not]
doff[1]
dog[3] ~-eared ~fight ~fish ~house
dogged ~ly
doggy[4] ~I paddle
dogma ~tic ~tically ~tism
dogsbody[4]
doh *[musical note]   dough *[bread][+],
                                  doe *[deer]
doj   dodge[2+]
dojem   dodgem[+]
dok   dock[1+]
dokter   doctor[1+]
doldrums
dole[2] ~ful ~fully ~I queue
dolfin   dolphin
doll ~'s house   dolly[4]
dollar
dollop
dolomite
dolphin ~arium
domain ~I name

---

dome *[shape] ~d   doom[1] *[destruction]
Domesday Book
domestic ~l science ~l violence
domestic ~ally ~ity
domesticate[2]
domicile ~d
dominance   dominant
dominate[2]   domination
domineer[1]
dominion
domino[5] ~l effect
dominyun   dominion
don[3]
donate[2]   donation
done *[finished]   dun *[colour]
donkey ~l derby ~l work
donor
don't [do not]
doodle[2]
doom[1] *[destruction]   dome *[shape][+]
Doomsday Book   Domesday Book
door ~bell ~knob ~knocker
door ~step ~way
dope[2]   dopey
dorb   daub[1]
dordul   dawdle[2]
dormant
dormitory[4]
dormouse   dormice
dorn   dawn[+]
dornt   daunt[1][+]
dorsal
dorter   daughter[+]
DOS *[program]   doss[1] *[stay]
dosage
dose[2] *[medicine]   doze[2] *[sleep]
doss[1] ~house
dossier

dot[3] ~.com
dotty[4]
double[2] ~l agent ~l back
double ~-barrelled ~l bass
double ~-check ~-click ~-cross ~-decker
double ~-jointed ~-park ~-quick ~l standard
doubly
doubt[1] ~ful ~fully ~less ~lessly
douche[2]
dough *[bread] ~y ~nut   doe *[deer]
dour
dourey   dowry[4]
douse[2] *[drench]   dowse[2] *[search]
dove ~cote
dovetail[1]
dowager
dowdy
dowdy[4]
dowel

☞ Can't find your word here? Take off **down** and look again

down[1] ~y ~-and-out ~-at-heel ~cast
down ~fall ~grade ~-hearted ~hill
down ~play ~pour ~right
down ~stairs ~stream
down ~time ~-to-earth ~trodden ~turn
down ~wards ~wind
downsize[2]
dowry[4]
dowse[2] *[search]   douse[2] *[drench]
dowtful   doubtful[+]
doze[2] *[sleep]   dose[2] *[medicine][+]
dozen
dozy[4]
drab ~ly ~ness
draft[1] *[bank, work]   draught *[air]
drag[3]

---

draggen	dragon *[monster]+
dragon ~fly	
dragoon[1]	
drain[1] ~age ~pipe	
drake	
dram	
drama ~tist	
dramatic ~al ~ally	
dramatise[2] dramatisation	
drank	
drape[2]	
drapery[4]	
drastic ~ally	
draught *[air]	draft *[bank, work]
draughtsman ~ship	
draughty[4]	
draul	drawl[1]
draw *[pull, art] ~back ~bridge	
drawer *[storage]	
drawing ~I pin ~I room	
drawl[1]	
drawn ~-out	
dray *[cart]	drey *[nest]
dread[1] ~ful ~fully	
dread ~locks ~nought	
dream[1] dreamt dreamy[4]	
dreary[4]	
dred	dread[1+]
dredge[2]	
dreem	dream[1+]
dregs	
drej	dredge[2]
dreme	dream[1+]
drench[1]	
dresarje	dressage
dress[1] ~es ~maker	
dress ~I rehearsal ~I shirt	
dressage	

dressing ~-down ~I gown ~I room ~-up	
dressy[4]	
drew	
drey *[nest]	dray *[cart]
dribble[2]	
dribs and drabs	
dride	dried
drie	dry[4+]
dried	
drier *[less wet]	dryer *[machine]
drift[1] ~I net ~wood	
drill[1] ~I sergeant ~I team	
drily	
drink ~able ~-driving	
drinking ~I chocolate ~I water	
drip[3] ~-dry ~-feed ~-feeding	
drive[2] ~-by ~-in driven	
drivel[3]	
drizzle[2]	
droll	
dromedary[4]	
drone[2]	
drool[1]	
droop[1] *[down]	
drop[3] *[let fall] ~I back ~I by	
drop ~-down menu ~I goal	
drop ~I kick ~let ~-off	
drop ~out ~I round ~I shot	
drore	draw[1] *[pull, art]+,
	drawer *[storage]
drorl	drawl[1]
drought	
droup	droop[1] *[down]
drove	
drown[1]	
drowse[2] drowsy[4]	
drowt	drought
drubbing	

KEY TO SUFFIXES AND COMPOUNDS

These rules are explained on pages ix to x.

1 Keep the word the same before adding ed, er, est, ing
e.g. cool[1] → cooled, cooler, coolest, cooling
2 Take off final e before adding ed, er, est, ing
e.g. fine[2] → fined, finer, finest, fining
3 Double final consonant before adding ed, er, est, ing
e.g. thin[3] → thinned, thinner, thinnest, thinning

4 Change final y to i before adding ed, er, es, est, ly, ness
e.g. tidy[4] → tidied, tidier, tidies, tidiest, tidily, tidiness
Keep final y before adding ing e.g. tidying
5 Add es instead of s to the end of the word
e.g. bunch[5] → bunches
6 Change final f to ve before adding s
e.g. calf[6] → calves

drudge² drudgery	
drue	drew
drug³	
Druid	
drule	drool¹
drum³ ~stick ~l major	
drummedary	dromedary⁴
drunk ~ard ~en ~enly ~enness	
dry⁴ ~ness ~l dock ~-clean ~run	
dryer *[machine]	drier *[less wet]
dryve	drive²⁺
du	dew *[drops],
	do *[get done]⁺,
	due *[owing]⁺
dual *[two] ~ism ~ity	duel³ *[fight],
	jewel *[gem]⁺
dub³	
dubble	double⁺
dubious ~ly ~ness	
duche	douche²
duchy⁴ duchess⁵	
duck¹ ~ling	
duct *[tube] ~ile ~l tape	ducked *[dodged]
dud	
due *[owing, expected]	dew *[drops],
due ~l process	do *[get done]⁺,
	Jew *[religion]⁺
duel³ *[fight]	dual *[two]⁺
duet	
duffel ~l bag ~l coat	
dug ~out	
duke	
dukebox	jukebox
dukt	duct⁺
dulcet	
dull¹ ~ish ~ness	
dully *[not bright]	duly *[due]
dulset	dulcet

duly *[due]	dully *[not bright]
dum	dumb¹
dumb¹	
dumb ~ly ~ness ~bell ~l down	
dumb ~found ~struck ~l waiter	
dummy⁴	
dump¹ ~y	
dumpling	
dumpy	
dun *[colour]	done *[finished]
dunce	
dune	
dung	
dungarees	
dungeon	
duniper	juniper
dunjon	dungeon
duns	dunce
duo	
duodenal	
dupe²	
Dupiter	Jupiter
duplex	
duplicate² duplication	
duplicity duplicitous	
durable durability	
duration	
duress	
Durex™	
duride	deride²
during	
durisdicshun	jurisdiction
durishun	derision⁺
durisprudens	jurisprudence⁺
durmatitis	dermatitis
durmatology	dermatology⁺
durt	dirt⁺
durth	dearth

KEY TO SPELLING RULES

Red words are wrong. **Black** words are correct.

~   Add the suffix or word directly to the main word, without a space or hyphen
     e.g. ash ~en ~tray → **ashen ashtray**

~-   Add a hyphen to the main word before adding the next word
     e.g. blow ~-dry → **blow-dry**

~l   Leave a space between the main word and the next word
     e.g. decimal ~l place → **decimal place**

+   By finding this word in its **correct** alphabetical order, you can find related words
     e.g. about⁺ → **about-face about-turn**

*   Draws attention to words that may be confused

TM   Means the word is a trademark

durty	dirty[4]
durvish	dervish
dury	jury[4] *[in court]+, Jewry *[Jews]
dusc	dusk+
dusk	dusky[4]
dust[1] ~bin ~cart ~| jacket	
dust ~man ~pan ~| sheet	
dust ~| storm	
dusty[4]	
Dutch ~| auction ~| barn ~| cap	
Dutch ~| elm disease ~man	
dutiful ~ly	
duty[4] ~-bound ~-free	
duv	dove+
duvay	duvet
duvet	
duvtale	dovetail[1]
duwel	dual *[two]+, duel[3] *[fight]
duz	does
duzn't	doesn't
duzzen	dozen
DVD ~| player	
dwarf[1] ~| star	
dwel	dwell+
dwell[1]	dwelt

dwindle[2]	
dworf	dwarf[1+]

☞ Can't find your word here? Look under **di**

dye *[colour] ~d	**die** *[death]*
dyeing *[colour]	
dying *[death]	
dyjerati	digerati
dyjerido	didgeridoo
dyke	
dylate	dilate[2+]
dylute	dilute[2+]
dynamic ~ally	dynamism
dynamite[2]	
dynamo	
dynasty[4] dynastic	
dynosaur	dinosaur

☞ Can't find your word here? Look under **dis**

dysability	disability[4]
dysabul	disable[2+]
dysagrie	disagree[1+]
dysentery	
dysfunction ~al	
dyslexia dyslexic	
dyspraxia dyspraxic	
dystrophy	

KEY TO SUFFIXES AND COMPOUNDS

These rules are explained on pages ix to x.

1 Keep the word the same before adding **ed, er, est, ing**
   e.g. cool[1] → cooled, cooler, coolest, cooling
2 Take off final **e** before adding **ed, er, est, ing**
   e.g. fine[2] → fined, finer, finest, fining
3 Double final consonant before adding **ed, er, est, ing**
   e.g. thin[3] → thinned, thinner, thinnest, thinning

4 Change final **y** to **i** before adding **ed, er, es, est, ly, ness**
   e.g. tidy[4] → tidied, tidier, tidies, tidiest, tidily, tidiness
   Keep final **y** before adding **ing** e.g. tidying
5 Add **es** instead of **s** to the end of the word
   e.g. bunch[5] → bunches
6 Change final **f** to **ve** before adding **s**
   e.g. calf[6] → calves

e ~-book ~-business
~-cash ~-commerce
e ~-mail
each *[every] ~| other   etch[1] *[draw]
eager ~ly ~ness
eagle ~-eyed eaglet
ear *[body part]   ere *[before],
                                err[1] *[mistake][+]

ear ~ache ~drum ~lobe
ear ~phones ~plugs
ear ~ring ~shot ~wig
eara   era
earl ~dom
early[4] ~| bird
earmark[1]
earn[1] *[money] ~ings   urn *[vase]
earnest ~ly ~ness
earth[1] ~ly ~bound ~iness
earth ~-shattering ~works ~worm
earthen ~ware
earthquake
earthy[4]
eary   eerie *[scary][+]
                                eyrie *[nest]
ease[2] ~ment
easel
east ~bound ~erly ~ern
east ~wards ~wardly
Easter ~| Bunny ~| egg ~| Sunday
eastrogen   oestrogen
easy[4] ~-care ~-going
eat ~able ~en ~ing
eau-de-Cologne
eaves
eavesdrop[3]
ebb[1]
ebony ebonite
ebullience ebullient

eccentric ~ally ~ity
ecclesiastic ~al ~ally
ecconamise   economise[2+]
ech   each *[every],
                              etch[1] *[draw]
echelon
echo[1] ~es

☞ Can't find your word here? Look under **ex**

ecksact   exact[1+]
ecksamination   examination
ecksamine   examine[2]
ecksampul   example
ecksceed   exceed[1+]
eckscellence   excellence[+]
eckschange   exchange[2+]
eckscite   excite[2+]
eclair
eclectic
eclesiastic   ecclesiastic[+]
eclipse[2] ecliptic
eco ~climate ~-friendly
ecological ~ly
ecology ecologist
economic ~al ~ally ~s
economise[2] economist
economy[4]
ecosystem
ecoterrorism ecoterrorist
ecotourism ecotourist
ecsentric   eccentric[+]
ecstasy
ecstatic ~ally
ectopic ~| pregnancy
ectoplasm
ecumenical
eczema
eddy[4]

---

edebul	edible+
edge² ~ways ~wise	
edgy⁴	
edible edibility	
edict	
edifice	
edifiss	edifice
edify⁴ edification	
edit¹ ~or	
edition *[version]	addition *[sum]
editorial ~ise ~ly	
edj	edge²⁺
educashun	education+
educate² educator	
education ~al ~ally ~ist	
educative	
edukayt	educate²⁺
eego	ego+
eegocentric	egocentric+
eek *[exclamation]	eke² *[out]
eel	
eer	ear *[body part], ere *[before], err¹ *[mistake]+
eerie *[scary]	eyrie *[nest]
eerily eeriness	
eese	ease²⁺
eest	east+
Eester	Easter+
eestern	eastern+
eesy	easy⁴⁺
eet	eat¹⁺
eev	eve
eeves	eaves
eezee	easy⁴⁺
efect	effect¹ *[result]+, affect¹ *[influence]+
efemeral	ephemeral+

effeminacy	effeminacy
efervesce	effervesce²⁺
efface² ~ment	
effect¹ *[result]	affect¹ *[influence]+
effective *[producing results]	affective *[emotions]
effective ~ly ~ness	
effeminate ~ly effeminacy	
effervesce²	
effervescence effervescent	
efficacious ~ly ~ness	
efficacy	
efficiency	
efficient ~ly	
effigy⁴	
effikashus	efficacious+
effluence *[waste]	affluence *[wealth]
effluent *[waste]	affluent *[wealthy]
effort ~less ~lessly	
effrontery⁴	
effusive ~ly	
eficasee	efficacy
efijy	effigy⁴
efikashus	efficacious+
efishent	efficient+
efishuncy	efficiency
efort	effort+
efurvess	effervesce²⁺
efusiv	effusive+
eg	egg¹⁺
egalitarian ~ism	
ege	edge²⁺
egect	eject¹⁺
eger	eager+
egg¹ ~cup ~nog	
egg ~plant ~l roll ~shell	
egg ~l timer ~l white	
egiptology	Egyptology+

KEY TO SUFFIXES AND COMPOUNDS

These rules are explained on pages ix to x.

1 Keep the word the same before adding ed, er, est, ing
e.g. cool¹ → cooled, cooler, coolest, cooling
2 Take off final e before adding ed, er, est, ing
e.g. fine² → fined, finer, finest, fining
3 Double final consonant before adding ed, er, est, ing
e.g. thin³ → thinned, thinner, thinnest, thinning

4 Change final y to i before adding ed, er, es, est, ly, ness
e.g. tidy⁴ → tidied, tidier, tidies, tidiest, tidily, tidiness
Keep final y before adding ing e.g. tidying
5 Add es instead of s to the end of the word
e.g. bunch⁵ → bunches
6 Change final f to ve before adding s
e.g. calf⁶ → calves

ego ~ism ~tism ~l trip
egocentric ~ity
egoist ~ic ~ical ~ically
egomania ~c
egret

☞ Can't find your word here? Look under **ex**

egsacerbate   exacerbate[2+]
egsact   exact[1+]
egsaggerate   exaggerate[2+]
egsample   example
egsasserbayt   exacerbate[2+]
egsude   exude[2]
egul   eagle[+]
egy   edgy[4]
Egyptology   Egyptologist
eiderdown
Eiffel Tower
eight *[number]   ate *[food]
eighteen ~th
eighth
eighty[4]   eightieth
either *[or]   ether *[air, liquid][+]
ejaculate[2]   ejaculation
eject[1] ~ion ~or
eji   edgy[4]
ejis   aegis
ejucayt   educate[2+]

☞ Can't find your word here? Look under **ec**

ekcentrik   eccentric[+]
ekclesiastik   ecclesiastic[+]
eke[2] ~l out
eklektik   eclectic
eklesiastic   ecclesiastic[+]
eklipse   eclipse[2+]
eko   echo[1+]
ekology   ecology[+]

ekonomic   economic[+]
ekonomy   economy[4]
ekotourism   ecotourism

☞ Can't find your word here? Look under **ex**

eksact   exact[1+]
eksampul   example
eksentric   eccentric[+]
eksma   eczema

☞ Can't find your word here? Look under **equi**

ekwine   equine
ekwity   equity[4]
ekwivalent   equivalent[+]
ekzema   eczema
elaborate[2] ~ly   elaboration
elament   element[+]
elamentree   elementary[+]
elapse[2]
elastic ~ity
Elastoplast™
elated   elation
elavate   elevate[2+]
elayted   elated
elbow[1] ~l room
elc   elk
eldebury   elderberry[4]
elder ~ly   eldest
elderberry[4]
eldur   elder[+]
elect[1] ~ive ~or ~orate
election ~eering
electoral   electorate
electric ~al ~ally
electric ~chair ~l generator
electricity   electrician
electrify[4]   electrification
electrocardiogram

---

electrocute[2] electrocution
electrode
electrolysis
electrolyte electrolytic
electromagnet ~ic ~ism
electromotive
electron
electronic ~ally ~| mail ~| publishing ~s
electroplate[2]
electroscope
elefant   elephant[+]
elegance
elegant ~ly
elegy[4] elegiac

☞ Can't find your word here? Look under **elec**

elekshun   election[+]
elekt   elect[1+]
elektoral   electoral[+]
elektrify   electrify[4+]
elektrik   electric[+]
elektroad   electrode
element ~al
elementary ~| particle
elephant ~ine
elevate[2] elevator
elevation
eleven ~th
elf[6] ~in ~ish
elicit[1] *[get]   illicit *[illegal][+]
eligans   elegance[+]
eligibility
eligible [fitting]   legible *[clear]
eliksir   elixir
eliminate[2] eliminator
elimination
elips   ellipse[+]
eliptic   elliptic[+]

Elisabethun   Elizabethan
elision
elisit   elicit[1] *[get],
                         illicit *[illegal][+]
élite élitism élitist
eliterashun   alliteration
elixir
Elizabethan
elk
ellipse ellipsis
elliptic ~al ~ally
elm
eloap   elope[2+]
elocution ~ist
elokwence   eloquence[+]
elongate[2] elongation
elope[2] ~ment
eloquence eloquent
eloqushun   elocution[+]
else ~where
elucidate[2] elucidation
elude[2] *[avoid]   illude *[trick]
elushun   illusion *[false idea],
                         elusion *[escape],
                         allusion *[hint]
elusidate   elucidate[2+]
elusion *[escape]   illusion *[false idea],
                         elusion *[escape],
                         allusion *[hint]
elusive *[hard to find]   illusive *[deceptive]
emaciated emaciation
e-mail
emanate[2]
emancipate[2] emancipation
emasculate[2] emasculation
emasiate   emaciate[2+]
embalm[1]
embankment

---

embarass · **embarrass[1+]**
embargo[1] ~es
embark[1] ~ation
embarm · **embalm[1+]**
embarrass[1] ~ment
embassy[4]
embattle[2]
embed[3]
embellish[1] ~ment
embers
embezzle[2] ~ment
embitter[1] ~ment
emblazon[1]
emblem ~atic ~atically
embody[4] **embodiment**
embolden
embolism
emboss[1]
embrace[2]
embroider[1] ~y
embroil[1]
embroyder · **embroider[1+]**
embryo ~nic
embryology **embryologist**
emerald ~l green
emere · **emir**
emerge[2]
emergence **emergent**
emergency[4] ~l fund ~l room ~l services
emery ~l board ~paper
emetic
emfasis · **emphasis[+]**
emfatic · **emphatic[+]**
emfyseema · **emphysema**
emigrant *[exits] · **immigrant** *[arrives]
emigrate[2] *[exit] · **immigrate[2]** *[arrive]
emigration *[exit] · **immigration** *
· [arrival]

emigrayt · **emigrate[2+]**
émigré
emin · **eminence**
eminent *[notable] · **imminent** *[soon][+],
· **immanent** *
· [inherent]
eminently
emishun · **emission**
emissary[4]
emission
emit[3] *[give out] · **omit[3]** *[leave out]
emity · **enmity[4]**
emoshun · **emotion[+]**
emoticon
emotion ~al ~ally
emotive
empares · **impairs[+]**
emperor **empress**
emphasis **emphases**
emphasise[2]
emphatic ~ally
emphysema
empire *[lands] · **umpire** *[game]
empire ~-building
empirical ~ly
empiricism **empiricist**
emplacement
employ[1] ~able ~ee ~er
employment ~l agency
emporium **emporia**
empower[1] ~ment
emprer · **emperor[+]**
empty[4] ~-handed ~l nest
empuror · **emperor[+]**
empyre · **empire**
emrald · **emerald[+]**
emrie · **emery[+]**

---

emtee	empty[4+]
emu	
emulate[2] emulation	
emulshun	emulsion
emulsify[4] emulsification	
emulsion	
emurge	emerge[2+]
en route	
enabel	enable[2+]
enable[2] ~ment	
enact[1] ~able ~ment	
enamel[3]	
enamour[1]	
encamp[1] ~ment	
encapsulate[2] encapsulation	
encase[2] ~ment	
encephalitis	
encercul	encircle[2+]
enchant[1] ~ment ~ress	
enciclopeedia	encyclopaedia[+]
encircle[2] ~ment	
enclave	
enclose[2] enclosure	
encoar	encore[2]
encode[2]	
encompass[1]	
encore	
encounter[1]	
encourage[2] ~ment	
encownter	encounter[1]
encroach[1]~ment	
encrust[1]	
encrypt[1]~ion	
encumber[1] encumbrance	
encumpass	encompass[1]
encurige	encourage[2+]
encyclopaedia encyclopaedic	
end[1] ~less ~lessly ~l product	

endanger[1] ~ed species	
endaws	endorse[2+]
endear[1] ~ment	
endeavour[1]	
endeer	endear[1+]
endever	endeavour[1]
endive	
endorse[2] ~ment	
endow[1] ~ment	
endure[2] endurable endurance	
endyve	endive
enema	
enemy[4]	
energetic ~ally	
energise[2]	
energy[4] ~l transfer	
enerjetic	energetic[+]
enerjy	energy[4]
enfold[1]	
enforce[2] ~ment	
enforceable enforceability	
enforse	enforce[2+]
enfranchise[2] ~ment	
engage[2] ~ment	
engender[1]	
engine ~-driver	
engineer[1]	
English ~l breakfast ~l Channel	
English ~l language ~man ~woman	
engrave[2]	
engrayned	ingrained
engross[1]	
engulf[1]	
enhance[2] ~ment	
enigma ~tic	
enjender	engender[1]
enjine	engine[+]
enjineer	engineer[1]

KEY TO SUFFIXES AND COMPOUNDS

These rules are explained on pages ix to x.

1 Keep the word the same before adding **ed, er, est, ing**
e.g. cool[1] → *cooled, cooler, coolest, cooling*
2 Take off final **e** before adding **ed, er, est, ing**
e.g. fine[2] → *fined, finer, finest, fining*
3 Double final consonant before adding **ed, er, est, ing**
e.g. thin[3] → *thinned, thinner, thinnest, thinning*

4 Change final **y** to **i** before adding **ed, er, es, est, ly, ness**
e.g. tidy[4] → *tidied, tidier, tidies, tidiest, tidily, tidiness*
Keep final **y** before adding **ing** e.g. *tidying*
5 Add **es** instead of **s** to the end of the word
e.g. bunch[5] → *bunches*
6 Change final **f** to **ve** before adding **s**
e.g. calf[6] → *calves*

enjoin[1]
enjoy[1] ~ment
enjoyable   enjoyably
enjoyn   enjoin[1]
enjure   endure[2+]

☞ Can't find your word here? Look under **enc**

enkapsulate   encapsulate[2+]
enkourage   encourage[2+]
enkroach   encroach[1+]
enkumber   encumber[1+]
enlarge[2] ~ment
enlighten[1] ~ment
enlist[1]
enliten   enlighten[1+]
enliven[1]
enlyten   enlighten[1+]
enmie   enemy[4]
enmity[4]
ennoble[2] ~ment
ennui
ennumerate   enumerate[2+]
enobul   ennoble[2+]
enormity[4]
enormous ~ly ~ness
enough
enquire   enquiry
enrage[2]
enrapture[2]
enrich[1] ~ment
enrol[3] ~ment
ensconce[2]
ensemble
ensephalic   encephalic[+]
ensew   ensue[2]
enshrine[2]
ensign
ensime   enzyme

ensine   ensign
ensircul   encircle[2+]
enskonce   ensconce[2]
enslave[2] ~ment
ensnare[2]
ensue[2]
ensure[2] *[make sure]   insure[2] *[money]
ensyclopeedia   encyclopaedia[+]
entail[1]
entangle[2] ~ment
enter[1] *[go in]   inter[3] *[bury]
enteritis
enterprise   enterprising
entertain[1] ~ment
enterytis   enteritis
enthoosiasum   enthusiasm[+]
enthral[3] ~ment
enthrone[2] ~ment
enthuse[2]
enthusiasm   enthusiast
enthusiastic ~ally
entice[2] ~ment
entimology   entomology[+]
entire ~ly ~ty
entise   entice[2+]
entitee   entity[4]
entitle[2] ~ment
entity[4]
entomb[1] ~ment
entomologist
entomology   entomological
entoom   entomb[1+]
entrails
entrance *[way in] ~~-fee
entrance[2] *[delight] ~ment
entrant
entrap[3] ~ment
entray   entrée

KEY TO SPELLING RULES

Red words are wrong. **Black** words are correct.

~   Add the suffix or word directly to the main word,
     without a space or hyphen
     e.g. ash ~en ~tray → ashen ashtray
~~   Add a hyphen to the main word before adding the
     next word
     e.g. blow ~~-dry → blow-dry

~| Leave a space between the main word and the next
     word
     e.g. decimal ~| place → decimal place
+   By finding this word in its **correct** alphabetical
     order, you can find related words
     e.g. about+ → about-face about-turn
*   Draws attention to words that may be confused
TM   Means the word is a trademark

entreat[1] ~ingly
entreaty[4]
entrée *[meal]   entry[4] *[go into][+]
entreet   entreat[1+]
entrence   entrance
entrench[1] ~ment
entrent   entrant
entrepreneur ~ial
entrust[1]
entry[4] *[go into] ~-level   entrée *[meal]
entur   enter[1]
enturitus   enteritis
enturprise   enterprise[+]
enturtain   entertain[1+]
entwine[2]
entyce   entice[2+]
entyre   entire[+]
enuff   enough
enumerate[2] enumeration
enunciate[2] *[clearly]   annunciate[2] *[say]
enunciation *[clarity]   annunciation *
                                [announcement]
enurjetic   energetic[+]
enurjise   energise[2]
envee   envy[4+]
envelop[1] *[surround]
envelope *[paper]
envie   envy[4+]
envious ~ly ~ness
enviroment   environment
environment ~al ~alist ~ally
environmental ~l conditions
envisage[2]
envisige   envisage[2]
envlope   envelope
envoy *[official]
envy[4] *[jealous]   enviable
envyronment   environment[+]

eny   any[+]
enygma   enigma[+]
enzyme
epaulet
ephemeral ~ly
epic ~ally
epicentre
epicure   epicurean
epidemic
epidermis   epidermal
epidural
Epifany   Epiphany
epiglottis
epigram ~matic ~matically
epigraph ~ic
epigrarf   epigraph[+]
epik   epic[+]
epikure   epicure[+]
epilepsy   epileptic
epilogue
Epiphany
epiqure   epicure[+]
episcopacy
episcopal ~ian
episentre   epicentre
episewd   episode
episkopal   episcopal[+]
episode
episodic ~ally
epissel   epistle[+]
epistle   epistolary
epitaph
epitarf   epitaph
epithet
epitome
epitomee   epitome
epitomise[2]
epoch ~al ~-making

KEY TO SUFFIXES AND COMPOUNDS

These rules are explained on pages ix to x.

1 Keep the word the same before adding ed, er, est, ing
   e.g. cool[1] → cooled, cooler, coolest, cooling
2 Take off final e before adding ed, er, est, ing
   e.g. fine[2] → fined, finer, finest, fining
3 Double final consonant before adding ed, er, est, ing
   e.g. thin[3] → thinned, thinner, thinnest, thinning

4 Change final y to i before adding ed, er, es, est, ly, ness
   e.g. tidy[4] → tidied, tidier, tidies, tidiest, tidily, tidiness
   Keep final y before adding ing e.g. tidying
5 Add es instead of s to the end of the word
   e.g. bunch[5] → bunches
6 Change final f to ve before adding s
   e.g. calf[6] → calves

epoksy resin	epoxy resin
eporlet	epaulet
epycure	epicure[+]
epydemyc	epidemic
epydermys	epidermis[+]
epygram	epigram[+]
epygraph	epigraph[+]
epylepsy	epilepsy[+]
epysode	episode[+]
epythet	epithet
eqewstrian	equestrian
equable equably	
equait	equate[2+]
equal[3] ~ly	
equalise[2] equaliser	
equality[4]	
equanimity	
equate[2] equation	
equator ~ial	
equerry[4]	
equestrean	equestrian
equestrian	
equidistant	
equilateral	
equilibrium	
equine	
equinox	
equip[3] ~ment	
equitable equitably	
equity[4]	
equivalent equivalence	
equivocal ~ly	
equivocate[2] equivocation	
era *[time]	ere *[before]
erace	erase[2+]
eradicate[2] eradication eradicator	
erase[2] erasure	
eratic	erratic[+]

eratum	erratum[+]
ere *[before]	air *[breathe], ear *[body part][+], err[1] *[mistake][+]
erect[1] ~ion	
erer	error[+]
erk	irk[1+]
erly	early[4+]
ermine	
ernest	earnest[+]
erobatics	aerobatics
erobic	aerobic[+]
erode[2]	
erodrome	aerodrome
erodynamic	aerodynamic[+]
erofoil	aerofoil
eronaut	aeronaut[+]
eroneous	erroneous[+]
eroplane	aeroplane
eror	error[+]
erosion	
erosol	aerosol
erotic ~a ~ally ~ism	
err[1] *[mistake] ~ant	ear *[body part][+], ere *[before]
errand	
erratic *[varying] ~ally	erotic *[sexual][+]
erratum errata	
erroneous ~ly	
error ~l message	
errupt	erupt[1+]
erstwhile	
erth	earth[1+]
erthen	earthen[+]
erudite ~ly erudition	
erupt[1] ~ion	
ervre	oeuvre
esay	essay[1+]

---

escalate[2] escalator
escalation
escalope
escapade
escape[2] ~| clause ~| hatch
escapee
escapism escapist
escarpment
eschew[1]
eschuary   estuary[4]
eschue   eschew[1]
escort[1]
esens   essence
esenshul   essential[+]
eshelon   echelon
eskalate   escalate[2+]
eskallop   escalope
eskapayd   escapade
eskape   escape[2+]
eskapisum   escapism[+]
eskarpment   escarpment
Eskimo
eskort   escort[1]
eskwire   esquire
esoteric ~ally
especial ~ly
espie   espy[4]
espinarj   espionage
espionage
espouse[2] espousal
espresso
espy[4]
espyonnage   espionage
esquire
essay[1] ~ist
essence
essential ~ly
establish[1] ~ment

estate ~| agent ~| duty
estchuary   estuary[4]
esteem[1]
estern   eastern[+]
esthetic   aesthetic[+]
estimable
estimate[2] estimation
estime   esteem[1]
estimebul   estimable
estranged estrangement
estuary[4]
estymate   estimate[2+]
esy   easy[4+]
etch[1] *[draw]   each *[every]
eteeolayshun   etiolation
eternal ~ly
eternity[4]
ether *[air, liquid] ~eal   either *[or]
ethic ~al ~ally ~s
ethnic ~ity ~| cleansing
ethnology ethnological
ethos
ethur   either *[or],
                            ether *[air, liquid][+]
etiket   etiquette
etimology   etymology[+]
etiolation
etiquette
eturnity   eternity[4]
etymology etymologist
eucalyptus
Eucharist
Euclid
eufemistic   euphemistic[+]
eufemisum   euphemism
euforia   euphoria[+]
eugenics
eukalyptus   eucalyptus

---

eulogise[2] eulogism
eulogy[4]
eunuch
euphemism
euphemistic ~ally
euphoria euphoric
Eurasian
eurhythmy eurhythmics
euro
Euro ~centre ~sceptic
European ~| Commission ~| Union
Eurostar™
euthanasia
evacuate[2] evacuation evacuee
evade[2]
evaluate[2] evaluation
evangelic ~al ~ally
evangelise[2] evangelism
evangelist
evanjelic   evangelic[+]
evaporate[2] evaporation
evasion
evasive ~ly ~ness
eve
even[1] ~ly ~ness ~song ~tide
evenchual   eventual[+]
evenchuality   eventuality[4]
even-handed ~ly ~ness
evening ~| classes ~| dress
event ~ful
eventual ~ly
eventuality[4]
ever ~green ~lasting ~more
every ~body ~day ~one
every ~thing ~where
evict[1] ~ion
evidence evidential
evident ~ly

evikt   evict[1+]
evil ~ly ~minded
evning   evening[+]
evocative ~ly
evoke[2] evocation
evolution ~ary ~ist
evolve[2]
evon   even[1+]
evry   every[+]
evur   ever[+]
evury   every[+]
evydent   evident[+]
evyl   evil[+]
ewe *[sheep]   you *[person],
                             yew *[tree]
exacerbate[2] exacerbation
exact[1] ~ly ~ness
exaggerate[2] exaggeration
exale   exhale[2+]
exalt[1] ~ation
exam ~ination
examine[2]
example
exasperate[2] exasperation
exaut   exhort[1+]
excavate[2] excavator
excavation
exceed[1] ~ingly
excel[3]
excellence excellent
Excellency[4]
excepshun   exception[+]
except[1] [other than]   accept[1] [take]
exception ~al ~ally
excerpt *[extract]   exert[1] *[effort][+]
excershun   exertion *[effort],
                             excursion *[visit]
excess ~ive ~ively ~| baggage

---

exchange² ~able ~l rate
exchequer
excise²
excitable   excitability
excite² *[very happy]   exit¹⁺ *[out]
excite ~ment
excited *[very happy] ~ly   exited *[went out]
exclaim¹
exclamation   exclamatory
exclude²   exclusion
exclusive ~ly   exclusivity
excommunicate²   excommunication
excrement
excrete²   excretion
excruciating ~ly
excrushiating   excruciating⁺
excursion
excuse²   excusable
execute²   executor
execution ~er
executive ~l officer ~l order
exekushun   execution⁺
exekute   execute²⁺
exekutiv   executive⁺
exellent   excellent
exemplary
exemplify⁴
exempt¹ ~ion
exercise²
exert¹ *[effort] ~ion   excerpt *[extract]
exhale²   exhalation
exhaust¹ ~ion ~l pipe
exhaustible   exhaustive
exhibit¹ ~or
exhibition ~ism ~ist
exhilarate²   exhilaration
exhorst   exhaust¹⁺
exhort¹ ~ation

exhume²
exibishun   exhibition⁺
exibit   exhibit¹⁺
exigency⁴
exigense   exigence⁺
exile²
exilerate   exhilarate²⁺
exist¹ ~ence ~ent
exit¹ *[out]   excite² *[very happy]⁺
exit ~l poll ~l visa
exklude   exclude²⁺
exklusiv   exclusive⁺
exkrement   excrement⁺
exkurshun   excursion
exkuse   excuse²⁺
exkwisit   exquisite⁺
exonerate²   exoneration
exorbitance   exorbitant
exorcise²
exorcist   exorcism
exort   exhort¹⁺
exotic ~a ~ally ~ism
expand¹   expansion
expanse
expansive ~ly ~ness
expatriate²   expatriation
expect¹ ~ancy ~ation
expectant ~ly
expectayshun   expectation
expectorant
expedience
expediency
expedient
expedishun   expedition⁺
expedishus   expeditious⁺
expedite²
expedition
expeditionary ~l force

KEY TO SUFFIXES AND COMPOUNDS

These rules are explained on pages ix to x.

1 Keep the word the same before adding ed, er, est, ing
  e.g. cool¹ → cooled, cooler, coolest, cooling
2 Take off final e before adding ed, er, est, ing
  e.g. fine² → fined, finer, finest, fining
3 Double final consonant before adding ed, er, est, ing
  e.g. thin³ → thinned, thinner, thinnest, thinning

4 Change final y to i before adding ed, er, es, est, ly, ness
  e.g. tidy⁴ → tidied, tidier, tidies, tidiest, tidily, tidiness
  Keep final y before adding ing e.g. tidying
5 Add es instead of s to the end of the word
  e.g. bunch⁵ → bunches
6 Change final f to ve before adding s
  e.g. calf⁶ → calves

expeditious ~ly
expel³
expend¹ ~iture
expendable expendability
expense expensive
expergate   expurgate²
experience²
experiment¹ ~ation
experimental ~ly
expert ~ise ~ly
expertees   expertise
expiate² expiation
expire² expiration
expiry
explain¹ ~able
explanation explanatory
expletive
explicable
explicit ~ly
explisit   explicit⁺
exploar   explore²
explode²
exploit¹ ~ation
exploration exploratory
explore²
explosion explosive
exployt   exploit¹⁺
exponent
export¹ ~ation
exposay   exposé
expose² *[show] exposure
exposé *[story]
express¹ ~ly ~\| delivery
expression ~less
expressionism expressionist
expressive ~ly
expresso   espresso
expropriate² expropriation

expulshun   expulsion
expulsion
expunge²
expurgate²
expurt   expert⁺
exquisite ~ly ~ness

☞ Can't find your word here? Look under **exc**

exseed   exceed¹⁺
exsel   excel³
exsellense   excellence⁺
exsept   except¹
exsert   excerpt *[extract],
           exert¹ *[effort]⁺
ex-service
exsess   excess⁺
exsite   excite²⁺
extaut   extort¹
extemporaneous ~ly
extemporise²
extend¹ ~ible
extended ~\| family ~\| play
extension
extensive ~ly
extent
extenuating ~\| circumstances
exterior
exterminate² exterminator
extermination
external ~ly
externalise²
extinct ~ion
extinguish¹
extirior   exterior
extol³
extorshun   extortion⁺
extort¹
extortion ~ist

☞ Can't find your word here? Take off <u>extra</u> and look again

extra ~-curricular ~sensory perception
extra ~terrestrial ~l time
extract[1] ~ion
extradite[2] extradition
extramural
extraneous ~ly ~ness
extraordinary extraordinarily
extrapolate[2] extrapolation
extravagance extravagant
extravagantly
extravaganza
extream   extreme[+]
extredite   extradite[2+]
extreme ~ly extremist
extremity[4]
extricable
extricate[2] extrication
extrordinary   extraordinary[+]
extrovert ~ed
exturminate   exterminate[2+]
exturnal   external[+]

exuberance exuberant
exude[2]
exult[1] ~ant ~antly ~ation
exume   exhume[2+]
exurcise   exercise[2]
exurt   exert[1+]

☞ Can't find your word here? Take off <u>eye</u> and look again

eye[2] *[sight] ~ball   aye *[yes]
eye ~brow ~lash
eye ~l level ~lid ~liner
eye ~-opener ~piece
eye ~sight ~sore
eye ~l teeth ~wash ~witness
eyed *[watched]   I'd *[I had, should, would]

eyeful *[in your eye]   Eiffel *[Tower]
eyelet *[hole]   islet *[island]
Eyemax   Imax™
eye-o-you   IOU
eyether   either
eyrie *[nest]   eerie *[scary]

KEY TO SUFFIXES AND COMPOUNDS

These rules are explained on pages ix to x.

1 Keep the word the same before adding **ed, er, est, ing**
  e.g. cool[1] → cooled, cooler, coolest, cooling
2 Take off final **e** before adding **ed, er, est, ing**
  e.g. fine[2] → fined, finer, finest, fining
3 Double final consonant before adding **ed, er, est, ing**
  e.g. thin[3] → thinned, thinner, thinnest, thinning

4 Change final **y** to **i** before adding **ed, er, es, est, ly, ness**
  e.g. tidy[4] → tidied, tidier, tidies, tidiest, tidily, tidiness
  Keep final **y** before adding **ing** e.g. tidying
5 Add **es** instead of **s** to the end of the word
  e.g. bunch[5] → bunches
6 Change final **f** to **ve** before adding **s**
  e.g. calf[6] → calves

fable ~d
fabric
fabricate² fabricator
fabrication
fabulous ~ly ~ness
facade
face² *[head]   faze² *[bother],
                       phase² *[stage]
face ~-cloth ~l flannel ~-lift
face ~-mask ~-off
face ~l pack ~l paint ~-powder
face ~-saving ~-to-face ~l value
facesear   fascia
facet ~ed
facetious ~ly ~ness
fachen   fashion¹⁺
Fachisum   Fascism⁺
fachuous   fatuous⁺
facial *[face]
facile *[easy]
facilitate² facilitation
facility⁴
facinate   fascinate²⁺
facshun   faction
facsimile ~l transmission
fact ~-finding ~oid ~otum
fact ~ual ~ually
facter   factor
faction
factitious *[artificial] fictitious *[story]
factor
factory⁴ ~l floor ~l gate
factotum
facts *[realities]   fax¹ *[machine]
faculty⁴
fad faddish faddy
fade²
faeces faecal

fag³ ~l end
faggot
faheeta   fajita
Fahrenheit
faid   fade²
faik   fake²⁺
fail¹ ~ure ~-safe
fain *[gladly]   feign¹ *[deceive]
faint¹ *[weak] ~ly ~ness feint¹ *[move]
faint ~-hearted
fair *[event]   fare *[bus, food]
fair¹ *[just]   fare² *[manage]⁺
fair ~ly ~ness~l game ~ground
fair ~-haired ~-minded ~l play
fair ~sex ~l test ~way ~-weather
fairo   Pharoah
fairy⁴ *[sprite]   ferry⁴ *[boat]
fairy ~l cake ~-godmother
fairy ~land ~l lights ~l story ~tale
fait accompli
faite   fate
faith ~ful ~fully ~fulness
faith ~-healer ~less
fajita
fake²
fakir
fakshun   faction
faksimile   facsimile
fakt   fact⁺
faktion   faction
faktor   factor
faktory   factory⁴
fakulty   faculty⁴
falafel
falanx   phalanx⁵
falasy   fallacy⁴⁺
falcify   falsify⁴⁺
falcon ~er ~ry

KEY TO SPELLING RULES

Red words are wrong. **Black** words are correct.

~   Add the suffix or word directly to the main word, without a space or hyphen
    e.g. ash ~en ~tray → **ashen ashtray**
~- Add a hyphen to the main word before adding the next word
    e.g. blow ~-dry → **blow-dry**

~l Leave a space between the main word and the next word
    e.g. decimal ~l place → **decimal place**
+   By finding this word in its **correct** alphabetical order, you can find related words
    e.g. about⁺ → **about-face about-turn**
*   Draws attention to words that may be confused
TM Means the word is a trademark

fale	fail[1+]	fansiful	fanciful[+]
fall ~en ~back ~l guy ~out		fansy	fancy[+]
fallacy[4] fallacious		fantasia	
fallible fallibility		fantasise[2]	
fallic	phallic[+]	fantasum	phantasm[+]
fallopian ~l tube		fantastic ~ally	
fallow ~l deer		fantasy[4]	
falls *[down]	false *[not real][+]	fantisize	fantasise[2]
fallseto	falsetto	fantisy	fantasy[4]
falo	fallow[1]	fantom	phantom
false ~ly ~ness		faquir	fakir
false ~l alarm ~hood		far *[distant] ~away	fare *[bus, food]
false ~l pretences ~l start ~l teeth			fare[2] *[manage][+]
falsetto		far ~-fetched ~-flung	
falsify[4] falsification		far ~l gone ~-off ~-out	
falsity[4]		far ~-reaching ~-sighted	
falter[1]		farad	
falufel	falafel	faraday	
famas	famous[+]	faraoh	pharaoh
fame ~d		farce farcical farcically	
familial		fare *[bus, food]	fair *[event][+]
familiar ~ity		fare[2] [manage]	fair[1] [just][+]
familiarise[2] familiarisation		farewell	
family[4] ~l name ~l planning		Far East [the]	
family ~l practice ~l tree ~l values		Farenheight	Fahrenheit
famine		Farisee	Pharisee
famished		farm[1] ~l hand ~house	
famme fatal	femme fatale	farm ~land ~yard	
famous ~ly		farmaceutical	pharmaceutical
fan[3] ~l belt ~l club ~fare		farmacist	pharmacist
fan ~light ~mail ~zine		farmacy	pharmacy[4]
fanatic ~al ~ally ~ism		farrier	
fanciful ~ly		farse	farce[+]
fancy[4] ~l dress ~-free		farst	fast[1]
fandango		fart[1]	
fane	fain *[gladly],	farther *[distant]	father *[dad]
	feign[1] *[deceive]	farthest	
fang		farthing	

KEY TO SUFFIXES AND COMPOUNDS

These rules are explained on pages ix to x.

1 Keep the word the same before adding ed, er, est, ing
e.g. cool[1] → cooled, cooler, coolest, cooling
2 Take off final e before adding ed, er, est, ing
e.g. fine[2] → fined, finer, finest, fining
3 Double final consonant before adding ed, er, est, ing
e.g. thin[3] → thinned, thinner, thinnest, thinning

4 Change final y to i before adding ed, er, es, est, ly, ness
e.g. tidy[4] → tidied, tidier, tidies, tidiest, tidily, tidiness
Keep final y before adding ing e.g. tidying
5 Add es instead of s to the end of the word
e.g. bunch[5] → bunches
6 Change final f to ve before adding s
e.g. calf[6] → calves

117

fary	fairy[4+]
faryngeal	pharyngeal[+]
farynx	pharynx
fasade	facade
fascia	
fascinate[2] fascination	
fascism fascist	
fase	face[2] *[head][+],
	faze[2] *[bother],
	phase[2] *[stage]
faseeshus	facetious[+]
fasen	fasten[1+]
faset	facet[+]
fashall	facial
fashion[1] ~able ~ably	
fashion ~| house ~| show	
Fashisum	fascism[+]
fasile	facile
fasilitate	facilitate[2+]
fasility	facility[4]
fassinate	fascinate[2+]
fast[1] ~~-acting ~| food	
fast ~~-forward ~| lane	
fast ~~-talking ~| track	
fasten[1]	
fastidious ~ly ~ness	
fat[3] *[big] ~ness ~~-free	fate *[destiny][+],
	fête *[festival]
fatal ~ly	
fatalist ~ic ~ically fatalism	
fatality[4]	
fate *[destiny] ~ful ~fully	fête *[festival]
	fetid *[decaying]
fate akomplee	fait accompli
fated *[destined]	fêted *[honoured]
fateeg	fatigue[2+]
fateful ~ly	
faten	fatten[1+]

father[1] *[dad] ~ly ~hood	farther *[distant]
Father Christmas	
father-in-law	
fathom[1] ~less	
fatigue[2] ~s	
fatten[1] ~| up	
fatty[4] ~| acid	
fatuous ~ly	
fatwah	
fault[1] ~y ~~-finding ~less	
faun *[in myths]	fawn *[colour, deer]
	fawn[1] *[flatter]
fauna	
faux pas	
favour[1] ~able ~ably	
favourite favouritism	
fawlt	fault[1+]
fawn *[colour, deer]	faun *[in myths]
fawn[1] *[flatter]	
fawna	fauna
fax[1] *[machine]	facts *[realities]
fay *[fairy]	fey *[strange]
fayr	fair[1] *[just, event][+],
	fare *[bus, food],
	fare[2] [manage][+]
fayth	faith[+]
faze[2] *[bother]	phase[2] *[stage]
fead	feed[+]
feal	feel[+]
feald	field[1+]
fear[1] ~some	
fearful ~ly ~ness	
fearless ~ly ~ness	
feasant	pheasant
feasible feasibility	
feast[1]	
feat *[action]	feet *[walking]
feather ~ed ~y ~weight	

---

feature² ~l film	
featus	foetus⁺
Febrary	February
February	
fech	fetch¹⁺
feckless	
fed	
federal ~ly	
federalist federalism	
federation	
fedral	federal⁺
fee	
feeble² ~-minded feebly	
feecher	feature²⁺
feed ~er ~back	
feeding ~l bottle ~l frenzy ~l ground	
feefdom	fiefdom
feel ~er ~ing	
feeld	field⁺
feend	fiend⁺
feer	fear¹⁺
feerse	fierce²⁺
feesibul	feasible⁺
feest	feast¹
feet *[walking]	feat *[action]
feeture	feature²⁺
feetus	foetus
feign¹ *[deceive]	fain *[gladly]
feil	feel⁺
feild	field¹⁺
feind	fiend⁺
feint¹ *[move]	faint¹ *[weak]
feirce	fierce⁺
fekless	feckless
fekund	fecund⁺
felicity	
feline	
felisity	felicity⁺

fell	
fellow ~ship	
felon felony⁴	
felow	fellow⁺
felt ~-tip	
female ~l impersonator	
femer	femur
feminine femininity	
feminise²	
feminist feminism	
femme fatale	
femur	
fen ~land	
fence²	
fend¹	
feng shui	
fenix	phoenix
fennel	
feral ~l animal	
ferlong	furlong
ferm	firm¹⁺
ferment¹ *[yeast]	foment¹ *[trouble]⁺
fermentation	
fern	
fernace	furnace
fernish	furnish¹⁺
ferniture	furniture
ferocious ~ly ~ness	
ferocity	
feroshus	ferocious⁺
ferret¹ ~l about ~l around ~l out	
Ferris wheel	
ferry⁴ ~boat ~man	
ferst	first⁺
ferther	further¹⁺
ferthest	furthest
fertile	
fertilise² fertilisation	

KEY TO SUFFIXES AND COMPOUNDS

These rules are explained on pages ix to x.

1 Keep the word the same before adding ed, er, est, ing
e.g. cool¹ → cooled, cooler, coolest, cooling
2 Take off final e before adding ed, er, est, ing
e.g. fine² → fined, finer, finest, fining
3 Double final consonant before adding ed, er, est, ing
e.g. thin³ → thinned, thinner, thinnest, thinning

4 Change final y to i before adding ed, er, es, est, ly, ness
e.g. tidy⁴ → tidied, tidier, tidies, tidiest, tidily, tidiness
Keep final y before adding ing e.g. tidying
5 Add es instead of s to the end of the word
e.g. bunch⁵ → bunches
6 Change final f to ve before adding s
e.g. calf⁶ → calves

fertility ~l drug	
fertive	furtive[+]
fervent ~ly	
ferver	fervour
fervid ~ly ~ness	
fervour	
fes	fez[+]
fester[1]	
festival	
festive ~ly ~ness	
festivity[4]	
festoon[1]	
festun	festoon[1]
fet accomply	fait accompli
feta ~l cheese	
fetch[1]	
fête[2] *[festival]	fate *[destiny]
fêted *[honoured]	fated *[destined],
	fetid *[decaying]
fether	feather[+]
fetid *[decaying]	fêted *[honoured]
fetish[5] ~ism ~ist	
fetlock	
fetoocheenee	fettuccine
fetter[1] ~s	
fettle[2]	
fettuccine	
feud[1]	
feudal ~ism ~ist ~istic	
fever ~ed ~l pitch	
feverish ~ly ~ness	
few *[not many]	phew *[exclamation]
fewgitive	fugitive
fewl	fuel[3+]
fewm	fume[2]
fewmigate	fumigate[2+]
fewneral	funeral *[ceremony],
fewnerial	funereal *[gloomy]

fewnicular	funicular
fewrius	furious[+]
fewrori	furore
fewse	fuse[2+]
fewsha	fuchsia
fewshun	fusion
fewsilier	fusilier[+]
fewtile	futile[+]
fey *[strange]	fay *[fairy]
fez fezzes	
fezant	pheasant
fial	file[2] *[doc, tool, line][+],
	phial *[bottle]
fialty	fealty
fiancé *[man]	
fiancée *[woman]	
Fianna Fail	
fiansay	fiancé *[man],
	fiancée *[woman]
fiasco	
fib[3]	
fibre ~fill ~glass ~l optics	
fibroid ~s	
fibrosis	
fibrous	
fibula fibular	
fibur	fibre[+]
fices	faeces[+]
fichery	fishery[4]
fickle ~ness	
ficks	fix[1+]
ficksashun	fixation
fickst	fixed[+]
ficshun	fiction[+]
fiction ~al	
fictishus	fictitious[+]
fictitious ~ly	
fiddle[2] ~sticks	

---

fiddly [4]	
fidelity	
fidget [1] ~y	
field [1] ~| day ~| glasses	
field ~| marshal ~mouse	
field ~| sports ~| test ~| trial	
field ~| trip ~work	
fiend ~ish ~ishly ~ishness	
fier	fear *[afraid],
	fire [2] *[flame]+
fierce [2] ~ly ~ness	
fierse	fierce+
fiery [4]	
fiesta	
fifteen ~th	
fifth ~| column	
fifty [4] ~-fifty fiftieth	
fig ~| tree	
figer	figure [2]+
figerativ	figurative+
figet	fidget [1]+
fight ~ing	
figment	
figurative ~ly	
figure [2] ~head ~| of speech ~| skating	
fiksashun	fixation
fiksed	fixed+
fikshun	fiction+
filament	
filander	philander [1]+
filanthropy	philanthropy+
filately	philately+
filch [1]	
file [2] *[doc, tool, line]	phial *[bottle]
file ~| server	
filement	filament
filharmonic	philharmonic
filial	

filibuster [1]	
filigree	
filine	feline
filing ~| cabinet ~s	
filistine	philistine
fill [1] *[make full]	file [2] *[doc, tool, line]+
fillet	
filling ~| station	
fillip	
filly [4]	
film [1] ~| festival ~-maker	
film ~-making ~| star ~strip	
filmy [4]	

> ☞ Can't find your word here? Look under <u>philo</u>

filo ~| pastry	
filosofer	philosopher+
filosofical	philosophical+
filter [1] *[sieve]	philtre *[drug]
filth filthy [4]	
filtrashun	filtration
filtration	
filtre	filter [1] *[sieve],
	philtre *[drug]
fimale	female+
fimur	femur
fin *[fish]	Finn *[from Finland]+
final *[last] ~ist ~ly	
finale *[last event]	
finalise [2]	
finality	
finance [2] financier	
financial ~ly ~| year	
finanshal	financial+
finarlay	finale
finch [5]	
finck	think+
find ~er ~ing ~| out	

KEY TO SUFFIXES AND COMPOUNDS

These rules are explained on pages ix to x.

1 Keep the word the same before adding ed, er, est, ing
e.g. cool [1] → cooled, cooler, coolest, cooling

2 Take off final e before adding ed, er, est, ing
e.g. fine [2] → fined, finer, finest, fining

3 Double final consonant before adding ed, er, est, ing
e.g. thin [3] → thinned, thinner, thinnest, thinning

4 Change final y to i before adding ed, er, es, est, ly, ness
e.g. tidy [4] → tidied, tidier, tidies, tidiest, tidily, tidiness
Keep final y before adding ing e.g. tidying

5 Add es instead of s to the end of the word
e.g. bunch [5] → bunches

6 Change final f to ve before adding s
e.g. calf [6] → calves

☞ Can't find your word here? Look under **thi**

fine[2] ~ly ~| art
fine ~| print ~| toothcomb
fineness *[quality]   finesse *[skill]
finery
finesse *[skill]   fineness *[quality]
finger[1] ~| bowl ~nail ~print
finicky
finish[1]
finite
finly   finally
Finn *[from Finland]   fin *[fish]
finsh   finch[5] *[bird],
       finish[1] *[end]
fiord
fir * [tree]   fur[3] *[coat][+]
fire[2] *[flame] ~arm ~ball
fire ~break ~| brigade
fire ~cracker ~| drill ~| engine
fire ~| escape ~| extinguisher
fire ~fighter ~fly ~guard
fire ~| hydrant ~lighter ~man
fire ~place ~| power ~proof ~-resistant
fire ~side ~| station ~wood ~work
firing ~| line ~| squad

☞ Can't find your word here? Look under **fer**

firm[1] ~ly ~ness
firment   ferment[1] *[yeast][+],
       foment[1] *[trouble][+]
firn   fern
firnace   furnace
firry   furry[4]
first ~ly ~-aid ~-class
first ~-hand ~-rate
firther   further[1+]
firtile   fertile[+]

firtilise   fertilise[2+]
firtility   fertility
firtiv   furtive[+]
firvent   fervent[+]
firvor   fervour
firy   fiery[4]
fisabul   feasible[+]
fiscal ~| policy
fish[1] ~| cake ~| farming
fish ~| finger ~monger ~wife
fisherman   fishery[4]
fishun   fission
fishure   fissure
fishy[4]
fisical   physical[+]
fisics   physics[+]
fisiotherapist   physiotherapist[+]
fisique   physique
fission
fissure
fist
fit[3] *[clothes, strong] ~ness fight *[hit]
fite   fight
five
fiver *[money]   fever *[temperature][+]
fix[1] ~es
fixate[2]   fixation
fixative
fixed ~| assets
fixture
fizz[1]   fizzle[2]
fizzy[4]
fjord
flabbergast
flabby[4]
flaccid ~ly
flachulence   flatulence[+]
flag[3] ~| day ~pole ~ship

KEY TO SPELLING RULES

Red words are wrong. **Black words are correct.**

~   Add the suffix or word directly to the main word,
     without a space or hyphen
     e.g. ash ~en ~tray → **ashen ashtray**

~-   Add a hyphen to the main word before adding the
     next word
     e.g. blow ~-dry → **blow-dry**

~| Leave a space between the main word and the next
     word
     e.g. decimal ~| place → **decimal place**

+   By finding this word in its **correct** alphabetical
     order, you can find related words
     e.g. about[+] → **about-face about-turn**

*   Draws attention to words that may be confused

TM   Means the word is a trademark

flagrant
flair *[instinct]   flare *[light, widen]
flajelate   flagellate²⁺
flak ~| jacket
flake² flaky⁴
flamboyance   flamboyant
flame²
flamenco
flamingo
flammable   flammability
flan
flange
flank¹
flannel³
flap³ ~jack
flare² *[light, widen]   flair *[instinct]
flash¹ ~back ~bulb ~| card
flash ~| flood ~gun ~light ~point
flashy⁴
flask
flassid   flaccid⁺
flat³ ~ly ~bed ~-cap
flat ~-chested ~-footed ~iron
flat ~lands ~mate ~| rate
flatten¹
flatter¹ ~y
flatulence   flatulent
flaunt¹
flautist
flaver   flavour¹
flavour¹
flaw *[blemish] ~ed   floor¹ *[ground]⁺
flawless ~ly
flawtist   flautist
flea *[insect] ~-bitten   flee *[run away]⁺
flea ~| market
flebitis   phlebitis
fleck ~ed

flecks *[spots]   flex¹ *[muscles]⁺
flecksibul   flexible
fled
fledgling
flee *[run away] ~ing   flea *[insect]⁺
fleece² fleecy
fleet
fleeting ~ly
fleksibility   flexibility
flem   phlegm⁺
flerdelis   fleur-de-lis
flert   flirt¹⁺
flesh¹ ~y ~-coloured ~| out
fleur-de-lis
flew *[flight]   flu *[ill], flue *[pipe]
flewensy   fluency
flewid   fluid⁺
flewk   fluke²
flewt   flute⁺
flewvial   fluvial
flex¹ *[muscles] ~es   flecks *[spots]
flexible   flexibility
flexitime
flick¹
flicker¹
flick-knife⁶
flies
flight ~| attendant ~| deck
flight ~| lieutenant ~| path
flight ~| recorder ~| simulator
flighty⁴
fliing   flying⁺
flileaf   flyleaf⁶
flimsy⁴
flinch¹ ~es
fling ~ing
flint ~y
flip³ ~chart ~-flop ~side

KEY TO SUFFIXES AND COMPOUNDS

These rules are explained on pages ix to x.

1 Keep the word the same before adding ed, er, est, ing
e.g. cool¹ → cooled, cooler, coolest, cooling
2 Take off final e before adding ed, er, est, ing
e.g. fine² → fined, finer, finest, fining
3 Double final consonant before adding ed, er, est, ing
e.g. thin³ → thinned, thinner, thinnest, thinning

4 Change final y to i before adding ed, er, es, est, ly, ness
e.g. tidy⁴ → tidied, tidier, tidies, tidiest, tidily, tidiness
Keep final y before adding ing e.g. tidying
5 Add es instead of s to the end of the word
e.g. bunch⁵ → bunches
6 Change final f to ve before adding s
e.g. calf⁶ → calves

flippant ~ly   flippancy
flipper
flirt[1] ~ation ~atious
flisse   fleece[2]
flit[3] *[move quickly]   flight *[travel][+]
flity   flighty[4]
float[1] ~ation
flock[1]
flocks *[sheep]   phlox *[plant]
floe *[ice]   flow[1] *[river][+]
flog[3]
flood[1] ~gate ~light ~| plain
floor[1] *[ground] ~board   flaw *[blemish][+]
floor ~| lamp ~| plan ~| show
floot   flute[+]
flop[3]
floppy[4] ~| disk
flora
floral
florid
florist
flornt   flaunt[1]
flortist   flautist
floss[1]
flote   float[1+]
flotilla
flotsam
flounce[2]
flounder[1]
flour[1] *[food] ~y ~mill   flower[1] *[plant][+]
flourish[1]
flout[1]
flow[1] *[river] ~| chart   floe *[ice]
flow ~| diagram
flower[1] *[plant] ~y   flour *[food]
flower ~| bed ~| power
flown
flownder   flounder[1]

flownse   flounce[2]
flowt   flout[1]
flox   flocks *[animals],
                             phlox *[flower]
flu *[ill]   flew *[fly],
                             flue *[metal tube]
flucks   flux
fluctuate[2]   fluctuation
flud   flood[1+]
flue *[pipe]   flew *[fly], flu *[ill]
fluent ~ly   fluency
fluff[1]   fluffy[4]
fluid ~| mechanics ~| ounce
fluke[2]
fluks   flux
fluktuate   fluctuate[2+]
flume
flummox ~ed
flung
flunk[1]
flunky[4]
fluorescent ~| light
fluoride
flur-de-lis   fleur-de-lis
fluride   fluoride
flurish   flourish[1]
flurocarbon   fluorocarbon
flurry[4]
flush[1]
fluster[1]
flute ~d
flutter[1]
fluvial
flux
fluzy   floozy[4]
fly *[insect, travel] ~ing   flies
fly ~catcher ~ -fishing
fly ~-half ~leaf ~over ~paper

---

fly ~past ~-posting ~sheet

fly ~| swatter ~weight ~wheel

flying ~| doctor ~| fish ~| saucer

flying ~| squad ~| start ~| visit

foal¹

foam¹ ~| rubber   foamy⁴

fob³ ~| off

fobia   phobia⁺

focal ~| length ~| point

focus¹ ~es   foci

fodder

foe

foepar   faux pas

foetus⁵ foetal

fog³ ~horn ~| up

fogey *[old]

foible

foie gras

foggy⁴ *[misty]

foil¹

foist¹

fokal   focal

foke   folk⁺

foks   fox⁺

fokus   focus¹⁺

fold¹

fole   foal¹

foleeo   folio

foliage

folic ~| acid

folicul   follicle

folij   foliage

folio

folk ~| dance ~lore ~| song

folken   falcon⁺

follicle

follow¹ ~-through ~| up

folly⁴

---

folsify   falsify⁴⁺

folt   fault¹⁺

folter   falter¹

fome   foam¹⁺

foment¹ *[trouble]   ferment¹ *[yeast]⁺

foment ~ation

fond¹ ~ly

fondle²

fondue

☞ Can't find your word here? Look under **phon**

fone   phone²⁺

fonic   phonic⁺

font

fony   phoney

food *[eat]   feud¹ *[fight]

food ~| additive ~| book

food ~| chain ~| poisoning

food ~| processor ~| web

fooey   phooey

fool¹ ~proof

foolhardy⁴

foolish ~ly ~ness

fool's ~| gold ~| paradise

foolscap

foot¹ ~| and mouth disease

foot ~fall ~-fault ~hills ~hold

foot ~lights ~loose ~mark

foot ~note ~path ~print ~rest

foot ~sore ~step ~stool ~wear

foot ~work

footage

football ~er ~ing

fop   foppish

☞ Can't find your word here? Look under **fore** or **four**

for *[used by]   fore *[front],

                    four *[number]⁺

KEY TO SUFFIXES AND COMPOUNDS

These rules are explained on pages ix to x.

1 Keep the word the same before adding **ed, er, est, ing**
e.g. cool¹ → cooled, cooler, coolest, cooling

2 Take off final **e** before adding **ed, er, est, ing**
e.g. fine² → fined, finer, finest, fining

3 Double final consonant before adding **ed, er, est, ing**
e.g. thin³ → thinned, thinner, thinnest, thinning

4 Change final **y** to **i** before adding **ed, er, es, est, ly, ness**
e.g. tidy⁴ → tidied, tidier, tidies, tidiest, tidily, tidiness
Keep final **y** before adding **ing** e.g. tidying

5 Add **es** instead of **s** to the end of the word
e.g. bunch⁵ → bunches

6 Change final **f** to **ve** before adding **s**
e.g. calf⁶ → calves

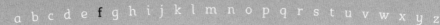

forage[2]

forbade

forbear *[not do] ~ing   forebear *[ancestor]

forebearance

forbid ~den ~ding

force[2] ~| majeure ~| meter

forced ~| labour ~| landing

forceful ~ly ~ness

forceps

forcible   forcibly

ford[1] ~able

☞ Can't find your word here? Look under **for**

fore *[front] ~arm ~cast   for *[used by][+],
                            four *[number][+]

fore ~court ~fathers

fore ~finger ~front ~ground

fore ~hand ~head ~knowledge

fore ~leg ~lock ~man ~most

fore ~name ~play ~runner

fore ~shorten ~sight ~skin

fore ~taste ~thought ~warn

forebear *[ancestor]   forbear *[not do][+]

foreboding ~ly

forecastle

foreclose[2]   foreclosure

foreign ~er ~| body ~| exchange

Foreign ~| Legion ~| Office ~| Secretary

foren   foreign[+]

forensic ~| medicine ~| science

foresaw

foresee ~able ~ing ~n

foreshadow[1]

forest ~ation ~er ~ry

forestall[1]

foretell ~ing   foretold

forever

foreword *[in book]   forward[1] *[advance]

forfeit[1] ~ure

forfit   forfeit[1+]

forgave

forge[2]   forgery[4]

forget ~ting ~~-me-not

forgetful ~ness

forgettable

forgivable

forgive ~n ~ness   forgiving

forgo ~ing

forgone ~| conclusion

forgot ~ten

forige   forage[2]

forj   forge[2]

forjery   forgery[4]

fork[1] ~~-lift truck

forlorn

forlt   fault[1+]

form[1] ~ation

formal   formality[4]

formaldehyde

formalise[2]   formalisation

formally *[officially]   formerly *[before]

formashun   formation

format[3]

formation   formative

forment   ferment[1] *[yeast][+],
                       foment[1] *[trouble][+]

former

formerly *[before]   formally *[officially]

Formica™

formidable   formidably

formula ~s   formulae

formulate[2]   formulation

forn   faun *[in myths],
                      fawn *[colour, deer]

forna   fauna

fornicate[2]   fornication

KEY TO SPELLING RULES

Red words are wrong. **Black** words are correct.

~   Add the suffix or word directly to the main word, without a space or hyphen
    e.g. ash ~en ~tray → **ashen ashtray**

~- Add a hyphen to the main word before adding the next word
    e.g. blow ~~-dry → **blow-dry**

~| Leave a space between the main word and the next word
    e.g. decimal ~| place → **decimal place**

+   By finding this word in its **correct** alphabetical order, you can find related words
    e.g. about[+] → **about-face about-turn**

*   Draws attention to words that may be confused

TM Means the word is a trademark

for-profit
forrest | forest[+]
forsake ~n   forsaking
forse | force[+]
forseps | forceps
forsithia | forsythia
forsook
forswear ~ing
forswore   forsworn
forsythia
fort *[castle] ~ress | fought *[battle],
 | thought *[think]
Fort Knox
fortay | forte
forte *[strong point] | fought *[battle],
 | forty[4] *[number]

☞ Can't find your word here? Look under **four**

forteen | fourteen[+]
forth *[forward] | fourth *[number][+]
forth ~coming ~right ~with
fortieth
fortify[4]   fortification
fortissimo
fortitude
fortnight ~ly
fortuitous ~ly ~ness
fortunate ~ly
fortune ~-hunter ~-teller
forty[4] *[number] | forte *[strong point]
fortyfie | fortify[4+]
forum
forward[1] *[advance] | foreword *[in book]
forward ~s ~l slash
forwent
fosfate | phosphate
fosforescent | phosphorescent
fosforus | phosphorus

fossil ~l fuel
fossilise[2]   fossilisation
foster[1] ~-child ~-parents
foto | photo[+]
fotograf | photograph[+]
foton | photon
fotosynthesis | photosynthesis
fought *[battle] | fort *[castle][+],
 | thought *[think]
foul[1] *[dirty] ~ly ~ness | fowl *[bird]
foul ~-mouthed
found[1] ~ation ~ling
foundry[4]
fountain ~l pen

☞ Can't find your word here? Look under **for**

four *[number] | for *[used by],
four ~-by-four ~-fold | fore *[front]
four ~-letter-word
four ~some ~-square ~-star
fourbare | forbear *[not do][+],
 | forebear *[ancestor]
fourbid | forbid[+]
fource | force[2+]
fourhand | forehand
fourm | form[1+]
fourmal | formal[+]
fourmula | formula[+]
fourmulate | formulate[2+]
fourt | fought *[battle],
 | fort *[castle][+],
 | thought *[think]
fourteen ~th
fourth *[number] | forth *[forward][+]
fourth ~l dimension
fourtnight | fortnight[+]
fow | foe
fowl *[bird] | foul[1] *[dirty][+]

KEY TO SUFFIXES AND COMPOUNDS

These rules are explained on pages ix to x.

1 Keep the word the same before adding **ed, er, est, ing**
 e.g. cool[1] → cooled, cooler, coolest, cooling
2 Take off final **e** before adding **ed, er, est, ing**
 e.g. fine[2] → fined, finer, finest, fining
3 Double final consonant before adding **ed, er, est, ing**
 e.g. thin[3] → thinned, thinner, thinnest, thinning

4 Change final **y** to **i** before adding **ed, er, es, est, ly, ness**
 e.g. tidy[4] → tidied, tidier, tidies, tidiest, tidily, tidiness
 Keep final **y** before adding **ing** e.g. tidying
5 Add **es** instead of **s** to the end of the word
 e.g. bunch[5] → bunches
6 Change final **f** to **ve** before adding **s**
 e.g. calf[6] → calves

fownd	found[1+]
fowndry	foundry[4]
fowntain	fountain[+]
fowpas	faux pas
fox[1] ~glove ~hound	
fox ~es ~y ~| hunting ~| terrier	
foxtrot[3]	
foybul	foible
foyer	
foyl	foil[1]
foyst	foist[1]
foyyay	foyer
fracas	
fractal	
fraction ~al ~ally	
fractious ~ly	
fracture[2]	
frael	frail[+]
fragile fragility	
fragment[1] ~ary ~ation	
fragrance fragrant	
fragrense	fragrance[+]
frail[1] frailty[4]	
frait	freight[+]
frajile	fragile[+]
fraksher	fracture[2]
frakshun	fraction[+]
frakshus	fractious[+]
frale	frail[+]
frame[2] ~| of mind	
frame ~| of reference ~work	
franc *[money]	frank *[blunt][+]
franchise[2]	
francincense	frankincense
Francophile	
Francophone	
frank[1] *[blunt] ~ly ~ness franc *[money]	
frankfurter	

frankincense	
frantic ~ally	
frappé	
frase	phrase[2] *[words][+], frays *[fights, wears out]
fraternal ~ly	
fraternise[2] fraternisation	
fraternity[4]	
fraud ~ster	
fraudulence fraudulent	
fraught	
frawd	fraud
frawght	fraught
fray[1]	
frayl	frail[+]
frays *[wears out, fights] phrase[2] *[words][+]	
frazzle[2]	
freak[1] ~ish ~ishly	
freckle ~d	
free ~d ~ing ~ly ~r ~st	
free ~| agent ~hand ~| house ~| kick	
free ~| love ~-market ~| radical	
free ~-range ~| speech	
free ~style ~| thinker	
free ~| trade ~| verse ~wheel ~| will	
freedom ~| of information ~| of speech	
freehold ~er ~ing	
freelance[2]	
Freemason ~ry	
Freephone™	
frees *[releases]	freeze *[cold][+], frieze *[pattern]
freesia	
freeze[2] *[cold]	frees *[releases], frieze *[pattern]
freeze ~-dried ~-frame	
freezha	freesia

KEY TO SPELLING RULES

Red words are wrong. **Black** words are correct.

~ Add the suffix or word directly to the main word, without a space or hyphen
e.g. ash ~en ~tray → ashen ashtray
~- Add a hyphen to the main word before adding the next word
e.g. blow ~-dry → blow-dry

~\| Leave a space between the main word and the next word
e.g. decimal ~\| place → decimal place
+ By finding this word in its **correct** alphabetical order, you can find related words
e.g. about[+] → about-face about-turn
* Draws attention to words that may be confused
™ Means the word is a trademark

128

freight [1] ~l train	frightful ~ly ~ness
frekwency	frequency [4]	frigid ~ity
frekwent	frequent [1+]	frijid	frigid[+]
french ~l bean ~l bread ~l dressing	frill [1] ~y
french ~l horn ~l kiss ~l letter ~l window	fringe [2] ~l benefit
french fry [4]	frippery [4]
frend	friend[+]	Frisbee™
frenetic	frisk [1]
frenology	phrenology[+]	frisky [4]
frenzy frenzied	fritter [1]
frequency [4]	frivolous ~ly frivolity [4]
frequent *[often] ~ly	frizz [1] frizzy [4]
frequent [1] *[go to]	frock ~coat
fresco [5]	frog ~man ~spawn
fresh [1] ~ly ~ness	frogmarch [1]
fresh ~-faced ~water	Froidian	Freudian[+]
freshen [1]	frolic frolicked frolicking
fresko	fresco [5]	from
fret [3] ~ful ~fully	frond
frete	freight[+]	frong	throng [1]
fretsaw	front [1] ~age ~al ~ally
Freudian ~l slip	front ~-bench ~-bencher
frew	threw *[ball],	front ~l burner ~l crawl
	through *[go through]	front ~-loader ~l line ~l man
frey	fray [1+]	front ~l office ~-page ~-row
friable	front ~-runner ~-wheel drive
friar *[religious] ~ly	fryer *[food]	frontier
frickshun	friction	frooishun	fruition
friction	froot	fruit[+]
Friday	frord	fraud [+]
fridge	frordulence	fraudulence[+]
fried *[cooked]	freed *[set free]	frorght	fraught
friend ~less ~ship	frost [1] ~bite ~bitten
friendly [4]	frosty [4]
frieze *[pattern]	freeze *[cold][+]	froth [1] frothy [4]
frigate ~l bird	frown [1]
fright *[fear]	freight *[goods]	Froydian	Freudian[+]
frighten [1]	froze ~n

---

fructose
frugal ~ity ~ly
fruit[1] ~| cake ~| cocktail
fruit ~| fly ~| machine ~| salad
fruitful ~ly ~ness
fruition
fruitless ~ly ~ness
fruity[4]
frump   frumpy[4]
frunt   front[+]
fruntier   frontier[+]
frustrate[2] frustration
frut   fruit[+]
fry[4] ~-up
fryer *[food]   friar *[religious]
frying pan
fryll   frill[1]
fryt   fright[+]
fryvolous   frivolous[+]
fucher   future[+]
fuchsia
fuchure   future[+]
fuddy-duddy[4]
fude   feud[1]
fudge[2]
fue   few
fuel[3] ~| cell ~-injection
fug *[bad air] ~gy   fugue *[music]
fugitive
fugue *[music]   fug *[bad air][+]
Führer
ful   fool[1] *[idiot][+],
                               full[1] *[complete][+]
fulcrum
fule   fuel[3+]
fulfil[3] ~ment
full[1] *[complete] ~ness   fool[1] *[idiot][+]
full ~back ~-blast ~-blooded

full ~-blown ~-face ~-frontal
full ~-length ~-page ~-scale
full ~-size ~| stop ~-time
fully ~-fledged ~-grown
fulsome ~ly ~ness
fumble[2]
fume[2]
fumigate[2] fumigator
fun
function[1]
functional ~ly
fund[1]
fundamental ~ist ~ly
fundraise[2]
funel   funnel[3]
funeral *[ceremony]
funereal *[gloomy]
fungus fungi fungicide
funicular
funk
funkshun   function[1]
funky[4]
funnel[3]
funny[4] ~| bone ~| business
fur[3] *[coat] ~| up   fir *[tree]
furious ~ly ~ness
furlong
furmament   firmament
furment   ferment[1] *[yeast][+],
                               foment[1] *[trouble][+]
furn   fern
furnace
furnish[1] ~ings
furniture
furore
furoshus   ferocious[+]
furrier
furrow[1]

---

furry⁴ *[hairy]	fury⁴ *[anger]
furst	first⁺
furth	firth
further¹ furthest	
furtherance	
furthermore	
furthermost	
furtile	fertile⁺
furtilise	fertilise²⁺
furtility	fertility
furtive ~ly ~ness	
furvent	fervent⁺
furver	fervour
furvour	fervour
fury⁴ *[anger]	furry⁴ *[hairy]
fuse² ~l box	
fuselage	
fushia	fuchsia
fusillade	
fusion	
fuss¹ *[worry] ~pot	fuzz *[fluff]
fussy⁴	
fusty⁴	
fut	phut *[sound],
	foot *[limb]⁺
futile futility	

futon	
future	
futurist ~ic ~ically	
fuzz¹	
fuzzy⁴ ~l logic	
fwa grar	foie gras

☞ Can't find your word here? Look under **fi**

fyasco	fiasco
fyfty	fifty⁴⁺
fylch	filch¹
fynale	final *[last]⁺,
	finale *[last event]
fynalyse	finalise²⁺
fynd	find¹
fyne	fine²⁺
fysical	physical⁺
fysician	physician
fysics	physics⁺
fysiognomy	physiognomy
fysiology	physiology⁺
fysiotherapist	physiotherapist⁺
fysique	physique
fyshun	fission
fyve	five

KEY TO SUFFIXES AND COMPOUNDS

These rules are explained on pages ix to x.

1 Keep the word the same before adding **ed, er, est, ing**
e.g. cool¹ → cooled, cooler, coolest, cooling

2 Take off final **e** before adding **ed, er, est, ing**
e.g. fine² → fined, finer, finest, fining

3 Double final consonant before adding **ed, er, est, ing**
e.g. thin³ → thinned, thinner, thinnest, thinning

4 Change final **y** to **i** before adding **ed, er, es, est, ly, ness**
e.g. tidy⁴ → tidied, tidier, tidies, tidiest, tidily, tidiness
Keep final **y** before adding **ing** e.g. tidying

5 Add **es** instead of **s** to the end of the word
e.g. bunch⁵ → bunches

6 Change final **f** to **ve** before adding **s**
e.g. calf⁶ → calves

G ~-string ~-suit
gab³
gabardine
gabble² *[talk]
gable *[on roof] ~d
gad³ ~| about
gadget ~ry
gael   gale⁺
Gaelic
gaffe *[mistake]
gaffer *[foreman]
gag³
gaga
gage   gauge²
gaggle²
Gaia ~| hypothesis
gaiety
gaily
gain¹ ~ful ~fully
gainsay ~ing   gainsaid
gaip   gape²
gait *[walk]   gate *[barrier]
gaiter ~ed
gajet   gadget⁺
gala
galactic
galant   gallant⁺
galaw   galore
galaxy⁴
gale ~-force
galery   gallery⁴
galivant   gallivant¹
gall¹ ~| bladder
gallant ~ry
galleon
gallery⁴
galley
gallivant¹

gallon
gallop¹ *[horse]   Gallup™ *[poll]
gallows
Gallup™ *[poll]   gallop³ *[horse]
galon   gallon
galop   gallop³ *[horse],
     Gallup™ *[poll]
galore
galoshes
galows   gallows
galvanise²
galy   gaily *[merrily],
     galley *[ship]
gambit
gamble² *[games]
gambol³ *[frolic]
game ~| bird ~keeper
game ~| plan ~| point
game ~| reserve ~| warden
gamesmanship
gamete
gaming
gammon
gamut
gander
gang¹ ~land ~plank ~way
gangling
gangrene   gangrenous
gangster ~ism ~| rap
gannet
gap *[space] ~-toothed
gape² *[look, open]
garage ~| sale
garantey   guarantee *[goods]⁺,
     guaranty *[debt]⁺
garb¹
garbage
garble²

---

gard   guard[1+]
garden[1] ~| centre ~| party ~| shed
gardenia
gardian   guardian+
gargantuan
gargle[2] *[throat]
gargoyle *[figure]
garige   garage+
garish
garland[1]
garlic ~ky
garment
garner[1]
garnet
garnish[1] ~es
garret
garrison
garrotte[2]
garrulous ~ly ~ness
garter
gas[3] ~es ~| chamber ~| fire
gas ~| mask ~| pressure ~works
gascet   gasket
gase   gaze[2]
gaselle   gazelle
gaseous
gasette   gazette
gash[1] ~es
gasket
gasp[1]
gaspacho   gazpacho
gastly   ghastly[4]
gastric   gastritis
gastronomic ~al
gastronomy
gate[2] *[barrier]   gait *[walk]
gate ~house ~keeper ~way
gateau   gateaux

gatecrash[1] ~es
gather[1]
gattoe   gateau
gauche
gaudy[4]
gauge[2]
gaugius   gorgeous+
gaunt ~let
gauze *[cloth]   gorse *[bush]
gave
gaw   gore[2+]
gawk[1] ~y
gay ~| rights
Gaya   Gaia+
gayety   gaiety
gaylic   Gaelic
gayly   gaily
gayn   gain[1+]
gaysha   geisha
gayt   gate *[barrier]+,
                              gait *[walk]
gayter   gaiter+
gaze[2]
gazebo
gazelle
gazette
gazpacho
gear[1] ~box ~stick
gecko
geek ~y
geese
Geiger ~| counter
geisha
geko   gecko
Gekyll   Jekyll+
gel[3]
gelatine   gelatinous
geld[1] *[horse] ~ing   gelled *[hair]

KEY TO SUFFIXES AND COMPOUNDS

These rules are explained on pages ix to x.

1 Keep the word the same before adding **ed, er, est, ing**
  e.g. cool[1] → cooled, cooler, coolest, cooling
2 Take off final **e** before adding **ed, er, est, ing**
  e.g. fine[2] → fined, finer, finest, fining
3 Double final consonant before adding **ed, er, est, ing**
  e.g. thin[3] → thinned, thinner, thinnest, thinning

4 Change final **y** to **i** before adding **ed, er, es, est, ly, ness**
  e.g. tidy[4] → tidied, tidier, tidies, tidiest, tidily, tidiness
  Keep final **y** before adding **ing** e.g. tidying
5 Add **es** instead of **s** to the end of the word
  e.g. bunch[5] → bunches
6 Change final **f** to **ve** before adding **s**
  e.g. calf[6] → calves

☞ Can't find your word here? Look under **je**

gelignite
gelly   jelly [4+]
gem
Gemini
gender ~-specific
gene ~| bank ~| pool
gene ~| therapy
genealogy   genealogist
general ~ly ~| anaesthetic
general ~| election ~| knowledge
general ~| practice ~| practitioner
general ~| public ~| strike
generalise [2] generalisation
generality [4]
generate [2] generator
generation ~al
generic ~ally
generosity [4]
generous ~ly ~ness
genes *[DNA]   jeans *[trousers]
genetic ~s ~| code ~| engineering
genetically ~| modified
genial ~ity
genie
genital ~ia ~s
genitive
genius [5]
genocide   genocidal
genome   genoytpe
genral   general [+]
genralise   generalise [2+]
genralist   generalist
genre
gent
genteel *[social class]   gentility
gentile *[not Jewish]

gentle [2] *[kind, soft]   gently
gentle ~ness
gentle ~man ~manly
gentrify [4] gentrification
gentry
genuine ~ly ~ness
genus   genera
geocentric
geodesic ~| dome
geofysical   geophysical
geofysics   geophysics [+]
geographic ~al ~ally
geography   geographer
geological ~ly
geology   geologist
geometric ~al ~ally
geometry
geophysical
geophysics   geophysicist
geranium
gerbil

☞ Can't find your word here? Look under **gi**

gerd   gird [1]
gerdul   girdle [2]
gergle   gurgle [2]
geriatric ~s
gerila   gorilla *[ape],
                                guerrilla *[war]
gerk   jerk [1+]
gerkin   gherkin
gerl   girl [+]
germ ~| warfare
German ~ic ~| measles ~| shepherd
germane ~ly ~ness
germicide
germinate [2] germination
gerontology   gerontologist

KEY TO SPELLING RULES

Red words are wrong. **Black** words are correct.

~ Add the suffix or word directly to the main word,
   without a space or hyphen
   e.g. ash ~en ~tray → ashen ashtray
~- Add a hyphen to the main word before adding the
   next word
   e.g. blow ~-dry → blow-dry

~| Leave a space between the main word and the next
    word
    e.g. decimal ~| place → decimal place
+   By finding this word in its **correct** alphabetical
    order, you can find related words
    e.g. about+ → about-face about-turn
*   Draws attention to words that may be confused
TM Means the word is a trademark

gerrymander[1]

gerth — girth

gerund ~ive

gess — guess[+]

gest — guessed *[estimated], guest *[visitor]

gestalt

Gestapo

gestate[2] gestation

gesticulate[2] gesticulation

gesture[2]

Gesuit — Jesuit

Gesus — Jesus[+]

get ~away getting

getsam — jetsam

gettison — jettison[1]

getto — ghetto[+]

Gew — dew *[drops], Jew *[religion][+]

gewel — jewel[3] *[gem][+], joule *[unit]

gewelry — jewellery

gewish — Jewish[+]

geyser

ghastly[4]

gherkin

ghetto ~l blaster

ghost[1] ~ly ~l town ~l train

ghost-write[2]

ghoul

ghoulish *[death] — goulash *[dish]

giant ~ess ~l panda

☞ Can't find your word here? Look under **ji**

gib — jib[3]

gibber[1] ~ish

gibbet

gibbon

giblets

gidanse — guidance

giddy[4]

gide — guide[+]

gier — gear[1+]

gift[1] ~-shop ~l voucher

gift ~-wrap

gig *[public performance] jig[3] *[dance][+]

gigabyte

gigantic ~ally

giggle[2] *[laugh] jiggle[2] *[move]

gigolo

gihad — jihad

gild[1] *[gold cover] guild *[association]

gilder — guilder

gile — guile

gill *[fish] guile *[cunning][+]

gillie

gilotine — guillotine[2]

gilt *[gold leaf] ~-edged guilt *[shame]

giltey — guilty[4]

gimlet

gimmick ~ry ~y

gin ~l and tonic ~l rummy

ginea — guinea[+]

ginecological gynaecological

ginecology gynaecology[+]

ginee — guinea[+]

ginger ~ly ~y ~l ale

ginger ~l beer ~bread

gingham

gingivitis

gingle — jingle[2]

gingo — jingo[5+]

Ginness — Guinness

ginseng

ginx — jinx[+]

giraffe

KEY TO SUFFIXES AND COMPOUNDS

These rules are explained on pages ix to x.

1 Keep the word the same before adding **ed, er, est, ing**
e.g. cool[1] → cooled, cooler, coolest, cooling

2 Take off final **e** before adding **ed, er, est, ing**
e.g. fine[2] → fined, finer, finest, fining

3 Double final consonant before adding **ed, er, est, ing**
e.g. thin[3] → thinned, thinner, thinnest, thinning

4 Change final **y** to **i** before adding **ed, er, es, est, ly, ness**
e.g. tidy[4] → tidied, tidier, tidies, tidiest, tidily, tidiness
Keep final **y** before adding **ing** e.g. tidying

5 Add **es** instead of **s** to the end of the word
e.g. bunch[5] → bunches

6 Change final **f** to **ve** before adding **s**
e.g. calf[6] → calves

gird[1]
girder
girdle[2]
girgle   gurgle[2]
girl ~ie ~ish ~friend ~l guide
giro *[banking]   gyro *[spins]+
girth
gise   guise
gist *[rough translation]   jest[1] *[joke]
gitar   guitar+
give ~n   giving
giy   guy+
Giy Forks   Guy Fawkes
gizmo
gizzard
glacial   glaciation
glacier *[ice]   glazier *[glass]
glad[3] *[happy] ~ly ~ness glade *[forest]
gladden[1]
glade *[forest]   glad[3] *[happy]+
gladiator
gladiolus gladioli
glaisha   glacier
glaishall   glacial+
glamorise[2] glamorisation
glamorous ~ly ~ness
glamour
glance[2]
gland ~ular fever
glanse   glance[2]
glare[2]
glars   glass
glasnost
glass[1] ~es ~ful ~-blower ~ware
glassy *[like glass]   glacé *[cherry]
glaucoma
glaze[2]
glazier *[glass]   glacier *[ice]

gleam[1]
glean[1]
glee ~ful ~fully
glen
glib ~ly ~ness
glicerine   glycerine
glide[2]
glimmer[1]
glimpse[2]
glint[1]
glisten[1]
glitch
glits   glitz+
glitter[1] ~ati
glitz   glitzy[4]
gloaming
gloat[1]
glob ~ule ~ular
global ~ly ~l village ~l warming
globalise[2] globalisation
globe ~trotter ~trotting
glockenspiel
gloom   gloomy[4]
glorify[4]   glorification
glorious ~ly ~ness
glory[4]
gloss[1] ~es   glossy[4]
glossary[4]
glottis
glove ~l compartment ~l puppet
glow[1] ~-worm
glowcoma   glaucoma
glower[1]
glucose
glue ~d ~ing ~y ~-sniffing
glukose   glucose
glum[3] ~ly ~ness
glut[3]

KEY TO SPELLING RULES

Red words are wrong. **Black** words are correct.

~ Add the suffix or word directly to the main word, without a space or hyphen
   e.g. ash ~en ~tray → ashen ashtray

~- Add a hyphen to the main word before adding the next word
   e.g. blow ~-dry → blow-dry

~l Leave a space between the main word and the next word
   e.g. decimal ~l place → decimal place

+ By finding this word in its **correct** alphabetical order, you can find related words
   e.g. about+ → about-face about-turn

* Draws attention to words that may be confused

TM Means the word is a trademark

gluten *[substance]   glutinous
glutton *[person] ~ous ~y
glycerine
gnarled
gnash¹ ~ers ~es
gnat
gnaw¹ *[bite]   nor *[neither]
gnome   gnomish
gnu
go⁵ ~er ~ing
go ~-ahead ~-between ~-kart ~slow
goad¹
goal ~ie ~keeper ~l kick
goal ~less ~l line ~mouth ~post
goat ~ee ~herd ~skin
gob³ ~smacked ~stopper
gobble² ~degook
goblet
goblin
goche   gauche
God
god ~dess ~ly ~child ~daughter
god ~father ~-forsaken ~-given
god ~head ~like ~mother ~parent
god ~send ~son ~speed
gofer   gopher
goggle² ~-eyed
goitre
gold ~digger ~finch ~fish ~l leaf
gold ~l medal ~l medalist
gold ~mine ~l rush ~smith
golden ~l age ~l eagle ~l girl
golden ~l handshake ~l jubilee
golden ~l oldie ~l retriever
golden ~l rule ~l syrup ~l wedding
golf¹ ~l course
gon   gone
gonad

gondola   gondolier
gone ~r
gong
gonorrhoea
good ~ly ~ness ~s
good ~l afternoon ~bye
good ~l day ~l evening ~l humoured
good ~-looking ~l morning
good ~-natured ~l Samaritan ~will
Good Friday
goody⁴ ~-bag
gooey
goose ~l bumps ~flesh ~l pimples ~step
gooseberry⁴
gopher
gord   gourd *[fruit],
                               gored *[bull]
Gordian knot
gordy   gaudy⁴
gore² gory⁴
gored *[bull]   gourd *[fruit]
gorge²
gorgeous ~ly ~ness
Gorgonzola
gorilla *[ape]   guerrilla *[war]
gork   gawk¹⁺
gormand   gourmand
gormay   gourmet⁺
gornt   gaunt⁺
gorse *[bush]   gauze *[cloth]
gory
gosh *[surprise]   gauche *[shy]
gosling
gospel
gossamer
gossip¹ ~y ~l column
gost   ghost¹⁺
gostwrite   ghostwrite²

KEY TO SUFFIXES AND COMPOUNDS

These rules are explained on pages ix to x.

1 Keep the word the same before adding ed, er, est, ing
  e.g. cool¹ → cooled, cooler, coolest, cooling
2 Take off final e before adding ed, er, est, ing
  e.g. fine² → fined, finer, finest, fining
3 Double final consonant before adding ed, er, est, ing
  e.g. thin³ → thinned, thinner, thinnest, thinning

4 Change final y to i before adding ed, er, es, est, ly, ness
  e.g. tidy⁴ → tidied, tidier, tidies, tidiest, tidily, tidiness
  Keep final y before adding ing e.g. tidying
5 Add es instead of s to the end of the word
  e.g. bunch⁵ → bunches
6 Change final f to ve before adding s
  e.g. calf⁶ → calves

gosumer	gossamer	
got		gram
Gothic		grammar ~ian ~l school
gouache		grammatical ~ly
Gouda		Grammy⁴
gouge²		gramophone
goul	ghoul *[spirit], goal *[target]	gran
		granade grenade⁺
		granary⁴
goulash *[dish]	ghoulish *[death]	granchild grandchild
gourd *[fruit]	gored *[bull]	grand¹ ~ly ~child ~children
gourmand		grand ~daughter ~father
gourmet ~l cook		grand ~ma ~mother ~pa ~parent
gout		grand ~l piano ~l slam ~son ~stand
govern¹ ~able ~ance		grandad
government ~al		grandeur
governor governess		grandiloquence grandiloquent
gowge	gouge²	grandiose grandiosity
gown		grange
gowt	gout	granite
grab³		granny⁴ ~l knot
grace² ~ful ~fully ~ness		grant¹ ~-making
gracious ~ly ~ness		granular ~ity
grade² gradation		granulate² granulation
gradient		granule
gradual ~ly		grape ~fruit ~seed ~shot ~vine
graduate² graduation		graph
graf	graph¹	grapheme
graffical	graphical⁺	graphic ~ally ~l novel
graffiti		graphical ~l user interface
grafic	graphic⁺	graphite
grafite	graphite	graphology
grafology	graphology⁴	grapple²
graft¹		grase grace² *[goodness]⁺, graze² *[feed, cut]
graid	grade²	
grail		grashus gracious⁺
grain ~y		grasp¹
grait	grate² *[fire], great¹ *[big]⁺	grass¹ ~y ~hopper ~land
		grass ~roots ~l snake

---

grate² *[fire, cheese]   great¹ *[big]⁺

grateful ~ly ~ness

grater *[cheese]   greater *[bigger]

gratest   greatest⁺

gratichewd   gratitude

gratify⁴ gratification

gratis

gratitude

gratuitous ~ly ~ness

gratuity⁴

grave² ~ly ~digger ~stone ~yard

gravel³ ~ly

gravitas

gravitate² gravitation

gravitational ~l attraction

gravity

gravy ~l boat ~l train

gray   grey

grayling

grayn   grain¹⁺

graze²

grease² ~paint ~proof

greasy⁴

great¹ *[big] ~ly ~ness   grate² *[fire, cheese]

greater *[bigger]   grater *[cheese]

greed   greedy⁴

green ~ery ~ness ~s

green ~gage ~grocer ~house ~tea

greenhouse ~l effect ~l gas

Greenwich ~l Mean Time

greese   grease²⁺

greet¹ ~ings

gregarious ~ly ~ness

greif   grief⁺

greive   grieve²⁺

gremlin

grenade grenadier

Grenitch   Greenwich⁺

Gretna Green

grew

grewl   gruel³

grewsome   gruesome⁺

grewyere   gruyère

grey¹ ~hound ~matter

greyling   grayling

grid

griddle²

gridiron

grief ~-stricken

grieve² grievance

grievous ~ly ~ness

griffin

grill¹ ~l room

grim³ *[harsh] ~ly ~ness   grime *[dirt]⁺

grimace²

grime *[dirt]   grim *[harsh]⁺

grimy⁴

grin³

grind¹ ~stone

grip³ *[hold]

gripe² *[pain, complain]

grisly⁴ *[horrid]   gristly *[meat],
                      grizzly⁴ *[bear]

grist

gristle *[meat]   grizzle² *[cry]

gristly

grit³ gritty⁴

grizzle² *[cry]   gristle *[on meat]

grizzly⁴ ~l bear   grisly⁴ *[horrid],
                     gristly *[meat]

groan¹ *[moan]   grown *[big]⁺

groap   grope²

groce   gross¹⁺

grocer ~ies ~y

groggy⁴

groin

---

grone   groan[1] *[moan],
                               grown *[big][+]

groom[1]
groop   group[1+]
groove[2] *[indent]   grove *[trees]
groovy[4]
grope[2]
groser   grocer
gross[1] ~ly ~ness ~l margin ~l profit
grotesque ~ly
grotto[5]
grotty
grouch grouchy[4]
ground[1] ~breaking ~less
ground ~sheet ~sman ~swell ~work
group[1] ~l practice ~l therapy ~ware
grouse[2]
grove *[trees]   groove[2] *[indent][+]
grovel[3]
grow ~er ~ing
growl[1]
grown *[bigger] ~-up   groan[1] *[moan]
grownd   ground[+]
growse   grouse[2]
growth ~l hormone ~l industry
grub[3] grubby[4]
grudge grudging grudgingly
grue   grew
gruel gruelling
gruesome ~ly ~ness
gruff[1] ~ly ~ness
gruge   grudge[2]
grumble[2]
grumpy[4]
grunge grungy[4]
grunt[1]
grupe   group[1+]
gruyère

☞ Can't find your word here? Look under **gri**

gryddle   griddle[2]
gryt   grit[3+]
guacamole
guano
guarantee *[goods] ~d ~ing
guaranty *[debt]   guarantor
guard[1] ~sman ~room
guardian ~l angel ~ship
guava
gud   good[+]
guerrilla *[war]   gorilla *[ape]
guess[1] ~timate ~work
guessed *[estimated]
guest *[visitor] ~l house
guest ~l room ~l worker
guffaw[1]
guidance
guide[2] ~book ~l dog ~lines
guided ~l missile ~l reading
guild *[association]   gild[1] *[gold cover]
guilder
Guildhall
guile ~less
guillotine[2]
guilt *[shame]   gilt *[gold leaf][+]
guilty[4]
guinea ~l fowl ~l pig
Guinness™ ~l Book of Records
guise *[pretence]   guys *[people]
guitar ~ist ~l player
guizer   geyser
Gulag
gulash   goulash
gulf
Gulf ~l stream ~l War Syndrome
gull

---

gullet

gullible   gullibility

gully[4]

gulp[1]

gum[3] ~drop ~shield ~l tree

gumption

gun[3] ~boat ~dog ~fight ~fire

gun ~man ~point ~powder

gun ~ship ~shot

gunnell   gunwale

gunner ~y

gunwale

gurbil   gerbil

gurd   gird[1]

gurdul   girdle[2]

gurgle[2]

gurkin   gherkin *[food],
                           jerkin *[jacket]

gurl   girl[+]

gurth   girth

guru

guseberry   gooseberry[4]

gush[1] ~es

gusse   goose[+]

gust[1]   gusty[4]

gusto

gut[3] ~tural ~turally

gutter ~ing ~snipe

guvern   govern[1+]

guverner   governor[+]

guvernment   government[+]

guy

Guy Fawkes

guynecology   gynaecology[+]

guys *[people]   guise *[pretence]

guzzle[2]

gwacamole   guacamole

gwano   guano

gwashe   gouache

gwava   guava

gybe[2] *[sailing]   jibe[2] *[taunt]

☞ Can't find your word here? Look under **gi**

gyblets   giblets

gyddy   giddy[4]

gyft   gift[1+]

gyg   gig[+]

Gygercounter   Geiger counter

gyggle   giggle[2]

gyld   gild[1] *[gold cover],
                           guild *[association]

gyll   gill[1]

gylt   gilt *[gold leaf][+],
                           guilt *[shame]

gym ~khana ~nasium

gymlet   gimlet

gymmyck   gimmick[+]

gymnast ~ic ~ics

gynaecological

gynaecology   gynaecologist

gypsum

gypsy[4]

gyrate[2]   gyration

gyro *[spins]   giro *[banking]

gyro ~compass ~scope

gyzmo   gizmo

H ~bomb

habeas corpus

haberdasher ~y

habit ~-forming

habitable

habitat ~ion

habitual ~ly

habius corpus   habeas corpus

hack¹ ~saw

hackle²

hackney ~ed

had   hadn't [had not]

haddock

Hades

hadj   hadji

haduck   haddock

haemoglobin

haemophilia   haemophiliac

haemorrhage²

haemorrhoids

hag

hage   hadj⁺

haggard

haggis

haggle²

haiku

hail¹ *[ice, salute] ~stone   hale *[hearty]

hair *[on head]   hare *[animal]⁺

hair ~brush ~cut ~do

hair ~dresser ~dressing ~line

hair ~net ~pin ~-raising

hair ~-splitting ~style

hairloom   heirloom

hairy⁴

halal

halcyon ~| days

hale *[hearty]   hail¹ *[ice, salute]⁺

half⁶ ~-baked ~-breed ~-day

half ~-hearted ~hour ~-life ~-light

half ~-mast ~-price ~-term

half ~-time ~way ~wit

halibut

hall *[room]   haul¹ *[pull]

hall ~mark ~way

hallelujah

hallowed

Halloween

hallucinate²   hallucination

hallucinogen

halo⁵ *[disc of light]   hello *[greeting]

halogen

halsyon   halcyon⁺

halt¹ ~ingly

halve²

ham³ ~burger ~-fisted

ham ~let ~string ~| up

hammer¹

hammock

hamper¹

hamster

hand¹ ~bag ~book ~ful

hand ~made ~shake ~rail ~stand

handcuff¹

handicap³

handicraft   handiwork

handkerchief

handky   hanky

handle² ~bar

hands ~~on ~-free

handsome *[looks] ~ly   hansom *[cab]

handwriting   handwritten

handy⁴ ~man

Hanekka   Hanukkah

hang¹ ~glider ~man ~over ~-up

hangar *[plane]

hanger *[clothes]

KEY TO SPELLING RULES

Red words are wrong. **Black** words are correct.

~   Add the suffix or word directly to the main word, without a space or hyphen
    e.g. ash ~en ~tray → **ashen ashtray**

~-   Add a hyphen to the main word before adding the next word
    e.g. blow ~-dry → **blow-dry**

~| Leave a space between the main word and the next word
    e.g. decimal ~| place → **decimal place**

+   By finding this word in its **correct** alphabetical order, you can find related words
    e.g. about⁺ → **about-face about-turn**

*   Draws attention to words that may be confused

TM   Means the word is a trademark

hanker[1]
hankercheif   handkerchief
hankuff   handcuff[1]
hanky ~-panky
hanriting   handwriting[+]
hanshake   handshake
hansom *[cab]   handsome *[looks][+]
Hanukkah
hapand   happened
haphazard ~ly ~ness
hapless ~ly ~ness
happen[1]
happy[4] ~-go-lucky
hara-kiri
harangue[2]
harass[1] ~ment
harbinger
harbour[1]
hard[1] ~ly ~ness
hard ~ball ~-bitten ~board ~-boiled
hard ~l disk ~-hearted ~ship ~ware
hard ~wearing ~- wired ~wood ~-working
harden[1]
hardy[4]
hare *[animal] ~bell   hair *[on head][+]
hare ~-brained ~-lip
harem
harf   half[6+]
hark[1] ~l back
harken   hearken[1]
harlequin
harlot
harm[1] ~ful ~fully
harmless ~ly ~ness
harmonic ~a ~ally
harmonious ~ly
harmonise[2]   harmonisation
harmony[4]

harness[1] ~es
harp[1] ~ist ~l on
harpoon[1]
harpsichord
harrier ~l jet
harrow[1]
harsh[1] ~ly ~ness
hart *[deer]   heart *[part of body][+]
harten   hearten[1]
harth   hearth
hartless   heartless[+]
harty   hearty[4]
harvest[1]
has ~-been   hasn't [has not]
hash[1] ~l up
hashish
hassle[2]
hassock
haste *[great speed]   hasten[1]
hasty[4] *[quick]
hat *[head] ~pin ~l trick   hate[2] *[dislike]
hatch[1] ~es ~back
hatchery[4]
hatchet ~l job ~l man
hate[2] *[dislike]   hat *[head][+]
hateful ~ly ~ness
hatred
haughty[4]
haul[1] *[pull]   hall *[room][+]
haunches
haunt[1]
haute couture
have   having   haven't [have not]
haven
haversack
havoc
hawd   horde *[swarm],
        hoard[1] *[collect]

KEY TO SUFFIXES AND COMPOUNDS

These rules are explained on pages ix to x.

1 Keep the word the same before adding **ed, er, est, ing**
  e.g. cool[1] → cooled, cooler, coolest, cooling
2 Take off final **e** before adding **ed, er, est, ing**
  e.g. fine[2] → fined, finer, finest, fining
3 Double final consonant before adding **ed, er, est, ing**
  e.g. thin[3] → thinned, thinner, thinnest, thinning

4 Change final **y** to **i** before adding **ed, er, es, est, ly, ness**
  e.g. tidy[4] → tidied, tidier, tidies, tidiest, tidily, tidiness
  Keep final **y** before adding **ing** e.g. tidying
5 Add **es** instead of **s** to the end of the word
  e.g. bunch[5] → bunches
6 Change final **f** to **ve** before adding **s**
  e.g. calf[6] → calves

hawk[1] ~-eyed ~ish

hawse — hoarse *[voice],
horse *[animal]+

hawser

hawthorn

hawticulcher — horticulture+

hay *[grass] ~l fever — hey *[greeting]

hay ~stack ~wire

hayl — hail[1] *[ice, salute]+,
hale *[hearty]

hazard[1] ~ous

haze   hazy[4]

hazel

he   he's [he is, has]

head[1] ~ache ~board ~l count ~dress

☞ Can't find your word here? Take off **head** and look
again

head ~l first ~gear ~land ~less ~light

head ~line ~master ~mistress ~-on

head ~-over-heels ~phones ~quarters

head ~rest ~room ~stone ~strong

head ~l teacher ~way ~l wind

headhunt[1]

heads ~l or tails ~-up

heal[1] *[cure] — heel *[foot]

health ~l care ~l centre

health ~l club ~l farm ~l food

health ~l insurance ~l service

healthy[4]

heamoglobin — haemoglobin

heap[1]

hear *[sound] ~ing ~say — here *[place]+

heard *[sound] — herd[1] *[animals]

hearken[1]

hearse

heart *[part of body] — hurt *[pain]+

heart ~l attack ~beat ~break

heart ~breaking ~broken ~burn

heart ~felt ~land ~-rending

heart ~sick ~strings ~-throb

hearten[1]

hearth

heartless ~ly ~ness

hearty[4]

heat[1] ~edly ~proof ~stroke ~wave

heath

heathen

heather

heave[2]

heaven ~ly ~ward

heavy[4] ~-duty ~-handed ~-hearted ~weight

Hebrew

heckle[2]

hectare

hectic ~ally

hecto ~gram ~litre ~ metre

he'd [he had, would]

hed — head+

hedge[2] ~hog ~row

hedonist ~ic   hedonism

heds — heads+

heed[1] *[take notice] ~ful — he'd *[he had, would]

heed ~less

heel *[foot] — he'll *[he will]

heeth — heath

heffer — heifer

hefty[4]

heifer

height

heighten[1]

Heimlich manoeuvre

heinous ~ly ~ness

heir *[inheritance] ~ess — hair *[on head]

heir ~l apparent

heirloom

KEY TO SPELLING RULES

Red words are wrong. **Black** words are correct.

~   Add the suffix or word directly to the main word,
    without a space or hyphen
    e.g. ash ~en ~tray → ashen ashtray

~- Add a hyphen to the main word before adding the
    next word
    e.g. blow ~-dry → blow-dry

~l Leave a space between the main word and the next
    word
    e.g. decimal ~l place → decimal place

+   By finding this word in its **correct** alphabetical
    order, you can find related words
    e.g. about+ → about-face about-turn

*   Draws attention to words that may be confused

TM Means the word is a trademark

heist

heksagon | hexagon[+]
heksahedron | hexahedron
held
helicopter helipad heliport
heliocentric
heliograph
heliotrope
helium
helix[5]
he'll [he will, shall]
hell ~bent ~hole | heal[1] *[cure]
hell | heel *[foot]
hellish ~ly ~ness
hello *[greeting] | halo *[disc of light]
helm ~sman
helmet ~ed
help[1] ~l desk ~line
helpful ~ly ~ness
helpless ~ly ~ness
helter-skelter
helth | health[+]
hem[3] ~-stitch
hemisphere
hemlock
hemofilia | haemophilia[+]
hemoroids | haemorrhoids
hemorrige | haemorrhage
hemp
hen ~pecked
hence ~forth ~forward
henchman henchmen
henna
hense | hence[+]
hepatitis
heptagon ~al
her *[female] ~self | here *[place][+]
herald[1] ~ic ~ry

herb ~al ~alist ~l garden
herbaceous ~l border
herbicide
herbivore   herbivorous
herd[1] *[animals] | heard *[sound]

☞ Can't find your word here? Look under **hur**

herdul | hurdle[2]
here *[place] ~abouts | hear *[sound][+],
here ~after | her *[female][+]
here ~by ~in ~with
hereditary *[handed down]
heredity *[handing down]
heresy[4]
heretic ~al
heritage
herl | hurl[1]
hermaphrodite
hermetic ~ally
hermit ~age
hernia
hero[5] ~ic ~ically ~-worship
heroin *[drug]
heroine *[hero]
heroism
heron
herpes
herring ~bone
herry | hairy[4]
hers *[possessive of 'she']
hert | hurt
hertul | hurtle[2]
hertz
hesitant ~ly hesitancy
hesitate[2] hesitation
hessian
heterogeneous
heterosexual

KEY TO SUFFIXES AND COMPOUNDS

These rules are explained on pages ix to x.

1 Keep the word the same before adding ed, er, est, ing
  e.g. cool[1] → cooled, cooler, coolest, cooling
2 Take off final e before adding ed, er, est, ing
  e.g. fine[2] → fined, finer, finest, fining
3 Double final consonant before adding ed, er, est, ing
  e.g. thin[3] → thinned, thinner, thinnest, thinning

4 Change final y to i before adding ed, er, es, est, ly, ness
  e.g. tidy[4] → tidied, tidier, tidies, tidiest, tidily, tidiness
  Keep final y before adding ing e.g. tidying
5 Add es instead of s to the end of the word
  e.g. bunch[5] → bunches
6 Change final f to ve before adding s
  e.g. calf[6] → calves

hether	heather
hetrogenious	heterogeneous
hetrosexual	heterosexual
heven	heaven[+]
hevy	heavy[4+]
hew[1] *[cut] ~n	hue *[tint, fuss]
hexagon ~al	
hexahedron	
hey *[greeting]	hay *[grass][+]
hi *[greeting] ~-fi ~-tech	high *[tall][+]
hiacinth	hyacinth
hiatus	
hibernate[2] hibernation	
hibrid	hybrid
hiccup[3]	
hid *[past of hide] ~den	
hide *[conceal] ~-and-seek ~out	
hideous ~ly ~ness	
hiding ~l place	

☞ Can't find your word here? Look under **hy**

hidrangea	hydrangea
hidrant	hydrant
hidrorlic	hydraulic[+]
hieght	height
hieghten	heighten[1]
hiena	hyena
hienous	heinous[+]
hier	hear *[sound][+],
	here *[place],
	higher *[taller],
	hire[2] *[employ]
hierarchical ~ly	
hierarchy[4]	
hieroglyph ~ic ~ics	
hiest	highest[+]
higenist	hygienist
higgledy-piggledy	

high *[tall] ~ly	hi *[greeting][+]
high ~brow ~chair ~-class	
high ~l command ~l court	
high ~-flyer ~-handed ~l jump	
high ~lands ~-level ~light	
high ~lighter ~-performance	
high ~-pitched ~l profile ~-ranking	
high ~-rise ~l school ~-speed	
high ~-spirited ~l street ~l tech	
higher *[taller]	hire *[employ]
highest ~l common denominator	
highlight[1]	
Highness	
highway ~man	
higiene	hygiene[+]
hijack[1]	
hike[2]	
hilarious ~ly hilarity	
hill ~side hilly[4]	
hilt	
him *[male] ~self	hymn *[song][+]
himen	hymen
Himlick manoover	Heimlich
	manoeuvre
hind ~quarters ~sight	
hinder[1]	
hindrance	
Hindu ~ism	
hinge[2]	
hint[1]	
hinterland	
hip ~- hop	
hiper	hyper[+]
hipothetical	hypothetical[+]
Hippocratic ~l oath	
hippodrome	
hippopotamus	
hippy[4]	

---

hir | her *[female]+,
 | hire[2] *[employ]
hirdel | hurdle[2]
hire[2] *[employ] | higher *[taller]
hirl | hurl[1]
his *[possessive of 'he']
Hispanic
hiss[1] *[sound] ~es
histerectomy | hysterectomy[4]
histeria | hysteria+
histerical | hysterical+
historian
historic ~al ~ally
history[4]
histrionic ~ally ~s
hit *[strike] ~~-and-run ~I list
hit ~ter ~ting ~~-and-miss
hitch[1] ~es
hitch-hike[2]
hite | height *[tallness]
hiten | heighten[1]
hither ~to
HIV *[disease]
hive[2] *[for bees]
hiway | highway+
ho *[shout] | hoe[2] *[dig]
hoaks | hoax[1+]
hoal | whole+
hoan | hone[2]
hoard[1] *[collect] | horde *[swarm]
hoar frost
hoarse *[voice] ~ly ~ness | horse *[animal]+
hoax[1] ~es
hob ~goblin ~nailed
hobble[2]
hobby[4] ~~-horse
hobnob[3]
Hobson's choice

hochpotch | hotchpotch
hock
hockey
hocus-pocus
hodgepodge
hoe[2] *[dig] | ho *[shout]
hog[3] ~shead ~wash
Hogmanay
hoist[1]
hojpoj | hodgepodge
hok | hock
hokey | hockey
hokus-pokus | hocus-pocus
hold ~all ~er ~ing
hold ~I out ~I up
hole[2] *[cavity] | whole *[complete]+
holegram | hologram
holey *[holes] | holy *[sacred],
 | wholly *[fully]
holiday[1]
Holiwood | Hollywood
hollandaise ~I sauce
hollow[1]
holly *[tree] ~hock | holy *[sacred],
 | wholly *[fully]
Hollywood
holocaust *[destruction of life]
Holocaust *[slaughter of Jews]
hologram
holster[1]
holy[4] *[sacred] | holly *[tree],
 | wholly *[fully]
Holy ~I Bible ~I Ghost
Holy ~I Grail ~I Land ~I See
Holy ~I Spirit ~I Trinity
homage
home ~ly ~coming ~I ground ~~-grown
home ~~-made ~I movie ~owner

KEY TO SUFFIXES AND COMPOUNDS

These rules are explained on pages ix to x.

1 Keep the word the same before adding **ed, er, est, ing**
 e.g. **cool[1] → cooled, cooler, coolest, cooling**
2 Take off final **e** before adding **ed, er, est, ing**
 e.g. **fine[2] → fined, finer, finest, fining**
3 Double final consonant before adding **ed, er, est, ing**
 e.g. **thin[3] → thinned, thinner, thinnest, thinning**

4 Change final **y** to **i** before adding **ed, er, es, est, ly, ness**
 e.g. **tidy[4] → tidied, tidier, tidies, tidiest, tidily, tidiness**
 Keep final **y** before adding **ing** e.g. **tidying**
5 Add **es** instead of **s** to the end of the word
 e.g. **bunch[5] → bunches**
6 Change final **f** to **ve** before adding **s**
 e.g. **calf[6] → calves**

home ~| page ~stead ~ward ~work
homeless ~ness
homely⁴ *[nice]   homily⁴ *[sermon]
home office *[work from home]
Home Office *[government]
homeopath ~ic ~y
homesick ~ness
homicide   homicidal
homige   homage
homily⁴ *[sermon]   homely⁴ *[nice]
homing ~| instinct ~| pigeon
homiopath   homeopath⁺
homiside   homicide⁺
homo sapiens
homofobia   homophobia⁺
homogeneous   homogeneity
homograph
homonym
homophobia   homophobic
homophone
homosexual ~ity
hone²
honer   honour¹⁺
honest ~ly ~y
honey ~ed ~comb ~suckle
honeymoon¹
honk¹
honorarium
honorific
honour¹ ~able ~ably
hoo   who⁺
hood¹
hoodlum
hoodwink¹
hoof⁶
hook¹ ~-up ~worm
hoolahoop   hula hoop
hooligan ~ism

hoop¹ *[circle]   whoop *[shout]
hoopla
hoot¹
hoover™¹
hop³ *[jump] ~scotch
hope² *[wish] ~ful ~fully
hopeless ~ly ~ness
hopital   hospital
horde *[swarm]   hoard¹ *[collect]
horer   horror⁺
horibul   horrible⁺
horid   horrid⁺
horific   horrific⁺
horify   horrify⁴
horizon
horizontal ~ly
hork   hawk¹⁺
horl   hall *[room]⁺,
                          haul¹ *[pull]

Horlicks™
hormone
horn¹ ~beam ~pipe ~-rimmed
hornches   haunches
hornet
hornt   haunt¹
horny⁴
horor   horror⁺
horoscope
horrible   horribly
horrid ~ness
horrific ~ally
horrify⁴
horror ~| film ~| story ~| struck
hors-d'oeuvre
horse *[animal] ~back   hoarse *[voice]
horse ~| box ~| chestnut
horse ~-drawn ~fly
horse ~hair ~man ~meat

---

horse ~play ~power

horse ~l riding ~shoe

horse ~-trading ~woman ~whip

horthorn — hawthorn

horticulturalist

horticulture   horticultural

horty — haughty[4]

hose[2] *[water] — hoes *[digs]

hosiery

hospitable   hospitably

hospital

hospitalise[2]   hospitalisation

hospitality

host[1] ~ess

hostage

hostel   hostelry[4]

hostile   hostility[4]

hot[3] ~ly ~-air balloon ~bed

hot ~-blooded ~l chocolate ~l dog

hot ~-headed ~house ~l key ~line

hot ~l pants ~l plate ~pot ~l potato

hot ~l rod ~shot ~-tempered

hotchpotch

hotel ~ier

hound[1]

hour *[time] ~ly ~glass   our *[possessive]+

hours *[time]   ours *[possessive]

house[2] ~boat ~ful

house ~hold ~holder ~keeper ~l party

house ~plant ~proud ~-sit ~-trained

house ~-warming ~wife ~work

House ~l of Commons ~l of Lords

hovel

hover[1] ~craft

how *[how much]   who *[who is it?]

however

howitzer

howl[1]

hownd — hound[1]

hows — house[2]+

howse — house+

howswife — housewife

howswork — housework

hoyst — hoist[1]

hu — hue *[tint, fuss],
    who *[who is it?]

hub ~bub ~cap

Hubble's ~l constant ~l law

huch — hutch[5]

hud — hood[1]+

huddle[2]

hudwink — hoodwink[1]

hue *[tint, fuss] — hew[1] *[cut]+,
    who *[question]+

huff[1] *[pant] — hoof[6] [animal foot]

huffy[4]

hug[3] *[embrace]

huge *[large] ~ly ~ness

Huguenot

huj — huge+

hula hoop

huligan — hooligan+

hulk ~ing

hull[1]

hullabaloo

hum[3]

human *[person] ~ly ~l being ~l rights

humane *[kindly] ~ly

humanise[2]

humanist ~ic ~ism

humanitarian ~ism

humanity[4]

humble[2] ~ness   humbly

humbug

humdrum

humer — humour[1]

KEY TO SUFFIXES AND COMPOUNDS

These rules are explained on pages ix to x.

1 Keep the word the same before adding ed, er, est, ing
  e.g. cool[1] → cooled, cooler, coolest, cooling

2 Take off final e before adding ed, er, est, ing
  e.g. fine[2] → fined, finer, finest, fining

3 Double final consonant before adding ed, er, est, ing
  e.g. thin[3] → thinned, thinner, thinnest, thinning

4 Change final y to i before adding ed, er, es, est,
  ly, ness
  e.g. tidy[4] → tidied, tidier, tidies, tidiest, tidily,
  tidiness
  Keep final y before adding ing e.g. tidying

5 Add es instead of s to the end of the word
  e.g. bunch[5] → bunches

6 Change final f to ve before adding s
  e.g. calf[6] → calves

humerus *[bone]   humorous *[funny]
humid ~ity
humidify⁴
humiliate²   humiliation
humility
humming ~bird
humorist
humorous *[funny]   humerus *[bone]
humour¹
hump¹ ~back
humus
hunch¹ ~es ~back
hundred ~th ~fold ~weight
huney   honey
hung ~over
hunger¹ ~| pang ~| strike
hungry⁴
hunk
hunny   honey
hunt¹ ~sman
hunta   junta
hunter ~-gatherer
hupe   hoop¹ *[circle]⁺

☞ Can't find your word here? Look under **her**

hurb   herb⁺
hurbivor   herbivore⁺
hurd   heard *[sound],
     herd¹ *[animals]
hurdle²
hurikane   hurricane
hurl¹
hurmafrodyte   hermaphrodite
hurmetic   hermetic⁺
hurmit   hermit
hurnia   hernia
hurpes   herpes
hurrah

hurray
hurricane
hurry⁴   hurriedly
hurse   hearse
hurt *[injure] ~ful ~ing   hut *[shed]
hurtle²
hurtz   hertz
husband¹ ~ry
hush¹ ~-hush ~| money
husk¹
husky⁴
hussel   hustle²
hussy⁴
hustle²
hut *[shed]   hurt *[injure]⁺
hutch⁵
huver   hoover™¹

☞ Can't find your word here? Look under **hi**

hy   hi⁺
hyacinth
hyatus   hiatus
hybernate   hibernate²⁺
hybrid
hyccup   hiccup¹
hychhike   hitch-hike²
hyd   hid⁺
hyddeous   hideous⁺
hyde   hide⁺
hydra
hydrangea
hydrant
hydraulic ~ally
hydrocarbon
hydrochloric ~| acid
hydrocortisone
hydroelectric   hydroelectricity
hydrofoil

Key to Spelling Rules

Red words are wrong. **Black** words are correct.

~   Add the suffix or word directly to the main word, without a space or hyphen
    e.g. ash ~en ~tray → **ashen ashtray**

~-   Add a hyphen to the main word before adding the next word
    e.g. blow ~-dry → **blow-dry**

~| Leave a space between the main word and the next word
    e.g. decimal ~| place → **decimal place**

+   By finding this word in its **correct** alphabetical order, you can find related words
    e.g. about⁺ → **about-face about-turn**

*   Draws attention to words that may be confused

™   Means the word is a trademark

hydrogen ~l bomb
hydrolysis
hydrometer
hydropath
hydrophobia
hydroplane
hydrostatic
hydrotherapy
hydrous
hydroxide
hyena

hyer | higher *[taller],
| hire[2] *[employ]
hyerarcky | hierarchy[4]
hyest | highest[+]
hyggledy-pyggledy | higgledy-piggledy
hygiene hygienist
hygienic ~ally
hyjack | hijack[1]
hyke | hike[2]
hylarious | hilarious[+]
hyll | hill[+]
hymen
hymn *[song] ~al | him *[male][+]
hynd | hind[+]
hynder | hinder[1]
hyndrance | hindrance
Hyndu | Hindu[+]
hynge | hinge[2]
hynt | hint[1]
hyper ~active ~inflation
hyper ~link ~market
hyper ~sensitive ~text
hyperbola *[curve]
hyperbole *[exaggeration]
hyperbolic ~al ~ally

hypercritical *[harsh]   hypocritical *[false]
hyperventilate[2]
hyphen
hyphenate[2]
hypnosis
hypnotic ~ally
hypnotise[2]
hypnotist hypnotism
hypoallergenic
hypochondria hypochondriac
hypocrisy[4]
hypocrite
hypocritical * | hypercritical *
     [false] | [harsh]
hypodermic ~l needle
hypotenuse
hypothermia
hypothesis hypotheses
hypothesise[2]
hypothetical ~ly
hyppodrome | hippodrome
hyppopotamus | hippopotamus
hyppy | hippy[4]
hyre | higher *[taller],
| hire[2] *[employ]
hyroglyph | hieroglyph[+]
Hyspanic | Hispanic
hyst | heist
hysterectomy[4]
hysteria hysterics
hysterical ~ly
hystoric | historic[+]
hystory | history[4]
hyt | height
hytch | hitch[1+]
hyway | highway[+]

KEY TO SUFFIXES AND COMPOUNDS

These rules are explained on pages ix to x.

1 Keep the word the same before adding ed, er, est, ing
  e.g. cool[1] → cooled, cooler, coolest, cooling
2 Take off final e before adding ed, er, est, ing
  e.g. fine[2] → fined, finer, finest, fining
3 Double final consonant before adding ed, er, est, ing
  e.g. thin[3] → thinned, thinner, thinnest, thinning

4 Change final y to i before adding ed, er, es, est, ly, ness
  e.g. tidy[4] → tidied, tidier, tidies, tidiest, tidily, tidiness
  Keep final y before adding ing e.g. tidying
5 Add es instead of s to the end of the word
  e.g. bunch[5] → bunches
6 Change final f to ve before adding s
  e.g. calf[6] → calves

☞ Can't find your word here? Look under **e**

I *[me]	aye *[yes],
	eye *[see]+
iambic ~l pentameter	
ibullience	ebullience+
ibuprofen	
ice² ~l age ~berg	
ice ~-cold ~l cream	
ice ~l hockey ~l lolly ~l pack	
ice ~l pick ~l rink ~-skate	
icee	icy⁴
ich	itch¹⁺
icicle	
icing ~l sugar	
iclair	éclair
iclectic	eclectic
iclispe	eclipse²⁺
icological	ecological+
icology	ecology+
icon ~oclast ~oclastic	
iconomy	economy⁴
icy⁴	
icycul	icicle
I'd [I had, would]	
idea	
ideal ~ism ~ly	
idealise²	
idear	idea
ideel	ideal+
ideelise	idealise²
ideer	idea
identical ~ly	
identify⁴ identifiable identification	
identity⁴ ~l card	
ideological ~ly	
ideology⁴	
iderdown	eiderdown

ides ~l of March	
idill	idyll+
idiocy	
idiological	ideological+
idiology	ideology⁴
idiom ~atic ~atically	
idiosincrasy	idiosyncrasy+
idiosy	idiocy
idiosyncrasy idiosyncratic	
idiot ~ic ~ically	
idium	idiom+
idle² *[lazy] ~ness idly	
idol *[worship]	
idolatry idolatrous	
idolise²	
idyll ~ic ~ically	
idyot	idiot+
ieght	eight *[number]+
ieghth	eighth+
ieghty	eighty⁴⁺
iery	eery⁴ *[strange],
	eyrie *[nest]
iether	either *[or],
	ether *[air, liquid]+
if	
iffy	
igalitarian	egalitarian+
Igiptology	Egyptology+
igloo	
igneminy	ignominy
igneous ~l rock	
igneramus	ignoramus
ignerence	ignorance
ignite² ignition	
ignius	igneous+
ignoble	
ignominie	ignominy
ignominious ~ly ~ness	

KEY TO SPELLING RULES

Red words are wrong. **Black** words are correct.

~   Add the suffix or word directly to the main word, without a space or hyphen
     e.g. ash ~en ~tray → ashen ashtray

~-   Add a hyphen to the main word before adding the next word
     e.g. blow ~-dry → blow-dry

~l   Leave a space between the main word and the next word
     e.g. decimal ~l place → decimal place

+   By finding this word in its **correct** alphabetical order, you can find related words
     e.g. about+ → about-face about-turn

*   Draws attention to words that may be confused

TM   Means the word is a trademark

ignominius	ignominious[+]
ignominy	
ignor	ignore[2]
ignoramus	
ignorance	
ignorant ~ly	
ignore[2]	
ignorens	ignorance
ignorent	ignorant[+]
ignyte	ignite[2+]
iguana	
igwana	iguana
ijaculate	ejaculate[2+]
iject	eject[1+]
iland	island[+]
ilapse	elapse[2+]
ilastic	elastic[+]
ilate	elate[2+]
ile	aisle *[passage], isle *[island]
I'le	I'll *[I will, shall]
ilegal	illegal[+]
ilegibul	illegible[+]
ilegitimacy	illegitimacy[4]
ilegitimate	illegitimate[+]
ilett	eyelet *[hole], islet *[island]
ilicit	elicit[1] *[get], illicit *[illegal]
iligitimasee	illegitimacy
iligitimate	illegitimate[+]
iliminate	eliminate[2+]
ilision	elision
iliterasee	illiteracy[+]
I'll *[I will, shall]	aisle *[passage], isle *[island]
ill ~-advised ~-bred	
ill ~-conceived ~-considered	

> ☞ Can't find your word here? Take off <u>ill</u> and look again

ill ~-defined ~-equipped ~-fated	
ill ~-l feeling ~-founded	
ill ~-l health ~-prepared	
illaborate	elaborate[2+]
illegal ~ly illegality[4]	
illegible illegibly illegibility	
illegitimacy	
illegitimate ~ly	
illicit *[illegal]	elicit[1] *[get]
illiteracy illiterate	
illness	
illogical ~ly	
illuminate[2] illumination	
illusion *[false idea]	allusion *[hint], elusion *[escape]
illusive *[deceptive]	allusive * [suggestive][+], elusive *[evasive][+]
illusory	
illustrate[2] illustrator	
illustration	
illustrative	
illustrious ~ly ~ness	
ilness	illness
ilogicul	illogical
ilongate	elongate[2+]
ilope	elope[2+]
iluminate	illuminate[2+]
ilusion	illusion *[false idea]
ilusive	illusive *[deceptive]
ilusory	illusory
ilustrate	illustrate[2+]
ilustrashun	illustration
ilustrius	illustrious[+]
I'm [I am]	
imaciate	emaciate[2+]

KEY TO SUFFIXES AND COMPOUNDS

These rules are explained on pages ix to x.

1 Keep the word the same before adding **ed, er, est, ing**
e.g. cool[1] → cooled, cooler, coolest, cooling
2 Take off final **e** before adding **ed, er, est, ing**
e.g. fine[2] → fined, finer, finest, fining
3 Double final consonant before adding **ed, er, est, ing**
e.g. thin[3] → thinned, thinner, thinnest, thinning

4 Change final **y** to **i** before adding **ed, er, es, est, ly, ness**
e.g. tidy[4] → tidied, tidier, tidies, tidiest, tidily, tidiness
Keep final **y** before adding **ing** e.g. tidying
5 Add **es** instead of **s** to the end of the word
e.g. bunch[5] → bunches
6 Change final **f** to **ve** before adding **s**
e.g. calf[6] → calves

☞ Can't find your word here? Look under **em**

Imacks	IMAX™
imaculate	immaculate+
image² imageable	imagery
imaginary ~I number	
imagine² imaginable	
imagination imaginative	
imam	
imanent	eminent * [notable]+,
	immanent * [inherent],
	imminent *[soon]+
imansipate	emancipate²+
imarm	imam
imasculate	emasculate²+
imatearial	immaterial
imature	immature+
IMAX™	
imbalance	
imbecile	
imbed³	
imbew	imbue²
imbibe²	

☞ Can't find your word here? Look under **imm**

imbicile	imbecile
imbue²	
imbybe	imbibe²
imedeate	immediate+
imediacy	immediacy
imemorial	immemorial
imens	immense+
imerse	immerse²+
imesurabul	immeasurable+
imige	image²
imigrant	immigrant

imigrate	immigrate²+
imij	image²
iminent	eminent * [notable],
	immanent * [inherent],
	imminent *[soon]+
imit	emit³
imitate² imitation	imitator
immaculate ~ly ~ness	
immanent *	imminent *[soon]+,
[inherent]	eminent *[notable]+
immaterial	
immature immaturity	
immeasurable immeasurably	
immediate ~ly	
immemorial	
immense ~ly immensity	
immerse² immersion	
immigrant *[arrives]	emigrant *[exits]
immigrate² *[arrive]	emigrate² *[exit]
immigration *[arrival]	emigration *[exit]
imminent *[soon] ~ly	eminent * [notable]+,
	immanent * [inherent]
immobile immobiliity	
immobilise² immobilisation	
immoderate ~ly	
immoral ~ity ~ly	
immortal immortality	
immortalise²	
immoshun	emotion+
immovable	
immune immunity	
immunise² immunisation	
immunology	
immutable	
imobilise	immobilise²+
imoderate	immoderate+

KEY TO SPELLING RULES

Red words are wrong. **Black** words are correct.

~   Add the suffix or word directly to the main word, without a space or hyphen
e.g. ash ~en ~tray → ashen ashtray

~-   Add a hyphen to the main word before adding the next word
e.g. blow ~-dry → blow-dry

~I   Leave a space between the main word and the next word
e.g. decimal ~I place → decimal place

+   By finding this word in its **correct** alphabetical order, you can find related words
e.g. about+ → about-face about-turn

*   Draws attention to words that may be confused

™   Means the word is a trademark

imoral	immoral⁺
imortalise	immortalise²⁺
imorul	immoral
imotiv	emotive
imovabul	immovable
imp ~ish ~ishly ~ishness	
impact¹	
impair¹ ~ment	
impakt	impact¹
impale²	
impalpable impalpably	
impare	impair¹⁺
imparshul	impartial⁺
impart¹	
impartial ~ity ~ly	
impashense	impatience
impasiv	impassive⁺
impasivity	impassivity
impassable	
impassabul	impassable
impasse	
impasshuned	impassioned
impassioned	
impassive ~ly ~ness	
impassivity	
impatience	
impatient ~ly	
impeach¹ ~able ~ment	
impeccable impeccably	
impechuous	impetuous⁺
impecunious ~ness	
impede²	
impediment ~a	
impeech	impeach¹⁺
impeeriel	imperial⁺
impekunious	impecunious⁺
impel³	
impending	

impenetrable	
impenitence	
imperative ~ly ~ness	
imperceptible imperceptibly	
imperetiv	imperative⁺
imperfect ~ly ~ion	
imperial *[empire]	imperil³ *[endanger]
imperial ~ism ~ly	
imperialist ~ic	
imperil³ *[endanger]	imperial *[empire]⁺
imperious ~ly ~ness	
impermeable	
imperseptibul	imperceptible⁺
impersonal ~ly	
impersonate²	
impersonation impersonator	
impertinence impertinent	
impervious ~ly ~ness	
impetuosity	
impetuous ~ly	
impetus⁵	
impinge²	
impirialist	imperialist⁺
impirious	imperious⁺
impish ~ness	
implacable implacably	
implament	implement¹⁺
implant¹ ~ation	
implausible	
implawsibul	implausible
implecate	implicate²⁺
implement¹ ~ation	
implicate² implication	
implicit ~ly ~ness	
implisit	implicit⁺
implore²	
implorsibul	implausible
imply⁴ implication	

KEY TO SUFFIXES AND COMPOUNDS

These rules are explained on pages ix to x.

1 Keep the word the same before adding **ed, er, est, ing**
e.g. cool¹ → cooled, cooler, coolest, cooling
2 Take off final **e** before adding **ed, er, est, ing**
e.g. fine² → fined, finer, finest, fining
3 Double final consonant before adding **ed, er, est, ing**
e.g. thin³ → thinned, thinner, thinnest, thinning

4 Change final **y** to **i** before adding **ed, er, es, est, ly, ness**
e.g. tidy⁴ → tidied, tidier, tidies, tidiest, tidily, tidiness
Keep final **y** before adding **ing** e.g. tidying
5 Add **es** instead of **s** to the end of the word
e.g. bunch⁵ → bunches
6 Change final **f** to **ve** before adding **s**
e.g. calf⁶ → calves

impolite ~ly ~ness
impolitic
imponderable
impondrabul   imponderable
imporchune   importune[2+]
import[1] ~able ~ation
importance *[value]   impotence *
                      [weakness][+]
important *[valuable]   impotent *[weak]
importantly
importune[2] importunity
impose[2] imposition
imposibility   impossibility[4]
impossibul   impossible[+]
impossibility[4]
impossible impossibly
impostor *[swindler]
imposture *[deception]
impotence *[weakness]   importance *[value]
impotent *[weak]   important *
                     [valuable][+]
impound[1]
impourt   import[1+]
impourtant   important
impoverish[1] ~ment
impoverished
impownd   impound[1]
impracticable
impractical ~ly
impracticality[4]
imprecise ~ly
impregnable
impregnate[2]
imprepryetie   impropriety[4]
impresario
impreshionism   impressionism[+]
impresise   imprecise[+]
impresiv   impressive[+]

impress[1]
impression ~able
impressionism impressionist
impressive ~ly ~ness
imprint[1]
imprison[1] ~ment
improbable improbability
impromptu
improper ~ly
impropriety[4]
impropur   improper[+]
improve[2] ~ment
improvident ~ly
improvise[2] improvisation
imprudence
imprudent ~ly
impruve   improve[2+]
impudence
impudent ~ly
impugn[1]
impulse impulsion
impulsive ~ly ~ness
impune   impugn[1]
impunity
impure
impurity[4]
impursonal   impersonal[+]
impursonate   impersonate[2+]
impurtinents   impertinence[+]
impurvious   impervious[+]
impyur   impure[+]
imulshun   emulsion
imulsify   emulsify[4+]
imune   immune[+]
imunise   immunise[2+]
imunology   immunology
imutabul   immutable
imyune   immune[+]

KEY TO SPELLING RULES

Red words are wrong. **Black** words are correct.

~   Add the suffix or word directly to the main word, without a space or hyphen
     e.g. ash ~en ~tray → **ashen ashtray**

~-   Add a hyphen to the main word before adding the next word
     e.g. blow ~-dry → **blow-dry**

~| Leave a space between the main word and the next word
     e.g. decimal ~| place → **decimal place**

+   By finding this word in its **correct** alphabetical order, you can find related words
     e.g. about[+] → **about-face about-turn**

*   Draws attention to words that may be confused

TM   Means the word is a trademark

in *[go in]	inn *[pub]+
in ~-box ~-fighting	
in ~l loco parentis	

☞ Can't find your word here? Take off <u>in</u> and look again

inability⁴	
inaccessible inaccessibility	
inaccuracy⁴	
inaccurate ~ly	
inacsessibul	inaccessible+
inaction	
inactive	
inactivity	
inacuracy	inaccuracy⁴
inacurate	inaccurate+
inadequacy⁴	
inadequate ~ly	
inadmissible inadmissibility	
inadvertent ~ly ~ness	
inaksessible	inaccessible+
inakshun	inaction
inaksuracy	inaccuracy⁴
inaktion	inaction
inaktive	inactive
inaktivity	inactivity⁴
inalienable	
inane ~ly ~ness	
inanimate	
inanity⁴	
inapplicable	
inappropriate ~ly ~ness	
inapt *[not suitable]	inept *[foolish]+
inarticulate	
inasmuch	
inate	innate+
inatenshun	inattention+
inattention inattentive	

inaudible inaudibility	
inaugerate	inaugurate²+
inaugural	
inaugurate² inauguration	
inauspicious ~ly	
inawdibel	inaudible+
inawganic	inorganic+
inawgurate	inaugurate²+
inawspishus	inauspicious+
in-between	
inbilt	inbuilt
inborn	
inbred inbreeding	
inbuilt	
incalculable	
incandescent	
incantation	
incapable	
incapacitate²	
incapacity	
incarcerate² incarceration	
incarnate² incarnation	
incarserate	incarcerate²+
incect	insect+
inceminate	inseminate²+
incendiary⁴	
incense²	
incensibul	insensible
incensitiv	insensitive+
incensitivity	insensitivity⁴
incentive	
inceprabul	inseparable
inception	
incequre	insecure+
incert	insert¹+
incertichude	incertitude
incertitude	
incesant	incessant+

KEY TO SUFFIXES AND COMPOUNDS

These rules are explained on pages ix to x.

1 Keep the word the same before adding **ed, er, est, ing**
e.g. cool¹ → cooled, cooler, coolest, cooling

2 Take off final **e** before adding **ed, er, est, ing**
e.g. fine² → fined, finer, finest, fining

3 Double final consonant before adding **ed, er, est, ing**
e.g. thin³ → thinned, thinner, thinnest, thinning

4 Change final **y** to **i** before adding **ed, er, es, est, ly, ness**
e.g. tidy⁴ → tidied, tidier, tidies, tidiest, tidily, tidiness
Keep final **y** before adding **ing** e.g. tidying

5 Add **es** instead of **s** to the end of the word
e.g. bunch⁵ → bunches

6 Change final **f** to **ve** before adding **s**
e.g. calf⁶ → calves

☞ Can't find your word here? Take off <u>in</u> and look again

inceschuous	incestuous⁺
incessant ~ly	
incest	
incestuous ~ly ~ness	
incet	inset³
inch¹ ~es	
inchoir	inquire
inchuitiv	intuitive⁺
incidence *[how often]	incidents *[events]
incident ~al ~ally	
incidiuss	insidious⁺
incignia	insignia
incignificanse	insignificance
incignificant	insignificant⁺
incincere	insincere⁺
incinerate² *[burn]	insinuate² *[imply]
incinerator	
incinuate	insinuate²⁺
incipid	insipid⁺
incipient	
incision	
incisive ~ly ~ness	
incisor	
incist	insist¹⁺
incite² *[stir up] ~ment	insight *[understand]
inclement	
incline² ~d inclination	
include² inclusion	
inclusive ~ly ~ness	
incognito	
incoherence incoherent	
income ~l tax	
incoming	
incommunicado	
incomparable incomparably	

incompatible
incompetence
incompetent ~ly ~ness
incomplete ~ly ~ness
incomprehensible
inconceivable inconceivably
inconcistent   inconsistent⁺
inconclusive ~ly ~ness
incongruity⁴
incongruous ~ly ~ness
inconseevabul   inconceivable⁺
inconsiderable
inconsiderate ~ness
inconsiderit   inconsiderate⁺
inconsidrabel   inconsiderable
inconsistency⁴
inconsistent ~ly
inconsolable
inconspicuous ~ly
inconstancy inconstant
incontestable
incontinence incontinent
incontrovertible incontrovertibly
inconvenience² inconvenient
incorporate² incorporation
incorrect ~ly ~ness
incorrigible
incorruptible
increase² increasingly
incredible incredibly
incredulity incredulous
increment ~al
incriminate² incrimination
incubashun   incubation
incubate² incubator
incubation
inculcate²
incumbency⁴ incumbent

☞ Can't find your word here? Take off **in** and look again

incur³
incurable   incurably
incursion
incynerate   incinerate²⁺
incypient   incipient
indebted ~ness
indecency
indecent ~ly ~l assault
indecipherable
indecision
indecisive ~ly ~ness
indecorous
indecorum
indeed
indefatigable
indefensible
indefinable
indefinite ~ly ~l article
indeks   index¹⁺
indelabul   indelible⁺
indelible   indelibly
indelicacy⁴
indelicate ~ly
indemnify⁴   indemnification
indemnity⁴
indent¹ ~ation ~ure
independence
independent ~ly
indescribable   indescribably
indesency   indecency
indesent   indecent⁺
indesiferabul   indecipherable
indesisiv   indecisive⁺
indeskribabul   indescribable⁺
indestructible

indeterminate ~ly
indetted   indebted⁺
indewbitably   indubitable⁺
indewse   induce²⁺
index¹ ~es   indices
index ~l card ~l finger
index ~-linked
Indian ~l ink ~l summer
indicate²   indication
indicative
indicator
indiciferable   indecipherable
indicision   indecision
indicisiv   indecisive⁺
indict¹ ~ment
indifatigabul   indefatigable
indifensabul   indefensible
indifferent ~ly   indifference
indifinabul   indefinable
indifrens   indifference⁺
indigenous
indigent
indigenus   indigenous
indigestible
indigestion   indigestive
indight   indict¹⁺
indignant ~ly   indignation
indignent   indignant⁺
indignity⁴
indigo
indijenous   indigenous
indijestibul   indigestible
indijestion   indigestion⁺
indikate   indicate²⁺
indikayshun   indication
indirect ~ly ~l speech
indiscreet *[careless]
indiscrete *[joined]

KEY TO SUFFIXES AND COMPOUNDS

These rules are explained on pages ix to x.

1 Keep the word the same before adding **ed, er, est, ing**
   e.g. cool¹ → cooled, cooler, coolest, cooling
2 Take off final **e** before adding **ed, er, est, ing**
   e.g. fine² → fined, finer, finest, fining
3 Double final consonant before adding **ed, er, est, ing**
   e.g. thin³ → thinned, thinner, thinnest, thinning

4 Change final **y** to **i** before adding **ed, er, es, est, ly, ness**
   e.g. tidy⁴ → tidied, tidier, tidies, tidiest, tidily, tidiness
   Keep final **y** before adding **ing** e.g. tidying
5 Add **es** instead of **s** to the end of the word
   e.g. bunch⁵ → bunches
6 Change final **f** to **ve** before adding **s**
   e.g. calf⁶ → calves

☞ Can't find your word here? Take off **in** and look again

indiscretion	
indiscribabul	indescribable+
indiscriminate	
indiskreshun	indiscretion
indispensable indispensably	
indisposed	
indisputable indisputably	
indistinct ~ly	
indistinguishable	
indistructabul	indestructible
inditerminat	indeterminate+
individual ~ity ~ly	
individualism indvidualist	
indivijalisum	individualism+
indivisible	
indoctrinate² indoctrination	
indolence indolent	
indomitable indomitably	
indoor ~s	
indubitable indubitably	
induce² ~ment	
induction	
indulge² indulgence indulgent	
induse	induce²⁺
industree	industry⁴
industrial ~ism ~ist ~ly	
industrialise² industrialisation	
industriel	industrial+
industrious ~ly ~ness	
industrlize	industrialise²⁺
industry⁴	
indycativ	indicative
indyrect	indirect+
indyte	indict¹⁺
inebriated	
ineckspensiv	inexpensive+

inecksperiens	inexperience+
inedible	
inefectiv	ineffective+
inefectual	ineffectual+
ineffective ~ly ~ness	
ineffectual ~ly	
inefficiency⁴	
inefficient ~ly	

☞ Can't find your word here? Look under **inex**

inekscusabul	inexcusable
inekserabul	inexorable
ineksorstibul	inexhaustible
inekspensiv	inexpensive+
ineksperience	inexperience+
inelegance inelegant	
ineligible ineligibility	
inelijibul	ineligible+
inept *[foolish] ~ly	inapt *[not suitable]
ineptitude	
inequality⁴	
inequity⁴ *[bias]	iniquity⁴ *[sin]
iner	inner+
inersha	inertia
inert ~ly ~l gas	
inertia	
inescapable inescapably	
inessential	
inestimable	
inevitable inevitably inevitability	
inexact ~itude	
inexaustibul	inexhaustible
inexcusable	
inexhaustible	
inexorable inexorably	
inexpensive ~ly	
inexperience ~d	
inexplicable inexplicably	

KEY TO SPELLING RULES

Red words are wrong. **Black** words are correct.

~   Add the suffix or word directly to the main word, without a space or hyphen
     e.g. ash ~en ~tray → ashen ashtray

~-   Add a hyphen to the main word before adding the next word
     e.g. blow ~-dry → blow-dry

~| Leave a space between the main word and the next word
     e.g. decimal ~| place → decimal place

+   By finding this word in its **correct** alphabetical order, you can find related words
     e.g. about+ → about-face about-turn

*   Draws attention to words that may be confused

TM   Means the word is a trademark

inexpressible
inextinguishable
inextricable
infachuated   infatuated
infallible infallibility
infamous ~ly
infamy
infancy
infant ~icide ~ile
infantry⁴
infatuated   infatuation
infect¹ ~ion
infectious ~ly ~ness ~l disease
infekshus   infectious⁺
infekt   infect¹⁺
infent   infant⁺
infentry   infantry⁴
infer³ ~ence
inferior ~ity
inferm   infirm
infermary   infirmary⁴
infernal ~ly
inferno
infertile   infertility
infest¹ ~ation
infidel
infidelity⁴
infighting
infiltrate² infiltration
infinite ~ly
infinitee   infinity⁴
infinitesimal ~ly
infinitive
infinity⁴
infirier   inferior⁺
infirm infirmary⁴
infirmity⁴
infirnel   infernal⁺

infirno   inferno
infirtile   infertile⁺
infiting   infighting
inflamabul   inflammable
inflamatry   inflammatory
inflame² inflammable
inflammation inflammatory
inflashun   inflation⁺
inflate² inflatable
inflation ~ary ~-proof
inflaym   inflame²⁺
inflayt   inflate²⁺
inflect¹ ~ion
inflekshun   inflection
infleksibul   inflexible⁺
inflekt   inflect¹⁺
inflewnce   influence²
inflewnza   influenza
inflexible inflexibility
inflict¹ ~ion
in-flight ~l entertainment
inflite   in-flight⁺
inflow
influcks   influx
influence²
influenshall   influential⁺
influential ~ly
influenza
influks   influx
influx
inform¹ ~ative
informal ~ity ~ly
informant
informashun   information⁺
information ~l retrieval ~l technology
infourm   inform¹⁺
infraction
infrakshun   infraction

KEY TO SUFFIXES AND COMPOUNDS

These rules are explained on pages ix to x.

1 Keep the word the same before adding **ed, er, est, ing**
   e.g. cool¹ → cooled, cooler, coolest, cooling
2 Take off final **e** before adding **ed, er, est, ing**
   e.g. fine² → fined, finer, finest, fining
3 Double final consonant before adding **ed, er, est, ing**
   e.g. thin³ → thinned, thinner, thinnest, thinning

4 Change final **y** to **i** before adding **ed, er, es, est, ly, ness**
   e.g. tidy⁴ → tidied, tidier, tidies, tidiest, tidily, tidiness
   Keep final **y** before adding **ing** e.g. tidying
5 Add **es** instead of **s** to the end of the word
   e.g. bunch⁵ → bunches
6 Change final **f** to **ve** before adding **s**
   e.g. calf⁶ → calves

infrared ~| astronomy ~| telescope
infrastructure
infrequency
infrequent ~ly
infrered   infrared⁺
infrestructure   infrastructure
infringe² ~ment
infuriate²
infurnal   infernal⁺
infurtile   infertile⁺
infuse² infusion
ingenious *[clever] ~ly   ingenuous *[fool]
ingenuity
ingenuous *[fool]   ingenious *[clever]
inglenook
inglorious ~ly
inglorius   inglorious⁺
ingot
ingrained
ingrashiate   ingratiate²
ingratiate²
ingratitude
ingredient
ingreedyent   ingredient
ingrow ~ing
ingrown ~| toenail
inhabit¹ ~ant
inhail   inhale²⁺
inhailunt   inhalant
inhalant
inhale² inhalation
inherent ~ly
inherit¹ ~ance ~or
inhewmane   inhuman⁺
inhibit¹ ~ion ~or
inhospitable
inhuman ~ity ~ly
inhumane

inhybit   inhibit¹⁺
inibriated   inebriated
inikwitus   iniquitous
inimical
inimitable
inings   innings
iniquitous
iniquity⁴ *[badness]   inequity⁴ *[bias]
inishiate   initiate²⁺
inishul   initial³⁺
initial³ ~ly
initialise² initialisation
initiate² initiation
initiative
inject¹ ~ion ~or
injenious   ingenious⁺
injenuity   ingenuity
injenuous   ingenuous⁺
injer   injure²⁺
injery   injury⁴
injuncshun   injunction
injunction
injure² injurious
injury⁴
injustice
ink¹ ~| y ~| in ~-jet
inkalkulable   incalculable

☞ Can't find your word here? Look under **inc**

---

inkling
inklude   include²⁺
inklusiv   inclusive⁺
inkrease   increase²
inkredibul   incredible⁺
inkur   incur³
inkurable   incurable⁺
inkurshun   incursion
inkwest   inquest

KEY TO SPELLING RULES

Red words are wrong. **Black** words are correct.

~   Add the suffix or word directly to the main word, without a space or hyphen
    e.g. ash ~en ~tray → ashen ashtray

~-   Add a hyphen to the main word before adding the next word
    e.g. blow ~-dry → blow-dry

~| Leave a space between the main word and the next word
    e.g. decimal ~| place → decimal place

+   By finding this word in its **correct** alphabetical order, you can find related words
    e.g. about⁺ → about-face about-turn

*   Draws attention to words that may be confused

TM   Means the word is a trademark

inland
in-laws
inlay inlaid
inlet
inlore in-law
inmate
inmost
inn *[pub] ~keeper in *[go in]

☞ Can't find your word here? Look under **in**

innability inability[4]
innaccurate inaccurate[+]
innactiv inactive
innate ~ly ~ness
innedible inedible
innept inept
inner ~I city ~most
innert inert[+]
innevitabul inevitable[+]
innings
innocence
innocent ~ly
innoculate inoculate[2+]
innocuous ~ly
innosent innocent[+]
innovate[2] innovation
innovative ~ly
innuendo
innumerable
innumeracy
innundate inundate[2+]
inocent innocent[+]
inoculate[2] inoculation
inocuous innocuous[+]
inoffensive ~ly ~ness
inokulate inoculate[2+]
inoperative
inopportune ~ly

inoprativ inoperative
inordinate ~ly
inorganic ~I chemistry
inorganic ~I compound
inorgural inaugural
inorgurate inaugurate[2+]
inormity enormity[4]
inormous enormous[+]
inorspishus inauspicious[+]
inovate innovate[2+]
inovativ innovative[+]
input[3]
inquest
inquire inquiry
inquisitive ~ly ~ness
inquisitor
inroads
insabordinashun insubordination
insane ~ly
insanitary
insanitry insanitary
insanity
insatiable insatiably
insayshabul insatiable[+]
inscrewtabul inscrutable
inscribe[2]
inscription
inscrutable
insect ~icide
insecure ~ly
insecurity[4]
insekt insect[+]
insekure insecure[+]
insekurity insecurity[4]
inseminate[2] insemination
insendury incendiary[4]
insense incense[2]
insensible

KEY TO SUFFIXES AND COMPOUNDS

These rules are explained on pages ix to x.

1 Keep the word the same before adding **ed, er, est, ing**
e.g. cool[1] → cooled, cooler, coolest, cooling
2 Take off final **e** before adding **ed, er, est, ing**
e.g. fine[2] → fined, finer, finest, fining
3 Double final consonant before adding **ed, er, est, ing**
e.g. thin[3] → thinned, thinner, thinnest, thinning

4 Change final **y** to **i** before adding **ed, er, es, est, ly, ness**
e.g. tidy[4] → tidied, tidier, tidies, tidiest, tidily, tidiness
Keep final **y** before adding **ing** e.g. tidying
5 Add **es** instead of **s** to the end of the word
e.g. bunch[5] → bunches
6 Change final **f** to **ve** before adding **s**
e.g. calf[6] → calves

163

insensitive ~ly
insensitivity[4]
insensybul — insensible
insentiv — incentive
inseparable
insepshun — inception
insergence — insurgence[+]
insermountabul — insurmountable
inserrecshun — insurrection
insert[1] ~ion
insertitude — incertitude
insessant — incessant[+]
insest — incest
insestuous — incestuous[+]
inset[3]
inshore *[coast] — ensure[2] *[be sure], insure[2] *[money]

inside ~I out
insidens — incidents *[events], incidence * [how often]
insident — incident[+]
insidents — incidents *[events]
insider ~I trading
insidious ~ly ~ness
insight *[understand] — incite[2] *[stir up][+]
insignia
insignificance
insignificant ~ly
insincere ~ly insincerity
insinuate[2] *[imply] — incinerate[2] *[burn][+]
insinuation
insipid ~ly ~ness
insise — incise[2+]
insishun — incision
insision — incision
insisive — incisive[+]
insisor — incisor

insist[1] ~ence ~ent ~ently
insite — incite[2] *[stir up][+], insight *[understand]
inskribe — inscribe[2]
inskripshun — inscription
inskrutable — inscrutable
insofar
insolant — insolent[+]
insolence
insolent ~ly
insoluble insolubility
insolvency insolvent
insolvensy — insolvency[+]
insomnia insomniac
insomuch
insomya — insomnia[+]
inspect[1] ~ion ~or
inspectorate
inspekt — inspect[1+]
inspektor — inspector
inspire[2] inspiration
instability
install[1] *[thing, person] — instil[3] *[idea]
installation
instalment
instance[2] *[example] — instants *[moments]
instant ~ly ~I messaging
instantaneous ~ly
instants *[moments] — instance[2] *[example]
instawl — install[1]
instawlment — instalment
instead
instep
instichute — institute[2]
instigate[2] instigator
instigation
instil[3] *[idea] — install[1] *[fix][+]
instinct ~ive ~ively

---

institushun	institution[+]	insyncere	insincere[+]
institute[2]		intact	
institution ~al		intake	
institutionalise[2]		intakt	intact
instrement	instrument[+]	intangible intangibly	
instruct[1] ~ion ~or		inteereer	interior
instructive ~ly		integer	
		integrait	integrate[2+]

> ☞ Can't find your word here? Take off **in** and look again

		integral ~ly	
instruement	instrument[+]	integrate[2] integration	
instrukt	instruct[1+]	integrated ~l circuit	
instrument ~ation		integrity	
instrumental ~ist		intejer	integer
instrumment	instrument[+]	intelecchual	intellectual[+]
insubordinate ~ly		intelekt	intellect[+]
insubordination		inteligense	intelligence
insufferable insufferably		inteligent	intelligent[+]
insufficiency[4]		inteligibul	intelligible
insufficient ~ly		intellect	
insufishensy	insufficiency[4]	intellectual ~ise ~ly	
insufishent	insufficient[+]	intellectual ~l property	
insufrabul	insufferable[+]	intelligence	
insular ~ity		intelligent ~ly ~sia	
insulate[2] insulator		intelligible intelligibility	
insulation		intemperance	
insulayt	insulate[2+]	intemperate ~ly	
insuler	insular[+]	intempranse	intemperance
insulin		intempurate	intemperate[+]
insult[1]		intence	intense[+]
insurance ~l policy ~l premium		intend[1]	
insure[2] *[money]	ensure[2] *[be sure],	intense ~ly	
	inshore *[coast]	intenshun	intention
insurgence insurgent		intenshunal	intentional[+]
insurmountable		intensify[4] intensification	
insurrection		intensity[4]	
insurt	insert[1+]	intensive ~ly ~ness ~l care	
insygnia	insignia	intent ~ly	
		intention ~al ~ally	

KEY TO SUFFIXES AND COMPOUNDS

These rules are explained on pages ix to x.

1 Keep the word the same before adding **ed, er, est, ing**
   e.g. cool[1] → cooled, cooler, coolest, cooling

2 Take off final **e** before adding **ed, er, est, ing**
   e.g. fine[2] → fined, finer, finest, fining

3 Double final consonant before adding **ed, er, est, ing**
   e.g. thin[3] → thinned, thinner, thinnest, thinning

4 Change final **y** to **i** before adding **ed, er, es, est, ly, ness**
   e.g. tidy[4] → tidied, tidier, tidies, tidiest, tidily, tidiness
   Keep final **y** before adding **ing** e.g. tidying

5 Add **es** instead of **s** to the end of the word
   e.g. bunch[5] → bunches

6 Change final **f** to **ve** before adding **s**
   e.g. calf[6] → calves

inter³ *[to bury]   enter¹ *[go in]
interact¹ ~ion
interactive ~| computing ~| video
interagayshun   interrogation
interbred   interbreeding
intercede²
intercept¹ ~ion ~or
intercession
interchange² ~able
intercom

> ☞ Can't find your word here? Take off **inter** and look again

interconnect¹ ~ion
intercontinental
intercourse
interdenominational
interdependence
interdict¹ ~ion
interdisciplinary
interest¹
interface
interfere²   interference
interferon
interim
interior
interject¹ ~ion
interkom   intercom
interleave²
interlock¹
interlocutor
interloper
interlude
intermarry⁴
intermediary⁴
intermediate
interment *[burial]   internment *[jail]
interminable   interminably

intermingle²
intermission
intermittent ~ly
intermix¹
intern¹   internee
internal ~ly
internashunal   international⁺
international ~ly
internaut
internecine
Internet ~| café ~| service provider
internment *[prison]   interment *[burial]
internought   internaut
interogate   interrogate²⁺
interogator   interrogator
interplanetary
interplay¹
Interpol
interpolate²
interpret¹ ~ation ~ive
interrelate²
interrogate²   interrogator
interrogation
interrogative
interrupt¹ ~ion
intersect¹ ~ion
intersept   intercept¹⁺
intersperse²
intertwine²
interval
intervene²   intervention
interview¹
intervue   interview¹
interweave   interweaving
interwove ~n
intestine   intestinal
intimacy
intimait   intimate⁺

KEY TO SPELLING RULES

Red words are wrong. **Black** words are correct.

~   Add the suffix or word directly to the main word, without a space or hyphen
    e.g. ash ~en ~tray → ashen ashtray

~- Add a hyphen to the main word before adding the next word
    e.g. blow ~-dry → blow-dry

~| Leave a space between the main word and the next word
    e.g. decimal ~| place → decimal place

+   By finding this word in its **correct** alphabetical order, you can find related words
    e.g. about⁺ → about-face about-turn

*   Draws attention to words that may be confused

TM Means the word is a trademark

intimasee	intimacy
intimate[2] ~ly	
intimidate[2]	intimidation
intirier	interior
into	
intocksicant	intoxicant
intocksicate	intoxicate[2+]
intolerable	intolerably
intolerance	intolerant
intolrabul	intolerable[+]
intolrance	intolerance[+]
intonation	
intone[2]	
intoxicant	
intoxicate[2]	intoxication
intractable	
intramuscular	
intranet *[internal]	Internet *[global][+]
intransigence	intransigent
intransitive	
intravenous ~ly	
intreegue	intrigue[2]
intrepid ~ly ~ness	
intreplanetary	interplanetary
Intrepol	Interpol
intricacy[4]	
intricate ~ly	
intrigue[2]	
intrikasee	intricacy[4]
intrikate	intricate[+]
intrinsic ~ally	
introduce[2]	
introduction	introductory
introjuce	introduce[2]
introod	intrude[2]
introoshun	intrusion[+]
introspection	introspective
introvert ~ed	

intrude[2]	
intrushun	intrusion[+]
intrusion	intrusive
intuishun	intuition
intuition	
intuitive ~ly	

☞ Can't find your word here? Look under **inter**

inturakt	interact[1+]
inturcors	intercourse
inturest	interest[1]
inturface	interface
inturfeer	interfere[2+]
inturim	interim
inturlude	interlude
inturmishun	intermission
inturn	intern[1+]
inturnal	internal
Inturnet	Internet
inturplanetary	interplanetary
Inturpol	Interpol
inturpret	interpret[1+]
intursept	intercept[1+]
inturvue	interview[1]
Inuit	
inumerabul	innumerable
inumeracy	innumeracy
inundate[2]	inundation
inure[2]	
inursha	inertia
inurtia	inertia
invade[2]	
invaigle	inveigle[2]
invalid ~ity	
invalidate[2]	
invaluable	
invariable	invariably
invaryabul	invariable[+]

---

invashun	invasion
invasion	
invay	inveigh[1]
invayd	invade[2]
invective	
inveigh[1]	
inveigle[2]	
invektiv	invective
invent[1] ~ion ~or	
inventive ~ness	
inverse ~ly inversion	
invert[1] ~ed comma	
invest[1] ~ment ~or	

☞ Can't find your word here? Take off **in** and look again

investicher	investiture
investichure	investiture
investigate[2] investigation	
investigator	
investiture	
inveterate	
invey	inveigh[1]
invidious ~ly ~ness	
invidius	invidious[+]
invight	invite[2+]
invigilate[2] invigilator invigilation	
invigorate[2]	
invijilate	invigilate[2+]
invincible	
inviolate	
invirse	inverse
invirt	invert[1+]
invirtibrate	invertebrate
invisibility	
invisible invisibly	
invite[2] invitation	
in-vitro fertilisation	

invoak	invoke[2]
invoice[2]	
invoke[2]	
involuntary involuntarily	
involuntry	involuntary[+]
involve[2] ~ment	
invoys	invoice[2]
invulnerable invunerability	
invurse	inverse
invurt	invert[1+]
invurtebrate	invertebrate
invyolate	inviolate
inward ~ly ~ness ~s	
inwud	inward[+]
inymical	inimical
inymitabul	inimitable
iodine	
iodise[2]	
iodyne	iodine
iodyse	iodise[2]
ion ~ic	
ionise[2]	
ionosfere	ionosphere
ionosphere	
ionyse	ionise[2]
iota	
IOU	
iradiate	irradiate[2+]
iradicate	eradicate[2+]
irait	irate[+]
irascible irascibility	
irase	erase[2+]
irassibul	irascible[+]
irate ~ly ~ness	
irational	irrational[+]
ire	
ireconcilabul	irreconcilable
iregular	irregular

☞ Can't find your word here? Look under **irre**

iregularity	irregularity[4]
irelevent	irrevelant[+]
ireparabul	irreparable
ireplaceable	irreplaceable
iresistibul	irresistible[+]
iresponsibul	irresponsible[+]
ireversibul	irreversible
irevocabul	irrevocable
irideamabul	irredeemable
iridium	
irigate	irrigate[2+]
iris	
Irish ~l coffee ~l stew	
iritabul	irritable[+]
iritant	irritant[+]
iritate	irritate[2+]
iritent	irritant[+]
irk[1] ~some	
irl	earl[+]
irly	early[4+]
irmine	ermine
irn	earn[1] *[money], urn *[vase]
irnest	earnest[+]
irning	ironing[+]
iron[1] ~l age ~clad ~l curtain	
iron ~l lung ~monger's ~mongery ~work	
ironic ~al ~ally	
ironik	ironic[+]
ironing ~l board	
irony[4]	
irradiate[2] irradiation	
irrashunal	irrational[+]
irrate	irate[+]
irrational ~ly	
irreconcilable	

irrecoverable
irredeemable
irrefutable   irrefutably
irregular ~ly
irregularity[4]
irrelevancy[4]
irrelevant ~ly   irrelevance
irreligious
irremediable
irremovable
irreparable
irreplaceable
irrepressible   irrepressibly
irreproachable
irresistible   irresistibly
irrespective
irresponsibility
irresponsible   irresponsibly
irretrievable
irreverence
irreverent ~ly
irreversible
irrevocable

irrigate[2] irrigation	
irritable irritably irritability	
irritant	
irritate[2] irritation	
irth	earth[1+]
irthen	earthen[+]
irydium	iridium
irys	iris
ise	ice
ishue	issue[2+]
isicul	icicle
ising	icing[+]
Islam ~ic ~icist	
island ~er	
isle *[island]	aisle *[passage]

KEY TO SUFFIXES AND COMPOUNDS

These rules are explained on pages ix to x.

1 Keep the word the same before adding **ed, er, est, ing**
e.g. cool[1] → cooled, cooler, coolest, cooling
2 Take off final **e** before adding **ed, er, est, ing**
e.g. fine[2] → fined, finer, finest, fining
3 Double final consonant before adding **ed, er, est, ing**
e.g. thin[3] → thinned, thinner, thinnest, thinning

4 Change final **y** to **i** before adding **ed, er, es, est, ly, ness**
e.g. tidy[4] → tidied, tidier, tidies, tidiest, tidily, tidiness
Keep final **y** before adding **ing** e.g. tidying
5 Add **es** instead of **s** to the end of the word
e.g. bunch[5] → bunches
6 Change final **f** to **ve** before adding **s**
e.g. calf[6] → calves

islet *[island]	eyelet *[hole]	ithos	ethos
isn't [is not]		itinerant	
isobar		itinerary[4]	
isolashun	isolation[+]	it'll [it will, shall]	
isolate[2]		its *[possessive]	it's *[it is, has]
isolation ~ism ~ist		itself	
isometrics isometrically		itsy-bitsy	
isosceles ~l triangle		iturnity	eternity[4]
isosulees	isosceles	itynerant	itinerant
isotherm		ivacuate	evacuate[2+]
isotope		ivade	evade[2+]
issue[2]		ivaluate	evaluate[2+]
isthmus		ivangelic	evangelic[+]
isue	issue[2]	ivangelise	evangelise[2+]
it *[preposition]		ivaporate	evaporate[2+]
IT *[information technology]		ivasive	evasive[+]
italicise[2]		I've [I have]	
italics		ivoke	evoke[2]
italiks	italics	ivolve	evolve[2]
italisize	italicise[2]	ivory ~l tower	
itch[1] itchy[4]		ivry	ivory[+]
item		ivy[4]	
itemise[2]		iyambic	iambic[+]
itemize	itemise[2]	iye	I *[me],
itemyse	itemise[2]		aye *[yes],
iternal	eternal[+]		eye *[see][+]
iternity	eternity[4]	iyota	iota
ither	either[+]	iznt	isn't [is not]

KEY TO SPELLING RULES

Red words are wrong. **Black** words are correct.

~   Add the suffix or word directly to the main word,
     without a space or hyphen
     e.g. ash ~en ~tray → ashen ashtray
~-   Add a hyphen to the main word before adding the
     next word
     e.g. blow ~-dry → blow-dry

~l   Leave a space between the main word and the next
     word
     e.g. decimal ~l place → decimal place
+   By finding this word in its **correct** alphabetical
     order, you can find related words
     e.g. about+ → about-face about-turn
*   Draws attention to words that may be confused
TM   Means the word is a trademark

170

☞ Can't find your word here? Look under **g**

jab³
jabber¹
jack¹ ~ass ~boot ~daw
jack ~-in-the-box
jack ~knife ~pot
jackal
jacket¹ ~l potato
jackul   jackal
Jacobean Jacobite
Jacobin
Jacuzzi™
jade ~d
Jaffa ~l orange
jagged ~ly ~ness
jaguar
jaid   jade
jail¹ ~bird ~break
jain
jak   jack⁺
jakdoor   jackdaw
jaket   jacket¹
Jakobean   Jacobean⁺
jakul   jackal
jakuzzi   Jacuzzi™
jale   jail⁺
jam³ *[food, squeeze] jammy
jamb *[side post]
jamboree
Janery   January
jangle²
janitor
January
jar³
jargon
jasmine
jasper

jaundice ~d
jaunt jaunty⁴
javelin
jaw ~bone
jawntee   jaunty⁴
jazz¹ ~y ~l musician
jealous ~ly ~y

☞ Can't find your word here? Look under **ge**

jeans *[trousers]   genes *[DNA]
jeehad   jihad
Jeep™
jeer¹
Jeeves
Jehovah ~'s Witness
Jekyll ~l and Hyde
jelly⁴ ~l baby ~fish
jelus   jealous⁺
jemmy⁴
jenital   genital
jeopardise² jeopardy
jeperdise   jeopardise⁺
jeriatric   geriatric⁺
jerk¹ jerky⁴
jerkin
jernal   journal⁺
jerney   journey¹
jeroboam
jerry-built
jerrycan
jersey
jest¹ jester
Jesuit
Jesus ~l Christ
jet³ ~l engine ~l lag ~-lagged
jet ~-propelled ~l set ~l stream
jetsam
jettison¹

KEY TO SUFFIXES AND COMPOUNDS

These rules are explained on pages ix to x.

1 Keep the word the same before adding **ed, er, est, ing**
e.g. cool¹ → cooled, cooler, coolest, cooling
2 Take off final **e** before adding **ed, er, est, ing**
e.g. fine² → fined, finer, finest, fining
3 Double final consonant before adding **ed, er, est, ing**
e.g. thin³ → thinned, thinner, thinnest, thinning

4 Change final **y** to **i** before adding **ed, er, es, est, ly, ness**
e.g. tidy⁴ → tidied, tidier, tidies, tidiest, tidily, tidiness
Keep final **y** before adding **ing** e.g. tidying
5 Add **es** instead of **s** to the end of the word
e.g. bunch⁵ → bunches
6 Change final **f** to **ve** before adding **s**
e.g. calf⁶ → calves

jetty[4]

Jew *[religion]

jewel[3] *[gem] ~lery

Jewish ~ness

jewn

Jewry *[Jews]

dew *[drops],
due *[owing, expected]

dual *[two][+],
duel *[fight],
joule *[energy]

June

jury[4] *[court][+]

☞ Can't find your word here? Look under ge

jewt

jib[3]

jibe[2] *[taunt]

jier

jiffy ~l bag

jig[3] ~saw

jiggle[2]

jihad

jilt[1]

jingle[2]

jingoism jingoistic

jinks *[high]

jinx[1] ~es *[spell]

jirarf

jitter[1] ~s jittery

jive[2]

job[3] ~l application ~l centre

job ~l description ~less ~l lot ~l satisfaction

job ~l security ~l seeker ~- sharing

jockey[1]

jockstrap

jocular ~ly ~ity

jodhpurs

jog[3]

join[1] ~ery ~l up

joint[1] ~ly ~l venture

joist[1]

jute

gybe[2] *[sailing]

jeer[1]

giraffe

joke[2] jokingly

jokuler

jolly[4] jollity

jolt[1]

jonkwil

jonquil

joos

joot

jorndiss

jornty

josel

joss ~l stick

jostle[2]

jot[3] ~tings

joule *[energy]

journal ~ese ~ism ~ist ~istic

journey[1]

joust[1]

jovial ~ly ~ity

jowl

jowst

joy ~ful ~fully ~stick

joyn

joynt

joyous ~ly ~ness

joy-ride[2]

joyst

joyus

jubilant ~ly jubilance

jubilee jubilation

jucuzi

Judaism

Judas

judder[1]

judge[2] ~ment ~mental

judicial ~ly

jocular[+]

jonquil

deuce *[card],
juice[2] *[drink][+]

jute *[cloth],
jut *[stick out]

jaundice

jaunty[4]

jostle[2]

duel *[fight]

joust[1]

join[1+]

joint[1+]

joist[1]

joyous[+]

Jacuzzi™

KEY TO SPELLING RULES

Red words are wrong. **Black** words are correct.

~   Add the suffix or word directly to the main word,
    without a space or hyphen
    e.g. ash ~en ~tray → ashen ashtray

~- Add a hyphen to the main word before adding the
    next word
    e.g. blow ~-dry → blow-dry

~l Leave a space between the main word and the next
    word
    e.g. decimal ~l place → decimal place

+   By finding this word in its **correct** alphabetical
    order, you can find related words
    e.g. about[+] → about-face about-turn

*   Draws attention to words that may be confused

TM Means the word is a trademark

172

judiciary⁴
judicious ~ly ~ness
judishery   judiciary⁴
judishul   judicial⁺
judishus   judicious⁺
judo
juel   duel *[fight],
       joule *[energy]
jug³
juggernaut
juggle²
juggler *[throws]
jugular *[vein]
juice² *[drink]   deuce *[card]
juicy⁴
jujitsu
jukebox
jukstapose   juxtapose²⁺
jule   joule *[energy],
       jewel *[gem]⁺
July
jumble²
jumbo ~| jet
jump¹ ~-start ~suit
jumper
jumpy⁴
juncshun   junction⁺
juncshure   juncture
junction ~| box
juncture
June *[month]   dune *[sand]
jungle   jungly
junior
juniper

junk¹ ~| bond ~| food
junk ~| mail ~| shop
junket¹
junkie
junksher   juncture
junkshun   junction
junta
junyer   junior
Jupiter
jurisdiction
jurisprudence   jurisprudent
jurist
jurkin   jerkin
jurnal   journal⁺
jurney   journey¹
juror
jursey   jersey
jury⁴ *[court] ~| box   Jewry *[Jews]
juse   juice² *[drink],
       Jews *[people]
just ~ly ~ness ~deserts
justice
justifiable   justifiably
justify⁴   justification
justiss   justice
jut³ *[stick out]
jute *[cloth]
juvenile ~| delinquent
juvenile ~| delinquency
juwel   jewel *[gem],
       joule *[unit]
juxtapose²   juxtaposition
Juze   Jews *[people],
       juice² *[drink]

KEY TO SUFFIXES AND COMPOUNDS

These rules are explained on pages ix to x.

1 Keep the word the same before adding **ed, er, est, ing**
e.g. cool¹ → cooled, cooler, coolest, cooling
2 Take off final **e** before adding **ed, er, est, ing**
e.g. fine² → fined, finer, finest, fining
3 Double final consonant before adding **ed, er, est, ing**
e.g. thin³ → thinned, thinner, thinnest, thinning

4 Change final **y** to **i** before adding **ed, er, es, est, ly, ness**
e.g. tidy⁴ → tidied, tidier, tidies, tidiest, tidily, tidiness
Keep final **y** before adding **ing** e.g. tidying
5 Add **es** instead of **s** to the end of the word
e.g. bunch⁵ → bunches
6 Change final **f** to **ve** before adding **s**
e.g. calf⁶ → calves

☞ Can't find your word here? Look under **c**

kab	**cab**⁺
kabbige	**cabbage**
kache	**cache**²
kael	**kale**
kafé	**café**
kaftan	
kage	**cage**²⁺
kail	**kale**
Kaiser	
kaki	**khaki**
Kalashnikov	
kalculate	**calculate**²⁺
kalculater	**calculator**
kalculus	**calculus**
kale	
kaleidoscope	**kaleidoscopic**
kalender	**calendar**
kalidoscope	**kaleidoscope**⁺
Kama Sutra	
kame	**came**
kameez	
kamikaze	
kamp	**camp**¹⁺
kan	**can**³ *[be able, tin]⁺
kanga	
kangaroo ~l court	
kanji	
kanoo	**canoe**⁺
kaolin	
kapchur	**capture**²
kaput	
karahtee	**karate**
karaoke	
karate	
kareer	**career** *[job],
	carrier *[carrying]⁺

karet	**carat** *[gold],
	carrot *[vegetable]
karioke	**karaoke**
karki	**khaki**
karma	
karnival	**carnival**
kart karting	
kasett	**cassette**⁺
kaution	**caution**¹⁺
kave	**cave**²⁺
kavity	**cavity**⁴
kayak ~ing	
keal	**keel**¹⁺
kean	**keen**¹⁺
Keanti	**Chianti**⁺
keap	**keep**⁺
kebab	
kech	**ketch**⁵
kechup	**ketchup**
kee	**key**¹ *[lock, PC, main]
	quay *[dock]

keel¹ ~l over
keen¹ ~ly ~ness
keep ~er ~ing ~l fit ~sake

keesh	**quiche**⁺
keg	
kelidoscope	**kaleidoscope**⁺
kelp	
kelvin	
kennel	
kept	
keratin *[protein]	**carotene** *[carrots]
kerb *[edge] ~-crawling	**curb**¹ *[stop]
kerb ~stone	
kerfuffle	
kernel *[seed]	**colonel** *[officer]
kerosene	
kestrel	

☞ Can't find your word here? Look under **c**

ketch[5]
ketchup
kettle ~drum
key[1] *[lock, PC, main]   quay *[dock]+
key ~board ~hole ~pad
key ~l ring ~stroke ~word
keynote ~l speech ~l speaker
khaki
kibab   kebab
kibbutz   kibbutzim
kibosh
kic   kick+
kiche   quiche
kichen   kitchen+
kick[1] ~back ~l boxing
kick ~-off ~stand ~-start
kid[3] ~l gloves
kiddy[4]
kidnap[3]
kidney ~l bean
kiel   keel[1]+
kight   kite
kik   kick+
kill[1] ~joy ~l off
killer ~l bee ~l instinct ~l whale
kiln
kilo ~byte ~gram ~hertz
kilo ~litre ~metre ~watt
kilt
kilter
kimera   chimera+
kimono
kin ~sfolk ~ship ~sman ~swoman
kinaesthetic ~ally
kind[1] ~ly ~ness ~-hearted
kindergarten

kindle[2]
kindred ~l spirit
kinetic ~l art ~l energy
king ~ly ~dom ~fisher ~pin
king ~-size ~-sized
kink
kinky[4]
kiosk
kipper
kirb   curb[1] *[stop],
                                 kerb *[edge]+
kirsch
kiss[1] ~es ~l of death ~l of life
kit[3] *[equipment]   kite *[flying toy]
kitchen ~ette ~ware
kite *[flying toy]   kit[3] *[equipment]
kith ~l and kin
kitten
kitty[4]
kiwi ~l fruit
Kleenex™
kleeshay   cliché
kleptomania   kleptomaniac
klorafill   chlorophyll+
klutz ~y
knack
knackered
knacker's yard
knapsack
knave *[Jack]   nave *[church]
knead[1] *[dough]   kneed *[knee],
                                 need *[must have]
knee ~ing ~l brace ~cap
knee ~-deep ~-high ~-jerk ~-length
kneed *[knee]   knead *[dough],
                                 need *[must have]
kneel ~ing
knell

KEY TO SUFFIXES AND COMPOUNDS

These rules are explained on pages ix to x.

1 Keep the word the same before adding ed, er, est, ing
e.g. cool[1] → cooled, cooler, coolest, cooling
2 Take off final e before adding ed, er, est, ing
e.g. fine[2] → fined, finer, finest, fining
3 Double final consonant before adding ed, er, est, ing
e.g. thin[3] → thinned, thinner, thinnest, thinning

4 Change final y to i before adding ed, er, es, est, ly, ness
e.g. tidy[4] → tidied, tidier, tidies, tidiest, tidily, tidiness
Keep final y before adding ing e.g. tidying
5 Add es instead of s to the end of the word
e.g. bunch[5] → bunches
6 Change final f to ve before adding s
e.g. calf[6] → calves

knelt
knew *[information]   new *[not old]
knickerbocker glory
knickerbockers
knickers
knick-knack
knife⁶ ~-edge
knight *[rank] ~hood   night *[dark]⁺
knit³ *[with needles]   nit *[insect]
knob³ ~bly
knock¹ ~back ~I off ~-on ~out
knock ~-kneed
knoll
knot³ *[tie] ~ty   not *[no]
know *[information]   no *[not]⁺
know ~ing ~ingly
know ~-all ~-how
knowledge ~able ~ably
known
knuckle² ~I down ~-duster
koala ~I bear
kobalt   cobalt⁺
kochineel   cochineal
Kodak™
kollekshun   collection⁺
kookaburra
Koran
kore   core² *[centre],
               corps *[army]
korespondens   correspondence⁺
korgi   corgi
koridor   corridor *[passage],
               corrida *[bullfight]
kornflower   cornflour *[cooking]
               cornflower *[flower],
koroshun   corrosion⁺
korps   corps *[army, ballet],
               corpse *[body]

kort   caught *[ball],
               court *[law]
korum   quorum
kosher
kosine   cosine
Kouran   Koran
kowtow¹
krate   crate²
krater   crater
krave   crave²⁺
Kremlin [the]
krew   crew¹⁺
krews   crews *[teams],
               cruise² *[trip]⁺
krill
Krishna
krone *[money]   crone *[old woman]
kroner
krugerrand
krypton
kudos
kukaburra   kookaburra
kumlawday   cum laude⁺
kumquat
kung fu
kurb   curb *[stop],
               kerb *[edge]⁺
kurfuffel   kerfuffle
kurnel   kernel *[seed],
               colonel *[officer]

☞ Can't find your word here? Look under **qu**

kwack   quack¹
Kweezanair rods   Cuisenaire™ rods
kwerty   QWERTY⁺
kwestshun   question¹⁺
kwestshunaire   questionnaire
kwiert   quiet¹⁺

L ~-plate
label
laber   labour[1+]
labirinth   labyrinth
laboratory[4]
laborious ~ly ~ness
labour[1] ~-intensive
Labour ~| Party
Labrador
laburnum
labyrinth
lace[2] lacy[4]
lacerate[2] laceration
lack[1] ~lustre
lackadaisical ~ly
lackey
lacksativ   laxative
laconic ~ally
lacquer[1]
lacrosse
lactate[2] lactation
lactic ~| acid
lactose ~| intolerance ~| intolerant
lad
ladder[1]
laden
ladies' ~| man ~| room ~| wear
ladle[2]
lady[4] ~bird ~killer ~like ~ship
laff   laugh[1+]
lag[3]
lager *[beer] larger *[bigger]
lagging
lagoon
lagubrius lugubrious[+]
lagune   lagoon
laid ~-back
lain *[down] lane *[path]

lair *[den] layer[1] *[thickness]
laird
laissez-faire
laity
lak   lack[1+]
lakadaisical lackadaisical[+]
lake ~side
lakonik laconic[+]
lakrosse lacrosse
laks   lax[+]
laktation lactation
laktik   lactic
laktose lactose
lam[3] *[hit] lamb[1] *[sheep][+]
lama *[Tibetan monk] llama *[animal]
lamb[1] *[sheep] ~skin lam[3] *[hit]
lambast[2]
lame[2] *[weak] ~ly ~ness ~| duck.
lamé *[gold cloth]
lament[1] ~ation
lamentable lamentably
laminate[2] laminator
lamp ~light ~| post ~shade
lampoon[1] ~ist
lance[2] ~-corporal
lancet

☞ Can't find your word here? Take off **land** and look
 again

---

land[1] ~fall ~fill ~form ~holding
land ~lady ~locked ~lord ~lubber
land ~mark ~mine ~owner ~scape ~slide
Land Rover™
landau
landing ~| gear ~| place ~| stage ~| strip
landscape[2] ~| gardening
lane *[path] lain *[down]
langer   languor[+]

KEY TO SUFFIXES AND COMPOUNDS

These rules are explained on pages ix to x.

1 Keep the word the same before adding **ed, er, est, ing**
 e.g. cool[1] → cooled, cooler, coolest, cooling
2 Take off final **e** before adding **ed, er, est, ing**
 e.g. fine[2] → fined, finer, finest, fining
3 Double final consonant before adding **ed, er, est, ing**
 e.g. thin[3] → thinned, thinner, thinnest, thinning

4 Change final **y** to **i** before adding **ed, er, es, est, ly, ness**
 e.g. tidy[4] → tidied, tidier, tidies, tidiest, tidily, tidiness
 Keep final **y** before adding **ing** e.g. tidying
5 Add **es** instead of **s** to the end of the word
 e.g. bunch[5] → bunches
6 Change final **f** to **ve** before adding **s**
 e.g. calf[6] → calves

language
languid ~ly
languish[1]
languor ~ous ~ously ~ousness
langwid   languid[+]
langwij   language
langwish   languish[1]
lank ~ly ~ness
lanky[4]
lanolin
lanse   lance[2+]
lantern
lanyard
lap[3] ~-dance ~l dog ~top ~wing
lapel
lapis lazuli
lapse[2]
larceny[4]   larcenist
larch[5]
lard[1]
larder
larf   laugh[1+]
large ~ly ~ness
larger *[bigger]   lager *[beer]
largesse *[kindness]   largest *[biggest]
largo
larinx   larynx[+]
larj   large[+]
lark[1] ~l about
larmay   lamé
larseny   larceny[4+]
larva *[insect]   lava *[volcano]
larvae
laryngitis
larynx larynges laryngeal
lasagne
lasanya   lasagne
lascivious ~ly ~ness

lase   lace[2] *[shoes][+],
                                 laze[2] *[not work][+]
laser ~l disk ~l gun ~l printer
laserate   lacerate[2+]
lash[1] lashings
lass ~ie
lassitude
lassivius   lascivious[+]
lasso[1] ~es
last[1] ~ly ~-ditch ~-gasp
last ~-minute ~l name ~l orders
last ~l post ~l rites ~l straw
Last Supper
lasue   lasso[1+]
latch[1] ~l key
late[2] ~ly ~ness ~comer
latency
latent ~l heat
later *[afterwards]   latter *[last][+]
lateral ~l thinking
latex
lath *[wooden strip]
lathe *[machine]
lather[1]
Latin ~l America ~l American
latiss   lattice[+]
latitude
latrine
latté
latter *[last]   later *[afterwards]
latter ~-day ~ly
lattice ~d ~l window ~work
laud[1] *[praise]   lord[1] *[noble][+]
laudable laudably laudatory
laugh[1] ~able ~ingly
laughing stock
laughter
launch[1] ~es ~l pad

launder[1] ~ette

laundry[4] ~| basket ~| list

laureate

laurel[3]

lava *[volcano]   larva *[insect][+]

lavatory[4]

lavender ~| oil

lavish[1] ~es ~ly ~ness

law *[rule] ~-abiding   lore *[tradition]

law ~| court~| enforcement ~suit

Law ~| Lord ~| Society

lawful ~ly ~ness

lawless ~ness

lawn ~mower ~| tennis

lawyer

lax ~ity ~ness

laxative

lay ~ing   laid

lay ~about ~-by ~man

lay ~out ~person

layer[1] *[thickness]   lair *[den]

laysay fair   laissez faire

laze[2] *[not work]   lace[2] *[shoes][+]

laze ~| around

lazer   laser[+]

lazy[4] ~bones

lea *[open ground]   lee *[shelter][+]

leach[1] *[drain away] ~es   leech[5] *[worm]

lead *[substance]   led *[guided, resulted]

lead ~ed ~en

lead ~| balloon ~-free

lead *[guide, result] ~ing

lead ~| time ~-up

leader ~ship

leading ~| article ~| edge

leading ~| lady ~| man

leaf[6] *[trees] ~y

leaf[1] *[turn pages] ~| through

leaflet[1]

league ~| tables

leak[1] *[hole]   leek *[vegetable]

leakage

leaky[4]

lean[1] *[bend, thin]   lien *[legal hold]

leant *[past of lean]   lent *[past of lend],
                                lent *[before Easter]

lean-to

leap[1] ~frog ~| year

leapt

learn[1] ~t

learning ~| curve ~| disability ~| support

lease[2] ~back ~hold ~holder

leash[1] ~es

least ~ways ~wise

leather[1] ~y ~| goods

leave   leaving

leavened ~| bread

leccher   lecture[2+]

lecher ~ous ~y

lectern

lecture[2] ~ship ~| theatre

lecturn   lectern

led *[past of lead]   lead *[substance][+]

leding   leading[+]

ledge

ledger[1]

lee *[shelter]   lea *[open ground]

lee ~ward ~way

Leebra   Libra

leece   lease[2+]

leech[5] *[worm]   leach[1] *[drain away][+]

leed   lead[+]

leeder   leader[+]

leef   leaf[6+]

leeg   league[+]

leeje   liege

---

leek *[vegetable]   leak¹ *[hole]⁺
leer¹
leera   lira
leery⁴
leesay   lycée
leeshun   lesion
left ~-field ~-footer ~-handed
left ~l over ~overs ~-wing
leftenant   lieutenant⁺
leftist
leg³ ~l iron ~room ~-up ~work
legacy⁴
legal ~ly
legal ~l action ~l aid ~l system
legalise² legalisation
legality⁴
legend ~ary
leger   ledger
leggings
leggy
legible *[clear]   eligible *[fitting]
legibility legibly
legion legionary⁴
legionnaire ~'s disease
legislate² legislator legislation
legislature
legitimacy
legitimate ~ly
legitimise² legitimisation
Lego™
legume leguminous
legyoom   legume
leisure ~ly ~l centre
leitmotif
lej   ledge
lejion   legion⁺
lejislashun   legislation
lejislate   legislate²⁺

lejitimise   legitimise²⁺
lejonair   legionnaire⁺
leksicon   lexicon
lemming
lemon ~ade ~l curd ~grass
lemur
lend ~er ~ing   lent
lene   lean¹⁺
length ~ways ~wise
lengthen¹
lengthy⁴
leniency
lenient ~ly
lens⁵
lent *[past of lend]   leant *[past of lean]
Lent *[before Easter]
lentil
lento
Leo
leopard
leotard
lepard   leopard
leper ~l colony
lepidopterous
lepracorn   leprechaun
leprechaun
leprosy   leprous
lept   leapt
lerch   lurch¹⁺
lerk   lurk¹
lern   learn¹⁺
lernt   learnt
lesbian ~ism
lesher   leisure⁺
lesion *[injury]   lesson *[learnt]
less
lessee
lessen¹ *[make less]   lesson *[learnt]

---

lesser *[smaller]
lesson *[learnt]
lessor *[landlord]
lest
let letting
lethal ~ly ~l injection
lethargic ~ally lethargy
lether leather[1]
letiss lettuce
letter[1] ~l bomb ~l box ~head
lettuce
leucocyte
leukaemia
Levant
levee
level[3] ~-crossing ~-headed ~-pegging
levened leavened[+]
lever[1] ~age ~aged
leviathan
Levis™
levitate[2] levitation
levity
levvay levee
levy[4]
lewd ~ly ~ness
lexicographer lexicography
lexicon
lexis lexical
lezbien lesbian[+]
liability[4]
liable *[likely, responsible] libel[3] *[lies]
liaise[2]
liaison ~l officer
liar *[tells lies] lyre *[musical][+]
liase liaise[2]
liason liaison[+]
libel[3] *[lies] liable *[likely, responsible]

lessor *[landlord]
lessen[1] *[make less]
lesser *[smaller]

libellous ~ly
liberal ~ly ~ism ~l arts ~l studies
Liberal ~l Democrat ~l Party
liberalise[2] liberalisation
liberate[2] liberator
liberation
libertine
liberty[4]
libido libidinous
Libra
libral liberal[+]
librarian ~ship
library[4]
libretto librettist
librury library[4]
lice
licence *[document] ~l plate
license[2] *[give permit]
licensee *[someone with permit]
licensing ~l hours ~l laws
licentiate
licentious ~ly ~ness
lichen
lick[1]
licker liquor
lickoriss liquorice
lid lidded
lide lied[+]
lido
lie *[down, untruth] lye *[chemical]
lie ~l detector
liebraree library[4]
lied
liege
lien *[legal hold] lean[1] *[thin][+]
lier leer[1]
lieu *[in lieu of] loo *[toilet]
lieutenant lieutenancy[4]

KEY TO SUFFIXES AND COMPOUNDS

These rules are explained on pages ix to x.

1 Keep the word the same before adding **ed, er, est, ing**
e.g. cool[1] → cooled, cooler, coolest, cooling
2 Take off final **e** before adding **ed, er, est, ing**
e.g. fine[2] → fined, finer, finest, fining
3 Double final consonant before adding **ed, er, est, ing**
e.g. thin[3] → thinned, thinner, thinnest, thinning

4 Change final **y** to **i** before adding **ed, er, es, est, ly, ness**
e.g. tidy[4] → tidied, tidier, tidies, tidiest, tidily, tidiness
Keep final **y** before adding **ing** e.g. tidying
5 Add **es** instead of **s** to the end of the word
e.g. bunch[5] → bunches
6 Change final **f** to **ve** before adding **s**
e.g. calf[6] → calves

☞ Can't find your word here? Take off <u>life</u> and look again

life⁶ ~belt ~boat ~blood ~buoy
life ~l cycle ~l force ~l guard
life ~l insurance ~l jacket
life ~less ~like ~line ~long
life ~l peer ~l raft
life ~saver ~l sciences ~l sentence
life ~-size ~-sized ~span
life ~l story ~style ~l support
life ~time ~-threatening
lift¹ ~-off
ligament
ligature
light¹ ~ly ~ness ~l bulb
light ~-fingered ~-footed
light ~l gate ~-headed ~-hearted
light ~house ~l intensity ~l meter
light ~l relief ~weight ~l year
lighten¹
lightmotif   leitmotif
lightning *[flash]   lightening *[making
                                      lighter]
lightning ~l conductor ~l strike
ligneous
ligue   league⁺
liing   lying⁺
like² ~able ~ness
like ~-minded ~wise
likely ~hood
liken¹
likwessent   liquescent
likwid   liquid⁺
likwidate   liquidate²⁺
lilac
Lilliputian
lilt¹

lily⁴ ~l pad ~-white
lima bean
limb ~ed ~less
limber¹ ~l up
limbo¹ ~es
lime² ~light ~stone ~l tree
Lime disease   Lyme disease
limerick
limf   lymph⁺
limit¹ ~ation ~less
limousine
limozeen   limousine
limp¹ ~ly ~ness
limpet
limpid
linage *[number of lines]   lineage *[ancestry]
linch   lynch¹⁺
linchpin
line² ~l graph ~l manager ~sman
lineage *[ancestry]   linage *[number of
                                      lines]
lineament *[features]   liniment *[ointment]
linear ~l accelerator
linen ~l basket ~l cupboard
linger¹
lingerie
lingo⁵
lingua franca
linguist ~ic ~ics
liniment *[ointment]   lineament *[features]
lining
linjerie   lingerie
link¹ ~age ~-up
links *[joins]   lynx *[animal]
linnet
lino ~cut
linoleum
linseed ~-oil

KEY TO SPELLING RULES

Red words are wrong. **Black** words are correct.

~   Add the suffix or word directly to the main word, without a space or hyphen
    e.g. ash ~en ~tray → **ashen ashtray**
~- Add a hyphen to the main word before adding the next word
    e.g. blow ~-dry → **blow-dry**

~l Leave a space between the main word and the next word
    e.g. decimal ~l place → **decimal place**
+   By finding this word in its **correct** alphabetical order, you can find related words
    e.g. about⁺ → **about-face about-turn**
*   Draws attention to words that may be confused
TM Means the word is a trademark

lint		litany⁴	
linx	lynx	lite *[food label]	light¹ *[all meanings]⁺
lion ~ess ~-hearted ~ise		litel	little²⁺
lip³ ~l gloss ~-read		litemoteef	leitmotif
lip ~l service ~stick		liten	lighten¹
lipid		literacy literate	
liquefaction		literal ~ly	
liquefy⁴		literary	
liquescent		literature	
liqueur *[sweet alcohol]		litergy	liturgy⁺
liquid ~ity ~l asset		litewait	lightweight
liquidate² liquidator		lithe ~ly ~some	
liquidation		lithium ~l battery	
liquidise³ liquidiser		lithograph lithography	
liquor *[alcohol, liquid]	liqueur *[sweet alcohol]	litigant	
		litigate² litigator	
liquorice		litigation	
lirch	lurch¹⁺	litigious ~ly ~ness	
lire	liar *[tells lies], lyre *[musical]⁺	litly	lightly
		litmus ~l paper	
liric	lyric⁺	litning	lightening *[making lighter],
liricist	lyricist⁺		lightning *[flash]⁺
lirk	lurk¹		
lise	lease²⁺	litre *[measurement]	
lisence	licence *[document]⁺, license² *[give permit]	litter¹ *[rubbish]	lighter *[fire, colour, weight]
lisensheate	licentiate	little² ~l finger	
lisenshus	licentious⁺	littrit	literate
lisp¹		liturgy⁴ liturgical	
lissen	listen¹	live² ~-in	
lissom		live ~l rail ~stock ~l wire	
list¹ ~l price		livelihood	
listen¹		lively⁴	
listening ~l device ~l post		liven¹ ~l up	
listeria		liver ~ish ~l sausage	
listless ~ly ~ness		liver ~l spot ~wort	
lit		livery⁴ ~l stable	
		livid	

KEY TO SUFFIXES AND COMPOUNDS

These rules are explained on pages ix to x.

1 Keep the word the same before adding ed, er, est, ing
  e.g. cool¹ → cooled, cooler, coolest, cooling
2 Take off final e before adding ed, er, est, ing
  e.g. fine² → fined, finer, finest, fining
3 Double final consonant before adding ed, er, est, ing
  e.g. thin³ → thinned, thinner, thinnest, thinning

4 Change final y to i before adding ed, er, es, est, ly, ness
  e.g. tidy⁴ → tidied, tidier, tidies, tidiest, tidily, tidiness
  Keep final y before adding ing e.g. tidying
5 Add es instead of s to the end of the word
  e.g. bunch⁵ → bunches
6 Change final f to ve before adding s
  e.g. calf⁶ → calves

living ~| death ~| fossil ~| hell
living ~| quarters ~| room
living ~| wage ~| will
livry   livery⁴⁺
lizard
llama *[animal]   lama *[monk]
load¹ *[weight]   lode *[mineral]⁺
loaf⁶ *[bread]
loaf¹ *[laze] ~| around
loam *[rich soil] ~y
loan¹ *[lend] ~| shark   lone *[alone]⁺
loath *[reluctant]
loathe² *[hate] ~some
lob³
lobby⁴ ~ist
lobe
lobelia
lobotomy⁴
lobster ~| pot
local ~ly ~| anaesthetic ~| authority
localise² localisation
locality⁴
locate² locator
location
loch *[lake]   lock¹ *[door]⁺
Loch Ness Monster
lock¹ *[door, canal]   loch *[lake]
lock ~jaw ~smith
locket
locomotion locomotive
locum
locus loci
locust
lode *[mineral] ~stone   load¹ *[weight]
lodge² ~ings ~ment
loft¹ lofty⁴
log³ ~book ~| cabin ~-jam
log ~| off ~-on ~| out

loganberry⁴
logarithm ~ic
loge   lodge²⁺
loggerheads
logic ~al ~ally ~ian
logistics
logo *[sign]
LOGO™ *[computer language]
loin ~cloth
loiter¹
lojic   logic⁺
lok   loch *[lake],
                              lock¹ *[door]⁺
lokal   local⁺
lokalise   localise²⁺
lokality   locality⁴
lokate   locate²⁺
lokomoshun   locomotion⁺
lokum   locum
lokust   locust
lokwacious   loquacious⁺
loll¹
lollipop lolly⁴
lone *[alone]   loan¹ *[lend]⁺
lone ~| some ~| wolf
lonely⁴
loner
lonjeree   lingerie

☞ Can't find your word here? Take off **long** and look
again

long¹ ~-distance ~| division
long ~hand ~| haul ~| johns
long ~| jump ~-lasting ~-life
long ~-lived ~-lost ~-range ~-sighted
long ~-standing ~-suffering
long ~-term ~| wave ~-winded
longevity

KEY TO SPELLING RULES

Red words are wrong. **Black** words are correct.

~   Add the suffix or word directly to the main word,
    without a space or hyphen
    e.g. ash ~en ~tray → ashen ashtray
~- Add a hyphen to the main word before adding the
    next word
    e.g. blow ~-dry → blow-dry

~| Leave a space between the main word and the next
    word
    e.g. decimal ~| place → decimal place
+   By finding this word in its **correct** alphabetical
    order, you can find related words
    e.g. about⁺ → about-face about-turn
*   Draws attention to words that may be confused
TM Means the word is a trademark

longing ~ly
longitude
longitudinal ~ly
lonjevity   longevity
loo *[toilet]   lieu *[in lieu of]
lood   lewd+
loofah
look[1] ~alike ~-in ~ism ~out
looker ~-on
looking glass
loom[1] *[large, weaving]
loominessens   luminescence
loonatic   lunatic+
loony[4]
loop[1] ~hole
loopy[4]
loose[2] *[not tight]   lose *[not win]+
loose ~ly ~ness ~-leaf
loosen[1] ~ up
loot[1] *[goods]   lute *[musical]
loova   louvre
lop[3] *[cut] ~sided
lope[2] *[run]
loquacious ~ly ~ness
lord[1] *[noble] ~ly ~ship   laud[1] *[praise]
Lord ~ Justice ~ Mayor
Lords [the]
Lord's Prayer
lordable   laudable+
lore *[tradition]   law *[rule]+
loreful   lawful+
lorgnette
lorless   lawless+
lornch   launch[1]+
lornder   launder[1]+
lorndry   laundry[4]+
lornmower   lawnmower
lornyet   lorgnette

lorreate   laureate
lorrel   laurel[3]
lorry[4]
lose *[not win]   loose[2] *[not tight]+
loser   losing
loshun   lotion
loss *[thing lost] ~ adjuster
loss ~ leader ~-making
lost *[past of lose]
lost ~-and-found ~ property
lot
lotion
lottery[4]
lotto
lottree   lottery[4]
lotus
loud[1] ~ly ~ness
loud ~mouth ~speaker
lounge[2] ~ suit
louse[2] ~ up
lousy[4]
lout ~ish
louvre ~d
lovable
love[2] ~ affair ~bird ~bite
love ~ letter ~ life
love ~making ~sick ~song
lovely[4]
loving ~ly
low[1] ~ness ~-cal ~-cut ~down
low ~-fat ~-flying ~-key
low ~lander ~lands ~life ~-lying
low ~-paid ~-pressure ~ profile
low ~-risk ~ season ~-spirited
low ~ tech ~ tide
lowd   loud+
lower[1] ~ case ~ class
lowly[4]

KEY TO SUFFIXES AND COMPOUNDS

These rules are explained on pages ix to x.

1 Keep the word the same before adding ed, er, est, ing
    e.g. cool[1] → cooled, cooler, coolest, cooling
2 Take off final e before adding ed, er, est, ing
    e.g. fine[2] → fined, finer, finest, fining
3 Double final consonant before adding ed, er, est, ing
    e.g. thin[3] → thinned, thinner, thinnest, thinning

4 Change final y to i before adding ed, er, es, est, ly, ness
    e.g. tidy[4] → tidied, tidier, tidies, tidiest, tidily, tidiness
    Keep final y before adding ing e.g. tidying
5 Add es instead of s to the end of the word
    e.g. bunch[5] → bunches
6 Change final f to ve before adding s
    e.g. calf[6] → calves

lownge	lounge² ⁺	lull¹	
lowse	louse² ⁺	lullaby⁴	
lowsy	lousy⁴	lumbago	
lowt	lout⁺	lumbar *[back] ~| puncture	
loyal ~ism ~ist ~ly		lumber¹ *[move]	
loyalty⁴		lumberjack	
loyer	lawyer	lume	loom¹
loyn	loin	luminary⁴	
loyter	loiter¹	luminescence luminescent	
lozenge		luminous luminosity	
lu	lieu *[in lieu of],	lump¹ lumpy⁴	
	loo *[toilet]	lunacy⁴	
lubricant		lunar ~| calendar	
lubricate² lubricator		lunar ~| module ~| month	
lubrication		lunasy	lunacy⁴
lucid ~ity ~ly ~ness		lunatic ~| asylum ~| fringe	
Lucifer		lunch¹ ~es ~| hour ~time ~voucher	
luck lucky⁴		luncheon	
lucksuriate	luxuriate² ⁺	luner	lunar⁺
lucksurius	luxurious⁺	luney	loony⁴
lucksury	luxury⁴	lung *[breathing]	
lucosite	leucocyte	lunge² *[move]	
Lucozade™		lunj	lunge²
lucrative ~ly		lunshun	luncheon
lucre		lupin	
Luddite		lurch¹ ~es	
ludicrous ~ly		lure²	
lufa	loofah	Lurex™	
lug³ ~| around ~hole		lurid ~ly	
luge		lurk¹	
luggage ~| rack		lurn	learn¹ ⁺
luggige	luggage⁺	lurning	learning⁺
lugubrious ~ly ~ness		luscious ~ly ~ness	
luj	luge	luse	loose² *[not tight],
lukemia	leukaemia		lose *[not win]⁺
luker	lucre	lush¹ ~ly ~ness	
lukewarm		lushus	luscious⁺
lukrative	lucrative⁺	lusid	lucid⁺

Lusifer	Lucifer	lybrary	library[4]
lusse	loose[2+]	lyce	lice
lussen	loosen[1+]	lycée	
lust[1] ~ful ~fully		lychee	
lustre lustrous		lychen	lichen[+]
lusty[4]		Lycra™	
lute [musical]	loot[1] *[goods]	lydo	lido
Lutheran		lye *[chemical]	lie *[down, untruth][+]
luv *[term of address]	love[2] *[all meanings][+]	lyer	liar *[tells lies],
luvly	lovely[4]		lyre *[musical][+]
luxuriant ~ly luxuriance		lying ~-in-state	
luxuriate[2]		lyme	lime[2+]
luxurious ~ly ~ness		Lyme disease	
luxury[4]		lymph ~atic ~l node ~oma	

☞ Can't find your word here? Look under **ly**

ly	lie *[down, untruth][+],	lynch[1] ~l mob	
	lye *[chemical]	lynx[5] *[animal]	links *[joins]
lyaise	liaise[2+]	lyon	lion[+]
lybel	libel[3+]	lyre *[musical] ~bird	liar *[tells lies]
lyberal	liberal[+]	lyric ~al	
		lyricist lyricism	
		lyrics	

KEY TO SUFFIXES AND COMPOUNDS

These rules are explained on pages ix to x.

1 Keep the word the same before adding **ed, er, est, ing**
   e.g. cool[1] → cooled, cooler, coolest, cooling
2 Take off final **e** before adding **ed, er, est, ing**
   e.g. fine[2] → fined, finer, finest, fining
3 Double final consonant before adding **ed, er, est, ing**
   e.g. thin[3] → thinned, thinner, thinnest, thinning

4 Change final **y** to **i** before adding **ed, er, es, est, ly, ness**
   e.g. tidy[4] → tidied, tidier, tidies, tidiest, tidily, tidiness
   Keep final **y** before adding **ing** e.g. tidying
5 Add **es** instead of **s** to the end of the word
   e.g. bunch[5] → bunches
6 Change final **f** to **ve** before adding **s**
   e.g. calf[6] → calves

ma
ma'am
mac *[raincoat]   Mach *[unit of speed]
macabre
macadam
macadamia ~| nut
macaroni
macaroon
macaw
mace *[spice, stick]   maize *[corn],
                         maze *[labyrinth]
Mach *[unit of speed]   mac *[raincoat]
machete
Machiavellian
machinations
machine² ~| gun ~-made
machine ~-readable ~| translation
machinery   machinist
macho   machismo
machure   mature²⁺
mackerel
mackintosh⁵
macor   macaw
macramé
macro ~biotic ~cosm ~economics
macroscopic
mad³ *[crazy] ~ly   made *[built],
mad ~ness ~cap ~man   maid *[girl, servant]
madam
madden¹
made *[built]   mad *[crazy],
made ~-to-measure   maid *[girl, servant]
made ~-to-order
Madeira
Madonna
madrigal
maelstrom
maer   mayor⁺

maestro
mafia   mafioso
maffs   maths
magazine
magenta
mager   major¹⁺
magestic   majestic⁺
magesty   majesty⁴
maggot
Magi
magic ~al ~ally
magician
magisterial ~ly
magistrate
magma
Magna Carta
magnanimity   magnanimous
magnate *[person]   magnet *[iron]
magnesia   magnesium
magnet *[iron]   magnate *[person]
magnetic ~ism ~| tape
magnetise²   magnetisation
magnificence
magnificent ~ly
magnify⁴   magnification
magnifying glass
magnitude
magnolia
magnum ~| opus
magpie
maharaja   maharani
Maharishi
mah-jong
mahm   ma'am
mahogany
maid *[girl, servant] ~en   made *[built, did]
mail¹ *[post] ~bag   male *[man]⁺
mail ~box ~| order ~shot

KEY TO SPELLING RULES

Red words are wrong. **Black** words are correct.

~   Add the suffix or word directly to the main word,
     without a space or hyphen
     e.g. ash ~en ~tray → ashen ashtray
~-   Add a hyphen to the main word before adding the
     next word
     e.g. blow ~-dry → blow-dry

~| Leave a space between the main word and the next
     word
     e.g. decimal ~| place → decimal place
+   By finding this word in its **correct** alphabetical
     order, you can find related words
     e.g. about⁺ → about-face about-turn
*   Draws attention to words that may be confused
TM   Means the word is a trademark

maim[1]
main *[chief]   mane *[hair]
main ~ly ~l clause ~land
main ~line ~stay ~stream
maintain[1]
maintenance
mais   mace *[spice, stick]
maisonette
mait   mate[2]
maître d'
maize *[corn]   mace *[spice, stick],
                                 maze *[labyrinth]
majenta   magenta
majestic ~ally
majesty[4]
majic   magic[+]
majishun   magician
majistrate   magistrate
majong   mah-jong
major[1] ~ette
majority[4]
mak   Mach *[unit of speed],
                                 make *[build][+]
makaber   macabre
makadam   macadam[+]
makaroni   macaroni
makaroon   macaroon
make   maker
make ~-believe ~shift ~-up
makerel   mackerel
Makiavellian   Machiavellian
making
makintosh   mackintosh[5]
makramay   macramé
makro   macro[+]
makroskopik   macroscopic
maksi   maxi
maksim   maxim

maksimise   maximise[2]
maksimum   maximum
malachite
maladjusted   maladjustment
maladroit ~ness
malady[4]
malaise
malajusted   maladjusted[+]
malakite   malachite
malapropism
malard   mallard[+]
malaria
malcontent
male *[man]   mail[1] *[post][+]
male ~-dominated
malediction
malevolence   malevolent
malform[1] ~ation
malfunction[1]
malice
malicious ~ly ~ness
malign[1]
malignancy[4]
malignant ~l tumour
maline   malign[1]
malinger[1]
malishus   malicious[+]
maliss   malice
mall *[shops]   maul[1] *[hurt]
malladroyt   maladroit
mallard
malleable   malleability
mallet
malnewtrishun   malnutrition
malnourished
malnutrition
malodorous
Malpighian layer

KEY TO SUFFIXES AND COMPOUNDS

These rules are explained on pages ix to x.

1 Keep the word the same before adding **ed, er, est, ing**
  e.g. cool[1] → cooled, cooler, coolest, cooling
2 Take off final **e** before adding **ed, er, est, ing**
  e.g. fine[2] → fined, finer, finest, fining
3 Double final consonant before adding **ed, er, est, ing**
  e.g. thin[3] → thinned, thinner, thinnest, thinning

4 Change final **y** to **i** before adding **ed, er, es, est, ly, ness**
  e.g. tidy[4] → tidied, tidier, tidies, tidiest, tidily, tidiness
  Keep final **y** before adding **ing** e.g. tidying
5 Add **es** instead of **s** to the end of the word
  e.g. bunch[5] → bunches
6 Change final **f** to **ve** before adding **s**
  e.g. calf[6] → calves

malpractice

malt ~ed ~| extract

malt ~| liquor ~| whisky

maltreat[1] ~ment

mame   maim[1]

mammal ~ian

mammary ~| gland

mammon

mammoth

man[3] ~eater ~fully ~hole ~hood ~hunt

man ~kind ~-of-war ~power

manacle[2]

manage[2] *[cope] ~able   ménage *[household]

management

manager *[person]   manger *[crib]

manager ~ess ~ial

managing ~| director ~| partner

mandarin

mandatary *   mandatory *

  [receives mandate]   [compulsory]

mandate[2]

mandatory *   mandatary *

  [compulsory]   [receives mandate]

mandible

mandolin

mane *[hair]   main *[chief][+]

manequin   mannequin

maner   manner *[method],

          manor *[estate]

manewer   manure[2]

manganese

mange   mangy

manger *[crib]   manager *[person]

mangle[2]

mango[5]

mangrove

manhandle[2]

mania

maniac *[mad person]   manioc *[root]

manic *[mad] ~| depressive

manicure[2]   manicurist

manifest[1] ~ation ~ly

manifesto

manifold[1]

manikin *[little man]   mannequin *[model]

manila ~| envelope

manioc *[root]   manic *[mad],

          maniac *[mad person]

manipulate[2]

manipulation   manipulative

manipulator

maniqure   manicure[2+]

manjer   manger

Manks   Manx

manly[4]

manna *[food]   manner *[method],

          manor *[estate]

mannequin *[model]   manikin *[little man]

manner *[method]   manna *[food],

          manor *[estate]

mannered

mannerism

manners

mannifest   manifest[1+]

manoeuvre[2]   manoeuvrable

manor *[estate]   manna *[food],

          manner *[method]

manshun   mansion

mansion

manslaughter

manslorter   manslaughter

mantel *[fireplace]   mantle[2] *[cloak]

mantelpiece

mantilla

mantis

mantle[2] *[cloak]   mantel *[fireplace][+]

KEY TO SPELLING RULES

Red words are wrong. **Black** words are correct.

~   Add the suffix or word directly to the main word, without a space or hyphen
    e.g. ash ~en ~tray → **ashen ashtray**

~--   Add a hyphen to the main word before adding the next word
    e.g. blow ~-dry → **blow-dry**

~| Leave a space between the main word and the next word
    e.g. decimal ~| place → **decimal place**

+   By finding this word in its **correct** alphabetical order, you can find related words
    e.g. about[+] → **about-face about-turn**

*   Draws attention to words that may be confused

TM   Means the word is a trademark

manual ~ly ~l work ~l worker	
manufacture[2]	
manure[2]	
manuscript	
manuver	manoeuvre[2+]
Manx ~l cat	
many	
Maoism	
Maori	
map[3]	
maple ~l leaf ~l syrup	
mar[3]	
maraschino ~l cherry	
marathon	
maraud[1]	
marble[2]	
march[1] *[walk] ~es ~-past	
March *[month]	
mare *[horse]	mayor *[official][+]
margarine	
margarita	
margin ~al ~ally	
marige	marriage[+]
marigold	
marijuana	
marina *[harbour]	marine *[soldier, sea]
marinade	
marinate[2]	
marine[1] *[soldier, sea]	marina *[harbour]
marionette	
marital *[marriage]	martial *[war][+]
maritime	
marjarin	margarine
marjin	margin[+]
marjoram	
mark[1] ~edly	
market[1] ~l place ~l research ~l share	
markey	marquee

Marksism	Marxism[+]
marksman ~ship	
markwis	marquis
marlin *[fish]	merlin *[bird]
marmalade	
Marmite™	
maroon[1]	
marord	maraud[1+]
marquee *[tent]	
marquis *[nobleman]	
marriage ~able ~l certificate	
marriage ~l licence	
marriwahna	marijuana
marrow ~bone	
marry[4] married	
Mars Martian	
Marseillaise	
marsewpial	marsupial
marsh ~mallow marshy	
marshal[3] *[arrange]	martial *[war][+]
Marshan	Martian
marsipan	marzipan
marsupial	
marten *[animal]	martin *[bird]
marterise	martyrise[2]
martial *[war]	marshal[3] *[arrange],
martial ~l arts ~l law	marital *[marriage]
Martian	
martin *[bird]	marten *[animal]
Martini™	
martyr[1] ~dom	
martyrise[2]	
marune	maroon[1]
marvel[3]	
marvellous ~ly	
Marxism Marxist	
marzipan	
masaker	massacre[2]

KEY TO SUFFIXES AND COMPOUNDS

These rules are explained on pages ix to x.

1 Keep the word the same before adding **ed, er, est, ing**
e.g. cool[1] → cooled, cooler, coolest, cooling
2 Take off final **e** before adding **ed, er, est, ing**
e.g. fine[2] → fined, finer, finest, fining
3 Double final consonant before adding **ed, er, est, ing**
e.g. thin[3] → thinned, thinner, thinnest, thinning

4 Change final **y** to **i** before adding **ed, er, es, est, ly, ness**
e.g. tidy[4] → tidied, tidier, tidies, tidiest, tidily, tidiness
Keep final **y** before adding **ing** e.g. tidying
5 Add **es** instead of **s** to the end of the word
e.g. bunch[5] → bunches
6 Change final **f** to **ve** before adding **s**
e.g. calf[6] → calves

masarge   massage[2]

mascara

mascot

masculine   masculinity

mash[1]

mashetee   machete

mashinations   machinations

mashine   machine[2+]

mashinery   machinery[+]

mask[1] *[cover]   masque *
                         [entertainment]

maskara   mascara

maskerade   masquerade[2]

masking tape

maskot   mascot

maskuline   masculine[+]

masochism

masochist ~ic ~ically

mason *[builder] ~ry   Mason *[society]

masonic

masque *[entertainment]   mask[1] *[cover][+]

masquerade[2]

masqulin   masculine[+]

mass[1] *[amount] ~es

mass ~| media ~-produced ~| production

Mass *[church]

massacre[2]

massage[2]

massectomee   mastectomy

masseur   masseuse

Massia   Messiah[+]

massive ~ly

mast ~| head

mastectomy

master[1] ~ly ~y ~| key

master ~mind ~piece ~| plan

Master ~| of Arts ~| of the Rolls ~| of Science

masterbate   masturbate[2+]

masterful ~ly

mastermind[1]

masticate[2]   mastication

mastiff

masturbate[2]   masturbation

mat[3] *[rug]   mate[2] *[partner],
                          matt *[dull]

matador

match[1] ~es ~box ~less ~maker

match ~| point ~stick ~wood

mate[2]

matedor   matador

material ~ly

materialise[2]   materialisation

materialist ~ic   materialism

maternal ~ly

maternity ~| leave ~| ward

mathematician

mathematics   mathematical

maths

matinée

matins

matiriel   material[+]

matirielise   materialise[2+]

matriarch ~al ~y

matriculate[2]   matriculation

matrimony   matrimonial

matrix   matrices

matron ~ly

matt *[dull] ~| finish   mat[3] *[rug]

matter[1]

matting

mattress[5]

mature[2] ~ly   maturity

maturnal   maternal[+]

maturnity   maternity[+]

matzo

maul[1] *[hurt]   mall *[shops]

KEY TO SPELLING RULES

Red words are wrong. **Black** words are correct.

~   Add the suffix or word directly to the main word, without a space or hyphen
    e.g. ash ~en ~tray → ashen ashtray

~-   Add a hyphen to the main word before adding the next word
    e.g. blow ~-dry → blow-dry

~| Leave a space between the main word and the next word
    e.g. decimal ~| place → decimal place

+   By finding this word in its **correct** alphabetical order, you can find related words
    e.g. about+ → about-face about-turn

*   Draws attention to words that may be confused

TM   Means the word is a trademark

mausoleum
mauve
maverick
mawkish ~ness
mawl   maul[1] *[hurt],
                         maul *[shops]
mawrayz   mores
maxi
maxim
maximal ~ly
maximise[2]
maximum
may *[perhaps] ~be
May *[month] mayfly[4] maypole
mayce   mace
mayday *[call for help]
May Day *[1st May]
mayde   made *[built],
                   maid *[girl, servant][+]
Mayflower [the]
mayhem
maym   maim[1]
mayonnaise
mayor *[official] ~al ~ess mare *[horse]
maysonet   maisonette
mayt   mate[2]
maze *[labyrinth]   maize *[corn]
me
mea culpa
mead
meadow
meagre ~ly
meal ~time
mealy ~-mouthed ~ing
mean *[average, imply]
mean[1] *[nasty] ~ie ~ly ~ness
meander[1]
meaning ~ful ~fully ~less

means ~-tested
meant
meantime
meanwhile
measles
measly
measurable   measurably
measure[2] ~less ~ment
meat *[flesh] ~ball ~loaf   meet *[encounter][+],
                              mete[2] *[out]
meatier *[more meaty]   meteor *[rock][+]
meaty[4]
mecanic   mechanic[+]
mecanise   mechanise[2+]
Mecca
mechanic ~al ~ally ~s
mechanise[2]   mechanisation
mechanism
medal *[award]   meddle[2] *[interfere][+]
medallion
medallist
meddle[2] *[interfere]   medal *[award]
meddler *[interferes]   medlar *[fruit]
meddow   meadow
media ~l coverage ~l hype
median
mediate[2] mediation mediator
medic
medical ~ly ~l practitioner ~l school
medicament
medicate[2] medication
medicine medicinal
medieval
mediocre mediocrity[4]
meditate[2] meditation
Mediterranean
medium ~-sized ~-term ~l wave
medlar *[fruit]   meddler *[interferes]

KEY TO SUFFIXES AND COMPOUNDS

These rules are explained on pages ix to x.

1 Keep the word the same before adding **ed, er, est, ing**
e.g. cool[1] → cooled, cooler, coolest, cooling
2 Take off final **e** before adding **ed, er, est, ing**
e.g. fine[2] → fined, finer, finest, fining
3 Double final consonant before adding **ed, er, est, ing**
e.g. thin[3] → thinned, thinner, thinnest, thinning

4 Change final **y** to **i** before adding **ed, er, es, est, ly, ness**
e.g. tidy[4] → tidied, tidier, tidies, tidiest, tidily, tidiness
Keep final **y** before adding **ing** e.g. tidying
5 Add **es** instead of **s** to the end of the word
e.g. bunch[5] → bunches
6 Change final **f** to **ve** before adding **s**
e.g. calf[6] → calves

medley	memorabilia
medulla	memorable memorably
meek ~ly ~ness	memorandum
meet *[encounter] ~ing meat *[flesh],	memorise[2]
mete[2] *[out]	memory[4] memorial
mega ~bit ~byte ~cycle	memrabilia memorabilia
mega ~dose ~hertz	men
mega ~phone ~star ~ton	menace[2]
megafone megaphone	ménage ~| à trois
megalith ~ic	menagerie
megalomania megalomaniac	menarj ménage[+]
Meka Mecca	mend[1]
mekanic mechanic[+]	mendacious ~ly mendacity
mekanise mechanise[2+]	menial ~ly
mekanistic mechanistic	meningitis
melancholic	meniss menace[2]
melancholy melancholia	menopause menopausal
melancolick melancholic	menshun mention[1]
melanoma	menstrual ~| period
melay mêlée	menstruate[2] menstruation
meld[1]	menswear
mêlée	mental ~ly ~| arithmetic
melen melon	mentality[4]
mellifluous	menthol
mellow[1]	mention[1]
melodic	mentor[1]
melodrama melodramatic	menu
melody[4] melodious	meny many
melon	mer myrrh
melstrom maelstrom	merang meringue
melt[1] ~down	mercantile mercantilism
melting pot	mercenary[4]
member ~ship	merchandise[2]
Member of Parliament	merchant ~| bank ~| navy
membrane	merciful ~ly
memento[5]	merciless ~ly ~ness
memo	mercury *[metal] mercurial
memoirs	Mercury *[planet]

<u>**Key to Spelling Rules**</u>

Red words are wrong. **Black** words are correct.

~   Add the suffix or word directly to the main word, without a space or hyphen
e.g. ash ~en ~tray → ashen ashtray

~-   Add a hyphen to the main word before adding the next word
e.g. blow ~-dry → blow-dry

~| Leave a space between the main word and the next word
e.g. decimal ~| place → decimal place

+   By finding this word in its **correct** alphabetical order, you can find related words
e.g. about+ → about-face about-turn

*   Draws attention to words that may be confused

TM   Means the word is a trademark

mercy[4]

merder   murder[1+]

mere ~ly   merest

merge[2]   merger

meridian

meridional

meringue

merit[1]

merlin *[bird]   marlin *[fish]

mermaid   merman

mermer   murmur[1]

merriment

merry[4] ~go-round ~-making

mersiless   merciless+

mersinary   mercenary[4]

merth   mirth+

mesels   measles

mesh[1]

meshurabul   measurable

meshure   measure[2+]

mesia   messiah+

mesige   message

mesmerise[2]

mess[1]   messy[4]

message ~l board

messaging

messenger

Messiah   Messianic

met

metabolic   metabolism

metacarpal

metadata

metafor   metaphor+

metafysics   metaphysics

metafysicul   metaphysical+

metal *[material]   mettle *[spirit]

metal ~l fatigue ~work

metallic

metallurgist

metallurgy   metallurgical

metamorphose[2]   metamorphosis

metaphor ~ic ~ical ~ically

metaphysical ~ly

metaphysics

mete[2] *[out]   meat *[flesh]+,
                   meet *[encounter]

meteor ~ological ~ologist ~ology

meteoric

meteorite

meter[1] *[machine]   metre *[measure]+

methadone

methane

method ~ical ~ically

Methodist   Methodism

methodology[4]

methylated spirits   meths

meticulous ~ly

metior   meteor

metre *[measure]   meter[1] *[machine]

metric ~al ~ation

metronome

metropolis   metropolitan

metsosoprano   mezzo-soprano

mettle *[spirit]   metal *[material]+

mew[1]

mewchual   mutual+

mewl[1] *[cry]   mule *[donkey]

mewnicipal   municipal+

mewral   mural

mews *[cat, stable]   muse[2] *[think]

mewseum   museum

mewsik   music+

mewsishan   musician

mewt   mute[2+]

mewtate   mutate+

mewtilate   mutilate[2+]

KEY TO SUFFIXES AND COMPOUNDS

These rules are explained on pages ix to x.

1 Keep the word the same before adding **ed, er, est, ing**
e.g. cool[1] → cooled, cooler, coolest, cooling

2 Take off final **e** before adding **ed, er, est, ing**
e.g. fine[2] → fined, finer, finest, fining

3 Double final consonant before adding **ed, er, est, ing**
e.g. thin[3] → thinned, thinner, thinnest, thinning

4 Change final **y** to **i** before adding **ed, er, es, est,
ly, ness**
e.g. tidy[4] → tidied, tidier, tidies, tidiest, tidily,
tidiness
Keep final **y** before adding **ing** e.g. tidying

5 Add **es** instead of **s** to the end of the word
e.g. bunch[5] → bunches

6 Change final **f** to **ve** before adding **s**
e.g. calf[6] → calves

mewtinear	mutineer[+]
mewtiny	mutiny[4]
mezzanine	
mezzo ~-soprano	
miander	meander[1]
miaow[1]	
mica	
mice	
Michaelmas ~l daisy	
micro ~biology ~biologist ~chip	
micro ~cosm ~economic	
micro ~electronics ~fiche ~film	
micro ~light ~management ~meter	
micro ~phone ~processor ~scope	
micro ~scopic ~wave	
microbe microbial	
micron	
mid ~day ~night ~point ~riff	
mid ~shipman ~summer ~way	
middle ~l age ~-aged ~l class	
middle ~man ~l school ~weight	
Middle ~l Ages ~l East	
middling	
midge	
midget	
midia	media[+]
midian	median
midiate	mediate[2+]
midium	medium[+]
Midlands [the]	
midst *[middle]	mist *[fog],
	missed *[did not get]
midwife[6] midwifery	
mien *[appearance]	mean *[nasty, imply,
	average][+]
miget	midget
might *[strength, may]	mite *[small child,
	parasite]

mighty[4]	
migraine	
migrant	
migrate[2] migration	
migratory	
migt	might
mika	mica
Mikalmus	Michaelmas
mike	
mikro	micro[+]
mikrobiology	microbiology[+]
mikron	micron
mikroskope	microscope[+]
miksamatosis	myxomatosis
mild[1] ~ly ~ness	
mildew	
mile ~age ~stone	
militancy militant	
military[4] ~l service militarism	
militate[2]	
militia	
milk[1] ~l fever ~l float	
milk ~man ~l round	
milk ~shake ~l tooth	
milky[4]	
Milky Way	
mill[1] ~pond ~stone	
millennium millennia	
millet ~l seed	
milligram millilitre millimetre	
milliner millinery	
million ~aire ~airess ~th	
millipede	
millivolt milliwatt	
milometer	
mime[2]	
mimic mimicked mimicking	
mimicry	

---

mimosa
minaret
mince[2] ~meat ~l pie
mind[1] ~ful ~-bending ~-blowing
mind ~-boggling ~l reader ~set
mindless ~ly ~ness
mine[2] ~field ~sweeper
miner *[worker]   minor *[lesser]
mineral
mineralogy   mineralogist
minestrone
mingle[2]
mingy[4]
mini ~beast ~bus ~l series ~skirt
miniature   miniaturist
miniaturise[2]
minim
minimal   minimalise[2]
minimise[2]
minimum
minion
minister[1] ~ial
ministration
ministronee   minestrone
ministry[4]
mink
minks *[animals]   minx[5] *[girl]
minnow
minor *[lesser] ~l league   miner *[worker]
minority[4]
minster
minstrel
mint[1] ~l sauce
minuet
minus ~l sign
minuscule
minute *[time]
minute[2] *[small] ~ly ~ness

minutiae
minx[5]
miopia   myopia[+]
miracle
miraculous ~ly
mirage
mirarj   mirage
mire[2]
mirge   merge[2]
miriad   myriad
mirk   murk[+]
mirmade   mermaid
mirmer   murmur[1]
mirror[1] ~l image
mirth
mirtle   myrtle

> ☞ Can't find your word here? Take off **mis** and look again

misadventure
misanthrope   misanthropic
misanthropist   misanthropy
misapply[4]
misapprehension
misappropriate[2]   misappropriation
misbehave[2]   misbehaviour
miscalculate[2]   miscalculation
miscarry[4]   miscarriage
miscast
miscellany[4]   miscellaneous
mischance
mischief   mischievous
misconceive[2]
misconception
misconduct
misconstrue[2]
miscount[1]
miscreant

KEY TO SUFFIXES AND COMPOUNDS

These rules are explained on pages ix to x.

1 Keep the word the same before adding **ed, er, est, ing**
   e.g. cool[1] → cooled, cooler, coolest, cooling
2 Take off final **e** before adding **ed, er, est, ing**
   e.g. fine[2] → fined, finer, finest, fining
3 Double final consonant before adding **ed, er, est, ing**
   e.g. thin[3] → thinned, thinner, thinnest, thinning

4 Change final **y** to **i** before adding **ed, er, es, est, ly, ness**
   e.g. tidy[4] → tidied, tidier, tidies, tidiest, tidily, tidiness
   Keep final **y** before adding **ing** e.g. tidying
5 Add **es** instead of **s** to the end of the word
   e.g. bunch[5] → bunches
6 Change final **f** to **ve** before adding **s**
   e.g. calf[6] → calves

misdemeanour

mise   mice

miser   miserly[4]

miserable   miserably

misery[4]

misfire[2]

misfit

misfortune

misgide   misguide[2]+

misgivings

misgovern[1] ~ment

misguide[2]   misguidance

mishandle[2]

mishap

mishear   misheard

mishun   mission+

misinform[1] ~ation

misinterpret[1] ~ation

misjudge[2] ~ment

miskondukt   misconduct

miskonseev   misconceive[2]

miskonstrue   misconstrue[2]

miskreant   miscreant

miskwote   misquote[2]

mislay ~ing   mislaid

mislead *[deceive] ~ing

misled *[past of mislead]

mismatch ~ed

misnomer

misogyny   misogynist

misplace[2] ~ment

misprint[1]

mispronounce[2]

mispronunciation

misquote[2]

misread ~ing

misrepresent[1] ~ation

misrule[2]

miss[1] ~es

missal *[prayer book]   missile *[weapon]

missed *[did not get]   midst *[middle],

                             mist *[fog]

missellany   miscellany[4]+

missel thrush

misshapen[1]

missile *[weapon]   missal *[prayer book]

missing ~l in action

missing ~l link ~l person

mission   missionary[4]

missive

misspell[1]   misspelt

misspend ~ing   misspent

misstate[2] ~ment

mist *[fog]   midst *[middle],

                            missed *[did not get]

mistake ~n ~nly   mistaking

mistakable

misterius   mysterious+

mistic   mystic

mistify   mystify[4]+

mistime[2]

mistique   mystique

mistletoe

mistook

mistreat[1] ~ment

mistress[5]

mistrust[1] ~ful

mistry   mystery[4]

misty[4]

misunderstand ~ing

misunderstood

misuse[2]

mite *[small child,   might *[strength,

         parasite]   may]

mith   myth+

mitigate[2]   mitigation

---

mitre² *[hat, joint]   meter¹ *[machine]

mitten

mity   mighty⁴

mix¹ ~ture ~-up

mixametosis   myxomatosis

mixed ~l blessing ~l doubles ~l grill

mizer   miser⁺

mizery   misery⁴

mizrabul   miserable⁺

mnemonic

moan¹ *[complain]   mown *[grass]

moat *[castle] ~ed   mote *[small speck]

mob³ ~l rule

mobile ~l phone

mobilise² mobilisation

mobility

moccasin

mocha

mock¹ ~ery ~-up

mode   modish

model³

modem

moderate² ~ly   moderator

moderation

modern ~ism ~ity

modernise² modernisation

modest ~ly ~y

modicum

modify⁴   modification

modulate²   modulator

modulation

module   modular

modurn   modern⁺

modurnise   modernise²⁺

modus ~l operandi ~l vivendi

mohair

moist¹ ~ness ~ure

moisten¹

moka   mocha

mokasin   moccasin

molar

molasses

molde   mould¹⁺

mole ~hill

molecule   molecular

molest¹ ~ation

mollify⁴

mollusc

mollycoddle²

molte   moult¹

molten

moment ~ous ~um

momentary⁴

monaky   monarchy⁴

monarch ~ic ~ical

monarchy⁴   monarchist

monastery⁴

monastic ~ism

Monday

monetary   monetarism

money ~ed   monies

money ~lender ~-making

mongoose

mongrel

monie   money⁺

monies

monitor¹ ~ing system

monk ~ish ~fish

monkey ~l business

☞ Can't find your word here? Take off **mono** and look again

---

monochrome   monochromatic

monocle

monogamous

monogamy   monogamist

KEY TO SUFFIXES AND COMPOUNDS

These rules are explained on pages ix to x.

1 Keep the word the same before adding **ed, er, est, ing**
e.g. cool¹ → cooled, cooler, coolest, cooling

2 Take off final **e** before adding **ed, er, est, ing**
e.g. fine² → fined, finer, finest, fining

3 Double final consonant before adding **ed, er, est, ing**
e.g. thin³ → thinned, thinner, thinnest, thinning

4 Change final **y** to **i** before adding **ed, er, es, est, ly, ness**
e.g. tidy⁴ → tidied, tidier, tidies, tidiest, tidily, tidiness
Keep final **y** before adding **ing** e.g. tidying

5 Add **es** instead of **s** to the end of the word
e.g. bunch⁵ → bunches

6 Change final **f** to **ve** before adding **s**
e.g. calf⁶ → calves

monogram   monograph

monokrome   monochrome⁺

monokside   monoxide

monolingual

monolith ~ic

monologue

monoplane

monopolisation

monopolise² monopolist

monopoly⁴

monorail

monosodium ~| glutamate

monosyllable   monosyllabic

monotone

monotonous ~ly   monotony

Monotype™

monoxide

monsewer   monsieur

monsieur

monsoon

monster   monstrous

monstrosity⁴

monsyer   monsieur

month ~ly

monument ~al ~ally

moo¹

mood *[temper]   mooed *[cow]

moody⁴

moon¹ ~beam ~light ~lit

moon ~scape ~shine ~stone

moor¹ *[ground, boat]   more *[greater

moor ~hen   quantity]⁺

moose *[deer]   mouse *[rat]⁺,

                        mousse *[pudding]

mooslee   muesli

moot¹ *[for debate]   mute² *[silent]⁺

moot ~| point

moove   move²

---

moovee   movie⁺

mop³ *[clean]

mope² *[do nothing]

moped *[bike]

mopped *[cleaned]

moral *[good] ~ly ~| majority

morale *[confidence]

moralise²

morality⁴

morass

moratorium

morbid ~ly ~ity

more *[greater quantity]   moor¹ *[ground, boat]

moreover

mores

morf   morph¹

morfeem   morpheme

morfia   morphia

morfine   morphine *[drug]

                           morpheme *
                           [unit of meaning]

morg   morgue

morgige   mortgage²

morgue

moribund

morkish   mawkish⁺

morl   mall *[shops],
                           maul¹ *[hurt]

morn *[morning]   mourn¹ *[grieve]

mornful   mournful⁺

morning

moron ~ic

morose ~ly

morph¹

morpheme *[unit of meaning] morphine *[drug]

morphia

morphine *[drug]   morpheme *
                           [meaning]

Morse ~| code

morsel

morsoleum   mausoleum

mortal ~ity ~ly

mortar[1] ~| board

mortgage[2]

mortify[4]   mortification

mortuary[4]   mortician

mosaic

Moses ~| basket

mosey[1] ~| along

moshun   motion[1+]

mosk   mosque

moskito   mosquito[5+]

mosque

mosquito[5] ~| net

moss[5] ~y

most ~ly

mote *[small speck]   moat[1] *[castle][+]

motel

moth ~eaten

mother[1] ~board ~hood ~-in-law

mother ~less ~| tongue

Mother ~| Earth ~| Nature

motherly[4]

Mother's Day

motif *[pattern]   motive *[cause]

motion[1] ~less

motivate[2]   motivator

motivation ~al

motive *[cause]   motif *[pattern]

motley ~| crew

motor[1] ~bike ~boat ~cade

motor ~| car ~cycle ~cyclist

motor ~home ~| racing

motor ~ist ~| vehicle ~way

motorise[2]

motto[5]

mould[1]   mouldy[4]

moult[1]

mound[1]

mount[1]

mountain ~ous

mountaineer[1]

Mountie

mourn[1] *[grieve]   morn *[morning]

mournful ~ly

mouse *[computer, rodent] mousse *[pudding]

mouse ~trap

moussaka

mousse *[pudding]   moose *[deer],
                           mouse *[computer,
                                       rodent][+]

moustache

mousy

mouth[1] ~ful ~| organ ~piece ~wash

mouth-to-mouth

movable ~| feast

move[2] ~ment

movie ~| star

mow ~er ~ing

mowed *[grass]   mode *[fashion][+]

Mowism   Maoism

mown *[grass]   moan[1] *[complain]

mownd   mound[1]

mowntain   mountain[+]

Mowri   Maori

mowse   mouse

mowsy   mousy

mowth   mouth[1+]

moyst   moist[1+]

MS-DOS

much ~-heralded ~ness

muck[1] ~-raking   mucky[4]

mucous *[containing slime] ~| membrane

mucus *[slime]

KEY TO SUFFIXES AND COMPOUNDS

These rules are explained on pages ix to x.

1 Keep the word the same before adding **ed, er, est, ing**
  e.g. **cool**[1] → cooled, cooler, coolest, cooling
2 Take off final **e** before adding **ed, er, est, ing**
  e.g. **fine**[2] → fined, finer, finest, fining
3 Double final consonant before adding **ed, er, est, ing**
  e.g. **thin**[3] → thinned, thinner, thinnest, thinning

4 Change final **y** to **i** before adding **ed, er, es, est, ly, ness**
  e.g. **tidy**[4] → tidied, tidier, tidies, tidiest, tidily, tidiness
  Keep final **y** before adding **ing** e.g. **tidying**
5 Add **es** instead of **s** to the end of the word
  e.g. **bunch**[5] → bunches
6 Change final **f** to **ve** before adding **s**
  e.g. **calf**[6] → calves

mud ~bath ~guard ~| pie
muddle²
muddy⁴
mue   mew¹⁺
muel   mewl¹ *[cry],
           mule *[donkey]
muesli
muff
muffin
muffle²
mufti
mug³ ~shot
muggins
muggy⁴
mujarhaddeen   mujaheddin
mujaheddin
mukus   mucous
mulberry⁴
mulch¹
mule *[donkey]   mewl¹ *[cry]
mullah
mulsh   mulch¹

> ☞ Can't find your word here? Take off **multi** and look
> again

multicoloured
multicultural ~ism
multifarious
multilateral ~ly
multilingual
multimedia ~player
multi-millionaire
multinational
multiple ~-choice ~| sclerosis
multiplex⁵
multiplicity
multiply⁴ multiplication
multiracial

multi-storey
multi-tasking
multitude multitudinous
multi-user
mum
mumble²
mumbo-jumbo
mummify⁴ mummification
mummy⁴
mumps
munch¹
munches *[eats]
munchies *[desire to eat]
mundane
Mundy   Monday
mune   moon¹⁺
munetry   monetary⁺
muney   money⁺
mungrel   mongrel
municipal
municipality⁴
munificence munificent
munitions
munk   monk⁺
munkey   monkey
munsh   munch¹
mural
murang   meringue
murcantile   mercantile⁺
murcenary   mercenary⁴
murchandise   merchandise²
murchant   merchant
murcury   mercury⁺
murcy   mercy⁴
murder¹ ~er ~ess ~ous
murge   merge²
murk murky⁴
murmaid   mermaid

---

murmur[1]

murr   myrrh

mursee   mercy[4]

mursiful   merciful[+]

murtel   myrtle

musarka   moussaka

muscat

muscle[2] *[in body]   mussel *[shellfish]

muscular   muscularity

muse[2] *[think]   mews *[cat, stable]

museum ~l piece

mush   mushy[4]

mushroom[1]

music ~al ~ally ~l video

musician ~ship

musik   music[+]

musishan   musician[+]

musium   museum[+]

musk ~y ~rat

muskat   muscat

musket ~eer ~ry

Muslim *[religion]

muslin *[cloth]

musse   moose *[deer],
              mousse *[pudding]

mussel *[shellfish]   muscle[2] *[in body]

must   mustn't [must not]

mustang

mustard *[spice] ~l gas   mustered *[grouped]

mustash   moustache[+]

muster[1]

mustered *[grouped]   mustard *[spice][+]

musty[4]

mutant

mutate[2]   mutation

mute[2] *[silent] ~ly   moot[1] *[for debate][+]

mutilate[2]   mutilation

mutineer   mutinous

mutiny[4]

mutter[1]

mutton

mutual ~ly ~l fund

muvabul   movable

muve   move[2+]

muvy   movie[+]

muzzle[2]

muzzy[4]

my ~self

myaow   miaow[1]

myld   mild[+]

mynah *[bird]   minor *[lesser]

myopia   myopic

myre   mire[2]

myriad

myrrh

myrth   mirth[+]

myrtle

mysterious ~ly ~ness

mystery[4]

mystic *[spiritual]   mystique *[mystery]

mystic ~al ~ism

mystify[4]   mystification

mystique *[mystery]   mystic *[spiritual][+]

mystro   maestro

myth ~ical

mythology[4]   mythological

mytre   mitre[2] *[hat, joint]

myxomatosis

KEY TO SUFFIXES AND COMPOUNDS

These rules are explained on pages ix to x.

1 Keep the word the same before adding **ed, er, est, ing**
e.g. cool[1] → cooled, cooler, coolest, cooling

2 Take off final **e** before adding **ed, er, est, ing**
e.g. fine[2] → fined, finer, finest, fining

3 Double final consonant before adding **ed, er, est, ing**
e.g. thin[3] → thinned, thinner, thinnest, thinning

4 Change final **y** to **i** before adding **ed, er, es, est, ly, ness**
e.g. tidy[4] → tidied, tidier, tidies, tidiest, tidily, tidiness
Keep final **y** before adding **ing** e.g. tidying

5 Add **es** instead of **s** to the end of the word
e.g. bunch[5] → bunches

6 Change final **f** to **ve** before adding **s**
e.g. calf[6] → calves

nab

☞ Can't find your word here? Look under **nat**

nacher	nature[+]
nacheral	natural[+]
nacherist	naturist[+]
nachos	
nachural	natural[+]
nachure	nature[+]
nadir	
naftha	naphtha
nag[3]	
nail[1] ~-biter ~-biting	
naive *[trusting] ~ly ~ty	nave *[church], knave *[Jack]
naked ~ness	
nale	nail[1+]
namby-pamby	
name[2] ~ly ~less ~plate ~sake	
name-drop[3]	
nanny[4] ~| goat	
nanosecond	
nanotechnology	
nap[3] *[sleep]	nape *[back of neck]
napalm	
nape *[back of neck]	nap[3] *[sleep]
naphtha ~lene	
napkin ~| ring	
nappy[4]	
narcissist ~ic narcissism	
narcolepsy	
narcosis	
narcotic	
nark	
narkosis	narcosis
narkotik	narcotic
narled	gnarled
narrate[2] narrator	

narration narrative	
narrow[1] ~ly ~ness	
narrow ~band ~boat	
narrow ~-gauge ~-minded	
narsissist	narcissist[+]
narsissisum	narcissism
nasal ~ly	
nascent	
nash	gnash[1+]
nashnalise	nationalise[2+]
nashnalist	nationalist[+]
nashnalisum	nationalism
nashos	nachos
nashun	nation[+]
nashunality	nationality[4]
nasty[4]	
nat	gnat
nation ~| state ~wide	
national ~| anthem ~| costume	
national ~| curriculum ~| debt	
national ~| park ~| security ~| service	
National Health Service	
nationalise[2] nationalisation	
nationalist ~ic nationalism	
nationality[4]	
native ~| speaker	
Nativity	
natty	
natural ~ly ~ist ~ized ~| gas	
natural ~| history ~| selection	
naturalise[2] naturalisation	
nature ~| reserve ~| study ~| trail	
naturist naturism	
naught	
naughty[4]	
nausea nauseous	
nauseate[2]	
nautical	

---

naval *[navy]   navel *[stomach]+
nave *[church]   naive *[trusting]+,
    knave *[Jack]
navel *[stomach]   naval *[navy]
navel ~-gazing
navey   navy⁴
navigable   navigability
navigate²   navigator
navigation
navul   naval *[navy],
    navel *[stomach]+
navvy⁴ *[worker]
navy⁴ *[fleet]
naw   gnaw¹ *[bite],
    nor *[neither]
nawghty   naughty⁴
nawsea   nausea+
nawtical   nautical
nay *[no]   neigh¹ *[horse]
naybor   neighbour+
naytiv   native+
nayv   nave *[church],
    naive *[trusting]+
nazel   nasal+
Nazi   Nazism
nead   knead *[dough],
    need *[must have]+,
    kneed *[with knee]
neadle   needle²+
Neanderthal
Neapolitan
near¹ ~by ~ly ~ness
neat¹ *[orderly]   net *[mesh, web]
neat ~ly ~ness
nebula   nebulous
necessary   necessarily
necessitate²
necessity⁴

neck ~lace ~line ~tie
neckst   next+
necrofilia   necrophilia
necrophilia
necropolis
nectar   nectarine
need¹ *[must have] ~ful   knead *[dough]
needle² ~point ~work
needless ~ly ~ness
needy⁴
nee   knee+
neel   kneel¹+
neer   near+
ne'er-do-well
neese   niece
nefarious ~ly ~ness
nefew   nephew
negate²   negation
negative ~ly   negativity
neglect¹ ~ful
negligee
negligence   negligent
negligible
neglijay   negligee
negotiable
negotiate²   negotiator
negotiation
neigh¹
neighbour ~ing ~ly
neighbourhood ~l watch
neither
nek   neck+
nekst   next+
neksus   nexus
nel   knell
nelt   knelt
nemesis
nemonic   mnemonic+

KEY TO SUFFIXES AND COMPOUNDS

These rules are explained on pages ix to x.

1 Keep the word the same before adding **ed, er, est, ing**
e.g. cool¹ → cooled, cooler, coolest, cooling
2 Take off final **e** before adding **ed, er, est, ing**
e.g. fine² → fined, finer, finest, fining
3 Double final consonant before adding **ed, er, est, ing**
e.g. thin³ → thinned, thinner, thinnest, thinning

4 Change final **y** to **i** before adding **ed, er, es, est, ly, ness**
e.g. tidy⁴ → tidied, tidier, tidies, tidiest, tidily, tidiness
Keep final **y** before adding **ing** e.g. tidying
5 Add **es** instead of **s** to the end of the word
e.g. bunch⁵ → bunches
6 Change final **f** to **ve** before adding **s**
e.g. calf⁶ → calves

neolithic
neon ~l lights
neo-Nazi
nephew
nepotism   nepotist
Neptune
nercher   nurture[2]
nerse   nurse[2+]
nersing   nursing[+]
nerve ~l centre ~l gas ~-racking
nervous ~ly ~ness
nervy
nesessary   necessary[+]
nesessitate   necessitate[2]
nesessity   necessity[4]
nest[1] ~ling
nestle[2]
net[3] *[mesh, web]   neat[1] *[orderly][+]
net ~ball ~work ~speak
net ~speak
nether
netizen
nettle[2] ~rash
neumatic   pneumatic[+]
neumonia   pneumonia
neural ~l net ~l network
neuralgia
neurological   neurology
neurologist
neuron
neurosis   neuroses
neurotic ~ally
neuter[1]
neutral ~ity
neutralise[2]   neutralisation
neutrel   neutral[+]
neutron ~l bomb
never ~-ending ~more ~theless

new[1] *[not old]   knew *[information]
new ~ly ~ness
new ~-age ~born ~comer
New ~l Testament ~l Year's Day ~l Year's Eve

☞ Can't find your word here? Look under **nu**

newance   nuance
newbile   nubile
newclear   nuclear[+]
newcleus   nucleus[+]
newdist   nudist[+]
newgar   nougat
newmeracy   numeracy
newmerus   numerous[+]
news ~agent ~l bulletin ~l conference
news ~desk ~flash ~group
news ~letter ~paper ~print
news ~reader ~room ~-stand
newsans   nuisance
newt
newton
newtrishus   nutritious
newtrishun   nutrition[+]
next ~l door ~-of-kin
nexus
niacin
Nianderthal   Neanderthal
Niapolitan   Neapolitan
niasin   niacin
nib
nibble[2]
nice[2] *[pleasant] ~ly   niece *[relative]
nicety[4]
niche ~l market
nick[1]
nickel
nickers   knickers
nickname ~d

KEY TO SPELLING RULES

Red words are wrong. **Black** words are correct.

~   Add the suffix or word directly to the main word,
     without a space or hyphen
     e.g. ash ~en ~tray → **ashen ashtray**
~-   Add a hyphen to the main word before adding the
     next word
     e.g. blow ~-dry → **blow-dry**

~l   Leave a space between the main word and the next
     word
     e.g. decimal ~l place → **decimal place**
+   By finding this word in its **correct** alphabetical
     order, you can find related words
     e.g. about[+] → **about-face about-turn**
*   Draws attention to words that may be confused
TM   Means the word is a trademark

☞ Can't find your word here? Look under **kni**

nicotine ~l gum ~l patch

niece *[relative]

nieghbour   neighbour+

nier   near+

niese   niece+

nife   knife[2]+

nifty[4]

niggard ~ly ~liness

niggle[2]   niggly

nigh

night *[dark] ~ly   knight *[soldier]+

night ~club ~dress ~fall

night ~gown ~life ~l light

night ~shade ~l shift ~shirt

night ~time ~watchman

nightingale

nightmare   nightmarish

nikel   nickel

nikname   nickname+

nikotine   nicotine+

nil

nilon   nylon

nimble ~ness   nimbly

nimbus   nimbi

nimf   nymph+

nincompoop

nine   ninth

nineteen ~th

ninety[4]   ninetieth

ninja

ninny[4]

nip[3]   nippy[4]

nipple

nircher   nurture[2]

nirve   nerve+

nirvos   nervous+

nice *[relative]   nice *[pleasant]+

nise   nice[1] *[pleasant]+

nisety   nicety[4]

nit *[insect]   knit[3] *[wool]

nite   knight *[soldier]+,

       night *[dark]

nither   neither

nitingale   nightingale

nitrate

nitric ~l acid

nitrogen

nitroglycerine

nitrous ~l oxide

nitty-gritty

nitwit

☞ Can't find your word here? Look under **kno**

no *[not]   know *[information]

no ~body ~~brainer

no ~~claims bonus

no ~~fly zone

no ~~go area ~man's land

no ~l one

no ~~show ~way ~where

nob *[cribbage]   knob *[door handle]

Nobel *[prize]   noble *[class, worthy]

nobility[4]

noble *[class, worthy]   Nobel *[prize]

noble ~man

nobly

nock   knock[1]+

nocturnal

nod[3] *[bow head] ~l off

node *[lump, in computing]

nodule

noise ~less ~lessly

noisy[4]

nollij   knowledge+

nomad ~ic

KEY TO SUFFIXES AND COMPOUNDS

These rules are explained on pages ix to x.

1 Keep the word the same before adding **ed, er, est, ing**
e.g. cool[1] → cooled, cooler, coolest, cooling
2 Take off final **e** before adding **ed, er, est, ing**
e.g. fine[2] → fined, finer, finest, fining
3 Double final consonant before adding **ed, er, est, ing**
e.g. thin[3] → thinned, thinner, thinnest, thinning

4 Change final **y** to **i** before adding **ed, er, es, est, ly, ness**
e.g. tidy[4] → tidied, tidier, tidies, tidiest, tidily, tidiness
Keep final **y** before adding **ing** e.g. tidying
5 Add **es** instead of **s** to the end of the word
e.g. bunch[5] → bunches
6 Change final **f** to **ve** before adding **s**
e.g. calf[6] → calves

nome	gnome[+]
nominal ~ly	
nominate[2] nomination	

> ☞ Can't find your word here? Take off **non** and look again

noncense	nonsense[+]
non-commital	
nonconformist nonconformism	
nonconformity	
nondescript	
none *[not any]	nun *[religious][+]
nonentity[4]	
non-existent	
non-ferrous	
non-fiction	
non-flammable	
non-human	
non-negotiable	
nonplussed	
non-profit -making	
non-returnable	
nonsense nonsensical	
non-standard	
non-starter	
non-stop	
non-volatile	
noodle	
noon *[midday] ~day	
no one *[not any person]	
noose	
nor *[neither]	gnaw[1] *[bite]
norghty	naughty[4]
norm	
normal ~cy ~ity ~ly	
normalise[2] normalisation	
Norman ~l Conquest	
norsea	nausea[+]

norseus	nauseous
north ~bound ~~east ~~easterly	
north ~erly ~ern ~erner	
north ~l pole	
north ~wards ~~west ~l westerly	
nortical	nautical
norty	naughty[4]
nose *[on face]	knows *[information]
nosedive[2]	
noshun	notion[+]
nostalgia nostalgic	
nostril	
nosy[4]	
not *[no]	knot *[tie],
	note[2+] *[remark]
notable notably	
notarise[2]	
notch	
note[2] ~book ~card	
note ~pad ~paper ~worthy	
nothing ~ness	
notice[2] ~able ~board	
notion ~al	
notiss	notice[2+]
notorious ~ly notoriety	
nougat	
nought ~s-and-crosses	
noun *[grammar]	known *[information]
noun ~l phrase	
nourish[1] ~ment	
nova novae	
novel ~ist novella	
novelty[4]	
November	
novice	
now ~adays	
nowere	nowhere
nowlege	knowledge[+]

---

nown	**known** *[information],
	noun *[grammar]+
noyse	**noise**+
noze	**knows** *[information],
	nose *[on face]
nozzle	
nuance	
nubile	
nuckel	**knuckle**[2+]
nuclear ~l energy ~l fission	
nuclear ~l physics ~l power	
nucleus nuclei	
nude nudity	
nudge[2]	
nudist nudism	
nue	**knew** *[information]
nues	**news**+
nugar	**nougat**
nugget	
nuisance	
nuj	**nudge**[2]
null ~l and void	
nullify[4]	
numatic	**pneumatic**+
numb[1] ~ly ~ness	
number[1] ~l plate	
numeracy	
numeral	
numerasee	**numeracy**
numerate	
numeration	
numerator	
numerical	
numerous ~ly	
numonia	**pneumonia**
numskull	
nun *[religious] ~nery	**none** *[not any],
	noon *[midday]+

nupshals	**nuptials**
nuptials	
nural	**neural**+
nurological	**neurological**+
nurologist	**neurologist**
nuron	**neuron**
nurosis	**neurosis**+
nurotic	**neurotic**+
nurrish	**nourish**[1+]
nurse[2] ~l practitioner	
nursery[4] ~l rhyme ~l school	
nursing ~l home	
nurture[2]	
nurve	**nerve**+
nurvous	**nervous**+
nurvy	**nervy**
nussance	**nuisance**
nut ~cracker ~meg ~shell	
nute	**newt**
nuter	**neuter**
nutralise	**neutralise**[2+]
nutrient	
nutrishus	**nutritious**
nutrition ~al ~ally ~ist	
nutritious	
nutron	**neutron**+
nutty[4]	
nuzzle[2]	

☞ Can't find your word here? Look under **ny**

ny	**nigh**
nylon	
nymph ~omaniac	
nytrate	**nitrate**
nytrogen	**nitrogen**
nytroglyceryne	**nitroglycerine**
nytrus	**nitrous**+

KEY TO SUFFIXES AND COMPOUNDS

These rules are explained on pages ix to x.

1 Keep the word the same before adding **ed, er, est, ing**
e.g. cool[1] → cooled, cooler, coolest, cooling
2 Take off final **e** before adding **ed, er, est, ing**
e.g. fine[2] → fined, finer, finest, fining
3 Double final consonant before adding **ed, er, est, ing**
e.g. thin[3] → thinned, thinner, thinnest, thinning

4 Change final **y** to **i** before adding **ed, er, es, est, ly, ness**
e.g. tidy[4] → tidied, tidier, tidies, tidiest, tidily, tidiness
Keep final **y** before adding **ing** e.g. tidying
5 Add **es** instead of **s** to the end of the word
e.g. bunch[5] → bunches
6 Change final **f** to **ve** before adding **s**
e.g. calf[6] → calves

oad	ode *[poem], owed *[money]
oaf ~ish	
oak ~en	
oan	own
oar *[boat]	awe *[wonder], or *[alternative], ore *[mineral]
oar ~sman ~swoman	
oasis oases	
oat ~cake ~meal	
oath[1]	
obay	obey[1]
obchuse	obtuse[+]
obdurate ~ly obduracy	
obedient ~ly obedience	
obedyans	obedience[+]
obeece	obese[+]
obelisk	
obese obesity	
obey[1]	
obichuary	obituary[4]
obidyant	obedient[+]
obise	obese[+]
obituary[4]	
objaydar	objet d'art
object[1] objector	
object ~-oriented ~l program	
objection ~able	
objective ~ly objectivity	
objekt	object[1+]
objet d'art	
objurate	obdurate[+]
obleek	oblique[+]
obligation	
oblige[2] obligatory	
oblique ~ly ~ness	
obliterate[2] obliteration	

oblivious ~ly oblivion	
oblong	
oblyge	oblige[2]
obnoxious ~ly	
oboe oboist	
obow	oboe[+]
obsalessence	obsolescence[+]
obscene ~ly obscenity[4]	
obscure[2] ~ly obscurity[4]	
obsequious ~ly ~ness	
observant observance	
observatory[4]	
observe[2] observation	
obsessed obsession obsessive	
obsidian	
obskure	obscure[2+]
obsolescence obsolescent	
obsolete	
obsqure	obscure[2+]
obsqurity	obscurity[4]
obstacle ~l course	
obstetric ~ian ~s	
obstinacy	
obstinate ~ly	
obstreperous	
obstruct[1] ~ion ~ive ~ively	
obsurd	absurd
obsurvabul	observable
obsurvance	observance[+]
obsurvatory	observatory[4]
obsurve	observe[2+]
obtain[1] ~able	
obtrusive	
obtuse ~ly ~ness ~l angle	
obverse	
obvious ~ly ~ness	
ocashun	occasion[1+]
occasion[1] ~al ~ally	

---

occident ~al
occlude² occlusion
occular   ocular⁺
occult
occupant   occupancy
occupation
occupational ~l hazard ~l therapy
occupy⁴
occur³   occurrence
ocean ~ography ~l current ~l ridge
ocelot
ochre *[colour]   okra *[vegetable]
ockur   occur³⁺
o'clock
ocsident   occident⁺
octagon ~al
octahedron
octain   octane
octajenerian   octogenarian
octane ~l rating
octave
octet ~l rule
octive   octave
October
octogenarian
octopus⁵
ocular   oculist
ocupant   occupant⁺
ocupashun   occupation⁺
ocupie   occupy⁴
ocur   occur³⁺
odd¹ ~ly ~ness ~-job ~ment
oddity⁴
odds ~-on ~l and ends
ode *[poem]   owed *[money]
oder   odour⁺
odious ~ly ~ness
odity   oddity⁴

odium
odius   odious⁺
odometer
odorous ~ly ~ness
odour ~less
ods   odds⁺
odyum   odium
Oedipus complex
oesophagus
oestrogen
oeuvre
of *[belonging to]   off *[away from]⁺
of course
ofal   awful *[terrible],
                          offal *[meat]
ofe   oaf⁺
ofen   often
ofend   offend¹
ofense   offence
ofensive   offensive⁺
ofer   offer¹
off *[away from]   of *[belonging to]
off ~-air ~-balance
off ~-centre ~-chance ~-colour ~-duty
off ~hand ~-licence ~line ~load
off ~peak ~-road ~-season
off ~-screen ~shoot ~shore ~side
off ~spring ~stage ~-the-cuff
off ~-the-record ~-the-wall ~-white
offal *[meat]   awful *[terrible]⁺
offence
offend¹
offensive ~ly ~ness
offer¹
offhand ~ed ~edness
office ~r
official ~dom ~ly
officiate²

KEY TO SUFFIXES AND COMPOUNDS

These rules are explained on pages ix to x.

1 Keep the word the same before adding **ed, er, est, ing**
  e.g. **cool¹** → cooled, cooler, coolest, cooling
2 Take off final **e** before adding **ed, er, est, ing**
  e.g. **fine²** → fined, finer, finest, fining
3 Double final consonant before adding **ed, er, est, ing**
  e.g. **thin³** → thinned, thinner, thinnest, thinning

4 Change final **y** to **i** before adding **ed, er, es, est, ly, ness**
  e.g. **tidy⁴** → tidied, tidier, tidies, tidiest, tidily, tidiness
  Keep final **y** before adding **ing** e.g. **tidying**
5 Add **es** instead of **s** to the end of the word
  e.g. **bunch⁵** → bunches
6 Change final **f** to **ve** before adding **s**
  e.g. **calf⁶** → calves

211

officious ~ly ~ness	
offing	
offset[3]	
offten	often
ofhand	offhand[+]
ofice	office
ofing	offing
ofiser	officer
ofishall	official[+]
ofishally	officially
ofishiate	officiate[2]
ofishus	officious[+]
ofline	offline
ofprint	offprint
ofset	offset[+]
ofspring	offspring
ofsyd	offside
often	
ofthalmic	ophthalmic
ofthalmologist	ophthalmologist[+]
ogel	ogle[2]
oger	ogre[+]
ogle[2]	
ogre ~ss	
oh *[exclamation]	owe[2] *[money]
ohm ~ic	
Ohm's ~| law	
oil[1] ~can ~cloth ~| crop ~field	
oil ~| rig ~skin ~| spill ~| well	
oily[4]	
ointment	
oister	oyster[+]
OK	

☞ Can't find your word here? Look under <u>oc</u>

okcult	occult[1+]
okcupancy	occupancy[+]
okcupation	occupation[+]

okcupy	occupy[4]
okcur	occur[3+]
o'klock	o'clock
okra *[vegetable]	ochre *[colour]
oksidise	oxidise[2]
okstail	oxtail
oksygen	oxygen[+]
oktagon	octagon[+]
oktane	octane
oktet	octet
Oktober	October
oktogenarian	octogenarian
oktopus	octopus[5]
okular	ocular[+]
old ~| age ~~-fashioned	
Old ~| Bailey ~| Testament	
olden ~| days	
olfactory	
oligarchy[4]	
Olimpic	Olympic[+]
olive ~| branch ~~-oil	
Olympic ~| Games Olympian	
om	ohm[+]
Oman *[country]	omen *[sign]
ombudsman	
omega	
omelette	
omen	
omiga	omega
ominous ~ly	
omishun	omission
omission	
omit[3] *[leave out]	emit[3] *[give out]
omlet	omelette
omminus	ominous[+]
ommit	omit[3]
omnibus[5]	
omnipotence omnipotent	

KEY TO SPELLING RULES

Red words are wrong. **Black words are correct.**

~   Add the suffix or word directly to the main word, without a space or hyphen
     e.g. ash ~en ~tray → ashen ashtray

~-   Add a hyphen to the main word before adding the next word
     e.g. blow ~~-dry → blow-dry

~\| Leave a space between the main word and the next word
     e.g. decimal ~\| place → decimal place

+   By finding this word in its **correct** alphabetical order, you can find related words
     e.g. about[+] → about-face about-turn

*   Draws attention to words that may be confused

TM   Means the word is a trademark

omnipresence omnipresent	
omniscience omniscient	
omnivore	
omnivorous ~ly ~ness	
omnybus	omnibus[5]
omnypresense	omnipresence[+]
omnyscience	omniscience[+]
omyshun	omission
on ~-air ~-coming ~-going	
on ~-rush ~-screen ~-set	
on ~-shore ~-slaught	
once *[one time] ~-over	wants *[would like]
oncology oncologist	
oncor	encore
one *[single] ~l another	wan *[pale],
	won *[victory]
one ~-piece ~-self	
one ~-sided ~-to-one ~-track	
one ~-upmanship ~-way	
oner	owner[+]
onerous	
ones *[these ones]	once *[upon a time]
onest	honest
onion ~l ring	
onix	onyx
online ~l system	
onlooker	
only	
onlyne	online
onomatopoeia onomatopoeic	
onous	onus
onroot	en route
onse	once[+]
onset	
onslort	onslaught
onto	
ontray	entrée
onus	

onward ~s	
onwee	ennui
onyun	onion[+]
onyx	
oodles	
ooze[2]	
opacity	
opake	opaque[+]
opal ~ine	
opan	open[1+]
opaque ~ly	
opasity	opacity
open[1] ~ly ~l air ~-ended ~l house	
open ~-market ~l minded ~ness	
opera ~tic ~tically	
operable	
operashun	operation[+]
operate[2] operative operator	
operating ~l system ~l theatre	
operation ~al	
operetta	
ophthalmic	
ophthalmologist ophthalmology	
opiam	opium
opiate	
opinion ~ated ~l poll	
opium	
oponent	opponent
oportune	opportune[+]
oportunism	opportunism[+]
oportunity	opportunity[4]
opose	oppose[2]
oposit	opposite[+]
opossum	
opous	opus
opponent	
opporchune	opportune[+]
opporchunism	opportunism[+]

KEY TO SUFFIXES AND COMPOUNDS

These rules are explained on pages ix to x.

1 Keep the word the same before adding **ed, er, est, ing**
e.g. cool[1] → cooled, cooler, coolest, cooling

2 Take off final **e** before adding **ed, er, est, ing**
e.g. fine[2] → fined, finer, finest, fining

3 Double final consonant before adding **ed, er, est, ing**
e.g. thin[3] → thinned, thinner, thinnest, thinning

4 Change final **y** to **i** before adding **ed, er, es, est, ly, ness**
e.g. tidy[4] → tidied, tidier, tidies, tidiest, tidily, tidiness
Keep final **y** before adding **ing** e.g. tidying

5 Add **es** instead of **s** to the end of the word
e.g. bunch[5] → bunches

6 Change final **f** to **ve** before adding **s**
e.g. calf[6] → calves

213

opporchunity   opportunity⁴

opportune ~ly ~ness

opportunism

opportunist ~ic ~ically

opportunity⁴

oppose²   opposition

opposite ~| angles

opposum   opossum

oppress¹ ~ion ~ive

oppressor

opra   opera⁺

oprabul   operable⁺

opress   oppress¹⁺

opretta   operetta

opshun   option⁺

opt¹ ~| out

optic ~s

optical ~ly ~| disc

optical ~| fibre ~| illusion

optician

optimise²   optimisation

optimist ~ic ~ically   optimism

optimum

option ~al ~ally

optishun   optician

optometrist

opulence   opulent

opurable   operable⁺

opurate   operate²⁺

opuration   operation⁺

opus

opyate   opiate

or *[alternative]   awe *[wonder],
                       oar *[boat],
                       ore *[mineral]

oracle *[prophesy]   auricle *[ear, heart]

oral *[mouth] ~ly   aural *[ear]⁺

oral ~| contraceptive

---

orange ~ade ~| juice

orang-utan

orashun   oration

oration   orator

oratorio

oratory⁴   oratorical

orb¹

orbit¹ ~al

orchard

orchestra   orchestral

orchestrate²   orchestration

orchid

ordain¹

ordeal

order¹ *[command]   ordure *[rubbish]

order ~| of reactivity

orderly⁴

ordinal ~| number

ordinance *[rule]   ordnance *
                              [army, map]

ordinary   ordinarily

ordination

ordinnal   ordinal

ordnance *[army,   ordinance *[rule]
           map]

ordnary   ordinary⁺

ordnense   ordinance *[rule],
                      ordnance *
                          [army, map]

ordur   order¹ *[command]

ordure *[rubbish]   order¹ *[command]

ore *[mineral]   awe *[wonder],
                       oar *[boat],
                       or *[alternative]

oregano

orel   oral⁺

orfan   orphan¹⁺

organ ~ist ~-grinder

---

organic ~ally ~l chemistry ~l farming	
organise² organisation	
organism	
organophosphate	
orgasm ~ic	
Orgust	August
orgy⁴ orgiastic	
oriant	orient¹⁺
orient¹ ~al ~ally ~eering	
orientate² orientation	
orientayt	orientate²⁺
orifice	
orifiss	orifice
origami	
origin	
original ~ity ~ly	
originate² origination originator	
orijin	origin
orijinal	original⁺
orijinate	originate²⁺
oriole	
Orion ~'s belt	
orkestra	orchestra⁺
orkestrate	orchestrate²⁺
orl	all *[every], awl *[tool]
ornait	ornate⁺
ornament¹ ~al ~ation	
ornate ~ly	
ornithology ornithological	
ornithologist	
orphan¹ ~age	
ort	aught *[anything], ought *[should]
orthodontist	
orthodox orthodoxy⁴	
orthography	
orthopaedic ~s orthopaedist	

ortistic	autistic
ortum	autumn
Oscar	
oscillate² oscillation oscillator	
oscilloscope	
oselot	ocelot
oshun	ocean⁺
osmosis	
osofogus	oesophagus
osprey	
ossify⁴	
ost	oast
ostensible ostensibly	
ostentatious ~ly ostentation	
osteo-arthritis	
osteopath ~y	
osteoporosis	
ostinato	
ostio-arthritis	osteo-arthritis
ostiopath	osteopath⁺
ostracise² ostracism	
ostrich⁵	
ote	oat⁺
ote kootewer	haute couture
othe	oath¹ *[promise], other *[different]⁺
other ~l half ~wise ~worldly	
otoman	ottoman
otter	
ottoman	
ought *[should]	aught *[anything]
oughtn't *[should not]	
Ouija™ ~l board	
oul	owl⁺
ounce	
our *[belonging] ~selves	are *[we are], hour *[time]⁺
ourang-outang	orang-utan

---

ours *[possessive]   hours *[time]
oust¹
out¹ ~back ~bid ~break

> ☞ Can't find your word here? Take off **out** and look again

out ~board ~burst ~cast ~come ~cry
out ~dated ~distance ~door
out ~fit ~going ~grow ~house ~last
out ~law ~let ~line ~look ~lying
out ~number ~patient ~post ~put
out ~rage ~rageous ~rageously
out ~rank ~reach ~right ~run
out ~set ~side ~sider ~skirts ~weigh ~wit
outdo ~ing outdoes outdone
outer ~most ~| space ~wear
outspoken
outstanding ~ly
outward ~ly ~s ~-bound
ova *[eggs]   over *[above]⁺
oval
ovarian
ovary⁴
ovashun   ovation
ovation
ovel   oval
ovem   ovum
oven ~proof ~ware

> ☞ Can't find your word here? Take off **over** and look again

over *[above] ~act   ova *[eggs]
over ~arm ~awed ~board
over ~cast ~coat ~come ~do ~dose
over ~draft ~due ~fish ~flow
over ~grown ~hang ~haul ~head
over ~hear ~heat ~joyed ~land ~lap
over ~lay ~look ~night ~power ~ride

over ~run ~seas ~shadow ~sight ~sleep
over ~spent ~throw ~time ~tone ~turn
over ~weight ~winter ~work ~wrought
overall ~| majority
overrort   overwrought
oversee ~n ~ing
overtake ~n overtaking
overture
overwait   overweight
overwelm   overwhelm¹⁺
overwerk   overwork¹
overwhelm¹ ~ingly
overy   ovary⁴
oviduct
ovulate² ovulation
ovule
ovum ova

> ☞ Can't find your word here? Look under **over**

ovurall   overall⁺
ovursee   oversee⁺
ovurtime   overtime
ovurwork   overwork¹
ovyule   ovule
ow *[pain]
owe² *[money]   oh *[exclamation]
owed *[money]   ode *[poem]
owl ~ish
own¹ ~| goal ~| up
ownce   ounce
owner ~-occupier ~ship
owtberst   outburst

> ☞ Can't find your word here? Look under **out**

owtbilding   outbuilding
owtdoor   outdoor⁺
owter   outer⁺
owtstanding   outstanding⁺

KEY TO SPELLING RULES

Red words are wrong. **Black** words are correct.

~   Add the suffix or word directly to the main word, without a space or hyphen
    e.g. ash ~en ~tray → ashen ashtray

~- Add a hyphen to the main word before adding the next word
    e.g. blow ~-dry → blow-dry

~| Leave a space between the main word and the next word
    e.g. decimal ~| place → decimal place

+   By finding this word in its **correct** alphabetical order, you can find related words
    e.g. about⁺ → about-face about-turn

*   Draws attention to words that may be confused

TM Means the word is a trademark

ox ~en ~tail

oxbow ~l lake

Oxbridge

oxi-asetileen   oxyacetylene

oxidation ~l number

oxide

oxidise[2] oxidisation

oxigen   oxygen[+]

oximoron   oxymoron

Oxo™

oxyacetylene

oxyde   oxide[+]

oxygen ~l mask ~l tent

oxygenate[2] oxygenation

oxymoron

oyel   oil[1+]

oyntment   ointment

oyster ~-bed ~-catcher

ozone ~-depletion ~l layer

KEY TO SUFFIXES AND COMPOUNDS

These rules are explained on pages ix to x.

1 Keep the word the same before adding **ed, er, est, ing**
e.g. cool[1] → cooled, cooler, coolest, cooling
2 Take off final **e** before adding **ed, er, est, ing**
e.g. fine[2] → fined, finer, finest, fining
3 Double final consonant before adding **ed, er, est, ing**
e.g. thin[3] → thinned, thinner, thinnest, thinning

4 Change final **y** to **i** before adding **ed, er, es, est, ly, ness**
e.g. tidy[4] → tidied, tidier, tidies, tidiest, tidily, tidiness
Keep final **y** before adding **ing** e.g. tidying
5 Add **es** instead of **s** to the end of the word
e.g. bunch[5] → bunches
6 Change final **f** to **ve** before adding **s**
e.g. calf[6] → calves

pa *[dad]

pace[2] ~maker ~setter

paced *[walked]

pachyderm

pacific *[peaceful]

Pacific *[Ocean]

pacifism pacifist

pacify[4] pacification

pack[1] ~horse ~| ice

package[2]

packed *[case]

packet

packiderm

pact *[agreement]

pad[3] *[cloth]

paddle[2] ~| wheel

paddock

paddy[4] ~| field

pade

padlock[1]

padray

padre

paediatric ~ian ~s

paedophile paedophilia

paella

pagan ~ism

page[2]

pageant ~ry

paginate[2] pagination

pagoda

paid

pail *[bucket]

pain[1] *[suffering] ~less

pain ~free ~killer ~staking

painful ~ly

paint[1] ~box ~brush

pair[1] *[two]

par *[on a par with]

paste[2] *[food, glue]

specific *[particular]

pact *[agreement]

packed *[case]

paid *[money]+

paid+

padre

pachyderm

pale[2] *[lose colour]+

pane *[of glass]

pare[2] *[trim],

pear *[fruit]

paj

pajent

pajinate

pakage

paket

pakiderm

pal *[friend] ~ly

palace palatial

palamino

palatable

palate *[mouth]

palaver

pale[2] *[colour] ~ness

paleolithic

paleontology

palette *[board] ~| knife

palindrome

palisade

paliss

pall[1] ~bearer

palladium

pallet *[stack]

palliative

pallid

pallitabul

pallor

palm[1] ~ist ~istry

Palm ~| Sunday

palomino

palpable palpably

palpitate[2] palpitation

palsy[4]

paltry[4]

palyative

page[2]

pageant+

paginate[2]+

package[2]

packet

pachyderm

pail *[bucket],
pale[2] *[colour]+

palomino

pallet *[stack],
palette * [board]

pail *[bucket]

palate *[mouth],
pallet *[stack]

palace+

palate *[mouth],
palette *[board]+

palatable

palliative

---

palysade   palisade
pamflet   pamphlet⁺
pampas ~I grass
pamper¹
pamphlet¹ ~eer
pan³ ~cake
panacea
panache
Panama ~I hat
panasea   panacea
panash   panache
pancreas   pancreatic
panda *[animal]   pander¹ *[indulge]
pandemonium
pander¹ *[indulge]   panda *[animal]
Pandora's Box
pane *[glass]   pain¹ *[suffering]⁺
panel³
panellist
panestaking   painstaking
pang
panic ~I attack ~-stricken
panicked   panicking   panicky
pankreas   pancreas⁺
pannier
panoply⁴
panorama   panoramic
pansy⁴
pant¹ *[breathe loudly]   paint¹ *[colour]⁺
pantheon *[gods]
Pantheon *[the]
panther
pantomime²
pantry⁴
pants
panty⁴ ~hose
panyer   pannier
papacy⁴   papal   papist

paparazzi
papaya
paper¹ ~back ~chase ~I clip
paper ~knife ~weight ~work
paperatzi   paparazzi
papier-mâché
papirus   papyrus
papoose
paprika
papyrus
par
parable
parabola   parabolic
parabul   parable
parachute²   parachutist
parade²
paradigm
paradime   paradigm
paradise
paradox ~ical ~ically
paraffin
parafinaylia   paraphernalia
paragliding
paragon
paragraph
parakeet
parallel¹   parallelogram
paralyse²
paralysis   paralytic
parameter
paramilitary
paramount
paramour
paranoia   paranoiac
paranoid
paranormal
parapet
paraphernalia

KEY TO SUFFIXES AND COMPOUNDS

These rules are explained on pages ix to x.

1 Keep the word the same before adding ed, er, est, ing
e.g. cool¹ → cooled, cooler, coolest, cooling
2 Take off final e before adding ed, er, est, ing
e.g. fine² → fined, finer, finest, fining
3 Double final consonant before adding ed, er, est, ing
e.g. thin³ → thinned, thinner, thinnest, thinning

4 Change final y to i before adding ed, er, es, est, ly, ness
e.g. tidy⁴ → tidied, tidier, tidies, tidiest, tidily, tidiness
Keep final y before adding ing e.g. tidying
5 Add es instead of s to the end of the word
e.g. bunch⁵ → bunches
6 Change final f to ve before adding s
e.g. calf⁶ → calves

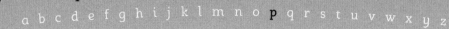

paraphrase[2]	
paraplegic	
parasailing	
parashoot	parachute[2+]
parasite	
parasitic ~al ~ally	
parasol	
paratrooper	
parboil[1]	
parcel[3]	
parch[1] ~ment	
pardon[1] ~able	
pardray	padre
pare[2] *[trim]	pair[1] *[two],
	pear *[fruit]

☞ Can't find your word here? Look under **para**

parebul	parable
paredice	paradise
parelise	paralyse[2]
parellel	parallel[1+]
parenoya	paranoia[+]
parenoyd	paranoid[+]
parent ~age ~al ~ing ~hood	
parenthesis parentheses	
parepet	parapet
pariah	
paribul	parable
parish[5] ~ioner	
Parisian *[person from Paris]	
Parisienne *[woman from Paris]	
parity[4]	
park[1] ~l and ride ~l keeper	
park ~land ~l ranger	
parka	
parkay	parquet
parking ~l meter ~l ticket	
Parkinson's ~l disease	

parlance	
parlement	parliament[+]
parlense	parlance
parler	parlour[+]
parley[1]	
parliament ~arian ~ary	
parlour ~l game ~maid	
parm	palm[1+]
parmesan	
parochial ~ism	
parocksisum	paroxysm
parody[4]	
parole[2] *[release]	payroll *[pay]
paroxysm	
parquet	
parrot[1]	
parry[4]	
parscher	pasture
parse[2]	
parsel	parcel[3]
parshialitee	partiality[4]
parshul	partial[+]
parsimonious parsimony	
parsley	
parsnip	
parson	
parsonage	
part[1] ~ly ~l exchange ~-time	
partake ~n partaking	
partial ~ly partiality[4]	
participant	
participate[2] participation	
participative	
participle	
particle ~l physics	
particular ~ity ~ly	
particularise[2]	
partisan ~ship	

---

partishun   partition[1]
partisipant   participant
partisipate   participate[2+]
partisipul   participle
partition[1]
partner[1] ~ship
partook
partridge
party[4] ~| line ~| pooper
partysan   partisan[+]
pashence   patience *[calmness],
                patients *[doctor's]
pashent   patient[+]
pashun   passion[+]
pasific   pacific *[peaceful],
                Pacific *[Ocean],
                specific *[particular][+]
pasifisum   pacifism[+]
pasify   pacify[4+]
pass[1] ~es ~book ~| key
pass ~port ~word
passable   passably
passage ~way
passay   passé
passé
passed *[did pass]   past *[time, beyond][+]
passenger
passer ~-by
passige   passage[+]
passion ~ate ~ately ~fruit
passive ~ly ~ness
Passover *[Jewish]   pass over *[go over]
past *[time, beyond]   passed *[did pass]
past ~| master
past ~| participle ~| tense
pasta *[noodles]   pastor *[religious][+]
paste[2] *[glue]   paced *[walked]
pasteesh   pastiche

pastel *[colour]   pastille *[suck]
paster   pasta *[noodles],
                pastor *[religious][+]
pasteurise[2]   pasteurisation
pastiche
pastille *[suck]   pastel *[colour]
pastime
pastor ~al
pastrami
pastry[4]
pasture
pasturise   pasteurise[2+]
pasty[4]
pat[3]
patay   pâté
patch[1] ~es ~work
patchy[4]
pâté
patella
patent[1] ~able ~ly
patent ~| leather
paternal ~ism ~ly
paternalist ~ic
paternity
path ~finder ~way
pathetic ~ally
pathological ~ly
pathology   pathologist
pathos
patience *[calmness]   patients *[doctor's]
patient ~ly
patina
patio ~| door
pâtisserie
patois
patriarch ~al
patricide
patrimony[4]

KEY TO SUFFIXES AND COMPOUNDS

These rules are explained on pages ix to x.

1 Keep the word the same before adding ed, er, est, ing
e.g. cool[1] → cooled, cooler, coolest, cooling
2 Take off final e before adding ed, er, est, ing
e.g. fine[2] → fined, finer, finest, fining
3 Double final consonant before adding ed, er, est, ing
e.g. thin[3] → thinned, thinner, thinnest, thinning

4 Change final y to i before adding ed, er, es, est, ly, ness
e.g. tidy[4] → tidied, tidier, tidies, tidiest, tidily, tidiness
Keep final y before adding ing e.g. tidying
5 Add es instead of s to the end of the word
e.g. bunch[5] → bunches
6 Change final f to ve before adding s
e.g. calf[6] → calves

patriot ~ism
patriotic ~ally
patriside   patricide
patrol³
patron ~age ~ess ~l saint
patronise²
patter¹
pattern¹
paturnal   paternal⁺
paturnalist   paternalist⁺
paturnity   paternity
patwah   patois
paucity
paunch ~y
pauper
pause² *[stop]   paws *[feet]
pave² ~ment
pavilion
paw¹ *[foot]   poor¹ *[needy]⁺,
                  pore² *[skin, over],
                  pour¹ *[liquid]
pawch   porch⁵
pawkupine   porcupine
pawn¹ *[money, chess] porn *[sex]
pawn ~broker ~shop
paws *[feet]   pause² *[stop]
pawshun   portion¹
pawtiko   portico
pawtmontoe   portmanteau
pawtray   portray¹⁺
pay ~able paid
pay ~ee ~er ~ing ~ment
pay ~l cheque ~l day
pay ~-off ~load
pay ~l packet ~phone
paynt   paint¹⁺
payroll *[pay]   parole² *[release]
pea *[vegetable] ~nut pee¹ *[toilet]

pea ~-shooter
peace *[calm] ~ably   piece *[part]
peace ~-loving ~-offering ~time
peaceful ~ly ~ness
peacekeeping peacekeeper
peach⁵
peacock peahen
peak¹ *[top]   peek¹ *[glance]
peal¹ *[bells]   peel¹ *[skin]
pear *[fruit] ~-shaped pare² *[trim],
                  peer¹ *[look, noble],
                  pier *[harbour]
pearl *[gem] ~y   purl¹ *[knitting]
peasant ~ry
peat
peaved   peeved
peavish   peevish⁺
pebble pebbly
pecan
peccadillo
peck¹ ~ish
pecking order
pecks *[bird]
pecs *[muscles]
pectin
pectoral
peculiar ~ly peculiarity⁴
pedagogic ~al pedagogy
pedal³ *[bicycle]   peddle² *[sell]
pedalo
pedant ~ic
peddle² *[sell]   pedal³ *[bicycle]
pederast ~y
pedestal
pedestrian ~l crossing ~l precinct
pediatrix   paediatrics
pedicure pedicurist
pedigree ~d

---

pedikure	pedicure⁺
pedlar	
pedofile	paedophile⁺
pedometer	
pee¹ *[toilet]	pea *[vegetable]⁺
peeadahtair	pied-à-terre
peece	peace *[calm]⁺,
	piece² *[part]
peech	peach⁵
peecock	peacock⁺
peek¹ *[glance]	peak¹ *[top]
peel¹ *[skin]	peal¹ *[bells]
peenalize	penalise²
peep¹	
peer¹ *[look, noble] ~less	pier *[harbour]
peerage	
peeriodd	period⁺
peet	peat
peeved	
peevish ~ly ~ness	
peewit	
peeza	pizza
peg³ ~board ~-leg	
peice	peace *[calm]⁺,
	piece² *[part]⁺
pejorative	
Pekinese	
pektin	pectin
pektoral	pectoral
pekuliar	peculiar⁺
pekuliarity	peculiarity⁴
pelava	palaver
pelican ~l crossing	
pellet	
pell-mell	
pelmet	
pelota	
pelt¹	

pelvis pelvic	
pen³ ~-friend ~knife ~l name	
penal ~l code	
penalise²	
penalty⁴	
penance *[repentance]	pennants *[flags]
penanse	penance *
	[repentance]
pence *[money]	pens *[writing]
penchant	
pencil³	
pendant	
pending	
pendulous ~ly	
pendulum	
pendulus	pendulous⁺
penery	penury
penetrable	
penetrate² penetration	
penguin	
pengwin	penguin
penicillin	
peninsula	
penis	
penisillin	penicillin
penitence *[remorse]	penance *[task]
penitenshury	penitentiary⁴
penitent ~ly	
penitentiary⁴	
pennants *[flags]	penance *[task]
pennife	penknife⁶
penniless ~ness	
pennitent	penitent⁺
penny⁴ ~-pinching	
pens *[writing]	pence *[money]
penshant	penchant
penshun	pension¹⁺
penshuner	pensioner

KEY TO SUFFIXES AND COMPOUNDS

These rules are explained on pages ix to x.

1 Keep the word the same before adding **ed, er, est, ing**
e.g. cool¹ → cooled, cooler, coolest, cooling

2 Take off final **e** before adding **ed, er, est, ing**
e.g. fine² → fined, finer, finest, fining

3 Double final consonant before adding **ed, er, est, ing**
e.g. thin³ → thinned, thinner, thinnest, thinning

4 Change final **y** to **i** before adding **ed, er, es, est, ly, ness**
e.g. tidy⁴ → tidied, tidier, tidies, tidiest, tidily, tidiness
Keep final **y** before adding **ing** e.g. tidying

5 Add **es** instead of **s** to the end of the word
e.g. bunch⁵ → bunches

6 Change final **f** to **ve** before adding **s**
e.g. calf⁶ → calves

pensil   pencil³
pension¹ ~able
pensioner
pensive ~ly ~ness
pent ~-up
pentagon *[shape] ~al
Pentagon *[the]
pentameter
pentathlon
Pentecost ~al
penthouse
penultimate
penury
peony⁴
people²
pepper¹ ~y ~corn ~mint
pepperoni
pepsin
pep-talk
peptic
peptide
per *[rate]   purr¹ *[cat]
per ~| annum ~| capita
peralisis   paralysis⁺
peramiter   parameter
percalator   percolator
perceive²
percent ~age
percentile
perceptible   perceptibly
perception   perceptual
perceptive ~ly ~ness
perch¹ ~es
perchance
perchase   purchase²⁺
percolate²   percolator
percussion ~ist   percussive
perdah   purdah

perdition
peregrine ~| falcon
peremptory
perennial ~ly
perenthesis   parenthesis⁺
perfect¹ ~ly perfection perfectionist
perforate²   perforation
perform¹ ~ance
perfume²   perfumery⁴
perfunctory⁴
pergatory   purgatory
perge   purge²
pergola
perhaps
peria   pariah
perifery   periphery⁺
peril ~ous ~ously
perimeter
period ~ical ~ically
periodic ~| table
peripatetic
periphery   peripheral
periscope
perish¹ ~able
peritonitis
perjure²   perjury
perk¹ perky⁴
perloin   purloin¹
perm¹ ~afrost
permanence   permanency
permanent ~ly
permanganate
permeable
permeate²
permission   permissible
permissive ~ness
permit³
permutation

---

pernicious ~ly ~ness
pernickety[4]
pernishus   pernicious[+]
peroxide
perpendicular
perpetrate[2] perpetrator
perpetual ~ly ~l motion
perpetuate[2]
perpetuity[4]
perple   purple
perplex[1] ~ingly
perplexity[4]
perposs   purpose[+]
perr   per *[rate],
                             purr[1] *[cat]
perrogativ   perogative
perse   purse[2]
persecute[2] *[harass]   prosecute[2] *[court][+]
persecution   persecutor
perseev   perceive[2]
persevere[2] perseverance
Persian
persimmon
persist[1] ~ent ~ently
persistence   persistency
person ~able ~age
persona ~l non grata
personal *[private] ~ly   personnel *
                                    [employees]
personality[4]
personify[4] personification
personnel *[employees]   personal *[private][+]
perspective
perspex
perspicacious   perspicacity
perspire[2]   perspiration
persuade[2]   persuadable
persuant   pursuant

persuasion
persuasive ~ly ~ness
persue   pursue[2]
persute   pursuit
perswade   persuade[2+]
perswadeabul   persuadable
perswasive   persuasive[+]
pert ~ly ~ness
pertain[1]
pertinence   pertinent
perturb[1]
peruse[2] perusal
pervade[2] pervasive
perverse ~ly ~ness
perversion   perversive   perversity
pervert[1]
pervey   purvey[1+]
pervious
pesant   peasant[+]
peseta
peso
pessary[4]
pessel   pestle
pessimism
pessimist ~ic ~ically
pest ~icide
pestel   pestle
pester[1]
pestilence   pestilent
pestiside   pesticide
pestle
pestur   pester[1]
pet[3] ~l name
petal[3]
peter[1] ~l out
petishun   petition[1]
petite
petition[1]

KEY TO SUFFIXES AND COMPOUNDS

These rules are explained on pages ix to x.

1 Keep the word the same before adding **ed, er, est, ing**
  e.g. **cool**[1] → cooled, cooler, coolest, cooling
2 Take off final **e** before adding **ed, er, est, ing**
  e.g. **fine**[2] → fined, finer, finest, fining
3 Double final consonant before adding **ed, er, est, ing**
  e.g. **thin**[3] → thinned, thinner, thinnest, thinning

4 Change final **y** to **i** before adding **ed, er, es, est, ly, ness**
  e.g. **tidy**[4] → tidied, tidier, tidies, tidiest, tidily, tidiness
  Keep final **y** before adding **ing** e.g. tidying
5 Add **es** instead of **s** to the end of the word
  e.g. **bunch**[5] → bunches
6 Change final **f** to **ve** before adding **s**
  e.g. **calf**[6] → calves

petrel *[bird] petrol *[fuel]+
petrify[4]
petrol *[fuel] ~eum petrel *[bird]
petrology petrologist
petteet petite
petticoat
petty[4]
petulance
petulant ~ly
petunia
pew
pewny puny[4]
pewpa pupa+
pewpil pupil
pewralunt purulent
pewter
pewtrid putrid
pewtrify putrefy[4]

☞ Can't find your word here? Look under **f**

phalanx[5]
phallic phallus[5]
phantasm ~agoric ~agorical
Phantom
pharaoh
Pharisee
pharmaceutical
pharmacology[4]
pharmacy[4] pharmacist
pharyngeal pharyngitis
pharynx
phase[2]
pheasant
phenix phoenix[5]
phenomenal ~ly
phenomenon phenomena
phew *[exclamation] few *[not many]
phial *[bottle] file[2] *[doc, tool, line]

philander[1] ~er
philanthropic ~ally
philanthropy philanthropist
philately philatelist
philharmonic
philistine
philology philologist
philosopher ~'s stone
philosophical ~ly
philosophise[2]
philosophy
philtre *[love potion] filter[1] *[sieve]
phlegm phlegmatic
phloem
phlox *[flower] flocks *[animals]
phoan phone[2] *[telephone]+
phobia phobic
phoenix[5]
phon *[unit of loudness]
phone[2] *[telephone] ~I card ~I number ~I line
phoneme phonemic
phonetic ~ally ~s
phonic ~s
phonograph
phonology phonological
phoney
phooey
phosphate
phosphorescence phosphorescent
phosphorus
photo ~copier ~-finish ~genic
photo ~journalism ~journalist
photo ~I opportunity ~I shoot
photocopy[4] photocopiable
photoelectric ~I cell
photofit
photograph
photographer photography

photographic ~| memory
photon
photosensitive
photosynthesis
phrasal ~| verb
phrase[2] *[words]   frays *[wear out]
phraseology
phrenetic   frenetic
phrenology   phrenologist
physical ~| education
physical ~| examination ~| force
physical ~| geography ~| sciences
physically
physician
physics   physicist
physiognomy
physiology   physiological   physiologist
physiotherapist   physiotherapy
physique
phyzeek   physique
pi *[number]   pie *[food][+]
pianissimo
piano ~forte   pianist
picador
pican   pecan
Piccadilly ~| Circus ~| station
piccher   picture[2+]
piccherresk   picturesque[+]
piccolo
pich   pitch[1+]
pichfork   pitchfork
pichuitary   pituitary[+]
pick[1] *[select] ~y   pique *[anger]
pick ~axe ~pocket
pick ~-your-own
picket[1]
pickings
pickle[2]

picksee   pixie
picksel   pixel
picnic ~| basket ~| hamper
picnicked   picnickers   picnicking
pictogram
pictorial ~ly
picture[2] ~| book ~~-perfect
picture ~~-postcard ~| rail
picturesque ~ly ~ness
piddle[2]
pide   pied[+]
pidgin *[language]   pigeon *[bird][+]
pidiatrics   pediatrics
pidiatrishun   pediatrician
pidofile   paedophile[+]
pie *[food]   pi *[number]
pie ~| chart ~crust
piebald
piece[2] *[part]   peace *[calm][+]
piece ~meal ~work
pied-à-terre
pied ~| piper
pieneer   pioneer[1]
pier *[jetty]   peer[1] *[look, noble][+]
pierage   peerage
pierce[2]
pierse   pierce[2]
piety
piffle   piffling
pig[3] ~~-iron ~let ~skin ~tail
pigeon *[bird] ~hole   pidgin *[language]
pigeon ~~-toed
piggery
piggy[4] ~back ~bank
pigheaded ~ness
pigin   pidgin *[language]
                                   pigeon *[bird]
pigmee   pygmy[4]

---

pigment[1] ~ation	
pigsty[4]	
pijarmas	pyjamas
pik	pick[1] *[select]+,
	pike[2] *[fish, weapon]
pikador	picador
pikant	piquant+
pikcher	picture[2+]
pike[2] *[fish, weapon]	pick[1] *[select]+,
	pique *[anger]
pikestaff	
piket	picket[1]
piksel	pixel
pikturesque	picturesque+
pilchard	
pile[2]	
pilfer[1] ~age	
pilgrim ~age	
pilige	pillage[2]
pill ~box	
pillage[2]	
pillar ~box	
pillery	pillory[4]
pillion	
pillory[4]	
pillow ~case	
pilon	pylon
pilot[1] ~| light	
pilyon	pillion
pimento	
pimpernel	
pimple pimply	
pin[3] *[point]	pine[2] *[tree, sad]+
pin ~ball ~| cushion	
pin ~hole ~point ~prick	
PIN *[Personal Identification Number]	
pinafore	
pincers	

pinch[1] ~es	
pine[2] ~apple ~| cone	
pine ~| needle ~| nut	
ping-pong	
pinion[1]	
pink[1] ~ish	
pinkie	
pinking shears	
pinnacle	
pinpoint[1]	
pinsers	pincers
pinstripe ~d	
pint ~-sized	
pioneer[1]	
pious ~ly ~ness	
pip[3] *[seed] ~squeak	
pipe[2] *[tube]	
pipe ~| dream ~line	
pipette	
piquant piquancy	
pique *[anger]	pick[1] *[select]+
piramid	pyramid+
piranha	
pirate[2] piracy	
pire	pyre
Pirex	Pyrex™
piriod	period+
piromaniac	pyromaniac
pirotechnics	pyrotechnics
pirouette[2]	
Pirric	Pyrrhic+
piruwette	pirouette[2]
Pisces	
piss[1]	
pistachio	
piste *[skiing]	pissed *[drunk],
	psst *[attention]
pisten	piston

---

pistil *[flower]
pistol *[gun]
piston
pit³ ~I bull ~fall
pit-a-pat ~ter
pitabred   pitta bread
pitch¹ ~es ~-black ~dark
piteous ~ly ~ness
Pithagoras' thearum   Pythagoras'
                         theorum
pithon   python
pithy⁴
pitiful ~ly
pitiless ~ly
pitious   piteous⁺
pitta ~I bread
pittance
pituitary ~I gland
pity⁴   pitiable
pitza   pizza⁺
pitzeria   pizzeria
pitzicato   pizzicato
pius   pious⁺
pivot¹ ~al
pixel
pixie
pizza   pizzeria
pizzicato
placard
placate²
place² *[position]   plaice *[fish]
place ~I mat ~ment ~I value
placebo ~I effect
placenta
placid ~ity ~ly
plack   plaque
plagiarise²   plagiarist
plagiarism

plague²
plaice *[fish]   place² *[position]⁺
plaid *[cloth]   played⁴ [did play]
plain¹ *[basic, flatland]   plane² *[smooth,
                           aircraft]
plain ~ly ~ness ~-spoken
plain ~-clothes ~I sailing
plaintiff *[legal]
plaintive *[sad] ~ly
plait¹ *[braid]   plate² *[dish, sheet]⁺
plakard   placard
plakate   placate²
plaket   placket
plan³
plane² *[smooth, aircraft]   plain¹ *[basic,
                           flat land]⁺
planet ~arium ~ary
planetiff   plaintiff *[legal],
                 plaintive *[sad]⁺
plank
plankton
plant¹ ~ation
plantain
plaque
plark   plaque
plasebo   placebo⁺
plasenta   placenta
plasid   placid⁺
plasis   places
plasma
plaster¹ ~I cast ~I of Paris
plaster ~work
plastic ~I surgeon ~I surgery
Plasticine™
plasticity
plat   plait¹
plate² *[dish, sheet]   plait¹ *[braid]
plate ~ful ~I glass ~I tectonics

---

plateau		plebyan	plebeian
platelet		plecksus	plexus [+]
platform		pledge [2]	
platinum		plee	plea
platipus	platypus [5]	pleeze	please [2]
platitude		plenary [4]	
platonic ~ally		plenitude	
platoon		plentiful ~ly ~ness	
platter		plenty plenteous	
platune	platoon	pleral	pleural *[lungs],
platypus [5]			plural *[several]
plaudits		plesenta	placenta
plausible plausibility		plethora	
play [1] ~able ~back ~boy ~ground		pleural *[lungs]	plural *[several]
play ~group ~mate ~off ~pen ~room		pleurisy	
play ~scheme ~school ~script ~time		plezant	pleasant [+]
playd	plaid *[cloth],	plezure	pleasure [+]
	played *[did play]	pliable	
playful ~ly ~ness		pliant	
playg	plague [2]	plié	
playjarize	plagiarise [2+]	pliers	
playn	plane [+]	plight *[bad situation]	polite *[good] [+]
playrite	playwright	plimsolls	
playtlet	platelet	plinth	
playwright		plite	plight *[bad situation],
plazmer	plasma		polite *[good] [+]
plea		plod [3]	
plead [1] ~ingly		plonk [1] ~l down	
pleas *[appeals]	please [2] *[polite]	ploorel	plural
pleasant ~ly ~ness		plop [3]	
pleasantry [4]		plordits	plaudits
please [2] *[polite]	pleas *[appeals]	plorsibul	plausible [+]
pleasure pleasurable pleasurably		plot [3]	
pleat [1]		plough [1] ~share	
pleay	plié	ploughman's ~l lunch	
pleb		plow	plough [1+]
plebeian		ploy	
plebiscite		pluck [1] plucky [4]	

---

plug³ ~hole
plum *[fruit] ~l pudding   plume *[feather]⁺
plumb¹ *[weight, pipe] ~line
plumber
plume   plumage
plumit   plummet¹
plummer   plumber
plummet¹
plump¹ ~ness
plunder¹
plunge²
pluperfect
plural *[several]   pleural *[lungs]
pluralism
plurality
plurisy   pleurisy
plus
plush ~y
Pluto
plutocracy⁴
plutonium
pluvial
ply⁴ ~wood
plyable   pliable
plyant   pliant
plyers   pliers
plyght   plight
plymsolls   plimsolls
pneumatic ~l drill
pneumonia
poach¹
poak   poke²
poaker   poker⁺
poar   paw¹ *[foot],
                              poor¹ *[needy]⁺,
                              pore² *[skin, over],
                              pour¹ *[liquid]
poch   poach¹

pock ~-marked
pocket¹ ~ful
pocket ~l knife ~l money
pod³
podgy⁴
podium
poem
poet ~l Laureate
poetic ~ally ~l justice ~l licence
poetry
pogo¹ ~es ~l stick
pogy   podgy⁴
poignancy
poignant ~ly
point¹ ~edly
point ~-blank ~l duty
point ~l of order ~l of view
pointillism   pointillist
pointless ~ly ~ness
poise²
poison¹ ~ous ~ously
poitree   poetry
pok   pock⁺
poke²   pokey
poker ~l dice ~-faced
poket   pocket¹⁺
poks   pox
polar ~l bear
polarise²   polarisation
polarity⁴
Polaroid™
pole *[post, stick] ~l vault poll¹ *[vote]⁺
poleaxe²
polecat
polees   police²⁺
polemic ~al
poler   polar⁺
polerise   polarise²⁺

KEY TO SUFFIXES AND COMPOUNDS

These rules are explained on pages ix to x.

1 Keep the word the same before adding **ed, er, est, ing**
  e.g. cool¹ → cooled, cooler, coolest, cooling
2 Take off final **e** before adding **ed, er, est, ing**
  e.g. fine² → fined, finer, finest, fining
3 Double final consonant before adding **ed, er, est, ing**
  e.g. thin³ → thinned, thinner, thinnest, thinning

4 Change final **y** to **i** before adding **ed, er, es, est, ly, ness**
  e.g. tidy⁴ → tidied, tidier, tidies, tidiest, tidily, tidiness
  Keep final **y** before adding **ing** e.g. tidying
5 Add **es** instead of **s** to the end of the word
  e.g. bunch⁵ → bunches
6 Change final **f** to **ve** before adding **s**
  e.g. calf⁶ → calves

Pole Star

police² ~| constable ~| force ~man

police ~| officer ~| station ~woman

policy⁴ ~holder

poliester	polyester
poligamy	polygamy⁺
poliglot	polyglot
poligon	polygon
polihedron	polyhedron
polimer	polymer

polio ~myelitis

| polip | polyp |

polish¹ ~| off ~| up

| poliss | police²⁺ |
| polisy | policy⁴⁺ |

Politburo

polite² *[good] ~ly ~ness   plight *[bad situation]

| politeknic | polytechnic |
| politheen | polythene |

politic politicking

political ~ly

politician

politicise²

politics

| politishun | politician⁺ |
| politisize | politicise² |

polka ~dot

poll¹ *[vote] ~| tax   pole *[post, stick]⁺

pollard

pollen ~| count

pollinate² pollination

| pollstar | Pole Star |

pollster

pollute² pollution

polo

polo-neck

| poloot | pollute²⁺ |

poltergeist

poltiss	poultice
poltry	poultry
polturgist	poltergeist

polyester

polygamy   polygamous

polyglot

polygon

polyhedron

polymer

| polyo | polio⁺ |

polyp

| polysh | polish¹⁺ |

polystyrene

polysyllabic

| polyte | polite⁺ |

polytechnic

polythene

polyunsaturated

| pome | poem |

pomegranate

| pomel | pommel³ |

pommel³

pomp ~osity

pompom

pompous ~ly

poncho

pond

ponder¹ ~able

ponderous ~ly

| ponee | pony⁴⁺ |

pong¹

pontiff

pontificate²

pontoon

pony⁴ ~tail ~-trekking

poo¹ *[toilet]   pooh *[exclamation]

poodle

| pooerile | puerile |

---

pooh *[exclamation]

pool *[swimming]

poop¹

poor¹ *[needy] ~ly

pop³ ~| art

pop ~corn ~gun

Pope [the]

poplar *[tree]

poplarise

poppadom

poppet

poppy⁴ ~cock ~| seed

populace *[masses]

popular *[liked]

popular ~ity ~ly

popularise²

populate² population

populous *[crowded]

por

porcelain

porch⁵

porcity

porcupine

pore² *[skin, over]

pork ~er ~y

porlsy

porltry

porn *[sex]

pornch

pornographic

pornography pornographer

poo¹ *[toilet]

pull¹ *[move]

paw¹ *[foot],
pore² *[skin, over],
pour¹ *[liquid]

popular *[liked]⁺

popularise²

populous *[crowded]

poplar *[tree]

populace *[masses]

paw¹ *[foot],
poor¹ *[needy]⁺,
pore² *[skin, over],
pour¹ *[liquid]

paucity

paw¹ *[foot],
poor¹ *[needy]⁺,
pour¹ *[liquid]

palsy⁴

paltry⁴

pawn¹ *[money]⁺

paunch⁺

porous porosity

porpoise

porpuss   porpoise

porridge

porse   pause² *[stop],
                            paws *[feet]

porshun   portion¹

porslin   porcelain

port ~able ~hole

portal

portcullis

portend¹ *[foretell]

portent *[omen] ~ous

porter

portfolio

portico

portion¹

portly⁴

portrait ~ure

portray¹ ~al

poscher   posture²

poschulate   postulate²

pose² *[position]   posse *[group of men]

posess   possess¹⁺

posession   possession

poseur

posh¹

poshun   potion

posishun   position

position

positive ~ly ~ness

positivism

positron

posse *[group of men]   pose² *[position]

possess¹ ~or

possession

possessive ~ly ~ness

possible possibly possibility⁴

---

possum
possy   posse *[group of men],
                                           posy *[bunch]
post[1] ~bag ~box ~card ~code
post ~date ~graduate ~haste
Post ~-Impressionism
post ~man ~mark ~master
post ~mistress ~| office
postage ~| stamp
postal ~| order ~| vote
poster
posterior
posterity
posthumous ~ly
postige   postage[+]
postirior   posterior
postmodern ~ism
post-mortem
postnatal ~| depression
postoperative
postpone[2] ~ment
postscript
postulant
postulate[2]
posture[2]
posum   possum
posy[4]
posytiv   positive[+]
posytivisum   positivism
posytron   positron
pot ~-bellied ~| belly ~boiler
pot ~hole ~holing ~| luck
potash
potassium
potato[5]
potency[4]   potent
potenshul   potential[+]
potensy   potency[+]

potentate
potential ~ly
potion
pot-pourri
potpuri   pot-pourri
potter[1]   potter's wheel
pottery[4]   poetry
pottry   pottery[4]
potty[4] ~-train
pouch[1] ~es
poultice
poultry
pounce[2]
pound[1] ~| sterling
pour[1] *[liquid]   paw[1] *[foot],
                                           poor[1] *[needy][+],
                                           pore[2] *[skin, over]
pournograffy   pornography[+]
pourous   porous[+]
pourt   port[+]

pourtal   portal

☞ Can't find your word here? Look under **por**

pourtfolio   portfolio
pourtray   portray[1+]
pourtrayt   portrait[+]
pout[1]
poverty ~-stricken
powch   pouch[1+]
powder[1] ~y ~| keg
powder ~| puff ~| room
power[1] ~less
power ~boat ~house ~| station
powerful ~ly ~ness
power-share[2]
power-station
pownd   pound[1+]

KEY TO SPELLING RULES

Red words are wrong. **Black words are correct.**

~   Add the suffix or word directly to the main word, without a space or hyphen
    e.g. ash ~en ~tray → ashen ashtray

~- Add a hyphen to the main word before adding the next word
    e.g. blow ~-dry → blow-dry

~| Leave a space between the main word and the next word
    e.g. decimal ~| place → decimal place

+   By finding this word in its **correct** alphabetical order, you can find related words
    e.g. about[+] → about-face about-turn

*   Draws attention to words that may be confused

TM Means the word is a trademark

pownse — pounce[2]
powt — pout[1]
powur — power[1+]
pow-wow[1]
pox
poynansy — poignancy
poynant — poignant[+]
poynt — point[1+]
poyson — poison[1+]
poyze — poise[2]
poze — pose[2]
pozeur — poseur
pozy — posy[4]
practicable   practicability
practical ~ity ~ly
practice *[a run-through]
practise[2] *[to practise]
practishuner — practitioner
practitioner
praer — prayer[+]
pragmatic   pragmatism
prairie
praise[2] ~worthy
praktikabul — practicable[+]
praktikal — practical[+]
pram
prance[2]
prank ~ster
pranse — prance[2]
prattle[2]
praun — prawn[1]
prawn[1]
pray[1] *[say prayers] — prey[1] *[devour]
prayer ~l book
prayse — praise[2+]
praysi — précis
preach[1] ~es
preamble[2]

☞ Can't find your word here? Take off **pre** and look
again

prearrange[2]
precarious ~ly ~ness
precaution ~ary
precawtion — precaution[+]
precede[2] *[go before] — proceed[1] *[go on]
precedence *[priority] — precedents *[before]
precedent *[example] — president *[leader][+]
precept
precinct
precious ~ly ~ness
precipice
precipitate[2]   precipitation
precipitous ~ly ~ness
précis *[summary]
precise *[exact] ~ly
precision
preclude[2]
precocious ~ly ~ness
preconceive[2]   preconception
preconseeve — preconceive[2]
precorshun — precaution[+]
precursor ~y
predator   predatory
predecessor
predestined   predestination
predetermine[2]
predicament
predicate[2]
predict[1] ~able ~ion ~or
predikament — predicament
predikayte — predicate[2]
predilecshun — predilection
predilection
predispose[2]   predisposition
predjudiss — prejudice[2]

KEY TO SUFFIXES AND COMPOUNDS

These rules are explained on pages ix to x.

1 Keep the word the same before adding **ed, er, est, ing**
e.g. cool[1] → cooled, cooler, coolest, cooling
2 Take off final **e** before adding **ed, er, est, ing**
e.g. fine[2] → fined, finer, finest, fining
3 Double final consonant before adding **ed, er, est, ing**
e.g. thin[3] → thinned, thinner, thinnest, thinning

4 Change final **y** to **i** before adding **ed, er, es, est, ly, ness**
e.g. tidy[4] → tidied, tidier, tidies, tidiest, tidily, tidiness
Keep final **y** before adding **ing** e.g. tidying
5 Add **es** instead of **s** to the end of the word
e.g. bunch[5] → bunches
6 Change final **f** to **ve** before adding **s**
e.g. calf[6] → calves

predjudishal	prejudicial[+]
predominance	
predominant ~ly	
predominate[2]	
preech	preach[1+]
pre-eminence pre-eminent	
pre-empt[1] ~ion ~ive	
preen[1]	
preest	priest[+]
pre-exist[1]	
prefabricate[2] prefabrication	
preface[2]	
prefect ~ure	
prefer[3] ~able ~ably	
preference	
preferential ~ly	
preferment	
prefiss	preface[2]
prefix[1]	
prefrence	preference
prefrenshall	preferential[+]
pregnancy[4]	
pregnant	
prehensile	
prehistoric ~ally prehistory	
prejudge[2]	
prejudice[2]	
prejudicial ~ly	
prejudishul	prejudicial[+]
preklude	preclude[2]
prekoshus	precocious[+]
prekursor	precursor[+]
prelate	
preliminary[4]	
prelims	
prelude[2]	
prelyud	prelude[2]
premarital ~l relations	

premature ~ly	
premeditate[2] premeditation	
premier *[prime minister] ~ship	
première *[first performance]	
premise	
premises	
premium	
Premium Bond	
premmiere	première
premonishun	premonition
premonition	
prenatal	
preoccupy[4] preoccupation	
preordained	
pre-packaged	
prepade	prepaid
prepaid	
preparation preparatory	
prepare[2]	
prepay ~ment	
preponderance preponderant	
preposition ~al	
preposterous ~ly ~ness	
prerequisite	
prerogative	
prery	prairie
Presbyterian	
pre-school ~-shrunk	
prescribe[2] *[medicine]	proscribe[2] *[outlaw]
prescription	
prescriptive ~ly	
presede	precede[2]
presedense	precedence
presedent	president *[leader][+]
	precedent *
	[happened before],
preseed	precede[2]
presence *[attendance]	presents *[gifts]

KEY TO SPELLING RULES

Red words are wrong. **Black** words are correct.

~   Add the suffix or word directly to the main word, without a space or hyphen
    e.g. ash ~en ~tray → ashen ashtray

~-   Add a hyphen to the main word before adding the next word
    e.g. blow ~-dry → blow-dry

~l   Leave a space between the main word and the next word
    e.g. decimal ~l place → decimal place

+   By finding this word in its **correct** alphabetical order, you can find related words
    e.g. about[+] → about-face about-turn

*   Draws attention to words that may be confused

TM   Means the word is a trademark

presens	presence
present[1] ~ly ~-day ~l tense	
presentable presentably	
presentation	
presentiment	
presept	precept
preservation ~ist	
preservative	
preserve[2]	
preshure	pressure[2+]
preshurise	pressurise[2+]
preshus	precious[+]
preside[2]	
presidency[4]	
president *[leader] ~ial	precedent *[example]
presinct	precinct
presipiss	precipice
presipitance	precipitance
presipitate	precipitate[2+]
presipitous	precipitous[+]
presise	precise[+]
press[1] ~l agency ~l agent	
press ~l baron ~l box	
press ~l conference	
press ~l corps ~l cutting	
press ~l gallery ~gang ~l pack	
press ~l release ~l room	
press ~l secretary ~l stud ~-up	
pressure[2] ~l cooker ~l group	
pressurise[2] pressurisation	
prestige prestigious	
prestij	prestige[+]
presto	
presume[2] presumably	
presumption presumptive	
presumptuous ~ly ~ness	
presumshus	presumptuous[+]
presuppose[2]	

presurvashun	preservation[+]
presurve	preserve[2]
pretect	protect[1+]
pretective	protective[+]
pretectorate	protectorate
pretence	
pretend[1]	
pretension	
pretentious ~ly ~ness	
preterite	
pretext	
pretsel	pretzel
pretty[4]	
pretzel	
prevail[1]	
prevalence prevalent	
prevaricate[2] prevarication	
prevent[1] ~able ~ion	
preventative	
preventive	
previde	provide[2+]
preview[1]	
previous ~ly	
prevlans	prevalence[+]
pre-war	
prey[1] *[devour]	pray[1] *[say prayers]
prezant	present[1+]
pricarious	precarious[+]
pricaushun	precaution[+]
price[2] *[cost]	prize[2] *[award][+]
price ~l control ~~-fixing ~l tag	
priceless ~ly ~ness	
prick[1]	
prickle[2] prickly[4]	
priconsepshun	preconception
pricoshus	precocious[+]
pride[2] *[self-respect]	pried *[curious]
pridesessor	predecessor

☞ Can't find your word here? Look under **pre**

pridestined	predestined+
pridetermin	predetermine[2]
pridict	predict[1+]
pridikshun	prediction
pridispose	predispose[2+]
pridominanse	predominance
pridominant	predominant+
pridominate	predominate[2]
pried *[curious]	pride[2] *[self-respect]
prier	prior
pries *[curious]	prize[2] *[award]+
priest ~ly ~ess ~hood	
prifer	prefer[3+]
prig priggish	
prihensile	prehensile
prihistoric	prehistoric+
prik	prick[1]
priliminary	preliminary[4]
prim[3] ~ly ~ness	
prima ballerina	
prima donna	
prima facie	
primacy	
primary[4] ~l colour ~l school ~l source	
primasy	primacy
primate	
prime[2] ~l factor ~l number	
prime minister	
primeditate	premeditate[2+]
primeval	
primitive primitivism	
primium	premium
primordial	
primrose	
primula	
prinatal	prenatal

prince ~ly   princess

principal *[chief] ~ly	principle *[rule, idea]
principality[4]	
principle *[rule, idea]	principal *[chief]+
prinse	prince+
prinsipality	principality[4]

print[1] ~l area ~out ~l run

prioccupy	preoccupy[4+]
prior	
prioritise[2]	
priority[4]	
priory[4]	
pripair	prepare[2]
prirequisit	prerequisite
priscribe	prescribe[2]
priscripshun	prescription+
prise[2] *[lever]	price[2] *[cost]+
priseed	precede[2] *[go before],
	proceed[1] *[go on]
prisentable	presentable+
prisentiment	presentiment
priservativ	preservative
priside	preside[2+]
prism	
prison ~er	
prissy[4]	
pristine	
prisumably	presumably
prisume	presume[2+]
prisupose	presuppose[2]
prisurve	preserve[2]
pritend	pretend[1]
pritense	pretence
pritenshun	pretension
pritenshus	pretentious+
prity	pretty[4]
privacy	
privale	prevail[1]

---

privaricate	prevaricate[2+]
private ~ly	
privateer	
privation	
privatise[2] privatisation	
privent	prevent[1+]
privet	
privilege[2]	
privvasee	privacy
privy	
Privy Council	
prize[2] *[award]	price[2] *[cost][+]
prize ~-fighter ~-giving	
pro ~| forma ~| tem	
proab	probe[2]
proan	prone[+]
probability ~| scale	
probable probably	
probashun	probation[+]
probate	
probation ~| officer probationary	
probe[2]	
problem	
problematic ~al ~ally	
proboscis	
procecute	prosecute[2+]
procecution	prosecution[+]
procedure	
proceed[1] *[go on] ~ings	precede[2] *[go before]
procelitise	proselytise[2]
procelyte	proselyte[2]
process[1] ~or	
procession ~al	
procksimate	proximate[+]
procksimity	proximity
procksy	proxy[4]
proclaim[1]	
proclamation	

procrastinate[2] procrastination	
procreate[2] procreation	
proctor	
procuration procurator	
procure[2] ~ment	
prod[3]	
prodigal	
prodigious ~ly ~ness	
prodigy[4]	
prodijus	prodigious[+]
prodijy	prodigy[4]
produce[2]	
product production	
productive ~ly	
productivity	
produse	produce[2]
profane[2] ~ly ~ness	
profanity[4]	
profer	proffer[1]
profesee	prophecy
profeshun	profession
profess[1]	
profession	
professional ~ism ~ly	
professor ~ial	
profet	prophet[+]
profetier	profiteer[1]
proffer[1]	
proffeshunal	professional[+]
proffesionalise	professionalise[2]
proffesor	professor[+]
proficiency proficient	
profile[2]	
profisiency	proficiency[+]
profit[1] ~| margin	
profit ~-sharing ~-taking	
profitable profitability profitably	
profiteer[1]	

---

profligate	prolong[1] ~ation
profound ~ly	promenade[2]
profundity	promenence · · · prominence[+]
profuse[2] ~ly · profusion	promethium
profylactic · · · prophylactic	prominade · · · promenade[2]
profyle · · · profile[2]	prominent ~ly · prominence
progect · · · project[1+]	promiscuous · promiscuity
progection · · · projection	promise[2] · promissory
progenitor	promiskuous · · · promiscuous[+]
progeny[4]	promiss · · · promise[2+]
progesterone	promithium · · · promethium
prognosis · prognoses	promontory[4]
program[3] *[computer]	promoshun · · · promotion[+]
programme *[events]	promote[2]
progress[1] ~ion	promotion ~al
progresshun · · · progression	prompt[1] ~ly ~ness
progressive ~ly	prone
prohibit[1] · prohibition	prong[1]
prohibitive ~ly	pronoun
projecshun · · · projection	pronounce[2] ~ment
project[1] ~ion ~ionist ~or	pronounciation · · · pronunciation
projectile	pronown · · · pronoun
projeny · · · progeny[4]	pronownsement · · · pronouncement
projesterone · · · progesterone	pronunciation
proklamation · · · proclamation	prood · · · prude[+]
proklaym · · · proclaim	proodense · · · prudence[+]
prokrastinate · · · procrastinate[2+]	proodenshal · · · prudential
prokreate · · · procreate[2+]	proof[1] *[evidence] · · · prove[2] *[show]
proksy · · · proxy[4]	proofread[1]
proktor · · · proctor	proon · · · prune[2]
prokuration · · · procuration[+]	prooriense · · · prurience
prokure · · · procure[2+]	proov · · · prove[2]
prolapse[2]	prop[3]
proletarian · proletariat	propaganda
proliferate[2] · proliferation	propagate[2] · propagator
prolific ~ally	propagation
prologg · · · prologue[2]	propane
prologue[2]	propegate · · · propagate[2+]

KEY TO SPELLING RULES

Red words are wrong. **Black** words are correct.

~   Add the suffix or word directly to the main word, without a space or hyphen
    e.g. ash ~en ~tray → ashen ashtray

~-   Add a hyphen to the main word before adding the next word
    e.g. blow ~-dry → blow-dry

~| Leave a space between the main word and the next word
    e.g. decimal ~| place → decimal place

+   By finding this word in its **correct** alphabetical order, you can find related words
    e.g. about[+] → about-face about-turn

*   Draws attention to words that may be confused

TM   Means the word is a trademark

propel[3] propeller

propellant

propelling pencil

propensity[4]

proper ~ly ~| fraction ~| noun

property[4]

prophecy[4] *[prediction]

prophesy[4] *[predict]

prophet ~ic ~ically

prophylactic

propishus   propitious[+]

propishiate   propitiate[2]

propitiate[2]

propitious ~ly ~ness

propolis

proporshun   proportion[1+]

proporshunal   proportional[+]

proportion[1]

proportional ~ity ~ly

proportionate ~ly

proposal

propose[2] proposition

propound[1]

proprietary *   propriety *
       [ownership]   [manners]

proprietor

propriety *   proprietary *
       [manners]   [ownership]

propryeter   proprietor

propryety   propriety

propulshun   propulsion[+]

propulsion propulsive

proqure   procure[2+]

Prosac   Prozac™

prosaic ~ally

prosciutto

proscribe[2] *   prescribe[2] *
       [outlaw]   [medicine]

prose

prosecute[2] *[court]   persecute[2] *[harass]

prosecution prosecutor

prosedure   procedure

proseed   proceed[1] *[go on],
                             precede[2] *[go before]

prosequte   prosecute[2+]

prosess   process[1]

prosession   procession[+]

prosessor   processor

proshooto   prosciutto

prospect[1] ~ive ~or

prospectus[5]

prosper[1] prosperity

prosperous ~ly

prostate *[gland]   prostrate[2] *[flat]

prosthesis prostheses

prosthetic ~ally ~s

prostitute[2] prostitution

prostrate[2] *[flat]   prostate *[gland]

protagonist

protecshun   protection

protect[1] ~ion ~or

protective ~ly ~ness

protectorate

proteen   protein

protégé *[man]

protégée *[woman]

protein

protejay   protégé *[man],
                             protégée *[woman]

protest[1] ~ation

Protestant ~ism

protocol

proton

protoplasm

prototype

protozoa

---

protract[1] ~or
protrude[2]   protrusion
protuberance
proud[1] ~ly
prove[2] *[show]   proof[1] *[evidence]
proven
provenance
proverb ~ial
provide[2]
providence
provident ~ial ~ially
province   provincial
provision ~al ~ally
proviso
provocative
provoke[2]   provocation   provocative
provost
provyso   proviso
prow
prowd   proud+
prowess
prowl[1]
proximate ~ly
proximity
proxy[4]
Prozac™
prozaic   prosaic+
proze   prose
prude   prudery   prudish
prudence   prudent
prudential
pruf   proof[1] *[evidence],
                            prove[2] *[show]
prufread   proofread[1]
prune[2]
prurience   prurient
prussic acid
pruve   prove[2]+

☞ Can't find your word here? Look under **pri**

pry[4]
pryde   pride[2]
pryer   prior
prymary   primary+
psalm ~ist
psalter
pseudo ~nym
psoriasis
psyche
psyched
psychedelic
psychee   psyche
psychiatric   psychiatrist   psychiatry
psychic ~ally
psycho
psychoanalyse[2]   psychoanalysis
psychoanalyst
psychodrama
psychological ~ly
psychology   psychologist
psychometric
psychopath ~ic
psychosis
psychosomatic
psychotherapist   psychotherapy
psychotic ~l illness
ptarmigan
pterodactyl
Ptolemaic ~l system
pub
puberty
pubescence   pubescent
pubic ~l hair
pubis   pubes
public ~ly ~l affairs ~l company
public ~l domain ~l house

KEY TO SPELLING RULES

Red words are wrong. **Black** words are correct.

~   Add the suffix or word directly to the main word,
     without a space or hyphen
     e.g. ash ~en ~tray → ashen ashtray
~-   Add a hyphen to the main word before adding the
     next word
     e.g. blow ~-dry → blow-dry

~l   Leave a space between the main word and the next
     word
     e.g. decimal ~l place → decimal place
+   By finding this word in its **correct** alphabetical
     order, you can find related words
     e.g. about+ → about-face about-turn
*   Draws attention to words that may be confused
™   Means the word is a trademark

public ~| inquiry ~| library
public ~| nuisance ~| relations
public ~| school ~| sector ~| servant
public ~| speaking ~| spending
public ~| transport ~| utility
publican
publication
publicise² publicist
publicity
publik   public⁺
publish¹ ~er
publisise   publicise²⁺
publisity   publicity
puce
puck
pucker¹ *[lips] ~| up   pukka *[good, real]
pudding ~| basin
puddle²
pudel   puddle²
puerile
pueter   pewter
puff¹ ~| pastry
puffin
puffy⁴
pug
pugnacious ~ly   pugnacity
pugnashus   pugnacious⁺
puk   puck *[hockey],
                         puke² *[vomit]
puke²
pukka *[good, real]   pucker¹ *[lips]⁺
pull¹ *[move]   pool *[swimming]
pullet
pulley
pullover
pulmonary
pulp¹ ~y
pulpit

pulsar
pulsate² pulsation
pulse²
pulverise²
puma
pumel   pummel³
pumice² ~| stone
pumiss   pumice²⁺
pumkin   pumpkin
pummel³
pump¹
pumpernickel
pumpkin
pumpurnickel   pumpernickel
pun³
puncchual   punctual⁺
punch¹ ~es ~bag ~| drunk
punch ~line ~up
punctilious ~ly ~ness
punctual ~ity ~ly
punctuate² punctuation
puncture²
pundit
pungent
punish¹ ~able ~ment
punitive ~ly
punjent   pungent
punktuate   punctuate²⁺
punkture   puncture²
punnet
punt¹
puny⁴
punytive   punitive⁺
pupa   pupae
pupil
puppet ~ry
puppeteer
puppy⁴

---

pur	per *[rate]+,
	pure² *[perfect]+,
	purr¹ *[cat]
puray	purée

☞ Can't find your word here? Look under **per**

purceive	perceive²
purcentage	percentage
purceptible	perceptible+
purception	perception+
purch	perch¹+
purchase²	
purcolate	percolate²
purcushon	percussion+
purdah	
purdishun	perdition
pure² ~ly	
purée	
purest *[most pure]	purist *[person]
purfect	perfect¹+
purfict	perfect¹+
purforate	perforate²+
purform	perform¹+
purfume	perfume²+
purfunctory	perfunctory⁴
purgatory	
purge²	
purhaps	perhaps
purify⁴ purification	
puritan ~ical Puritan	
purity	
purjer	perjure²+
purk	perk¹+
purl¹ *[knitting]	pearl *[gem]+
purloin¹	
purm	perm¹+
purmanence	permanence+
purmanent	permanent+

puroxide	peroxide
purpendicular	perpendicular
purpetrate	perpetrate²+
purple	
purplex	perplex¹+
purpose ~ly ~-built	
purposeful ~ly	
purr¹ *[cat]	per *[rate]+,
	pure² *[perfect]+
purrfikt	perfect¹+
purse²	
pursecute	persecute²+
pursevure	persevere²+
pursew	pursue²+
pursonality	personality⁴
pursuade	persuade²+
pursuant	
pursuasive	persuasive+
pursue² pursuable	
pursuit	
purt	pert+
purtain	pertain¹
purvade	pervade²+
purvey¹ ~or	
purvurse	perverse+
purytan	puritan+
pus *[infection]	puce *[colour],
	puss *[cat]
push¹ ~chair ~over	
pushy⁴	
pusillanimity pusillanimous	
puss *[cat]	puce *[colour],
	pus *[infection]
pussy⁴ ~l cat ~foot ~l willow	
put *[place] ~ting	putt¹ *[golf]
putative	
putrefy⁴ putrefaction	
putrid	

KEY TO SPELLING RULES

Red words are wrong. **Black** words are correct.

~   Add the suffix or word directly to the main word, without a space or hyphen
    e.g. ash ~en ~tray → ashen ashtray

~-   Add a hyphen to the main word before adding the next word
    e.g. blow ~-dry → blow-dry

~l   Leave a space between the main word and the next word
    e.g. decimal ~l place → decimal place

+   By finding this word in its **correct** alphabetical order, you can find related words
    e.g. about+ → about-face about-turn

*   Draws attention to words that may be confused

TM   Means the word is a trademark

putt[1] *[golf]   put *[place][+]
putty[4]
puzzle[2] ~ment
py   pi *[number],
                            pie *[food][+]

☞ Can't find your word here? Look under **pi**

pybald   piebald
pyed   pied[+]
pyella   paella
pyety   piety
pygmy[4]
pyjamas
pyke   pike[2+]

pyle   pile[2]
pylon
pynt   pint[+]
pyramid ~l selling
pyrate   pirate[2+]
pyre
Pyrex™
pyromaniac
pyrotechnics
Pyrrhic ~l victory
Pysees   Pisces
Pythagoras' theorem
python
pyur   pure[2+]

---

qake	quake
qarrel	quarrel
qarry	quarry[4]
qarter	quarter[1+]
qiche	quiche
qorum	quorum
quack[1]	

☞ Can't find your word here? Look under <u>quo</u>

quad ~rant
quadrangle   quadrangular
quadrat ~l sampling
quadratic ~l equation
quadratic ~l expression
quadratic ~l function
quadratic ~l sequence
quadriceps
quadrilateral
quadrille
quadriplegic
quadruple[2]   quadruplet
quadruplicate[2]
quaff[1]
quagmire
quail[1]
quaint[1] ~ly ~ness
quake[2]
Quaker ~ism
qualify[4]   qualification
quality[4]   qualitative
qualms
quandary[4]
quantify[4]
quantitative
quantity[4] ~l surveyor
quantum ~l leap ~l mechanics
quantum ~l theory
quarantine[2]

quark	
quarms	qualms
quarrel[3] ~some	
quarry[4]	
quart	
quarter[1] ~ly ~back	
quarter ~deck ~master	
quartet	
quarto	
quarts *[measure]	
quartz *[mineral] ~ite	
quary	quarry[4]
quasar	
quash[1]	
quasi	
quaternary[4]	
quatrain	
quaver[1]	
quay *[by the sea] ~side	key *[lock, PC, main]
que	cue *[billiards],
	queue[2] *[line up][+]
queasy[4]	
queen ~ly ~-size ~-sized	
queer[1] ~ly ~ness	
queery	query[4]
queezy	queasy[4]
queiten	quieten[1]
queitude	quietude
quell[1]	
quench[1] ~able	
Querty	QWERTY[+]
querulous ~ly ~ness	
query[4]	
quest[1]	
question[1] ~able ~ably ~l mark	
questionnaire	
queue[2] *[line] ~-jump	cue[2] *[billiards]
quibble[2]	

KEY TO SPELLING RULES

Red words are wrong. **Black** words are correct.

~   Add the suffix or word directly to the main word, without a space or hyphen
    e.g. ash ~en ~tray → **ashen ashtray**

~-   Add a hyphen to the main word before adding the next word
    e.g. blow ~-dry → **blow-dry**

~l   Leave a space between the main word and the next word
    e.g. decimal ~l place → **decimal place**

+   By finding this word in its **correct** alphabetical order, you can find related words
    e.g. about[+] → **about-face about-turn**

*   Draws attention to words that may be confused

TM   Means the word is a trademark

quiche	
quick[1] ~ly ~-freeze	
quick ~sand ~silver ~step	
quick ~-tempered ~-witted	
quicken[1] quickie	
quicley	quickly
quid ~l pro quo	
quier	queer[1+]
quiery	query[4]
quiescence quiescent	
quiet[1] *[no sound] ~ly quite *[almost, very]	
quieten[1]	
quiff	
quill[1]	
quilt[1]	
quin	
quince	
quinine	
quinse	quince
quintessence quintessential	
quintet	
quintuple ~t	
quip[3]	
quire *[paper]	choir *[singers]
quirk ~y	
quit *[leave, stop] ~ter ~ting	
quite *[almost, very]	quiet *[no sound]+
quiver[1]	
quixotic ~ally	
quiz[3] ~master	
quizzical ~ly	

☞ Can't find your word here? Look under **qua**

quodrangle	quadrangle+
quodratic	quadratic+

quoit	
quolify	qualify[1+]
quolity	quality[4+]
quondry	quandary[4]
quontify	quantify[4]
quontitativ	quantitative
quontity	quantity[4+]
quontum	quantum+
quorrel	quarrel[3+]
quorry	quarry[4]
quort	quart
quortenary	quaternary[4]
quorter	quarter[1+]
quortet	quartet
quorts	quarts *[measure], quartz *[mineral]+
quorum	
quoruntine	quarantine[2]
quoshent	quotient
quota	
quotable	
quotashun	quotation
quote[2] quotation	
quotient	

☞ Can't find your word here? Look under **qua** or **quo**

qwack	quack[1]
qwench	quench[1+]
QWERTY ~l keyboard	
qwick	quick+
qwit	quit+
quwod	quad+
qwodrangle	quadrangle
qworter	quarter[1+]
qwote	quote[2+]

KEY TO SUFFIXES AND COMPOUNDS

These rules are explained on pages ix to x.

1 Keep the word the same before adding ed, er, est, ing
e.g. cool[1] → cooled, cooler, coolest, cooling
2 Take off final e before adding ed, er, est, ing
e.g. fine[2] → fined, finer, finest, fining
3 Double final consonant before adding ed, er, est, ing
e.g. thin[3] → thinned, thinner, thinnest, thinning

4 Change final y to i before adding ed, er, es, est, ly, ness
e.g. tidy[4] → tidied, tidier, tidies, tidiest, tidily, tidiness
Keep final y before adding ing e.g. tidying
5 Add es instead of s to the end of the word
e.g. bunch[5] → bunches
6 Change final f to ve before adding s
e.g. calf[6] → calves

rabbi
rabbit[1] *[animal]   rarebit *[cheese]
rabble
rabeys   rabies
rabid ~ly
rabies
raccoon
race[2] *[contest] ~course   raise[2] *[lift]
race ~horse ~track ~way
rachet   ratchet[1]
racial ~ly   racism   racist
rack[1] *[shelf, pain]   rake[2] *[leaves]
racket[1] *[noise, swindle]   racquet[+] *[tennis]
racketeer
raconteur
racy[4]
radar
radial ~l tyre
radiance   radiant   radiantly
radiate[2]   radiator
radiation ~l sickness
radical *[political] ~ly   radicle *[root]
radicalise[2]
radicchio   radiccio
radiccio
radices
radicle *[root]   radical *[political][+]
radio[1] ~active ~activity
radio ~-astronomy ~-controlled
radio ~-isotope ~therapy ~l wave
radiographer   radiography
radiology   radiologist
radish[5]
radium
radius   radii
radon
radyal   radial[+]
radyans   radiance[+]

radyate   radiate[2] [+]
radyo   radio[+]
radyus   radius[+]
raffia
raffish ~ly
raffle[2]
raft[1]
rag[3] *[cloth] ~l doll   rage[2] *[anger]
rag ~time ~l trade ~wort
ragamuffin
rage[2] *[anger]
ragemuffin   ragamuffin
ragged *[torn, dirty]   raged *[anger]
ragout
ragu   ragout
raid[1]
rail[1] *[train, against]   râle *[sound]
rail ~card ~road ~way
raiment
rain[1] *[water] ~bow   reign[1] *[rule],
rain ~coat ~drop   rein[1] *[horse]
rain ~fall ~forest
rain ~proof ~storm
raindeer   reindeer
rainy[4]
raip   rape[2+]
raique   rake[2+]
raise[2] *[lift]   rays *[light],
                          race *[contest]
raisin *[fruit]
raison d'être *[reason]
Raj [the]
raje   rage[2]
rake[2] *[leaves]   rack[1] *[shelf, pain]
rakish ~ly
rakoon   raccoon
rale *[sound]   rail[1] *[train, against][+]
rally[4] *[together]   rely[4] *[trust]

KEY TO SPELLING RULES

Red words are wrong. **Black** words are correct.

~   Add the suffix or word directly to the main word, without a space or hyphen
     e.g. ash ~en ~tray → **ashen ashtray**

~-- Add a hyphen to the main word before adding the next word
     e.g. blow ~-dry → **blow-dry**

~l   Leave a space between the main word and the next word
     e.g. decimal ~l place → **decimal place**

+   By finding this word in its **correct** alphabetical order, you can find related words
     e.g. about[+] → **about-face about-turn**

*   Draws attention to words that may be confused

TM   Means the word is a trademark

rallying cry

ram³ *[hit, male sheep] ~rod

RAM *[random access   ROM *[read only
     memory]   memory]

Ramadan

ramble²

ramekin

ramerkin   ramekin

ramify⁴   ramification

ramp¹

rampage²

rampant ~ly rampancy

ramparts

ramshackle

ran

ranch¹ ~es

rancid ~ity

rancour

random ~ly ~ness ~| number ~| sampling

randomise²

rane   rain¹ *[water]+,
                             reign¹ *[rule],
                             rein¹ *[horse]

rang

range² ~finder

rank¹ ~ings ~| and file

rankel   rankle²

ranker   rancour

rankle²

ransack¹

ransid   rancid+

ransom¹

rant¹

rap³ *[music, knock]   wrap³ *[pack]

rapacious ~ly ~ness

rapcher   rapture+

rape² rapist

rapid ~ity ~ly ~| fire

rapier

rapore   rapport

rapped *[music, knocked]   rapt *[absorbed],
                             wrapped *[packed]

rapper *[singer]   wrapper *[packing]

rapport

rapsody   rhapsody⁴+

rapt *[absorbed]   wrapped *[packed],
                             rapped *[music,
                                      knocked]

rapture   rapturous

rare² ~ly ~ness

rarebit *[cheese]   rabbit¹ *[animal]

rarefy⁴

rarity⁴

rasberry   raspberry⁴

rascal ~ly

rash¹ ~ly ~ness

rashen   ration¹

rasher

rashio   ratio

rashnalise   rationalise²+

rashun   ration

rashunal   rational *[logical],
                             rationale *[reason]

rashunarle   rationale

rasisum   racism+

rasp¹

raspberry⁴

Rastafarian

rasy   racy⁴

raszmatasz   razzmatazz

rat³ ~-a-tat ~bag ~| race

ratan   rattan

ratchet¹

rate² ~| of interest ~payer

rather

ratify⁴   ratification

KEY TO SUFFIXES AND COMPOUNDS

These rules are explained on pages ix to x.

1 Keep the word the same before adding ed, er, est, ing
  e.g. cool¹ → cooled, cooler, coolest, cooling

2 Take off final e before adding ed, er, est, ing
  e.g. fine² → fined, finer, finest, fining

3 Double final consonant before adding ed, er, est, ing
  e.g. thin³ → thinned, thinner, thinnest, thinning

4 Change final y to i before adding ed, er, es, est,
  ly, ness
  e.g. tidy⁴ → tidied, tidier, tidies, tidiest, tidily,
  tidiness
  Keep final y before adding ing e.g. tidying

5 Add es instead of s to the end of the word
  e.g. bunch⁵ → bunches

6 Change final f to ve before adding s
  e.g. calf⁶ → calves

ratio
ration[1] ~| book
rational *[logical] ~ly
rationale *[reason]
rationalise[2] rationalisation
rationalist ~ic rationalism
rationality
rattan
rattle[2] ~snake
ratty[4]
raucous ~ly
ravage[2]
rave[2] ~| review
raven ~-haired
ravenous ~ly ~ness
ravige   ravage[2]
ravine
ravioli
ravish[1]
ravyoli   ravioli
raw[1] *[uncooked] ~ness   roar[1] *[sound]
raw ~| data ~hide ~| materials
ray ~| gun
rayd   raid[1]
raydar   radar
rayl   rail[1] *[train, against][+],
             rale *[sound]
raylery   raillery
rayment   raiment
rayn   rain[1] *[water][+],
             reign[1] *[rule],
             rein[1] *[horse]
rayny   rainy[4]
rayon
rays *[light]   raise[2] *[lift]
rayser   razor[+]
rayshal   racial[+]
raysond'etre   raison d'être

raze[2] *[demolish]   raise[2] *[lift]
razor ~bill ~| blade
razor ~-edged ~-sharp
razzmatazz
reach[1]

> ☞ Can't find your word here? Take off **re** and look
> again

react[1] ~ive ~or
reaction reactionary[4]
read *[book] ~able   reed *[plant]
read ~er ~ing ~out
readdress[1]
readmission
readmit[3] readmittance
readjust[1] ~ment
ready[4] ~-made ~-mix
reaffirm[1] ~ation
reafforestation
real *[actual]   reel[1] *[film, spin]
real ~| time ~| world
realise[2] realisable realisation
realism realist
realistic ~ally
reality[4]
reallocate[2] reallocation
really *[actually]   rely[4] *[depend]
realm
ream
reanimate[2] reanimation
reap[1]
reappear[1] ~ance
reappraise[2] reappraisal
rear[1] *[back, horse]   rare *[unusual][+]
rear ~-admiral ~-end ~guard
rearm[1] ~ament
rearrange[2] ~ment
reason[1] ~able ~ably

KEY TO SPELLING RULES

Red words are wrong. **Black** words are correct.

~   Add the suffix or word directly to the main word,
     without a space or hyphen
     e.g. ash ~en ~tray → ashen ashtray
~-   Add a hyphen to the main word before adding the
     next word
     e.g. blow ~-dry → blow-dry

~| Leave a space between the main word and the next
     word
     e.g. decimal ~| place → decimal place
+   By finding this word in its **correct** alphabetical
     order, you can find related words
     e.g. about[+] → about-face about-turn
*   Draws attention to words that may be confused
TM   Means the word is a trademark

reassemble[2] *[meet]   resemble[2] *[look like]

reassert[1] ~ion

reassess[1] ~ment

reassure[2]   reassurance

reassuringly

reawaken[1]

rebal   rebel[3+]

rebate[2]

rebel[3]   rebellion

rebellious ~ly ~ness

rebild   rebuild[+]

rebirth[1]   reborn

rebound[1]

rebuff[1]

rebuild ~ing   rebuilt

rebuke[2]

rebut[3] ~tal

recalcitrance   recalcitrant

recall[1]

recant[1] *[not true]   recent *[of late][+]

recap[3]

recapitulate[2]   recapitulation

recapture[2]

recast ~ing

recede[2]

receipt[1] *[document]   reseat[1] *[seat again]

receive[2]   receivable

received ~| pronunciation

receivership

recent *[just passed] ~ly   resent *[grudge][+]

receptacle

reception ~ist ~-room

receptive ~ness

receptivity

receptor

recess ~ed

recession ~ary

recessive ~ly ~ness

rech   reach[1] *[get],
                     retch[1] *[vomit]
                     wretch *[person]

recharge[2] ~able

recidivism   recidivist

recind   rescind[1]

recipe

recipient

reciprocal ~ly   reciprocity

reciprocate[2]   reciprocation

recite[2]   recital   recitation

reckless ~ly ~ness

reckon[1]

reclaim[1]   reclamation

recline[2]

recluse

recognisable   recognisably

recognise[2]   recognition

recoil[1]

recollect[1] ~ion

recommence[2]

recommend[1] ~able ~ation

recompense[2]

reconcile[2]   reconcilable   reconciliation

recondition[1]

reconnaissance

reconnect[1]

reconnoitre[2]

reconquer[1]

reconsider[1] ~ation

reconsile   reconcile[2+]

reconstitute[2]   reconstitution

reconstruct[1] ~ion

reconstructive ~| surgery

reconvene[2]

recooperate   recuperate[2+]

recooperativ   recuperative[+]

record[1] ~-breaking ~| player

---

re-count[1] *[count again]
recount[1] *[tell]
recoup[1] ~ment
recourse
recover[1] ~able   recovery[4]
re-create[2]
recreation ~al
recrimination
recruit[1] ~ment
rectangle   rectangular
rectify[4]   rectifiable   rectification
rectitude
rector   rectory[4]
rectum   rectal
recuperate[2]   recuperation
recuperative ~l powers
recur[3]
recurrence   recurrent
recurring ~l decimal
recycle[2]
red[3] *[colour]   read *[book][+]
red ~-blooded ~-brick ~coat
red ~-eye ~-eyed
red ~-faced ~-handed
red ~head ~l herring
red ~neck ~l tape ~wood
redden[1]
reddish
reddy   ready[4+]
redecorate[2]   redecoration
redeem[1] ~able
redemption   redemptive
redeploy[1] ~ment
redevelop[1] ~ment
redial[3]
redid
rediffusion
redirect[1] ~ion

redistribute[2]   redistribution
redo ~ing   redone
redolence   redolent
redouble[2]
redoubt
redress[1]
reduce[2]   reduction
redundancy[4]   redundant
reduse   reduce[2+]
reech   reach[1+]
reed *[plant]   read *[book][+]
reef[1] ~l knot
reefer *[cigarette]   refer[3] *[pass on][+]
reek[1] *[smell]   wreak *[havoc]
reel[1] *[film, spin]   real *[actual][+]
re-elect[1] ~ion

☞ Can't find your word here? Take off **re** and look again

re-enact[1] ~ment
re-engineer[1]
re-enter[1]
re-entry[4]
reeson   reason[1+]
re-establish[1] ~ment
re-examine[2]   re-examination
re-export[1]
refashion[1]
refectory[4]
refer[3] *[pass on]   reefer *[cigarette]
referee ~d ~ing
reference
referendum   referenda
referent ~ial
referral
refill[1] ~able
refine[2] ~ment
refinery[4]

refit[3]
reflate[2]
reflect[1] ~ive ~or
reflection ~| symmetry
reflex ~es ~ive
refloat[1]
reflux[1] ~es
reform[1] *[change] ~ation   Reformation [the]
re-form[1] *[exist again]
reformat[3]
refract[1] ~ion ~ive
refrain[1]
refresh[1] ~ment
refried ~| beans
refrigerate[2]   refrigerator
refrigeration
refuel[3]
refuge *[shelter]
refugee *[fugitive]
refund[1] ~able
refurbish[1]
refuree   referee[+]
refurendum   referendum[+]
refuse[2]   refusal
refute[2]   refutable   refutal
regain[1]
regal *[king] ~ly
regale[2] *[entertain]
regalia
regard[1] ~less
regatta
regay   reggae
reject   reject[1+]
regency[4]   regent
regenerate[2]   regeneration
regenerative
regergitate   regurgitate[2]
reggae

regicide   regicidal
regime   regimen
regiment[1] ~al ~ation
region ~al ~alism ~ally
register[1]   registration
registrar   registry[4]
reglate   regulate[2+]
reglater   regulator
regler   regular[+]
reglurise   regularise[2]
regress[1] ~ion ~ive
regret[3] ~ful ~fully
regrettable   regrettably
regular ~ity ~ly
regularise[2]
regulate[2]   regulator
regulation
regurgitate[2]
rehabilitate[2]   rehabilitation
rehash[1]
rehearse[2]   rehearsal
reheat[1]
rehouse[2]
Reich
reign[1] *[rule]   rain[1] *[water],
                                     rein[1] *[horse]
reimburse[2] ~ment
rein[1] *[horse]   rain[1] *[water],
                                     reign[1] *[rule]
reincarnate[2]   reincarnation
reindeer
reinforce[2] ~ment
reinforced ~| concrete
reinstate[2] ~ment
reinvent[1] ~ion
reinvest[1] ~ment
reiterate[2]   reiteration
reject[1] ~ion

---

rejicide	regicide[+]
rejime	regime[+]
rejiment	regiment[1+]
rejion	region[+]
rejister	register[1+]
rejistrar	registrar[+]
rejoice[2] rejoicingly	
rejoin[1] ~der	
rejoise	rejoice[2+]
rejuce	reduce[2+]
rejuvenate[2] rejuvenation	
rekindle[2]	
rekkanoyta	reconnoitre[2]
rekollekt	recollect[1+]
rekommend	recommend[1+]
rekommendable	recommendable
rekompense	recompense[2]
rekoncilabul	reconcilable
rekoncile	reconcile[2+]
rekonnaissance	reconnaissance
rekord	record[1+]
rekwest	request[1]
rekwiem	requiem
rekwisite	requisite[+]
rekwited	requited
relapse[2]	
relate[2]	
relation ~al ~less ~ship	
relative ~ly ~| frequency ~| pronoun	
relativity	
relax[1] ~es ~ation	
relay[1]	
release[2]	
relegate[2] relegation	
relent[1] ~less ~lessly	
relevance relevant	
reliable reliability reliably	
reliance reliant	

relic	
relief ~| effort	
relieve[2] relievable	
religion	
religious ~ly ~ness	
relijion	religion
relijious	religious[+]
relinquish[1] ~ment	
relish[1]	
relm	realm
reload[1]	
relocate[2] relocation	
reluctance	
reluctant ~ly	
rely[4] *[trust]	**really** *[actually]
remain[1] ~der	
remake remaking remade	
remand[1]	
remaniss	reminisce[2+]
remanissant	reminiscent
remark[1] ~able ~ably	
remarry[4]	
rematch	
reme	ream
remedial	
remedy[4] remediation	
remember[1] remembrance	
remind[1] ~er	
reminisce[2]	
reminiscence reminiscent	
remiss	
remission	
remit[3] ~tal ~tance	
remix[1]	
remnant	
remodel[3]	
remonstrance	
remonstrate[2] remonstration	

---

remorse ~ful ~fully
remorseless ~ly ~ness
remote[2] ~ly ~ness
removal
remove[2]   removable
remunerate[2]   remuneration
renaissance *[rebirth]
Renaissance *[historic period]
renal
renayg   renege[2]
rend[1]
rendayvoo   rendezvous
render[1]
rendezvous[1]
rendition
reneegosheate   renegotiate[2]
renegade
renege[2]
renegotiate[2]
renew[1] ~able ~al
renounce[2] ~ment
renovate[2]   renovation
renown ~ed
rent[1] ~~al ~~free
renunciation
reoccupy[4]
re-open[1]
reorganise[2]   reorganisation
re-orientate[2]   re-orientation
repaid
repair[1] ~| man
reparable   reparation
repartee
repatriate[2]   repatriation
repay ~able ~ing ~ment
repayd   repaid
repeal[1] *[law]   repel[3] *[keep away]
repeat[1] ~able ~edly

repel[3] *[keep away]   repeal[1] *[law]
repellent
repent[1]
repentance   repentant
repercussion
repertoire
repertory
repete   repeat[1]
repetition   repetitious
repetitive ~ly ~ness
replace[2] ~able ~ment
replay[1]
replenish[1] ~ment
replete
replica
replicate[2]   replication
reply[4]
report[1] ~able ~edly
repose[2]
repository[4]
repossess[1]
repreev   reprieve[2]
reprehend[1]   reprehension
reprehensible   reprehensibly
represent[1] ~ation ~ative
repress[1] ~ible ~ion ~ive
reprieve[2]
reprimand[1]
reprint[1]
reprise[2]   reprisal
reproach[1] ~ful ~fully
reprobate[2]
reproduce[2]   reproducible
reproduction   reproductive
reproof *[criticism]
reprove[2] *[criticise]   reprovingly
reptile   reptilian
republic   Republican

KEY TO SUFFIXES AND COMPOUNDS

These rules are explained on pages ix to x.

1 Keep the word the same before adding ed, er, est, ing
   e.g. cool[1] → cooled, cooler, coolest, cooling
2 Take off final e before adding ed, er, est, ing
   e.g. fine[2] → fined, finer, finest, fining
3 Double final consonant before adding ed, er, est, ing
   e.g. thin[3] → thinned, thinner, thinnest, thinning

4 Change final y to i before adding ed, er, es, est, ly, ness
   e.g. tidy[4] → tidied, tidier, tidies, tidiest, tidily, tidiness
   Keep final y before adding ing e.g. tidying
5 Add es instead of s to the end of the word
   e.g. bunch[5] → bunches
6 Change final f to ve before adding s
   e.g. calf[6] → calves

repudiate[2] repudiation
repugnance repugnant
repulse[2] repulsion
repulsive ~ly ~ness
reputation reputable
repute ~d ~dly
request[1]
requiem
require[2] ~ment
requisite requisition
requited

rere   rare[2] *[unusual][+],
          rear[1] *[back, horse]

rerify   rarefy
rerite   rewrite[+]
rerity   rarity[4]
rerote   rewrote
rescind[1]
rescue[2]
research[1] ~er
re-seat[1] *[seat again]   receipt[1] *[document]
reseeve   receive[2+]
reseevership   receivership
resemble[2] *[look like]   reassemble[2] *[meet]
resemblance
resent[1] *[grudge] ~ment   recent *[just passed]
               re-sent *[sent again]
resentful ~ly ~ness
resepshun   reception[+]
reseptacle   receptacle
reseptiv   receptive[+]
reseptivity   receptivity
reseptor   receptor
reserface   resurface[2]
resergence   resurgence[+]
reserrect   resurrect[1+]
reservation
reserve[2] reservist

reservoir
resess   recess[+]
resession   recession
reset ~ting
resettle[2] ~ment
reshape[2]
reshuffle[2]
reside[2]
residence residency[4]
resident
residential
residew   residue[+]
residivisum   recidivism[+]
residue residual
resign[1] *[leave]   resin *[sticky]
resignation
resilience
resilient ~ly
resin *[sticky]   resign[1] *[leave]
resipient   recipient
resiprocal   reciprocal[+]
resiprocate   reciprocate[2+]
resipy   recipe
resist[1]
resistable resistability resistably
resistance resistant
resistant ~l materials
resister *[person]
resistor *[electrical]
resit resat
resite   recite[2+]
resize[2]
reskue   rescue[2]
resolushun   resolution
resolute ~ly ~ness
resolution
resolve[2]
resonance resonant

---

resonate² resonator		resurvwa	reservoir
resondetre	raison d'être	resus	rhesus⁺
resonense	resonance⁺	resuscitate² resuscitation	
resort¹		resycle	recycle²
resound¹		retail¹	
resource ~ful ~fully		retain¹	
respect¹ ~ful ~fully		retake ~n retaking	
respectable respectability respectably		retaliate² retaliation	
respective ~ly		retaliatory	
respire² respirator respiratory		retard¹ ~ation	
respiration		retch¹ *[vomit]	wretch *[person]
respite		retention retentive	
resplendence resplendent		rethink ~ing	
respond¹ ~ence ~ent		reticence	
response		reticent ~ly	
responsibility⁴		retina	
responsible responsibly		retinue	
responsive ~ly ~ness		retire² ~ment	
resstront	restaurant	retisense	reticence
rest¹ *[calm, stay]	wrest¹ *[pull]	retold	
restate²		retook	
restaurant		retool¹	
restful ~ly ~ness		retoric	rhetoric⁺
restitution		retort¹	
restive ~ly ~ness		retouch¹	
restless ~ly ~ness		retrace²	
restorative		retract¹ ~able ~ion	
restore² restoration		retread *[walk again] ~ing	
restrain¹ ~ing order restraint		retread¹ *[tyre]	
restrict¹ ~ion ~ive		retreat¹	
restructure²		retrench¹ ~ment	
result¹ ~ant		retrial	
resume² *[restart]		retribution	
résumé *[summary]		retrieval ~l system	
resumption		retrieve² retrievable	
resurface²		retriever	
resurgence resurgent		retro ~active	
resurrect¹ ~ion		retrod ~den	

KEY TO SUFFIXES AND COMPOUNDS

These rules are explained on pages ix to x.

1 Keep the word the same before adding ed, er, est, ing
e.g. cool¹ → cooled, cooler, coolest, cooling
2 Take off final e before adding ed, er, est, ing
e.g. fine² → fined, finer, finest, fining
3 Double final consonant before adding ed, er, est, ing
e.g. thin³ → thinned, thinner, thinnest, thinning

4 Change final y to i before adding ed, er, es, est, ly, ness
e.g. tidy⁴ → tidied, tidier, tidies, tidiest, tidily, tidiness
Keep final y before adding ing e.g. tidying
5 Add es instead of s to the end of the word
e.g. bunch⁵ → bunches
6 Change final f to ve before adding s
e.g. calf⁶ → calves

retrograde
retrogress[1] ~ion ~ive
retrospect ~ion ~ive
retrovirus
return[1] ~able ~| match
reumatic   rheumatic[+]
reumatisum   rheumatism
reumatoid   rheumatoid[+]
reunion   reunite[2]
reuse[2]
Reuters
rev[3] *[engine]   Rev *[vicar]
revallee   reveille
revalue[2]   revaluation
revamp[1]
reveal[1]
reveille
revel[3] ~ler ~ry
revelation
revenge[2] ~ful ~fully
revenue
reverberate[2]   reverberation
revere[2]
reveree   reverie
reverence
Reverend *[priest]
reverent *[respectful] ~ly
reverie
reversal
reverse[2]   reversible
revert[1]   reversion
revery   reverie
review[1] *[survey]   revue *[show]
revile[2]
revise[2]
revision ~ist
revisit[1]
revitalise[2]   revitalisation

revival ~ist
revive[2]
revocation
revoke[2]   revocable
revolt[1]
revolution ~ise   revolutionary[4]
revolutionise[2]
revolve[2]
revrand   reverend
revrent   reverent[+]
revue *[show]   review[1] *[survey]
revulsion
rew   rue[2+]
reward[1]
rewbella   rubella
rewbicund   rubicund
rewbie   ruby[4]
rewbric   rubric
rewd   rude[2] *[offensive][+],
                rued *[regretted]
rewind ~ing
reword[1]
rework[1]
rewound
rewrite   rewriting   rewriter
rewritten
rewrote
rewse   ruse
rezzavwa   reservoir
rhapsody[4]   rhapsodise[2]
rhelm   realm
rhesus ~| monkey
rhetoric ~al
rheumatic ~| fever
rheumatism
rheumatoid ~| arthritis
rhinestone
rhino   rhinoceros[5]

KEY TO SPELLING RULES

Red words are wrong. **Black words are correct.**

~   Add the suffix or word directly to the main word, without a space or hyphen
    e.g. ash ~en ~tray → ashen ashtray
~-   Add a hyphen to the main word before adding the next word
    e.g. blow ~-dry → blow-dry

~| Leave a space between the main word and the next word
    e.g. decimal ~| place → decimal place
+   By finding this word in its **correct** alphabetical order, you can find related words
    e.g. about[+] → about-face about-turn
*   Draws attention to words that may be confused
TM   Means the word is a trademark

rhizome	
rhodium	
rhododendron	
rhomboid	
rhombus[5]	rhombi
rhubarb	
rhyme[2] *[poetry]	rime *[frost]
rhythm ~ic ~ical ~ically	

☞ Can't find your word here? Look under **re**

riacshun	reaction[+]
riact	react[1+]
riality	reality[4]
riappear	reappear[1+]
riawaken	reawaken[1]
rib[3]	
ribald ~ry	
ribate	rebate[2]
ribbon	
ribellious	rebellious[+]
rice *[food]	rise[2] *[up][+]
ricede	recede[2]
riceipt	receipt[1]
rich[1] ~ly ~ness	
richarge	recharge[2+]
richous	righteous[+]
Richter Scale [the]	
ricidivisum	recidivism[+]
ricipient	recipient
rick[1]	
rickets	
rickety	
rickoshay	ricochet[1]
rickshaw	
riclaim	reclaim[1+]
ricochet[1]	
ricoil	recoil[1]
rid[3] riddance	

ridden	
riddle[2]	
ride rider riding	
ridge ~d	
ridicule[2]	
ridiculous ~ly ~ness	
rife	
rifectory	refectory[4]
rifer	reefer *[cigarette], refer[3] *[pass on][+]
riff-raff	
rifill	refill[1+]
rifine	refine[2+]
rifinery	refinery[4]
rifit	refit[3]
riflate	reflate[2]
rifle[2] ~man ~l range	
riflect	reflect[1+]
rift ~l valley	
rig[3] ~l up	
right[1] *[correct]	rite *[ceremony], write *[text]
right ~ly ~ness ~l angle	
righteous ~ly ~ness	
rightful ~ly	
right-hand right-handed	
right-wing	
rigid ~ity ~ly	
rigmarole	
rigor *[stiffness] ~l mortis	
rigour *[severity]	
rile[2]	
rim[3] *[edge] ~less	rhyme[2] *[poetry]
rimain	remain[1+]
rimand	remand[1]
rimark	remark[1+]
rimedial	remedial
rimember	remember[1+]

KEY TO SUFFIXES AND COMPOUNDS

These rules are explained on pages ix to x.

1 Keep the word the same before adding ed, er, est, ing
e.g. cool[1] → cooled, cooler, coolest, cooling

2 Take off final e before adding ed, er, est, ing
e.g. fine[2] → fined, finer, finest, fining

3 Double final consonant before adding ed, er, est, ing
e.g. thin[3] → thinned, thinner, thinnest, thinning

4 Change final y to i before adding ed, er, es, est, ly, ness
e.g. tidy[4] → tidied, tidier, tidies, tidiest, tidily, tidiness
Keep final y before adding ing e.g. tidying

5 Add es instead of s to the end of the word
e.g. bunch[5] → bunches

6 Change final f to ve before adding s
e.g. calf[6] → calves

☞ Can't find your word here? Look under **re**

rimiss	remiss⁺
rimit	remit³⁺
rimorse	remorse⁺
rimorseless	remorseless⁺
rimote	remote²⁺
rimoval	removal
rimunerate	remunerate²⁺
rinal	renal
rinayg	renege²
rind	
rinestone	rhinestone
ring¹ *[circle]	wring *[squeeze]⁺
ring *[bell] ~ing	
ring ~leader ~master ~-pull	
ring ~| road ~side ~worm	
ringer *[horse]	wringer *[squeezer]
ringlet	
rink	
rinkle	wrinkle²
rino	rhino⁺
rinoserus	rhinoceros
rinounce	renounce²⁺
rinown	renown⁺
rinse²	
rinunsiayshun	renunciation
riot¹ ~ous ~ously	
rip³ *[tear] ~-cord	ripe² *[ready to eat]⁺
rip ~-off ~-roaring	
ripair	repair¹⁺
riparabul	reparable⁺
ripatriate	repatriate²⁺
ripe² *[ready to eat] ~ness	
ripeal	repeal¹
ripeat	repeat¹⁺
ripel	repel³
ripen¹	

ripent	repent¹
ripentant	repentant
riplace	replace²⁺
riplenish	replenish¹⁺
riply	reply⁴
riport	report¹⁺
ripose	repose²
ripository	repository⁴
ripple² ~| effect	
ripreeve	reprieve²
ripreshun	repression
riproach	reproach¹⁺
ripublic	republic⁺
ripudiate	repudiate²⁺
ripugnance	repugnance⁺
ripulsiv	repulsive⁺
ripute	repute⁺
riquest	request¹
riquire	require²⁺
riscind	rescind¹
rise *[up] rising	rice *[food]
risearch	research¹⁺
risemble	resemble²⁺
risen	
risent	resent¹ *[grudge]⁺, re-sent *[sent again]
risentful	resentful⁺
riserve	reserve²⁺
rishufful	reshuffle²
riside	reside²⁺
risilience	resilience
risine	resign¹
risist	resist¹
risistabul	resistible⁺
risistance	resistance⁺
risit	resit
risk¹ ~-averse ~-taking	
risky⁴ *[dangerous]	risqué [suggestive]

KEY TO SPELLING RULES

Red words are wrong. **Black** words are correct.

~   Add the suffix or word directly to the main word, without a space or hyphen
    e.g. ash ~en ~tray → **ashen ashtray**

~-   Add a hyphen to the main word before adding the next word
    e.g. blow ~-dry → **blow-dry**

~| Leave a space between the main word and the next word
    e.g. decimal ~| place → **decimal place**

+   By finding this word in its **correct** alphabetical order, you can find related words
    e.g. about⁺ → **about-face about-turn**

*   Draws attention to words that may be confused

TM   Means the word is a trademark

risolve	resolve[2]	roadster	
risort	resort[1]	roal	role *[actor][+],
risotto			roll[1] *[move][+]
risource	resource[+]	roam[1] *[wander around]	Rome *[city]
rispect	respect[1+]	roan	
rispectabul	respectable[+]	roar[1] *[sound]	raw[1] *[uncooked]
rispectiv	respective[+]	roast[1]	
rispire	respire[2+]	rob[3] robbery[4]	
rispite	respite	robe[2]	
rispond	respond[1+]	robin ~l redbreast	
risponse	response[+]	robot ~ics	
risponsibul	responsible[+]	robust ~ly ~ness	
rissole		rock[1] ~l and roll ~l bottom	
ritch	rich	rock ~l climbing ~l garden	
rite *[ceremony]	right[1] *[correct][+],	rock ~-hard ~l music ~l pool	
	write *[text][+]	rock ~-solid ~-steady	
rithum	rhythm[+]	rocker	
ritual ~ise ~ism ~istic		rockery[4]	
riturn	return[1+]	rocket[1] ~l science	
riunion	reunion[+]	rocketry	
rival[3] rivalry[4]		rocking ~l chair ~l horse	
riveal	reveal[1]	rockrey	rockery[4]
rivenge	revenge[2+]	rocky[4]	
river ~front ~side		rococo	
riverberate	reverberate[2+]	rod *[fishing]	
rivere	revere[2+]	rode *[bike]	road *[street],
rivet[1]			rowed *[boat]
Riviera [the]			
rivulet		☞ Can't find your word here? Look under **rho**	
rizome	rhizome	rodent	
ro	roe *[deer, fish][+],	rodeo	
	row[1] *[boat, column][+]	rodium	rhodium
roach[5]		rododendron	rhododendron
road *[street] ~block	rode *[bike],	rodyo	rodeo
	rowed *[boat]	roe *[deer, fish] ~buck	row[1] *[boat, column]
road ~hog ~runner		rog	rogue[+]
road ~show ~side		rogue roguish	
road ~way ~worthy		roial	royal[+]

KEY TO SUFFIXES AND COMPOUNDS

These rules are explained on pages ix to x.

1 Keep the word the same before adding **ed, er, est, ing**
e.g. cool[1] → cooled, cooler, coolest, cooling
2 Take off final **e** before adding **ed, er, est, ing**
e.g. fine[2] → fined, finer, finest, fining
3 Double final consonant before adding **ed, er, est, ing**
e.g. thin[3] → thinned, thinner, thinnest, thinning

4 Change final **y** to **i** before adding **ed, er, es, est, ly, ness**
e.g. tidy[4] → tidied, tidier, tidies, tidiest, tidily, tidiness
Keep final **y** before adding **ing** e.g. tidying
5 Add **es** instead of **s** to the end of the word
e.g. bunch[5] → bunches
6 Change final **f** to **ve** before adding **s**
e.g. calf[6] → calves

rojer	roger
rok	rock[+]
roker	rocker
roket	rocket[1] *[missile][+]
rokoko	rococo
roky	rocky[4]
role *[actor]	roll[1] *[move][+]
role ~| model ~| play	
rolipoly	roly-poly
roll[1] *[move] ~| call	role *[actor][+]
roll ~over ~-top	
roller ~| coaster ~| skate	
Rollerblade™	
rollick[1]	
rolling ~| contract ~| pin ~| stock	
Rolls-Royce™	
roly-poly	
ROM	
Roman ~| candle ~| Catholic ~| numerals	
romance[2] ~| language	
romanse	romance[2]
romantic ~ally ~ism	
Romany[4]	
rombus	rhombus[+]
Romen	Roman[+]
romeo	
romio	romeo
romp[1]	
romper suit	
rondayvoo	rendezvous
rondo	
rong	wrong[1+]
roobarb	rhubarb
roof[1] ~less	
roof ~| garden ~| rack	
roof ~| terrace ~top	
rook[1] rookery[4]	
rookie	

room ~ful roomy[4]	
roomer	rumour[+]
roomynate	ruminate[2+]
roon	ruin[1+]
roonous	ruinous[+]
roost[1]	
root[1] *[plant] ~less	route *[way]
root ~| directory ~| vegetable	
rope[2] ~| ladder	
ropy[4]	
rorcous	raucous[+]
rore	roar[1] *[noise],
	raw *[fresh]
rosary[4]	
rose *[flower, up]	rows *[boat, columns]
rose ~bud ~-coloured	
rose ~water ~| window ~wood	
rosemary	
rosette	
rosrey	rosary[4]
rost	roast[1]
roster	
rostrum	
rosy[4]	
rot[3]	
rota *[list]	rotor *[blade]
rotary[4] *[machine]	
Rotary *[club] Rotarian	
rotashun	rotation[+]
rotate[2] rotatable	
rotation ~| symmetry	
rote *[repetition]	wrote *[text]
rotor *[blade]	rota *[list],
	rotter *[bad person]
rotten[1] ~ly ~ness	
rotter *[bad person]	rota *[list],
	rotor *[blade]
Rottweiler	

---

rotund   rotunda

rouble

rouge[2]

rough[1] *[coarse] ~ly   ruff *[collar, bird]

rough ~ness ~neck ~shod

roughage

roughen[1]

roulette

round[1] ~ly ~ness

roundabout

rounders

Roundhead

round-table *[talks]

Round Table *[club]

rouse[2]

rout[1] *[defeat, out]   rout *[tool]

route *[way] ~| march   root[1] *[plant][+]

routine

rove[2]

row[1] *[boat, column]   roe *[deer, fish]

row[1] *[noise]

rowan ~| tree

rowdy[4]

rownd   round[1][+]

rows *[boat, column]   rose *[flower, up][+],

rows *[noise]   rouse[2] *[wake]

rowse   rouse[2]

rowt   rout[1]

royal ~ly ~ty

Royters   Reuters

rub[3]

rubarb   rhubarb

rubber ~ise ~y

rubber ~| band ~| dinghy

rubber-stamp[1]

rubbish[1] ~y

rubble

rubella

rubicund

rubric

rubul   rouble *[money],
                    rubble *[stones]

ruby[4]

rucksack

ructions

rudder

ruddy[4]

rude[2] *[offensive]   rued *[regretted]

rude ~ly ~ness

rudiment ~ary

rue[2] ~ful ~fully

rued *[regretted]   rude *[offensive][+]

ruel   rule[2][+]

ruff *[collar, bird]   roof[1] *[building][+],
                    rough[1] *[coarse][+]

ruffian

ruffle[2]

rug

Rugby ~| League ~| Union

ruge   rouge[2]

rugged ~ly ~ness

rugger

rugid   rugged[+]

ruin[1] *[destroy] ~ation   rune *[letter]

ruinous ~ly

rule[2] ~book

rulette   roulette

rum

rumatic   rheumatic[+]

rumatisum   rheumatism

rumatoid   rheumatoid[+]

rumba

rumble[2]

ruminate[2]   rumination

rummage[2]

rummige   rummage[2]

---

rummy	
rumour ~ed ~-monger	
rump ~| steak	
rumple²	
rumpus⁵	
rumynate	ruminate²⁺
run *[fast]	rune *[letter]
runabout	
runaway *[person]	runway *[airport]
rune *[letter]	ruin¹ *[destroy]
rung *[ladder, bell]	wrung *[squeezed]
runner ~| bean ~-up	
running ~| battle ~| commentary	
running ~| costs ~| joke	
running ~| mate ~| order	
running ~| repairs ~| total	
running ~| water	
runny⁴	
runt	
runway *[airport]	runaway *[person]
rupchure	rupture²
rupee	
rupture²	
rural ~ness	
rusc	rusk
ruse	

ruset	russet
rush¹ ~| hour	
Rushun	Russian⁺
rusk	
rusler	rustler
russel	rustle²⁺
russet	
Russian ~| roulette	
rust¹ ~-free ~-proof	
rustic	
rustle² ~| up	
rustler	
rusty⁴	
rut³	
rute	root¹ *[plant]⁺, route *[way]
ruthless ~ly ~ness	
rutine	routine

☞ Can't find your word here? Look under **ri**

rybald	ribald⁺
ryce	rice
rye *[grain] ~grass	wry *[humour]
ryme	rhyme
ryval	rival³⁺

---

sabbath
sabbatical
sabel   sable
sable
sabotage²   saboteur
sabre ~-rattling ~-toothed
sac *[cavity]   sack¹ *[bag, destroy]
saccharin
sachel   satchel
sachet *[small bag]   sashay¹ *[walk]
sachurate   saturate²⁺
sack¹ *[bag, destroy]   sac *[cavity]
sack ~cloth ~ful
sacrament
sacred ~ly ~ness
sacrifice²   sacrificial
sacrilege
sacrilegious ~ly ~ness
sacrin   saccharin
sacrosanct
sad³ ~ly ~ness
sadden¹
saddle² ~bag ~-sore
saden   sadden¹
sadist ~ic ~ically   sadism
sadomasochist
safari
safe² ~ly ~-conduct ~-deposit
safe ~l haven ~keeping
safeguard¹
safety ~l belt ~l catch
safety ~l glass ~l match
safety ~l net ~l pin ~l valve
saffire   sapphire
saffron
saftey   safety⁺
sag³
saga

sagacious ~l sagacity
sage ~ly ~ness
Sagittarius
said
saif   safe⁺
saifety   safety⁺
saik   sake
sail¹ *[boat] ~or   sale *[goods]⁺
saim   same⁺
sain   sane⁺
saint ~ly ~hood ~'s day
saiv   save²
saje   sage⁺
Sajittarius   Sagittarius
sak   sack¹ *[bag, destroy]⁺,
                           sake *[sake of]
sakarin   saccharin
sake
sakrament   sacrament
sakred   sacred⁺
sakrifise   sacrifice²⁺
sakrilij   sacrilege⁺
sakrilijus   sacrilegious⁺
salaam
salad ~l bar ~l cream ~l dressing
salami
salarmee   salami
salary⁴
sale *[goods] ~able   sail¹ *[boat]⁺
sale ~l price
salery   salary⁴
sales ~l force ~man ~person
sales ~l pitch ~l representative
sales ~woman
salient
saline   salinity
saliva
salivate²   salivation

KEY TO SUFFIXES AND COMPOUNDS

These rules are explained on pages ix to x.

1 Keep the word the same before adding **ed, er, est, ing**
e.g. cool¹ → cooled, cooler, coolest, cooling
2 Take off final **e** before adding **ed, er, est, ing**
e.g. fine² → fined, finer, finest, fining
3 Double final consonant before adding **ed, er, est, ing**
e.g. thin³ → thinned, thinner, thinnest, thinning

4 Change final **y** to **i** before adding **ed, er, es, est, ly, ness**
e.g. tidy⁴ → tidied, tidier, tidies, tidiest, tidily, tidiness
Keep final **y** before adding **ing** e.g. tidying
5 Add **es** instead of **s** to the end of the word
e.g. bunch⁵ → bunches
6 Change final **f** to **ve** before adding **s**
e.g. calf⁶ → calves

sallow
sally[4] ~| forth
salm   psalm[+]
salmon
salmonella
salon *[hair, beauty]
saloon *[car, bar]
salow   sallow
salsa
salt[1] ~| cellar ~| marsh
salter   psalter
salty[4]
salubrious ~ly ~ness
salune   saloon
salutary
salute[2] salutation
salvage[2] ~able
salvation
salve[2]
salvige   salvage[2+]
salvo
salyne   saline[+]
salyvate   salivate[2+]
Samaritan
samba
same ~ness ~-sex
samerai   samurai
samon   salmon
samovar
samosa
sample[2]
samurai
sanatorium sanatoria
sanchury   sanctuary[4]
sancshun   sanction[1]
sanctify[4] sanctification
sanctimonious ~ly ~ness
sanction[1]

sanctity[4]
sanctuary[4]
sanctum
sand[1] ~bag ~bank
sand ~blast ~box ~castle
sand ~paper ~pit ~stone
sandal ~wood
sandwich[1] ~es
sandy[4]
sane ~ly
sang
sangfroid
sangria
sanguine sanguinity
sangwin   sanguine[+]
sanitary[4] ~| towel
sanitashun   sanitation
sanitation
sanitree   sanitary[4+]
sanity
sank
sankshun   sanction[1]
sanktimonius   sanctimonious[+]
sanktity   sanctity
sanktum   sanctum
sans serif
Sanskrit
Santa Claus
sanwich   sandwich[1+]
sapeena   subpoena[1]
sap[3] ~ling
sapphire
sarcasm
sarcastic ~ally
sarcoffagus   sarcophagus[+]
sarcoma
sarcophagus sarcophagi
sardine

---

sardonic ~ally		sause	sauce *[liquid]+, source² *[origin]+
sari			
sarkasm	sarcasm	sauser	saucer
sarkastik	sarcastic+	sausery	sorcery
sarm	psalm+	sausy	saucy⁴
sarong		sauté¹ *[fry]	sortie *[outing]
sary	sari	savage² ~ly ~ry	
sash⁵		savannah	
sashabul	satiable	savant	
sashay¹ *[walk]	sachet *[small bag]	save²	
sasheate	satiate² +	saver *[one who saves]	savour *[flavour]
sashimi		savery	savoury⁴
sat		savige	savage²+
Satan ~ic		savings ~| account ~| bank	
satchel		saviour *[helper]	savour¹ *[flavour]
sate²		savoir-faire	
satellite ~| dish		savont	savant
Saterday	Saturday	savour¹ *[flavour]	saviour *[helper]
Satern	Saturn	savoury⁴	
satiate² satiable		savvy⁴	
satin ~wood		savwafair	savoir-faire
satire satirist		saw *[past of see]	soar¹ *[fly], sore² *[hurt]+
satirical ~ly			
satirise²		saw¹ *[cut] ~n ~dust	
satisfactory⁴		sawlt	salt¹+
satisfy⁴ satisfaction		sawna	sauna
saturate² saturation		sawnter	saunter¹
Saturday		sawsa	saucer
Saturn		saxhorn	
satyre	satire+	saxophone saxophonist	
sauce *[liquid]	source² *[origin]+	say ~ing said	
sauce ~| boat ~pan		sayber	sabre+
saucer		saym	same+
saucy⁴		saynt	saint+
saudust	sawdust	sayons	séance
sauna		sayvyer	saviour
saunter¹		scab³	
sausage ~| dog ~| meat ~| roll		scabbard	

---

scabies	
scaffold¹	
scair	scare²⁺
scald¹	
scale² ~l down ~l drawing	
scale ~l factor ~l up	
scalene	
scallop ~ed	
scallywag	
scalp¹	
scalpel	
scaly⁴	
scam³	
scamp	
scamper¹	
scampi	
scan³	
scandal scandalise²	
scandalous ~ly	
scanner	
scant scanty⁴	
scapegoat¹	
scar³ *[mark] ~-faced	scare² *[frighten]⁺
scarab	
scarce² ~ly ~ness	
scarcity⁴	
scare² *[frighten] ~crow scar³ *[mark]⁺	
scaremongering	
scarf⁶ ~l pin	
scarlet ~l fever	
scarper¹	
scarse	scarce²⁺
scarsity	scarcity⁴
scary⁴	
scate	skate²⁺
scathing ~ly	
scatter¹ ~brain ~brained	
scatter ~l graph	

scatty⁴	
scavenge²	
scaw	score²⁺
scawch	scorch¹
scawn	scorn¹⁺
scenario	
scene *[theatre]	seen *[eyes]
scenery	
scenic ~ally	
scent¹ *[smell]	sent *[gone]
	cent *[money]
sceptic ~ism	
sceptical ~ly	
sceptre ~d	
schedule²	
schema ~s schemata	
schematic ~ally	
scheme²	
schemer *[plotter]	schema *[plan]
scherzo	
schism	
schizoid	
schizophrenia schizophrenic	
schnapps	
schnitzel	
scholar ~ly ~ship	
scholastic ~ally	
school¹ ~boy ~child ~girl ~teacher	
schooner	
schwa	
sciatic ~l nerve sciatica	
science scientist	
scientific ~ally	

☞ Can't find your word here? Look under <u>ski</u>

scill	skill⁺
scim	skim³
scin	skin³⁺

---

scintillating
scip   skip[3+]
scism   schism
scissors
scitsofreenia   schizophrenia[+]
scitszoyd   schizoid
scittul   skittle[2]
sclerosis
Scoch   Scotch
scoff[1]
scolar   scholar[+]
scolastic   scholastic[+]
scold[1] *[tell off]   scald[1] *[burn]
scone
scool   school[1+]
scooner   schooner
scoop[1]
scoot[1]
scope[2]
scorch[1]
score[2] ~board ~card ~sheet
scorn[1] ~ful ~fully
Scorpio
scorpion
Scot   Scotch   Scottish
scot-free
scoundrel
scour[1]
scourge[2]
scout[1]
scowl[1]
scowndrel   scoundrel
scowt   scout[1]
scrabble[2]
scrach   scratch[1+]
scraggy[4]
scram[3]
scramble[2]

scrap[3] *[get rid of]   scrape[2] *[remove]
scrap ~book ~| heap
scrap ~| metal ~yard
scrape[2] *[remove]   scrap[3] *[get rid of]
scrappy[4]
scratch[1] ~card ~| pad
scraul   scrawl[1]
scrauny   scrawny[4]
scrawl[1]
scrawny[4]
screach   screech[1+]
scream[1]
scree
screech[1] ~es ~| owl
screed
screen[1] ~play ~writer
screme   scream[1]
screw[1] ~y ~driver
screwpel   scruple[2]
screwpulus   scrupulous[+]
screwtinise   scrutinise[2]
screwtiny   scrutiny[4]
scribble[2]
scribe[2]
scrimp[1]
scripcher   scripture
script[1] ~writer
scripture
scroll[1] ~bar
scrooge
scrotum
scrounge[2]
scrownge   scrounge[2]
scrub[3]
scrue   screw[1+]
scruff   scruffy[4]
scrum ~| half
scrummage[2]

Key to Suffixes and Compounds

These rules are explained on pages ix to x.

1 Keep the word the same before adding **ed, er, est, ing**
e.g. cool[1] → cooled, cooler, coolest, cooling
2 Take off final **e** before adding **ed, er, est, ing**
e.g. fine[2] → fined, finer, finest, fining
3 Double final consonant before adding **ed, er, est, ing**
e.g. thin[3] → thinned, thinner, thinnest, thinning

4 Change final **y** to **i** before adding **ed, er, es, est, ly, ness**
e.g. tidy[4] → tidied, tidier, tidies, tidiest, tidily, tidiness
Keep final **y** before adding **ing** e.g. tidying
5 Add **es** instead of **s** to the end of the word
e.g. bunch[5] → bunches
6 Change final **f** to **ve** before adding **s**
e.g. calf[6] → calves

scrumptious ~ly ~ness
scrunch[1] ~es   scrunchy[4]
scruple[2]
scrupulous ~ly ~ness
scrutinise[2]
scrutiny[4]   scrutineer
scuba ~| diver ~| diving
scud[3]
scuff[1]
scuffle[2]
sculery   scullery[4]
sculk   skulk[1]
scull[1] *[boat]   skull *[head][+]
scullery[4]
sculpcher   sculpture
sculpt[1]
sculptor *[artist]   sculptress
sculpture[2] *[carving]
scum[3] ~bag
scuner   schooner
scupper[1]
scurf
scurrilous ~ly
scurry[4]
scurvy
scute   scoot[1]
scuttle[2]
scythe[2]
sea *[waves]   see *[eyes][+]
sea ~| anenome ~bed ~food
sea ~front ~gull ~horse
sea ~| level ~| lion ~plane
sea ~| port ~shore ~sickness
sea ~side ~ward ~weed
sead   cede[2] *[give up],
                           said *[say]
                           seed[1] *[plant,
                                   number][+]

☞ Can't find your word here? Look under **ce**

seady   seedy[4]
seafarer   seafaring
seak   seek *[look for][+],
                           Sikh *[religion][+]
seal[1] ~skin
sealant
sealing *[fastening]   ceiling *[roof]
seam *[cloth]   seem[1] *[appear][+]
seaman *[sailor] ~ship   semen *[sperm]
seamstress[5]
seamy[4]
sean   scene *[theatre],
                           seen *[eyes]
séance
seap   seep[1+]
sear[1] *[scorch]   seer *[prophet]
search[1] ~es ~| engine ~light
seasaw   seesaw[1]
sease   cease[2] *[stop][+],
                           seize[2] *[grab hold][+]
seasick ~ness
season[1] ~able ~ably ~| ticket
seasonal ~ly
seat[1] ~| belt
seathe   seethe[2]
seaworthy[4]
sebaceous
sebashus   sebaceous
sec
secateurs
secede[2]   secession
seclude[2]   seclusion
second[1] ~ly ~~hand ~~rate
secondary[4] ~| data ~| school ~| source
secondment
secondry   secondary[4+]

☞ Can't find your word here? Look under <u>ce</u>

secrecy	
secret *[hidden] ~ly ~ive	secrete² *[produce]⁺
secretariat	
secretary⁴ ~| general	
secrete² *[produce]	secret *[hidden]⁺
secretion	
secshun	section⁺
sect ~arian	
section ~al sector	
secular ~ise ~isation	
secularism secularist	
secure² securable	
security⁴	
sed	said
sedait	sedate⁺
sedate ~ly ~ness	
sedative sedation	
sedentary	
Seder *[Jewish meal]	cedar *[tree]
sedilla	cedilla
sediment ~ary ~ation	
sedition seditious	
seduce² seduction	
seductive ~ly	
seduse	seduce²⁺
see *[eyes] ~ing ~n	sea *[waves]⁺
seed¹ *[plant, number]	cede² *[give up]
seed ~less ~| money	
seedar	cedar *[tree], Seder * [Jewish meal]
seedling	
seedy⁴	
seek *[look for] ~ing	Sikh *[religion]⁺
seel	seal¹⁺
seeling	ceiling *[roof], sealing *[shut]

seem¹ *[appear] ~ingly	seam *[cloth]
seeman	seaman *[sailor]⁺, semen *[sperm]
seemly⁴	
seen *[past of see]	scene *[theatre]
seep¹ seepage	
seepia	sepia
seer *[prophet]	sear¹ *[scorch]
seereez	series
seeriul	cereal *[grain], serial *[sequence]⁺
seesairean	Caesarian
seesaw¹	
seeson	season¹⁺
seesonal	seasonal⁺
seet	seat¹
seethe²	
seeworthy	seaworthy⁴
segment¹ ~ation	
segregate² segregation	
seismic seismograph	
seismology seismologist	
seize² *[grab hold]	cease² *[stop]
seizure	
sekateurs	secateurs
sekure	secure²⁺
sekurity	security⁴
sekwel	sequel
sekwence	sequence⁺
sekwestrate	sequestrate²⁺
sekwin	sequin⁺
seldom	
selebrate	celebrate²
selebrity	celebrity⁴
select¹ ~ion ~or	
selective ~ly	
selenium	
selery	celery

KEY TO SUFFIXES AND COMPOUNDS

These rules are explained on pages ix to x.

1 Keep the word the same before adding ed, er, est, ing
e.g. cool¹ → cooled, cooler, coolest, cooling

2 Take off final e before adding ed, er, est, ing
e.g. fine² → fined, finer, finest, fining

3 Double final consonant before adding ed, er, est, ing
e.g. thin³ → thinned, thinner, thinnest, thinning

4 Change final y to i before adding ed, er, es, est, ly, ness
e.g. tidy⁴ → tidied, tidier, tidies, tidiest, tidily, tidiness
Keep final y before adding ing e.g. tidying

5 Add es instead of s to the end of the word
e.g. bunch⁵ → bunches

6 Change final f to ve before adding s
e.g. calf⁶ → calves

271

selestial   celestial[+]
self[6] ~-centred ~-confessed
self ~confidence ~-confident

> ☞ Can't find your word here? Take off **self** and look
> again

self ~-conscious ~-contained
self ~-control ~-controlled ~-defence
self ~-discipline ~-employed ~-esteem
self ~-evident ~-expression
self ~-government ~-help ~-image
self ~-important ~-made ~-opinionated
self ~-pity ~-preservation
self ~-proclaimed ~-promotion
self ~-portrait ~-regulating
self ~-respect ~-righteous
self ~-seeking ~-service
selfish ~ly ~ness
selfless ~ly
selibate   celibate
sell *[goods] ~| off ~| out   cell *[prison, unit][+]
seller *[sales person]   cellar *[room]
sellestial   celestial[+]
sellophane   Cellophane™
Sellotape™
sellphone   cellphone
sellular   cellular
sellulite   cellulite
selluloid   celluloid™
sellulose   cellulose[+]
Selotape   Sellotape™
Selsius   Celsius
selves
semafore   semaphore
semantic ~ally ~s
semaphore
semblance
semblense   semblance

seme   seam *[cloth],
                     seem[1] *[appear][+]
semen *[sperm]   seaman *[sailor][+]
sement   cement[1+]
semester
semetery   cemetery[4]

> ☞ Can't find your word here? Take off **semi** and look
> again

semi ~-automatic ~breve
semi ~circle ~circular
semi ~colon ~conductor
semi ~conscious ~-detached
semi ~-final ~-finalist
semi ~-precious ~quaver
semi ~-skilled ~-skimmed
semi ~tone
seminal
seminar
seminary[4]
seminel   seminal
Semite Semitic
semmi   semi[+]
semmolina   semolina
semolina
Semtex™
Semyte   Semite[+]
senario   scenario
senate senator
send ~er ~ing sent
sene   scene *[theatre],
                     seen *[eyes]
senic   scenic[+]
senile senility
senior ~ity
senotaph   cenotaph
sensashunal   sensational
sensation ~al ~ism ~ly

☞ Can't find your word here? Look under <u>ce</u>

sensationalise[2]	
sense[2] *[become aware]	cents *[money],
	scents *[perfumes]
senseless ~ly	
sensibility[4]	
sensible sensibly	
sensitise[2]	
sensitive ~ly	
sensitivity[4]	
sensor *[detector]	censer *[incense],
	censor[1] *[restrict]
sensory	
sensual ~ist ~ity ~ly	
sensuous ~ly ~ness	
sensure	censure[2]
sensus	census
sensyewus	sensuous[+]
sent *[gone]	cent *[money],
	scent[1] *[smell]
senta	centre[2+]
sentaur	centaur
sentenarian	centenarian
sentenary	centenary[4]
sentence[2]	
sentencious	sententious[+]
sentennial	centennial
sentense	sentence[2]
sentenshus	sententious[+]
sententious	
senter	centre[2+]
sentigrade	centigrade
sentilitre	centilitre
sentiment	
sentimental ~ism ~ist ~ity ~ly	
sentimentalise[2]	
sentimetre	centimetre

sentinel	
sentipede	centipede
sentral	central[+]
sentralise	centralise[2+]
sentrie	sentry[4]
sentrifugal	centrifugal[+]
sentrifuge	centrifuge
sentry[4] ~I box	
senturion	centurion
sentury	century[4]
sepal	
separable	
separate[2] ~ly separator	
separation	
separatist separatism	
sepcis	sepsis
sephalitis	cephalitis
sepia	
sepret	separate[2+]
sepsis	
September	
septer	sceptre[+]
septic septicaemia	
septiseemia	septicaemia
septum	
sepulchre	
sepulker	sepulchre
seqewster	sequester[1]
sequel	
sequence sequential	
sequester[1]	
sequestrate[2] sequestration	
sequin ~ned	
ser	sir
seramic	ceramic
seraph	
serch	search[1+]
sercharge	surcharge[2]

KEY TO SUFFIXES AND COMPOUNDS

These rules are explained on pages ix to x.

1 Keep the word the same before adding **ed, er, est, ing**
   e.g. cool[1] → cooled, cooler, coolest, cooling
2 Take off final **e** before adding **ed, er, est, ing**
   e.g. fine[2] → fined, finer, finest, fining
3 Double final consonant before adding **ed, er, est, ing**
   e.g. thin[3] → thinned, thinner, thinnest, thinning

4 Change final **y** to **i** before adding **ed, er, es, est, ly, ness**
   e.g. tidy[4] → tidied, tidier, tidies, tidiest, tidily, tidiness
   Keep final **y** before adding **ing** e.g. tidying
5 Add **es** instead of **s** to the end of the word
   e.g. bunch[5] → bunches
6 Change final **f** to **ve** before adding **s**
   e.g. calf[6] → calves

☞ Can't find your word here? Look under <u>ce</u>

sereal	cereal *[grain], serial *[sequence]+
serebellum	cerebellum
serebrul	cerebral+
serebrum	cerebrum
seremonial	ceremonial+
seremony	ceremony[4]
serenade[2]	
serendipity	
serene ~ly serenity	
serf *[slave] ~dom	surf[1] *[sea]+
serface	surface[2]+
serfit	surfeit
sergeant * ~-major	
sergeon	surgeon
sergery	surgery[4]
sergical	surgical+
serial *[sequence]	cereal *[grain]
serial ~l killer	
serial ~l number ~l port	
serialise[2] serialisation	
seriel	serial *[sequence], cereal *[grain]
series	
serif	
serious ~ly ~ness	
serje	surge[2]
serloin	sirloin+
serly	surly[4]
sermise	surmise[2]
sermon	
sermonise[2]	
sermount	surmount[1]
sername	surname
serpass	surpass[1]
serpent ~ine	

serpliss	surplice *[robe], surplus[5] *[excess]
serprise	surprise[2]+
serrated ~l edge	
serrealism	surrealism
sertain	certain+
sertax	surtax+
sertifiabul	certifiable+
sertificate	certificate
sertify	certify[4]+
sertitude	certitude
serum	
servant	
serve[2]	
serveillance	surveillance
servey	survey[1]+
servical	cervical+
service[2] ~able	
service ~l charge ~l station	
serviette	
servile ~ly	
servility servitude	
servival	survival+
servive	survive[2]+
servix	cervix
sesame	
Sesarean	Caesarian+
sesashun	cessation
sesede	secede[2]+
sessation	cessation
sesshun	session+
session ~al	
sesspit	cesspit+
set *[put] ~ting	seat[1] *[sitting]
set ~-aside ~back	sett *[badger]
set ~l square ~-up	
settee	
setter	

---

settle² ~ment

seveir   severe⁺

seven ~teen ~teenth

seventh ~l heaven

seventy⁴   seventieth

sever¹ ~ance

several ~ly

severe ~ly   severity

sevrel   several⁺

sew¹ *[clothes] ~n   sow¹ *[seeds]⁺,
                              so *[in this way]

sewage

sewer   sewerage

sewn *[clothes]   sown *[seeds]

sewur   sewer

sex¹

sexism   sexist

sextant

sextet

sexton

sexual ~ity ~ly

sexual ~l abuse ~l intercourse

sexual ~l harassment

sexy⁴

sey   say⁺

sfere   sphere⁺

sfincter   sphincter

sfinx   sphinx⁵

shabby⁴

shack

shackle²

shade²   shady⁴

shaded ~l area

shadow¹ ~y

shaft¹

shaggy⁴

shah

shaid   shade²⁺

shaik   shake *[agitate]⁺,
                              sheikh *[Arab chief]

shaip   shape²⁺

shair   share²⁺

shake *[agitate]

shaken   shaking

shaky⁴

shale

shall

☞ Can't find your word here? Look under **ch**

shallay   chalet

shallot

shallow¹ ~ness

sham³ *[not real]   shame² *[guilty]

shaman ~ism

shamble²

shame² *[guilty] ~-faced   sham³ *[not real]

shameez   chemise

shameful ~ly

shameless ~ly

shamman   shaman⁺

shammi   chamois

shamois   chamois

shampain   champagne

shampoo¹

shamrock

shandy⁴

Shangri La

shank

shan't [shall not]

shanty⁴ ~l town

shape² ~less

shapely⁴

shaperon   chaperone²

sharard   charade

shard

share² ~holder ~ware

KEY TO SUFFIXES AND COMPOUNDS

These rules are explained on pages ix to x.

1 Keep the word the same before adding **ed, er, est, ing**
e.g. cool¹ → cooled, cooler, coolest, cooling

2 Take off final **e** before adding **ed, er, est, ing**
e.g. fine² → fined, finer, finest, fining

3 Double final consonant before adding **ed, er, est, ing**
e.g. thin³ → thinned, thinner, thinnest, thinning

4 Change final **y** to **i** before adding **ed, er, es, est, ly, ness**
e.g. tidy⁴ → tidied, tidier, tidies, tidiest, tidily, tidiness
Keep final **y** before adding **ing** e.g. tidying

5 Add **es** instead of **s** to the end of the word
e.g. bunch⁵ → bunches

6 Change final **f** to **ve** before adding **s**
e.g. calf⁶ → calves

☞ Can't find your word here? Look under <u>ch</u>

sharia
shark ~-infested
sharlatan   charlatan
sharp[1] ~ly ~ness
sharp ~-eared ~-eyed ~-witted
sharpen[1]
sharzhay da fair   chargé d'affaires
shassee   chassis
shatter[1]
shattow   chateau[+]
shauffer   chauffeur[+]
shaul   shawl
shave[2] ~| off
shaving ~| cream ~| gel ~| lotion
shaw   shore[2] *[sea, prop][+],
                                 sure[2] *[certain][+]
shawl
shawt   short[1+]
shay dervr   chef d'oeuvre
she   she's [she is, has]
sheaf[6]
sheap   sheep[+]
sheapish   sheepish[+]
shear[1] *[clip]   sheer[1] *[thin, steep]
sheat   sheet[1]
sheath *[covering]
sheathe[2] *[put away]
shed *[building, hair] ~ding
she'd *[she had, would]
shedule   schedule[2]
sheen
sheenyon   chignon
sheep ~dog ~skin
sheepish ~ly ~ness
sheer[1] *[thin, steep]   shear[1] *[clip]
sheet[1] ~| of lightning

sheeth   sheath *[covering],
                                 sheathe[2] *[put away]
sheikh *[Arab chief]   shake *[agitate][+]
sheild   shield[1]
Sheite   Shiite
shekel
shelf[6] ~| life
shell[1] [sea] ~fish   she'll *[she will]
shell ~-shocked
shelter[1]
shelve[2]
shemeez   chemise
shepherd[1] ~ess
shepherd's ~| crook ~| pie
sherbet
sheree   sherry[4]
sheriff
sheroot   cheroot
sherpa
sherry[4] *[drink]   cherry[4] *[fruit]
shert   shirt[+]
shertzo   scherzo
she's [she is, has]
Shetland ~| pony
shevvaleer   chevalier
shiatsu
shicanery   chicanery
shiek   chic *[elegant],
                                 sheikh *[Arab chief]
shield[1]
shier   sheer[1] *[thin, steep],
                                 shire *[place][+]
shiffon   chiffon
shift[1]   shifty[4]
Shiite
shilling
shilly-shally[4]
shimmer[1] ~y

KEY TO SPELLING RULES

Red words are wrong. **Black** words are correct.

~   Add the suffix or word directly to the main word,
     without a space or hyphen
     e.g. ash ~en ~tray → **ashen ashtray**
~-   Add a hyphen to the main word before adding the
     next word
     e.g. blow ~-dry → **blow-dry**

~| Leave a space between the main word and the next
     word
     e.g. decimal ~| place → **decimal place**
+   By finding this word in its **correct** alphabetical
     order, you can find related words
     e.g. about[+] → **about-face about-turn**
*   Draws attention to words that may be confused
TM   Means the word is a trademark

shin³ *[leg, up]

shine *[sun]   shining

shine² *[shoes]

Shin Fane   Sinn Fein

shingle

shiny⁴

ship³ ~builder ~load

ship ~ment ~shape ~yard

shipping ~l forecast ~l lane

shipwreck¹

shire *[place] ~l horse   shear¹ *[clip],

                             sheer¹ *[thin, steep]

shirk¹

shirt ~-sleeved

shirty⁴

shit³   shitty⁴

shivelry   chivalry⁺

shiver¹ ~y

shnaps   schnapps

shnitsel   schnitzel

sho   show¹⁺

shoal¹

shoar   shore² *[sea, prop]⁺,

                    sure² *[certain]

shock¹ ~-absorber ~-proof

shod

shoddy⁴

shoe *[foot] ~ing ~box   shoo¹ *[away]⁺

shoe ~horn ~lace ~string

shok   shock¹⁺

shole   shoal¹

shone *[lit up, polished]   shown *[displayed]

shoo¹ *[away]   shoe *[foot]⁺

shook

shoot *[weapon, goal] ~er   chute *[slide]

shooting ~l star

shop³ ~l floor ~keeper ~lifter

shop ~-soiled ~l steward

shoplift¹

shopping ~l centre

shopping ~l mall ~l trolley

shore² *[sea, prop] ~line   sure² *[certain]⁺

shority   surety

shorn

short¹ ~ly ~ness

short ~bread ~cake

short ~-change ~-circuit

short ~coming ~l cut ~fall

short ~hand ~-handed

short ~haul ~list ~-lived

short ~-range ~-sighted

short ~ -staffed ~l story

short ~ -tempered~-term

shortage

shorten¹

shot ~gun ~l put

should   shouldn't [should not]

shoulder¹ ~-high ~-length

shout¹

shove²

shovel³ ~ful

show¹ ~n ~boat ~case

show ~down ~girl ~ground

show ~l house ~jumper ~man ~off

show ~piece ~room ~stopper

shower¹ ~proof

showery⁴

showlder   shoulder¹⁺

shown *[displayed]   shone *[lit up, polished]

showt   shout¹

showvanist   chauvinist⁺

showy⁴

shpeel   spiel

shrank

shrapnel

shred³

KEY TO SUFFIXES AND COMPOUNDS

These rules are explained on pages ix to x.

1 Keep the word the same before adding **ed, er, est, ing**
e.g. cool¹ → cooled, cooler, coolest, cooling

2 Take off final **e** before adding **ed, er, est, ing**
e.g. fine² → fined, finer, finest, fining

3 Double final consonant before adding **ed, er, est, ing**
e.g. thin³ → thinned, thinner, thinnest, thinning

4 Change final **y** to **i** before adding **ed, er, es, est, ly, ness**
e.g. tidy⁴ → tidied, tidier, tidies, tidiest, tidily, tidiness
Keep final **y** before adding **ing** e.g. tidying

5 Add **es** instead of **s** to the end of the word
e.g. bunch⁵ → bunches

6 Change final **f** to **ve** before adding **s**
e.g. calf⁶ → calves

shreik	shriek[1]
shrew ~ish ~ishly	
shrewd[1] ~ly ~ness	
shriek[1]	
shrift	
shrill[1] ~y ~ness	
shrimp ~ing ~l cocktail	
shrine	
shrink ~ing ~-wrapped	
shrinkage	
shrivel[3]	
shroud[1]	
Shrove Tuesday	
shrowd	shroud[1]
shrub shrubbery[4]	
shrue	shrew+
shrued	shrewd+
shrug[3] ~l off	
shrunk ~en	
shryne	shrine
shud	should+
shudder[1]	
shudent	shouldn't [should not]
shuffle[2]	
shun[3]	
shunt[1]	
shurbet	sherbet
shurpa	sherpa
shush[1]	
shut *[close] chute *[slide],	
shut ~-eye	shoot *[weapon, goal]+
shutter ~ed	
shutting	
shuttle[2] ~cock	
shuv	shove[2]
shuvel	shovel[3+]
shy *[timid] ~ly ~ness	
shy[4] *[horse]	

shyre	shire
si	sigh[1]
Siamese ~l cat ~l twin	
siatica	sciatica
sibling ~l rivalry	
sic *[thus]	sick[1] *[ill]+

> ☞ Can't find your word here? Look under **sy**, **ci** or **psy**

sicada	cicada
sicadelic	psychedelic
sicamore	sycamore
sichuate	situate[2+]
sichuayshun	situation
siciatrist	psychiatrist+
sicick	psychic+
sick[1] *[ill] ~ly ~ness	sic *[thus],
	Sikh *[religion]+
sicken[1]	
sickle ~-cell anaemia	
sicoanalise	psychoanalyse[2+]
sicofant	sycophant+
sicology	psychology+
sicotic	psychotic+
sicreet	secrete[2+]
side[2] ~board ~burns ~car	
side ~l effect ~light ~line	
side ~long ~saddle ~show ~step	
side ~swipe ~track ~ways	
sidel	sidle[2]
sider	cider
sidle[2]	
siege ~l mentality	
siense	science+
siesta	
sieve[2]	
sifer	cipher[1]
sifon	siphon[1]
sift[1]	

---

sigar	cigar	silicosis	
sigaret	cigarette+	silium	cilium
sigh¹		silk ~en ~-screen ~worm	
sighkee	psyche+	silky⁴	
sight¹ *[seeing] ~read	site² *[place]	sill	
sightseeing sightseer		sillabul	syllable+
sign¹ *[pointer]	sine *[angle]	sillabus	syllabus⁵
sign ~I language ~post		sillogisum	syllogism
sign ~-writer		sillooet	silhouette²
signachure	signature+	silly⁴ ~-billy	
signal³ ~I box ~man		silo	
signatory⁴		silt¹	
signature ~I file ~I tune		silver ~I birch ~I cutlery ~fish	
signet *[ring]	cygnet *[swan]	silver ~I foil ~I medal ~I plate	
significance		silver ~smith ~ware ~I wedding	
significant ~ly		silvery⁴	
signify⁴		SIM card	
sik	sic *[thus],	simbol	cymbal *[music],
	sick¹ *[ill]+,		symbol *[sign]
	Sikh *[religion]+	simbolic	symbolic+
siken	sicken¹	simbolise	symbolise²+
sikey	psyche+	simese	Siamese+
Sikh *[religion] ~ism	seek *[look for]+,	simfony	symphony+
	sic *[thus]	similar ~ly	
sikle	sickle+	similarity⁴	
sikosis	psychosis+	simile	
siksteen	sixteen+	similitude	
siksth	sixth	simmer¹	
siksty	sixty+	simmetric	symmetric+
silage		simmetry	cemetery⁴ *[graves],
silee	silly⁴+		symmetry⁴ *[same]
silence²		simpathetic	sympathetic+
silent ~ly		simpathise	sympathise²
silf	sylph+	simpathy	sympathy
silhouette²		simper¹	
silica		simphony	symphony+
silicon *[element]		simple² simply	
silicone *[compound]		simple ~-minded	

KEY TO SUFFIXES AND COMPOUNDS

These rules are explained on pages ix to x.

1 Keep the word the same before adding ed, er, est, ing
e.g. cool¹ → cooled, cooler, coolest, cooling
2 Take off final e before adding ed, er, est, ing
e.g. fine² → fined, finer, finest, fining
3 Double final consonant before adding ed, er, est, ing
e.g. thin³ → thinned, thinner, thinnest, thinning

4 Change final y to i before adding ed, er, es, est, ly, ness
e.g. tidy⁴ → tidied, tidier, tidies, tidiest, tidily, tidiness
Keep final y before adding ing e.g. tidying
5 Add es instead of s to the end of the word
e.g. bunch⁵ → bunches
6 Change final f to ve before adding s
e.g. calf⁶ → calves

simplify[4] simplification	
simplisity	simplicity
simplistic ~ally	
simposium	symposium[+]
simpul	simple
simulate[2] simulator	
simulation	
simultaneous ~ly ~l equation	
sin[3] *[wrong]	sign[1] *[pointer],
	sine *[angle]
sinagog	synagogue
since *[from when]	sins *[wrong doings]
sincere[2] ~ly sincerity	
sinch	cinch[1+]
sinchronise	synchronise[2+]
sincopate	syncopate[2+]
sinder	cinder[+]
Sinderella	Cinderella
sindicalist	syndicalist
sindicate	syndicate[2+]
sindrome	syndrome
sine *[angle]	sign[1] *[pointer]
sinecure	
sinema	cinema[+]
sinematographer	cinematographer[+]
sine qua non	
sinew ~y	
sinfonia	
sinful ~ly ~ness	
sing *[music] ~er ~ing	
sing ~along ~-song	
singe[2] *[burn]	
single[2] ~-handed ~-minded	
singly	
singular ~ly ~ity	
sinister	
sink *[drop, basin] ~ing	sync *[together]
Sinn Fein	

sinnamon	cinnamon
sinnee	cine
sinner	
sinni kwa non	sine qua non
sinnus	sinus[5+]
sinod	synod
sinonim	synonym[+]
sinopsis	synopsis[+]
sinoptic	synoptic
sinovial	synovial
sinse	since
sintax	syntax[+]
sinthesis	synthesis[+]
sinthesise	synthesise[2]
sinthetic	synthetic[+]
sintillating	scintillating
sinue	sinew[+]
sinuous ~ly	
sinus[5] ~itis	
sinuus	sinuous[+]
sip[3]	
sipher	cipher[1]
siphilis	syphilis[+]
siphon[1]	
sir *[man]	sire[2] *[breed, king]

☞ Can't find your word here? Look under <u>cir</u>

sirca	circa
sircadian	circadian
sircul	circle[2]
sircus	circus[5]
sire[2] *[breed, king]	sir *[man]
siren	
siringe	syringe
sirloin ~l steak	
sirocco	
sirrocumulus	cirrocumulus
sirrosis	cirrhosis

---

sirrup	syrup⁺		

sirrup | syrup⁺
sirum | serum
sismic | seismic⁺
sismology | seismology⁺
sissy |
sistematic | systematic⁺
sistematise | systematise²
sister ~ly ~hood ~-in-law |
sistern | cistern
sistole | systole
sit *[down] | sight *[seeing]⁺, site² *[place]
sitadel | citadel
sitar |
sitcom |
site² *[place] | cite² *[quote]⁺, sight *[seeing]⁺
siteseeing | sightseeing⁺
sithe | scythe²
sitizen | citizen⁺
sitric | citric⁺
sitrus | citrus⁺
sitting ~l duck ~l room |
sitting ~l target ~l tenant |
situate² |
situation |
sity | city⁴⁺
sityooashun | situation
sive | sieve²
sivic | civic
sivil | civil⁺
sivilian | civilian
sivilisashun | civilisation
sivilise | civilise²
sivility | civility⁴
sivvet | civet
six ~fold ~-pack ~pence |
sixteen ~th |

sixth ~l sense
sixty⁴ sixtieth
size² ~able ~ably
sizzle²
skab | scab³⁺
skabbard | scabbard
skaffold | scaffold¹
skale | scale²⁺
skallop | scallop⁺
skalp | scalp¹⁺
skaly | scaly⁴
skam | scam³
skan | scan³
skate² ~board ~boarder
skeemata | schemata
skein
skeleton skeletal
skerge | scourge
skermish | skirmish¹⁺
skert | skirt¹
skervy | scurvy
sketch¹ ~es ~book
sketchy⁴
skew¹ ~bald ~-whiff
skewer¹
ski¹ *[sport] ~l jump | **sky** *[space]⁺
skid³ *[slip] | **skied** *[sport]
skiff
skilful ~ly ~ness
skill ~ed
skim³
skimmed milk
skimp¹
skimpy⁴
skin³ ~care ~-deep
skin ~flint ~head ~-tight
skinny⁴
skint

KEY TO SUFFIXES AND COMPOUNDS

These rules are explained on pages ix to x.

1 Keep the word the same before adding ed, er, est, ing
e.g. cool¹ → cooled, cooler, coolest, cooling
2 Take off final e before adding ed, er, est, ing
e.g. fine² → fined, finer, finest, fining
3 Double final consonant before adding ed, er, est, ing
e.g. thin³ → thinned, thinner, thinnest, thinning

4 Change final y to i before adding ed, er, es, est, ly, ness
e.g. tidy⁴ → tidied, tidier, tidies, tidiest, tidily, tidiness
Keep final y before adding ing e.g. tidying
5 Add es instead of s to the end of the word
e.g. bunch⁵ → bunches
6 Change final f to ve before adding s
e.g. calf⁶ → calves

skip³
skirmish¹ ~es
skirt¹
skirting ~| board
skit
skittish ~ness
skittle²
skizm   schism
sklerosis   sclerosis
skoff¹   scoff¹
skold   scald¹ *[burn],
              scold¹ *[tell off]
skone   scone
skool   school¹
skoop   scoop¹
skoot   scoot¹
skrimp   scrimp¹
skript   script¹⁺
skud   scud³
skufful   scuffle²
skulk¹
skull *[head] ~cap   scull¹ *[boat]
skunk
skurf   scurf
skuttle   scuttle²
skwall   squall¹
skwallor   squalor
skware   square⁺
skwaw   squaw
skwobble   squabble²
skwod   squad
skwodron   squadron
skwolid   squalid⁺
skwonder   squander¹
skwosh   squash¹
skwot   squat³
sky *[space]   ski¹ *[sport]⁺
sky ~-blue ~-diving

sky ~-high ~lark ~lights
sky ~line ~scraper ~wards
slab
slack¹ *[lazy, loose]   slake² *[thirst]
slack ~ly ~ness
slacken¹
slaik   slake²
slain
slait   slate²
slaiv   slave²⁺
slake² *[thirst]   slack¹ *[lazy, loose]⁺
slam³
slander¹ ~ous ~ ously
slane   slain
slang
slanging match
slant¹
slap³ ~-dash ~-happy ~stick ~-up
slash¹
slat *[thin strip]
slate² *[roof, criticise]
slaughter¹ ~house
slave² ~| driver ~| labour ~| trade
slavery
slavish ~ly ~ness
slay¹ *[kill]   sleigh *[reindeer]
sleap   sleep⁺
sleapless   sleepless⁺
sleat   sleet¹
sleave   sleeve⁺
sleaze
sleazy⁴
sledge ~hammer
sledging
sleek¹ ~ly ~ness
sleep ~er ~ing ~over ~walk
sleeping ~| bag ~| pill
sleepless ~ly ~ness

---

sleepy⁴ ~head		sloe *[fruit]	slow¹ *[not quick]⁺
sleet¹		slog³	
sleeve ~d ~less		slogan	
sleezy	sleazy⁺	sloop	
slege	sledge⁺	slop³ *[slosh]	
sleigh *[reindeer]	slay¹ *[kill]⁺	slope² *[surface]	
slender ~ness		sloppy⁴	
slep	sleep⁺	slorter	slaughter¹⁺
slept		slosh¹	
sler	slur³	slot³ ~l machine	
slerp	slurp¹	sloth ~ful	
sleuth		slouch¹	
slew		slough¹	
sley	slay¹ *[kill]⁺, sleigh * [reindeer]	sloup	sloop
		slovenly⁴	
slice²		slow¹ *[not quick] ~ly	sloe *[fruit]
slick¹ ~ly ~ness		slow ~coach ~-witted	
slid *[did slide]		slowworm	
slide *[slip] ~l rule		sludge² sludgy⁴	
sliding ~l door ~l scale		slue	slew
slight¹ ~ly ~ness		slug³	
slik	slick¹⁺	sluggish ~ly ~ness	
slim³ *[thin] ~line ~ness		sluice² ~l gate	
slime *[thick substance]	slimy⁴	slum³	
sling¹ ~back ~shot		slumber¹ ~l party	
slink ~ing		slump¹	
slinky⁴		slung	
slip³ ~l road ~shod		slunk	
slip ~-up ~way		slur³	
slippage		slurp¹	
slipper		slurry	
slippery⁴ slippy⁴		slush¹ slushy⁴	
slise	slice²⁺	slut	
slit *[cut] ~ting	slight¹ *[light]⁺	sluth	sleuth
slither¹ ~y		sluvenly	slovenly⁴
sliver		sly ~ly ~ness	
slob		slyme	slime⁺
slobber¹ slobbery		smack¹	

KEY TO SUFFIXES AND COMPOUNDS

These rules are explained on pages ix to x.

1 Keep the word the same before adding ed, er, est, ing
  e.g. cool¹ → cooled, cooler, coolest, cooling
2 Take off final e before adding ed, er, est, ing
  e.g. fine² → fined, finer, finest, fining
3 Double final consonant before adding ed, er, est, ing
  e.g. thin³ → thinned, thinner, thinnest, thinning

4 Change final y to i before adding ed, er, es, est, ly, ness
  e.g. tidy⁴ → tidied, tidier, tidies, tidiest, tidily, tidiness
  Keep final y before adding ing e.g. tidying
5 Add es instead of s to the end of the word
  e.g. bunch⁵ → bunches
6 Change final f to ve before adding s
  e.g. calf⁶ → calves

small[1] ~-minded ~pox
small ~-scale ~-town
smarmy[4]
smart[1] ~ly ~ness
smarten[1] ~l up
smash[1] ~l hit
smattering
smear[1] ~l campaign
smear ~l tactics ~l test
smell[1] smelt smelly[4]
smelling ~l salts
smelt[1]
smerk   smirk[1]
smidgen
smigen   smidgen
smile[2] ~y
smirk[1]
smite smiting
smith smithy[4]
smithereens
smitten
smock ~ed ~ing
smog
smoke[2] ~l bomb ~l detector ~-free ~less
smoke ~screen ~l signal ~stack
smoked ~l glass ~l salmon
smoking ~l area ~l gun
smoky[4]
smooch[1]
smooth[1] ~ly ~ness
smoothie
smorgasbord
smote
smother[1]
smoulder[1]
smudge[2]
smug[3] ~ly ~ness
smuggle[2]

smut smutty[4]
smyle   smile[2+]
snack[1] ~-bar
snaffle[2]
snag[3]
snaik   snake[2+]
snail ~l mail
snair   snare[2]
snak   snack[1+]
snake[2] ~bite ~skin
snakes ~l and ladders
snale   snail[+]
snap[3] ~dragon ~-on ~shot
snapper
snappy[4]
snare[2]
snarl[1] ~-up
snatch[1] ~es
snaw   snore[2]
snazzy[4]
sneak[1] ~l preview
sneaky[4]
sneer[1]
sneeze[2]
snick[1]
snide ~ly
snier   sneer[1]
snifel   sniffle
sniff[1] sniffer dog
sniffle[2]
snifter
snigger[1]
snip[3] *[cut]
snipe[2] *[criticise, shoot, bird]
sniper
snippet
snitch[1]
snivel[3]

KEY TO SPELLING RULES

Red words are wrong. **Black words are correct.**

~   Add the suffix or word directly to the main word,
       without a space or hyphen
       e.g. ash ~en ~tray → **ashen ashtray**

~-   Add a hyphen to the main word before adding the
       next word
       e.g. blow ~-dry → **blow-dry**

~l   Leave a space between the main word and the next
       word
       e.g. decimal ~l place → **decimal place**

+   By finding this word in its **correct** alphabetical
       order, you can find related words
       e.g. about+ → **about-face about-turn**

*   Draws attention to words that may be confused

TM   Means the word is a trademark

sno	snow[1+]
snob snobbery	
snobbish ~ly ~ness	
snog[3]	
snooker[1]	
snoop[1]	
snooty	
snooze[2]	
snorcul	snorkel[3]
snore[2]	
snorkel[3]	
snort[1]	
snot	
snotty[4] ~-nosed	
snout *[pig's nose]	
snow[1] ~ball ~boarding ~bound	
snow ~-capped ~l chains ~drift	
snow ~drop ~fall ~flake ~man	
snow ~plough ~shoe ~storm	
snow ~suit ~-white	
snowt	snout
snowy[4]	
snub[3] ~-nosed	
snuck	
snuff[1] ~box	
snuffle[2]	
snug[3]	
snuggle[2] ~l down ~l up	
snuker	snooker[1]
snupe	snoop[1]
snutey	snooty
snuze	snooze[2]
snyde	snide[+]
so *[in this way]	sew[1] *[clothes],
so ~-and-so ~-called	sow[1] *[seeds]
soak[1]	
soal	sole *[single, shoe][+],
	soul *[spirit][+]

soap[1] ~box ~suds soapy[4]	
soar[1] *[fly]	saw *[see, cut][+],
	sore[2] *[hurt][+]
sob[3] ~l story	
sober[1] ~ly	
sobriety	
sobriquet	
soccer	
sociable sociably sociability	
social ~ite ~ity ~ly	
social ~l climber ~l security	
social ~l services ~l worker	
socialise[2] socialisation	
socialism socialist	
socialite	
society[4] societal	
socio-economic	
sociology sociological sociologist	
socio-political	
sock[1]	
socker	soccer
socket	
sod sod's law	
soda ~l water	
sodden	
sodium	
sodomy	
sofa ~l bed	
soffen	soften[1]
sofist	sophist[+]
sofisticashun	sophistication
soft[1] ~ly ~ness	
soft ~ball ~-boiled	
soft ~l drink ~-spoken	
soften[1] ~er	
soft-pedal[3]	
software	
softy[4]	

KEY TO SUFFIXES AND COMPOUNDS

These rules are explained on pages ix to x.

1 Keep the word the same before adding **ed**, **er**, **est**, **ing**
e.g. cool[1] → cooled, cooler, coolest, cooling

2 Take off final **e** before adding **ed**, **er**, **est**, **ing**
e.g. fine[2] → fined, finer, finest, fining

3 Double final consonant before adding **ed**, **er**, **est**, **ing**
e.g. thin[3] → thinned, thinner, thinnest, thinning

4 Change final **y** to **i** before adding **ed**, **er**, **es**, **est**, **ly**, **ness**
e.g. tidy[4] → tidied, tidier, tidies, tidiest, tidily, tidiness
Keep final **y** before adding **ing** e.g. tidying

5 Add **es** instead of **s** to the end of the word
e.g. bunch[5] → bunches

6 Change final **f** to **ve** before adding **s**
e.g. calf[6] → calves

soggy⁴
Soho
soil¹
soirée
sojourn¹
sok   sock¹ *[foot]
         soak¹ *[water]
soket   socket
solace
solar ~ium
solar ~| plexus ~| system
solase   solace
sold
solder¹ *[join]   soldier¹ *[army]
soldering iron
soldier¹ *[army]   solder¹ *[join]
sole *[single, shoe] ~ly   soul *[spirit]⁺
solecism
solejur   soldier¹
solem   solemn⁺
solemise   solemnise²
solemn ~ity ~ly
solemnise²
solenoid
soler   solar⁺
solesism   solecism
solichude   solitude
solicit¹ ~ation
solicitor
solicitous ~ly   solicitude
solid ~ity ~ly
solidarity
solidify⁴
soliloquy⁴
solipsism
solisit   solicit¹⁺
solisitor   solicitor
solisitus   solicitous

solitaire
solitary⁴
solitude
solliss   solace²
solo ~ist
solstice
solt   salt¹⁺
solty   salty⁴
soluble   solubility
solution
solve²
solvency
solvent ~| abuse
sombre ~ly ~ness
sombrero
sombur   sombre⁺
some *[a quantity]   sum³ *[total]
some ~body
some ~how ~one
some ~thing ~times
some ~what ~where
somersault¹
somnambulism
somnolent
son *[boy] ~-in-law   sun *[shine]⁺
son et lumière
sonar
sonata
soner   sonar
sonet   sonnet
song ~bird ~book ~| writer
songfrwa   sangfroid
sonic ~| boom
sonnet
sonorous
soodoenym   pseudonym
sooflay   soufflé
soon¹

KEY TO SPELLING RULES

Red words are wrong. **Black** words are correct.

~   Add the suffix or word directly to the main word, without a space or hyphen
     e.g. ash ~en ~tray → **ashen ashtray**

~-   Add a hyphen to the main word before adding the next word
     e.g. blow ~-dry → **blow-dry**

~| Leave a space between the main word and the next word
     e.g. decimal ~| place → **decimal place**

+   By finding this word in its **correct** alphabetical order, you can find related words
     e.g. about⁺ → **about-face about-turn**

*   Draws attention to words that may be confused

TM   Means the word is a trademark

soop	soup	soshall	social+
soot *[black powder] ~y	suit[1] *[clothes]+	sosiety	society[4]+
soothe[2]		sosiology	sociology+
soothsayer soothsaying		sossige	sausage+
sop *[offer, liquid]	soap[1] *[washing]+	sot	
sopey	soapy[4]	sotay	sauté
sophist ~ry		sotto voce	
sophisticate[2] sophistication		soufflé	
sophisticated		sought *[looked for]	sort[1] *[kind]+
sophomore		souk	
soporific		soul *[spirit] ~less	sole *[single, shoe]+
sopping ~l wet		soul ~-destroying ~l food	
soppy[4]		soul ~-mate ~l music ~-searching	
soprano		soulful ~-ly	
sorce	sauce *[liquid]+,	sound[1] ~ly ~ness ~l barrier	
	source[2] *[origin]+	sound ~l effects ~track	
sorcer	saucer	soundless ~ly	
sorcerer sorceress sorcery		soundproof[1]	
sorcy	saucy[4]	soup	
sord	sword+	sour[1] ~ly ~ness	
sordid ~ly ~ness		sour ~-dough ~puss	
sore[2] *[hurt] ~ly ~ness	saw *[see, cut]+,	source[2] *[origin] ~l code sauce *[liquid]+	
	soar[1] *[fly]	souse[2] *[pickle]	
sorel	sorrel	south ~bound ~-east ~-easterly	
soriasis	psoriasis	south ~erly ~ern ~erner	
sorn	sawn	south ~-seeking ~l pole	
sorna	sauna	south ~-wards ~-west ~-westerly	
sornter	saunter[1]	souvenir ~l hunter	
sorow	sorrow+	sou'-wester	
sorrel		sovereign ~ty	
sorrow ~ful ~fully ~fulness		Soviet	
sorry		sovren	sovereign+
sorserer	sorcerer+	sow[1] *[seeds] ~n	sew[1] *[clothes]+,
sort[1] *[kind] ~l code	sought *[looked for]	sow *[pig]	so *[in this way]
sortie *[outing]	sauté[1] *[fry]	sown *[seeds]	sewn *[clothes]
sory	sorry[4]	sownd	sound[1]+
soshabul	sociable+	sowndprufe	soundproof[1]
soshalisum	socialism+	sowr	sour[1]+

sowse	souse[2]
sowth	south[+]
soy	
soya ~| bean ~| sauce	
sozzled	
spa *[spring]	spar[3] *[fight]
space[2] ~-age ~craft ~| flight	
space ~man ~| probe ~ship ~| shuttle	
space ~| station ~suit ~walk	
spachula	spatula
spacial	spatial
spacious ~ly ~ness	
spade ~work	
spaghetti	
spair	spare[2+]
spairingly	sparingly
spait	spate
spam *[meat, Internet]	
span[3]	
spaner	spanner
spangle ~d	
spaniel	
spank[1]	
spanner	
spanyel	spaniel
spar[3] *[fight]	spa *[spring],
	spare[2] *[give, extra][+]
sparcity	sparsity
spare[2] *[give, extra]	spar[3] *[fight]
sparingly	
spark[1] ~| plug	
sparkle[2]	
sparow	sparrow[+]
sparrow ~hawk	
sparse[2] ~ly ~ness	
sparsity	
spartan	
spase	space[+]

spashus	spacious[+]
spasm	
spasmodic ~ally	
spastic ~ally	
spat *[argument, past of spit]	
spate *[large number]	
spatial	
spatter[1]	
spatula	
spaun	spawn[1]
spaw	spoor[1] *[track],
	spore *[seed, germ]
spawn[1]	
spay[1]	
spayr	spare[2] *[give, extra][+]
speach	speech[+]
spead	speed[1+]
speady	speedy[4]
speak ~ing	
speaker ~phone	
spear[1] ~head ~mint	
spec *[on spec, info]	speck[1] *[spot]
speces	species
special ~ly ~ism ~ist	
specialise[2] specialisation	
speciality[4]	
specialty[4]	
species	
specific ~ally ~s	
specify[4] specification	
specimen	
specious ~ly ~ness	
speck[1] *[spot]	spec *[on spec, info]
speckle[2]	
spectacle	
spectacles spectacled	
spectacular ~ly	
spectator ~| sport	

KEY TO SPELLING RULES

Red words are wrong. **Black words are correct.**

~   Add the suffix or word directly to the main word, without a space or hyphen
     e.g. ash ~en ~tray → **ashen ashtray**

~-   Add a hyphen to the main word before adding the next word
     e.g. blow ~-dry → **blow-dry**

~| Leave a space between the main word and the next word
     e.g. decimal ~| place → **decimal place**

+   By finding this word in its **correct** alphabetical order, you can find related words
     e.g. about[+] → **about-face about-turn**

*   Draws attention to words that may be confused

TM   Means the word is a trademark

spectre

spectrum

speculate[2] speculation

speculative

speculator

sped *[past of speed]   speed *[move fast][+]

speech ~less ~| marks ~| therapy ~writer

speed[1] ~boat ~| bump ~| limit ~way

speedometer

speedy[4]

speek   speak[+]

speekerfone   speakerphone

speer   spear[1+]

speesheez   species

spektakel   spectacle

spektakular   spectacular[+]

spektator   spectator[+]

spekter   spectre

spektrum   spectrum

spekulate   speculate[2+]

spekulator   speculator

spell[1] ~checker spelt

spellbinding   spellbound

spend ~er ~ing spent

spend ~thrift

sper   spur[3+]

sperm ~atoza ~icide

sperm ~| bank ~| count ~-whale

spern   spurn[1]

spert   spurt[1]

speshul   special[+]

speshulise   specialise[2+]

speshulty   specialty[4]

speshus   specious[+]

spesies   species

spesific   specific[+]

spesify   specify[4+]

spesimen   specimen

spew[1]

sphere   spherical

sphincter

sphinx[5]

spice[2] spicy[4]

spick and span

spider ~'s web   spidery

spied *[looked]   speed[1] *[fast][+]

spiel

spigot

spike[2] spiky[4]

spill[1]

spillage

spilt

spin *[turn fast]   spine *[backbone][+]

spin ~ner ~| doctor

spin ~-dryer ~-off

spina bifida

spinach

spinal ~| column ~| cord ~| tap

spindle   spindly

spine *[backbone] ~less   spin *[turn fast][+]

spine ~-chilling ~-tingling

spineker   spinnaker

spiney   spinney *[trees],
                         spiny *[spines]

spinich   spinach

spining   spinning[+]

spinnaker

spinney *[trees]   spiny *[spines]

spinning ~| wheel

spin-off

spinster ~hood

spiny

spiral[3] ~-bound ~| staircase

spire

spirichual   spiritual[+]

spirit[1] ~| lamp ~| level

KEY TO SUFFIXES AND COMPOUNDS

These rules are explained on pages ix to x.

1 Keep the word the same before adding ed, er, est, ing
e.g. cool[1] → cooled, cooler, coolest, cooling

2 Take off final e before adding ed, er, est, ing
e.g. fine[2] → fined, finer, finest, fining

3 Double final consonant before adding ed, er, est, ing
e.g. thin[3] → thinned, thinner, thinnest, thinning

4 Change final y to i before adding ed, er, es, est, ly, ness
e.g. tidy[4] → tidied, tidier, tidies, tidiest, tidily, tidiness
Keep final y before adding ing e.g. tidying

5 Add es instead of s to the end of the word
e.g. bunch[5] → bunches

6 Change final f to ve before adding s
e.g. calf[6] → calves

spiritual ~ly ~ism ~ist ~ity
spise   spice[2+]
spit *[saliva] ~ting ~ball ~fire
spite[2] *[nasty, in spite of]
spiteful ~ly ~ness
spittle
splash[1] ~y ~-back ~-down
splatter[2]
splay[1] ~l out
spleen
splender   splendour
splendid ~ly
splendour
splerge   splurge[2]
splice[2]
splint[1]
splinter[1]
splise   splice[2]
split ~ting ~-level
split ~-screen ~l up
splodge[2] splodgy[4]
splurge[2]
splutter[1]
splyt   split[+]
spoak   spoke[+]
spoar   spoor[1] *[track],
                              spore *[seed, germ]
spoil[1] ~t ~sport
spoilage
spoke   spoken
spoke ~sman ~sperson ~swoman
sponge[2] ~bag ~l bath ~l cake
spongy[4]
sponser   sponsor[1+]
sponsor[1] ~ship
spontaneity
spontaneous ~ly
spontenaity   spontaneity

spoof[1]
spook[1] spooky[4]
spool[1]
spoon[1] ~ful
spoonerism
spoonfeed ~ing   spoonfed
spoor[1] *[track]   spore *[seed, germ]
sporadic ~ally
sporan   sporran
spore *[seed, germ]   spoor[1] *[track]
sporran
sport[1] ~y
sports ~l car ~l centre
sports ~l coat ~wear ~woman
sportsman ~like ~ship
spot[3] ~l check
spotless ~ly ~ness
spotlight[1]
spotty[4]
spoure   spoor[1] *[track],
                              spore *[seed, germ]
spourt   sport[1+]
spouse   spousal
spout[1]
spowse   spouse[+]
spowt   spout[1]
spoylige   spoilage
sprain[1]
sprang
sprawl[1]
spray[1] ~l gun ~l paint
spread ~er ~ing
spread ~sheet
spread-eagle[2]
spred   spread[+]
spree
sprig
sprightly[4]

KEY TO SPELLING RULES

Red words are wrong. **Black** words are correct.

~   Add the suffix or word directly to the main word,
     without a space or hyphen
     e.g. ash ~en ~tray → ashen ashtray

~-   Add a hyphen to the main word before adding the
     next word
     e.g. blow ~-dry → blow-dry

~l   Leave a space between the main word and the next
     word
     e.g. decimal ~l place → decimal place

+   By finding this word in its **correct** alphabetical
     order, you can find related words
     e.g. about[+] → about-face about-turn

*   Draws attention to words that may be confused

TM   Means the word is a trademark

spring ~er ~ing		spyn	spin[+]
spring ~board ~bok ~l chicken		spynal	spinal[+]
spring ~-clean ~-loaded		spyne	spine[+]
spring ~l onion ~l roll ~l tide		spyral	spiral[3+]
spring ~time		spyre	spire
springy[4]		squabble[2]	
sprinkle[2]		squad	
sprint[1]		squadron	
sprite ~ly		squalid ~ly squalor	
spritzer		squall[1] squally	
sprocket		squallor	squalor
sprog		squander[1]	
sprout[1]		square[2] ~ly ~l dance ~l meal	
spruce ~ly ~l up		square ~l root ~l up	
sprung		squash[1]	
spruse	spruce[+]	squat[3]	
spry *[energetic] ~ly	spree *[spending]	squaw	
spryte	sprite[+]	squawk[1]	
spud		squeak[1] squeaky[4]	
spue	spew[1]	squeal[1]	
spufe	spoof[1]	squeamish ~ly ~ness	
spuk	spook[1+]	squeek	squeak[1+]
spule	spool[1]	squeel	squeal[1]
spume[2]		squeemish	squeamish[+]
spun *[past of spin]	spoon[1] *[eat][+]	squeeze[2]	
spunk		squelch[1]	
spunky[4]		squerm	squirm[1]
spur[3] ~-of-the-moment		squert	squirt[1]
spurious ~ly ~ness		squib *[firework]	
spurm	sperm[+]	squid *[fish]	
spurmatoza	spermatozoa	squier	squire[2+]
spurn[1]		squigel	squiggle[2]
spurt[1]		squiggle[2]	
spuryius	spurious[+]	squint[1]	
sputter[1]		squire[2] ~archy	
sputum		squirel	squirrel
spy[4] ~-glass ~-hole		squirm[1]	
spyke	spike[2+]	squirrel	

KEY TO SUFFIXES AND COMPOUNDS

These rules are explained on pages ix to x.

1 Keep the word the same before adding ed, er, est, ing
e.g. cool[1] → cooled, cooler, coolest, cooling
2 Take off final e before adding ed, er, est, ing
e.g. fine[2] → fined, finer, finest, fining
3 Double final consonant before adding ed, er, est, ing
e.g. thin[3] → thinned, thinner, thinnest, thinning

4 Change final y to i before adding ed, er, es, est, ly, ness
e.g. tidy[4] → tidied, tidier, tidies, tidiest, tidily, tidiness
Keep final y before adding ing e.g. tidying
5 Add es instead of s to the end of the word
e.g. bunch[5] → bunches
6 Change final f to ve before adding s
e.g. calf[6] → calves

squirt¹		stak	stack¹
squish¹ squishy⁴		stakato	staccato
squork	squawk¹⁺	stake² *[post, share]	steak *[beef]⁺
stab³		stake ~holder ~-out	
stabel	stable²⁺	stalactite *[down]	
stabilise²		stalagmite *[up]	
stabilitie	stability	stale² ~mate	
stability		stalegmite	stalagmite *[up]
stable² ~l lad ~mate		stalektite	stalactite *[down]
staccato		stalk¹ *[follow]	stork *[bird]
stacher	stature	stall¹	
stachuary	statuary	stallion	
stachue	statue⁺	stalwart	
stachute	statute	stalyen	stallion
stack¹		stamen	
stadium ~s stadia		stamina	
staek	stake² *[post, share]⁺,	stammer¹	
	steak *[beef]⁺	stamp¹	
staer	stair *[step]⁺,	stampede²	
	stare² *[gaze]	stance	
staff¹ ~l nurse		stand ~ing ~-alone ~by	
stag *[deer]		stand ~point ~still	
stage² *[time, theatre] ~coach		standard ~-bearer ~-issue ~l lamp	
stage ~craft ~hand ~struck		standardise² standardisation	
stage-manage²		standedise	standardise²⁺
stagger¹		stand-off ~ish	
stagnait	stagnate²⁺	stane	stain¹
stagnant		stank	
stagnate² stagnation		stansa	stanza
staid *[prim]	stayed *[remained]	stanse	stance
staik	stake²⁺	stanza	
stail	stale²⁺	stapel	staple²
stain¹		staple²	
stained glass		star³ *[in sky, actor]	stare² *[gaze]
stainless steel		star ~board ~burst ~dom	
stair *[step] ~case	stare² *[gaze]	star ~dust ~fish ~gaze ~gazer	
stair ~way ~well		star ~less ~light ~ship	
stait	state²⁺	star ~struck ~-studded	

starch[1]	starchy[4]	stayje	stage[2+]
stare[2] *[gaze]	stair *[step][+]	staymin	stamen
staree	starry[4]	steadfast ~ly ~ness	
stark ~ers		steady[4]	
starlight		steak *[beef] ~-house	stake[2] *[post, share][+]
starling		steal *[take] ~ing	steel[1] *[iron][+]
starlit *[bright]	starlight *[light]	stealth stealthy[4]	
starry[4]		steam[1] ~l engine ~roller ~ship	
start[1] ~l up		steamy[4]	
startle[2]		stedfast	steadfast[+]
starve[2] starvation		stedy	steady[4]
stash[1]		steed	
stashun	station[1+]	steel[1] *[iron]	steal *[take][+]
stashuner	stationer	steely[4]	
state[2] ~ly ~hood		steep[1] ~ly ~ness	
state ~less ~ment		steeple ~chase ~jack	
state ~sman ~swoman		steer[1]	
stately[4] ~l home		steerage	
static ~ally		stellar	
statik	static[+]	stelth	stealth[+]
station[1] ~master		stem[3] *[grow] ~l cell	steam[1] *[hot air][+]
stationary *[still]	stationery *[paper]	stem-and-leaf diagram	
stationer		stench[5]	
stationery *[paper]	stationary *[still]	stencil[3]	
statistic ~ian ~s		stenography stenographer	
statistical ~ly		stensil	stencil[3]
statuary		step[3] *[pace]	steppe *[land]
statue		step ~brother ~child ~children	
statuesque		step ~daughter ~father	
statuette		step ~ladder ~mother	
stature		step ~parent ~sister ~son	
status		steppe *[land]	step[3] *[pace][+]
statute		ster	stir[3+]
staunch[1]		sterdy	sturdy[4]
stave[2]		stereo ~phonic ~scopic	
staw	store[2+]	stereotype[2] stereotypical	
stay[1] ~-at-home		stergeon	sturgeon
stayed *[remained]	staid *[prim]	sterile sterility	

KEY TO SUFFIXES AND COMPOUNDS

These rules are explained on pages ix to x.

1 Keep the word the same before adding **ed, er, est, ing**
e.g. cool[1] → cooled, cooler, coolest, cooling
2 Take off final **e** before adding **ed, er, est, ing**
e.g. fine[2] → fined, finer, finest, fining
3 Double final consonant before adding **ed, er, est, ing**
e.g. thin[3] → thinned, thinner, thinnest, thinning

4 Change final **y** to **i** before adding **ed, er, es, est, ly, ness**
e.g. tidy[4] → tidied, tidier, tidies, tidiest, tidily, tidiness
Keep final **y** before adding **ing** e.g. tidying
5 Add **es** instead of **s** to the end of the word
e.g. bunch[5] → bunches
6 Change final **f** to **ve** before adding **s**
e.g. calf[6] → calves

sterilise[2]   sterilisation

sterio   stereo[+]
steriotipe   stereotype[2+]
sterling
stern[1] ~ly ~ness
sternum
steroid
steryle   sterile[+]
sterylise   sterilise[2+]
stethoscope
stew[1]
steward ~ess ~ship
stewdent   student[+]
sticelback   stickleback[+]
stich   stitch[1+]
stick ~er ~ing ~l insect ~-up
stickleback
stickler
sticky[4]
stier   steer[1]
stifel   stifle[2]
stiff[1] ~ly ~ness
stiffen[1]
stifle[2]
stigma   stigmata
stigmatise[2]
stik   stick[+]
stikler   stickler
stiky   sticky[4]
stile *[steps]   style[2] *[appearance][+]
stiletto ~l heel
stilise   stylise[2]
stilist   stylist[+]
still ~ness ~-birth ~-born
still ~l image ~-life
stilted   stilting
Stilton ~l cheese
stilts

stilus   stylus[5]
stimie   stymie[+]
stimulant
stimulate[2]   stimulation
stimulus   stimuli
sting ~er ~ing ~-ray
stingy[4]
stink ~er ~ing   stinky[4]
stint[1]
stipend
stipple[2]
stipulate[2]   stipulation
stir[3] ~-crazy ~-fry
stirrup
stitch[1] ~es ~l up
sto   stow[1+]
stoal   stole[+]
stoan   stone[2+]
stoat
stoav   stove[2]
stock[1] ~ade ~broker
stock ~l car ~l exchange
stock ~l market ~l option
stock ~room ~l still ~taking
stocking
stockpile[2]
stocky[4]
stodge[2]   stodgy[4]
stoic ~al ~ally ~ism
stoking[2] *[making a fire]   stocking *[nylon]
stokpile   stockpile[2]
stole ~n
stolid ~ly
stolwort   stalwart
stoma   stomata
stomach[1] ~-ache ~l pump
stomp[1]
stomping ground

---

stone² ~-cold ~mason
stone ~wall ~ware ~work
Stone Age
Stonehenge
stony⁴ ~-faced
stood
stooge²
stook¹
stool
stoop¹ ~l down
stop³ ~cock ~gap ~light ~over
stop ~l press ~-start ~watch
stoppage
storage ~l capacity ~l facility ~l unit
store² ~house ~keeper
storey *[floor level]   story⁴ *[tale]
storeybord   storyboard¹
storige   storage
stork *[bird]   stalk *[follow]
storm¹ ~l cloud ~l damage ~-trooper
stormy⁴
stornch   staunch¹
story⁴ *[tale]   storey *[floor level]
story ~book ~line
story ~teller ~telling
storyboard¹
stote   stoat
stoup   stoop¹⁺
stourm   storm¹⁺
stout¹ ~ly ~ness
stove²
stow¹ ~away   stowage
stowick   stoic⁺
stowt   stout⁺
straddle²
straey   stray¹
strafe²
straggle² straggly

straight¹ *[not bent]   strait *[sea passage]
straight ~away ~-faced
straight ~forward ~jacket ~-laced
straighten¹
strain¹
strait *[sea passage]   straight¹ *[not bent]⁺
straiten   straighten¹
strand¹
strane   strain¹
strange² ~ly ~ness
stranger
strangle² ~hold
strangulated   strangulation
strap³ ~less
stratagem
strategic ~ally
strategy⁴ strategist
stratify⁴
stratosphere stratospheric
stratum   strata
straw ~-coloured ~l man ~-poll
strawberry⁴
stray¹
strayt   straight¹ *[not bent],
                             strait *[sea passage]
streak¹ streaky⁴
stream¹
streamline²
strech   stretch¹⁺
streek   streak¹⁺
streem   stream¹
street ~-cred ~lamp
street ~l value ~wise
strength ~l of evidence
strengthen¹
strenth   strength
strenuous ~ly ~ness
streptococcus streptococci

KEY TO SUFFIXES AND COMPOUNDS

These rules are explained on pages ix to x.

1 Keep the word the same before adding **ed, er, est, ing**
e.g. cool¹ → cooled, cooler, coolest, cooling

2 Take off final **e** before adding **ed, er, est, ing**
e.g. fine² → fined, finer, finest, fining

3 Double final consonant before adding **ed, er, est, ing**
e.g. thin³ → thinned, thinner, thinnest, thinning

4 Change final **y** to **i** before adding **ed, er, es, est, ly, ness**
e.g. tidy⁴ → tidied, tidier, tidies, tidiest, tidily, tidiness
Keep final **y** before adding **ing** e.g. tidying

5 Add **es** instead of **s** to the end of the word
e.g. bunch⁵ → bunches

6 Change final **f** to **ve** before adding **s**
e.g. calf⁶ → calves

stress[1] ~| fracture
stress ~full ~fully ~fulness
stretch[1] ~| mark ~| pants
stretcher ~-bearer
strew[1] ~n
strewth
striccher   stricture
stricken
stricnine   strychnine
strict[1] ~ly ~ness
stricture
stride[2]
strident ~ly
strife
strike[2]
strike ~-breaker ~-breaking
striken   stricken
strikt   strict[+]
string ~er ~ing ~y
stringent   stringency
strip[3] *[naked] ~-search
stripe[2] *[pattern]   stripy[4]
stripling
striptease
strive[2]   striven
stroad   strode
stroak   stroke[2]
strobe ~| lighting
strode
stroke[2]
stroll[1]
strong[1] ~ly ~-arm ~hold
strong ~-minded ~room
strontium
strop[3]   stroppy[4]
strorbury   strawberry[4]
strore   straw[+]
strove

struck
structural ~ly
structure[2]
strudel
strue   strew[1+]
strueth   strewth
struggle[2]
strum[3]
strung
strut[3]
strychnine
strydent   strident[+]
stryfe   strife
stryke   strike[+]
stryng   string[+]
stryngent   stringent[+]
stryve   strive[2+]
stub[3]
stubble   stubbly[4]
stubborn ~ly ~ness
stubel   stubble[+]
stuborn   stubborn[+]
stucco[1] ~es
stuck ~-up
stuco   stucco[1+]
stud[3]
studded *[decorated]   studied *[worked]
student ~| body
student ~| council ~| teaching
studie   study[4]
studied *[worked]   studded *[decorated]
studio
studious ~ly ~ness
study[4]
studyo   studio
stue   stew[1]
stueard   steward[+]
stuff[1]

---

stuffy[4]

stuge — stooge[2]

stule — stool

stultify[4]

stumack — stomach[1+]

stumble[2]

stumbling block

stump[1]

stun[3] ~| grenade ~| gun

stung

stunk

stunt[1] ~man ~woman

stupefy[4]

stupendous ~ly ~ness

stuper — stupor

stupid[1] ~ly   stupidity[4]

stupify — stupefy[4]

stupor

stur — stir[3+]

sturdy[4]

sturgeon

sturling — sterling

sturn — stern[+]

sturnum — sternum

stutter[1]

sty[4]

style[2] *[appearance]   stile *[steps]

stylise[2]

stylish ~ly ~ness

stylist ~ic ~ically ~ics

stylus[5]

stymie ~d

stypend — stipend

su — sue[2]

suave[2] ~ly ~ness

sub[3]

subcommittee

subconscious ~ly ~ness

☞ Can't find your word here? Take off <u>sub</u> and look again

subcontinent

subcontractor

subdew — subdue[2]

subdivide[2]   subdivision

subdue[2]

subedit[1] ~or

suberb — suburb *[town][+], superb *[great]

subheading

subject[1] ~| matter

subjective   subjectivity

subjugate[2]   subjugation

subjunctive

subkontracter — subcontractor

sublet[3]

sublimate[2]

sublime   subliminal

submachine-gun

submarine

submerge[2]

submersion   submersible

submission

submissive ~ly

submit[3]

submurge — submerge[2]

submurshun — submersion[+]

subordinate[2]   subordination

sub-plot

subpoena[1]

subscribe[2]   subscription

subsequent ~ly

subservience   subservient

subset

subside[2]   subsidence

subsidiary[4]

subsidise[2]

KEY TO SUFFIXES AND COMPOUNDS

These rules are explained on pages ix to x.

1 Keep the word the same before adding **ed, er, est, ing**
e.g. cool[1] → cooled, cooler, coolest, cooling
2 Take off final **e** before adding **ed, er, est, ing**
e.g. fine[2] → fined, finer, finest, fining
3 Double final consonant before adding **ed, er, est, ing**
e.g. thin[3] → thinned, thinner, thinnest, thinning

4 Change final **y** to **i** before adding **ed, er, es, est, ly, ness**
e.g. tidy[4] → tidied, tidier, tidies, tidiest, tidily, tidiness
Keep final **y** before adding **ing** e.g. tidying
5 Add **es** instead of **s** to the end of the word
e.g. bunch[5] → bunches
6 Change final **f** to **ve** before adding **s**
e.g. calf[6] → calves

subsidy[4]
subsist[1] ~ence
subsoil
subsonic
substance
sub-standard
substantial ~ly
substantiate[2] substantiation
substantive ~ly
substence   substance
substitute[2] substitution
substratum substrata
subsume[2]
subsurvience   subservience[+]
subtafuge   subterfuge
subteranean
subterfuge
subtitle[2]
subtle[2] subtly
subtlety[4]
subtotal
subtract[1] ~ion
subtropical
subturranean   subterranean
suburb ~an ~ia
subversion subversive
subvert[1]
subvursion   subversion[+]
subway
subzero
succeed[1]
success ~ful ~fully
success succession successor
successive ~ly
succinct ~ly
succour[1] *[help]   sucker *[victim, plant]
succulent succulence
succumb[1]

such -~like
suck[1] suction
sucker *[victim, plant]   succour[1] *[help]
suckle[2]
sucrose
sucseed   succeed[1]
sucsess   success[+]
sucshun   suction
suction
sudden ~ly ~ness
suds
sue[2]
suecrose   sucrose
sued *[claimed]
suede *[leather]
suet ~| pudding
sueur   sewer *[drain],
                             sure[2] *[certain][+]

suffer[1] ~ance ~er
suffice[2]
sufficiency
sufficient ~ly
sufficks   suffix[1+]
suffiss   suffice[2]
suffix[1] ~es
sufflay   soufflé
suffocate[2] suffocation
suffrage suffragette
suffuse[2]
sufice   suffice[2]
sufishency   sufficiency
sufishent   sufficient[+]
sufix   suffix[1+]
sufokate   suffocate[2+]
sufrage   suffrage[+]
sufuse   suffuse[2]
sugar[1] ~y
suggest[1] ~ion ~ive

---

suicide   suicidal
suit[1] *[clothes] ~case

suite *[rooms],
soot *[black powder]+,
sweet[1] [food]

suitability
suitable   suitably
suite *[rooms]

suit[1] *[clothes]+,
sweet[1] *[food]+

suitor *[for marriage]

suture[2] *[sew up]

sukculent

succulent

sukcumb

succumb[1]

suker

succour[1] *[help],
sucker *[victim, plant]

sukrose

sucrose

sukul

suckle[2]

sulen

sullen

sulffait

sulphate

sulffide

sulphide

sulffur

sulphur+

sulffuric

sulphuric+

sulk[1]   sulky[4]

sullen ~ly ~ness

sully[4]

sulphate

sulphide

sulphur ~ous

sulphuric ~l acid

sultan ~a

sultry[4]

suly

sully[4]

sum[3] *[total]

some *[a quantity]

sumchuous

sumptuous+

sumer

summer+

sumerily

summarily

sumerise

summarise[2]

sumersorlt

somersault[1]

sumery

summary *[quick],
summery *[warm]

summarily

summarise[2]

summary[4] *[quick]

summery *[warm]

summer ~time

summery *[warm]

summary[4] *[quick]

summit

summon[1] *[call forth]

summons[1] *[before court]

sump

sumptuous ~ly ~ness

sun[3] *[shine]

son *[boy]+

sun ~bathe ~beam

sun ~burn ~burnt ~dial

sun ~down ~dress

sun ~-dried ~fish

sun ~flower ~glasses

sun ~l hat ~-kissed ~lamp ~lit

sun ~light ~rise ~screen ~set

sun ~shade ~shine ~l spot ~stroke

sun ~tan ~tanned ~l worshipper

sundae *[ice cream]

Sunday *[day of week] ~l school

sundry[4]

sune

soon[1]

sung

sunk ~en

Sunni *[religion]

sunny[4] *[sun]

supafishal

superficial

super *[great]

supper *[meal]+

superabundance

superannuated   superannuation

superb ~ly

☞ Can't find your word here? Take off **super** and look again

supercargo[5]

supercede

supersede[2]

---

supercharger
supercilious ~ly ~ness
supercomputer
superconductor   superconductivity
superficial ~ly ~ity
superfluous ~ly ~ness
superhero⁵
superhuman
superimpose²
superintendent
superior ~ity
superlative ~ly
supermarket
supernatural ~ly
supernova
supernumerary
supersede²
supersillius   supercilious⁺
supersonic
superstition
superstitious ~ly ~ness
superstructure
supervise²   supervisor
supervision   supervisory
supine
suplant   supplant¹
suple   supple⁺
suplement   supplement¹⁺
suply   supply⁴
suport   support¹⁺
supose   suppose²⁺
suppeena   subpoena¹
supper *[meal] ~l time   super *[great]
supperb   superb⁺
suppervise   supervise²⁺
suppervision   supervision
supplant¹
supple ~ness

supplement¹ ~ary
supply⁴
support¹ ~ive
suppose² ~dly   supposition
suppository
suppress¹ ~ant ~ion ~or
supremacy   supremacist
supreme ~ly   supremo
supresor   suppressor
supress   suppress¹⁺
suprintendant   superintendent
supurfluous   superfluous⁺
supurhuman   superhuman
surcharge²
sure² *[certain] ~ly   shore² *[sea, prop]⁺
sure ~fire ~-footed
surealist   surrealist⁺
surely *[certainly]   surly⁴ *[rude]
surender   surrender¹
surene   serene⁺
sureptishus   surreptitious⁺
surety
surf¹ *[sea] ~board   serf *[slave]⁺
surface² ~l area ~l mail ~l tension
surfeit
surge²
surgeon *[doctor]
surgery⁴
surgical ~ly ~l spirit
surly⁴ *[rude]   surely *[certainly]
surmise²
surmon   sermon
surmonise   sermonise²
surmount¹
surname
surogate   surrogate⁺
suround   surround¹⁺
surpass¹

---

surpent	serpent+
surplice *[robe]	
surplus5 *[excess]	
surprise2	
surprisingly	
surrated	serrated
surrealism	
surrealist ~ic	
surrender1	
surreptitious ~ly ~ness	
surrogate ~l father ~l mother	
surround1 ~ings	
surtax5	
survalence	surveillance
survant	servant
surve	serve2
surveillance	
survey1 ~or	
survice	service2+
surviet	serviette
survile	servile+
survival ~l kit	
survive2 survivor	
sus	suss1+
susceptible susceptibility	
suspect1	
suspend1 ~ers	
suspense ~ful	
suspension ~l bridge	
suspicion	
suspicious ~ly ~ness	
suss1 ~l out	
sussinct	succinct+
sustain1 ~able ~ability	
sustenance	
sutch	such
sute	soot *[black powder]+, suit1 *[clothes]

suter	suitor
suttel	subtle2+
suttlety	subtlety
suttly	subtly
suture2 *[sew up]	suitor *[for marriage]
suvenear	souvenir+
svelte	
swab3	
swach	swatch *[sample], Swatch™ *[watch]
swaddle2	
swaddling ~l clothes	
swade	suede
swagger1	
swaith	swathe2
swallow1	
swam *[past of swim]	swarm1 *[of insects]
swamp1 swampy4	
swan3 ~song	
swank1 swanky4	
swap3	
swarm1 *[of insects]	swam *[past of swim]
swarthy4	
swarve	suave2+
swastika	
swat3 *[hit]	swot3 *[study]
swatch *[sample]	
Swatch™ *[watch]	
swathe2	
swaw	swore+
sway1	
swayd	suede
swaythe	swathe2
swear ~ing ~l word	
sweat1 *[hot]	suite *[rooms], sweet1 *[food]+
sweat ~band ~pants	
sweat ~shirt ~shop ~suit	

KEY TO SUFFIXES AND COMPOUNDS

These rules are explained on pages ix to x.

1 Keep the word the same before adding **ed, er, est, ing**
e.g. cool1 → cooled, cooler, coolest, cooling
2 Take off final **e** before adding **ed, er, est, ing**
e.g. fine2 → fined, finer, finest, fining
3 Double final consonant before adding **ed, er, est, ing**
e.g. thin3 → thinned, thinner, thinnest, thinning

4 Change final **y** to **i** before adding **ed, er, es, est, ly, ness**
e.g. tidy4 → tidied, tidier, tidies, tidiest, tidily, tidiness
Keep final **y** before adding **ing** e.g. tidying
5 Add **es** instead of **s** to the end of the word
e.g. bunch5 → bunches
6 Change final **f** to **ve** before adding **s**
e.g. calf6 → calves

sweater *[clothing]   sweeter *[sugary]

sweaty[4]

swede *[vegetable]

Swede *[from Sweden]

sweep ~er ~ing ~stake

sweet[1] *[food] ~ly ~ness   suite *[rooms]

sweet ~ly ~ness

sweet ~bread ~| chestnut ~corn

sweet ~heart ~meat ~| pea ~| pepper

sweet ~| potato ~-tempered ~| tooth

sweeten[1]

sweeter *[sugary]   sweater *[clothing]

swell[1]

swelter[1]

swept ~-back

swerl   swirl[1]

swerve[2]

swet   sweat[1] *[hot]+,
         sweet[1] *[food]+

swetter   sweater

swhere   swear+

swich   switch[1]+

swift[1] ~ly ~ness

swig[3]

swill[1]

swim ~mer ~suit ~wear

swimming ~| costume ~| pool

swindle[2]

swine

swing

swingeing *[far-reaching]

swinging *[moving]

swipe[2]

swirl[1]

swish[1]

Swiss ~| cheese ~| roll

switch[1] ~back ~blade ~board

swivel[3] ~| chair ~| round

swizzle[2] ~| stick

swob   swab[3]

swoddle   swaddle[2+]

swollen

swollow   swallow[1]

swomp   swamp[1+]

swon   swan[3+]

swoon[1]

swoop[1]

swoosh[1]

swopp   swap

sword ~fish ~sman

swore   sworn

sworthy   swarthy[4]

swostika   swastika

swot[3] *[study]   swat[3] *[hit]

swotch   swatch *[sample],
            Swatch™ *[watch]

swoth   swathe[2]

swoup   swoop[1]

swum

swung

swurve   swerve[2]

swyne   swine

swype   swipe[2]

☞ Can't find your word here? Look under <u>si</u>, <u>ci</u> or <u>psy</u>

syanide   cyanide

sybernetiks   cybernetics

sycamore ~| tree

syche   psyche+

sychedelic   psychedelic

sychiatrist   psychiatrist+

sychic   psychic+

sychoanalyse   psychoanalyse[2+]

sychotic   psychotic+

syclamen   cyclamen

sycle   cycle[2]

KEY TO SPELLING RULES

Red words are wrong. **Black** words are correct.

~   Add the suffix or word directly to the main word,
    without a space or hyphen
    e.g. ash ~en ~tray → ashen ashtray

~-   Add a hyphen to the main word before adding the
    next word
    e.g. blow ~-dry → blow-dry

~| Leave a space between the main word and the next
    word
    e.g. decimal ~| place → decimal place

+   By finding this word in its **correct** alphabetical
    order, you can find related words
    e.g. about+ → about-face about-turn

*   Draws attention to words that may be confused

TM   Means the word is a trademark

syclic	cyclic[+]	syncere	sincere[2+]
syclist	cyclist	synchronise[2]	synchronisation
syclone	cyclone	syncopate[2]	syncopation
Syclops	Cyclops	syndicalist	
syclotron	cyclotron	syndicate[2]	syndication
sycophant ~ic		syndrome	
syfilis	syphilis[+]	synic	cynic[+]
syft	sift[1]	synical	cynical[+]
sygn	sign[+]	synod	
sygnet	cygnet *[swan], signet *[ring]	synonym ~ous ~ously	
		synopsis synopses	
sygnpost	signpost	synoptic ~l nerve	
Sykh	Sikh[+]	synovial	
sylage	silage	syntax syntactic	
sylence	silence[2]	synthesis syntheses	
sylent	silent[+]	synthesise[2]	
sylinder	cylinder	synthetic ~ally	
sylindrical	cylindrical[+]	synus	sinus[5+]
sylk	silk[+]	syoodoenym	pseudonym
syllable syllabic		sypher	cypher
syllabus[5]		syphilis syphilitic	
syllogism		sypress	cypress
sylph ~like		syre	sire[2]
symbiosis symbiotic		syren	siren
symbol *[sign]	cymbal *[music]	Syrillic	Cyrillic
symbolic ~al ~ally		syringe	
symbolise[2] symbolism		syrup syrupy	
symfony	symphony[+]	sysop	
symmetric ~al ~ally		syst	cyst[+]
symmetry[4]		system ~l operator ~l 's analysis	
sympathetic ~ally		systematic *[planned] ~ally	
sympathise[2]		systematise[2]	
sympathy		systemic *[affecting all] ~ally	
symphony symphonic		syte	cite[2] *[quote][+], sight *[seeing][+], site[2] *[place]
symposium symposia			
symptom ~atic			
synagogue		sythe	scythe[2]
sync *[together]	sink[1] *[drop, basin][+]		

KEY TO SUFFIXES AND COMPOUNDS

These rules are explained on pages ix to x.

1 Keep the word the same before adding ed, er, est, ing
e.g. cool[1] → cooled, cooler, coolest, cooling

2 Take off final e before adding ed, er, est, ing
e.g. fine[2] → fined, finer, finest, fining

3 Double final consonant before adding ed, er, est, ing
e.g. thin[3] → thinned, thinner, thinnest, thinning

4 Change final y to i before adding ed, er, es, est, ly, ness
e.g. tidy[4] → tidied, tidier, tidies, tidiest, tidily, tidiness
Keep final y before adding ing e.g. tidying

5 Add es instead of s to the end of the word
e.g. bunch[5] → bunches

6 Change final f to ve before adding s
e.g. calf[6] → calves

T ~-junction ~-shirt ~-square
tab³ ~| stop
tabby⁴

tabel   table²⁺
tabelspoon   tablespoon⁺
tabernacle
table² ~cloth ~| manners
table ~| mat ~| tennis ~ware
tablespoon ~ful
tablet
tabloid ~| journalism
taboo¹
tabular
tabulate²   tabulation
taburnacle   tabernacle
tachograph
tachometer
tacit ~ly ~ness
taciturn
tack¹ *[nail, sailing]   take *[get]⁺
tackle²
tacks *[nails, sailing]   tax¹ *[money]⁺
tacksidermy   taxidermy⁺
tacksonomy   taxonomy⁴
tacky⁴
taco
tact ~ful ~fully ~less ~lessly
tactic ~al ~ally   tactician
tactile
tad ~pole
taek   take
taffeta
tag³ ~| along
tagliatelle
t'ai chi
tail¹ *[follow, dog]   tale *[story]
tail ~less ~back ~coat ~| light
tail ~piece ~spin ~wind

tailor¹ ~-made
taint¹
taip   tape²⁺
taiper   tapir *[animal]
                taper¹ *[narrow, burn]
tair   tear⁺
take   taken   taking
take ~away ~over
takle   tackle²
tako   taco
takometer   tachometer
taks   tacks *[nails],
                tax¹ *[money]⁺
taksi   taxi⁺
takt   tact⁺
taktik   tactic⁺
taktile   tactile
talc ~um powder
tale *[story]   tail¹ *[follow, dog]⁺
talen   talon
talent ~ed ~| scout
talisman
talk¹ ~ative ~back
tall ~ness ~| order
tallow
tally⁴
tally-ho
Talmud
talon
tamarisk
tambourine
tame² ~able ~ly ~ness
tam-o'-shanter
tamper¹
tampon
tan³
tandem
tang   tangy⁴

KEY TO SPELLING RULES

Red words are wrong. **Black** words are correct.

~   Add the suffix or word directly to the main word, without a space or hyphen
     e.g. ash ~en ~tray → ashen ashtray

~-   Add a hyphen to the main word before adding the next word
     e.g. blow ~-dry → blow-dry

~| Leave a space between the main word and the next word
     e.g. decimal ~| place → decimal place

+   By finding this word in its **correct** alphabetical order, you can find related words
     e.g. about⁺ → about-face about-turn

*   Draws attention to words that may be confused

TM   Means the word is a trademark

tangent ~ial

tangerine

tangible   tangibly

tangle²

tango¹

tanin   tannin

tanjent   tangent⁺

tanjerine   tangerine

tanjible   tangible⁺

tank¹ ~ard ~ful

tanner   tannery⁴

tannin

tannoy

tantalise²   tantalisingly

tantamount

tantra   tantric

tantrum

Tao ~ism

tap³ ~root

tapas

tap-dance²

tape² ~| measure ~-record ~worm

taper¹ *[narrow, burn]   tapir *[animal]

tapestry⁴

tapioca

tapir *[animal]   taper¹ *[narrow, burn]

tapistry   tapestry⁴

tappet

tapyoca   tapioca

tar³

tarantella *[dance]

tarantula *[spider]

tardy⁴

target¹ ~| area ~| market

tariff

tarmac

tarmigan   ptarmigan

tarn

tarnish¹

taro *[plant]

tarot *[cards]

tarpaulin

tarporlin   tarpaulin

tarragon

tarry⁴

tarsus   tarsi   tarsal

tart ~ly ~ness

tartan

tartar *[teeth]

tartare *[food] ~| sauce

tartaric acid

tartrate

tarty⁴

tasit   tacit⁺

tasiturn   taciturn

task ~| force ~master

tassel ~led

taste² ~bud ~less

tasteful ~ly ~ness

tasty⁴

tattered   tatters

tattoo¹ ~ist

tatty⁴

tatu   tattoo¹⁺

taudry   tawdry⁴

taught *[teach]   taut *[tight]⁺

taunt¹

taupe

Taurus

taut *[tight] ~ly ~ness   taught *[teach]

tautology   tautological

tavern ~a

tawdry⁴

tawn   torn

tawny⁴

tawso   torso

---

tawtology

tautology[+]

tax[1] *[money]

tacks *[nails, sailing]

tax ~able ~ation

tax ~-deductible ~l disc

tax ~-exempt ~l exile ~-free

tax ~l inspector ~payer

tax ~l relief ~l return

taxi[1] ~cab ~l stand

taxidermy   taxidermist

taxonomic ~l group

taxonomy[4]

taylor

tailor[1+]

TB

tea *[drink]

tee *[golf][+]

tea ~l bag ~cake ~cup

tea ~pot ~l room ~spoon

tea ~time ~l towel

teach ~able ~ing

teacher

teak

teal

team[1] *[group] ~mate

teem[1] *[swarm]

team   ~l player ~l spirit

teanage

teenage[+]

teanie

teeny[4]

tear *[cry]

tier *[layer]

tear ~ful ~fully ~drop ~l gas

tear *[rip] ~ing ~away

tearful ~ly ~ness

tease[2]

Teashert

T-shirt

teaspoon ~ful

Teasquare

T-square

teat

teater

teeter[1]

teatotal

teetotal[+]

techer

teacher

techie

technical ~ly

technicality[4]

technician

technicolour

technikality

technicality[4]

technique

technocrat ~ic

technological ~ly

technology[4]   technological

technophobe

tectonic ~l plates

teddy ~l bear

tedious ~ly ~ness

tedium

tedy

teddy[+]

tee *[golf] ~d ~ing ~l off   tea *[drink][+]

teejuncshun

T-junction

teek

teak

teel

teal

teem[1] *[swarm]

team[1] *[group][+]

teenage teenager   teens

teeny ~bopper ~-weeny

teese

tease[2]

Teeshert

T-shirt

teespoon

teaspoon[+]

Teesquare

T-square

teet

teat

teeter[1]

teeth *[plural of tooth]

teethe[2] *[develop teeth]

teetotal ~ism ~ler

Teflon™

tekie

techie

☞ Can't find your word here? Look under **tech**

tekilla

tequila

tekneek

technique

teknical

technical[+]

tekst · text[+]
tekstile · textile
tele ~communications ~gram
tele ~graph ~graphic ~marketing
tele ~operator ~port
telecommute[2]
telefone · telephone[2+]
telefoto · telephoto[+]
telekinesis · telekinetic
telepathy · telepathic
telephone[2] · telephonic · telephonist
telephoto ~l lens
telescope[2] · telescopic
teletext
telethon
televise[2]
television ~l licence ~l programme
telex[1]

☞ Can't find your word here? Look under **tele**

teligraf · telegraph[1]
teligram · telegram
telikinisis · telekinesis[+]
telivise · televise[2]
telivision · television[+]
tell ~er ~ing ~l off ~tale
telly[4]
temerity
temp[1] *[work] · tempt[1] *[seduce]
temper[1] ~l tantrum
temperament ~al ~ally
temperance
temperate
temperature
tempest ~uous ~uously
template
temple
tempo

tempoora · tempura
temporary[4]
tempracher · temperature
temprament · temperament[+]
tempranse · temperance
temprate · temperate
tempt[1] *[seduce] ~ation · temp[1] *[work]
tempul · temple
tempur · temper[1+]
tempura
ten ~th ~fold ~pin
tenable
tenacious ~ly
tenacity
tenament · tenement[+]
tenancy[4]
tenant ~l farmer
tenashus · tenacious[+]
tenasity · tenacity
tend[1]
tendency[4]
tender ~ly ~ness ~-hearted ~loin
tenderise[2]
tendon ~itis
tendril
tendur · tender[+]
tendurise · tenderise[2]
tenement
tenent · tenant
tener · tenner *[money], tenor *[voice]
tenet
tenner *[money] · tenor *[voice]
tennis ~l court ~l elbow ~l shoe
tenor *[voice] · tenner *[money]
tenpin ~l bowling
tense[2] ~ly
tenshun · tension

KEY TO SUFFIXES AND COMPOUNDS

These rules are explained on pages ix to x.

1 Keep the word the same before adding **ed, er, est, ing**
e.g. cool[1] → cooled, cooler, coolest, cooling

2 Take off final **e** before adding **ed, er, est, ing**
e.g. fine[2] → fined, finer, finest, fining

3 Double final consonant before adding **ed, er, est, ing**
e.g. thin[3] → thinned, thinner, thinnest, thinning

4 Change final **y** to **i** before adding **ed, er, es, est, ly, ness**
e.g. tidy[4] → tidied, tidier, tidies, tidiest, tidily, tidiness
Keep final **y** before adding **ing** e.g. tidying

5 Add **es** instead of **s** to the end of the word
e.g. bunch[5] → bunches

6 Change final **f** to **ve** before adding **s**
e.g. calf[6] → calves

tensile ~| strength
tension
tent
tentacle
tentative ~ly
tenterhooks
tenth
tenuous ~ly ~ness
tenure *[job] ~d   tenor *[voice],
                                    tenner *[money]
tepee
tepid
tequila
terakotta   terracotta

☞ Can't find your word here? Look under **tur**

terban   turban⁺
terbine   turbine
terbo   turbo
tereen   tureen
terer   terror⁺
tererise   terrorise²
terf   turf¹⁺
tergid   turgid
terier   terrier
terific   terrific⁺
terify   terrify⁴
teriss   terrace²
teritorial   territorial⁺
teritory   territory⁴⁺
terkey   turkey
Terkish delite   Turkish delight
term¹
terminal ~ly
terminate² termination
terminology⁴
terminus
termite

termoil   turmoil
tern *[bird]   turn¹ *[around]
ternary
terning   turning⁺
ternip   turnip
terodactil   pterodactyl
teror   terror⁺
terpentine   turpentine
terquoise   turquoise
terra firma
terrace²
terracotta
terrain
terrapin
terrestrial
terrible   terribly
terrier
terrific ~ally
terrify⁴
territorial ~ly
territory⁴
terror ~ism ~ist
terrorise²
terse ~ly ~ness
tershary   tertiary
tertiary
tertle   turtle⁺
tessellate²   tessellation
test¹ ~| ban ~| case ~| flight
test ~| match ~| pilot ~| tube
testament
testicle
testify⁴
testimony   testimonial
testis   testes
testosterone
testy⁴
tetanus

tetatet	tête-à-tête	theef	thief[5+]
tête-à-tête		theft	
tether[1]		their *[possession]	there *[place][+],
tetrahedron			they're *[they are]
tetsifly	tsetse fly	theirs *[belonging]	there's *[there is]
Teutonic		theism	
Tewder	Tudor	them ~selves	
tewlip	tulip	theme ~l park thematic	
tewn	tune[2+]	then	
tewnful	tuneful[+]	thence ~forth	
tewnic	tunic	theology[4] theologian theological	
Tewsday	Tuesday	theorem	
tewter	tutor[1+]	theoretical ~ly ~l probability	
tewtlige	tutelage	theorise[2]	
text[1] ~book ~l message		theory[4] theorist	
textile		theosophical ~ly theosophy	
textual		therapeutic ~ally	
texture[2]		therapy therapist	
thach	thatch[1]	there *[place] ~abouts	their *[possession],
		there ~after ~by ~fore	they're *[they are]

☞ Can't find your word here? Look under **f**

		thereputic	therapeutic[+]
Thalidomide		there's *[there is]	theirs *[belonging]
thallium		therfour	therefore[+]
than		thermal	
thank[1] ~less		thermodynamics	
thankful ~ly ~ness		thermoelectric ~ity	
thank ~l you		thermometer	
thanksgiving		thermonuclear	
that		Thermos™ ~l flask	
thatch[1]		thermostat ~ic ~ically	
thaw[1]		thers	there's *[there is],
thay	they[+]		theirs *[belonging]
the *[article]	thee *[you]	Thersday	Thursday
thearam	theorem	thesaurus	
thearetical	theoretical[+]	these	
thearise	theorise[2]	thesis theses	
theatre theatrical theatrics		thesorrus	thesaurus[+]
thee *[you]	the *[article]	thesys	thesis[+]

KEY TO SUFFIXES AND COMPOUNDS

These rules are explained on pages ix to x.

1 Keep the word the same before adding **ed, er, est, ing**
e.g. cool[1] → cooled, cooler, coolest, cooling

2 Take off final **e** before adding **ed, er, est, ing**
e.g. fine[2] → fined, finer, finest, fining

3 Double final consonant before adding **ed, er, est, ing**
e.g. thin[3] → thinned, thinner, thinnest, thinning

4 Change final **y** to **i** before adding **ed, er, es, est, ly, ness**
e.g. tidy[4] → tidied, tidier, tidies, tidiest, tidily, tidiness
Keep final **y** before adding **ing** e.g. tidying

5 Add **es** instead of **s** to the end of the word
e.g. bunch[5] → bunches

6 Change final **f** to **ve** before adding **s**
e.g. calf[6] → calves

they
they'd [they had, would]
they'll [they will, shall]
they're *[they are]   there *[place],
                             their *[possession]
they've [they have]
thick[1] ~ly ~ness ~-skinned
thicken[1]
thicket
thief[6]
thier   there *[place],
                             their *[possession],
thigh *[leg]   thy [+][your]
thik   thick[+]
thimble ~ful
thin[3] ~ly ~ness ~-skinned
thine
thing   thingy[4]
think ~er ~ing ~| tank
third ~ly ~-class
thirst[1]   thirsty[4]
thirteen ~th
thirty[4]   thirtieth
this
thistle ~down
thither
thong
thorax   thoracic
thore   thaw[1]
thorn   thorny[4]
thorough ~ly ~ness ~bred ~fare
thort   thought[+]
thortless   thoughtless[+]
those
thou *[you]
though *[but]
thought ~-provoking
thoughtful ~ly ~ness

thoughtless ~ly ~ness
thousand ~fold ~th
thow   thou *[you],
                             though *[but]
thowsand   thousand[+]
thrall
thrash[1]
thrawl   thrall
thread[1] ~bare
threat
threaten[1]
thred   thread[1+]
three ~-dimensional
three ~fold ~-legged
three ~-piece suite ~-point turn
three ~-quarters ~| R's ~-wheeler
thresh[1] ~hold
thret   threat
thretton   threaten[1]
threw *[ball]   through *[go through]
thrice
thrift   thrifty[4]
thrill[1]
thrive[2]
throat ~y
throb[3]
throes *[middle of]   throws *[ball]
thrombosis
throne *[chair]   thrown *[ball]
throng[1]
throrl   thrall
throttle[2]
through *[go through]   threw *[ball]
throughout
throw *[ball] ~ing   through *[go through]
thrown *[ball]   throne *[chair]
throws *[ball]   throes *[middle of]
thrush[5]

---

thrust ~ing

thryve — thrive[2]

thud[3]

thug ~gery ~gish

thum — thumb[1+]

thumb[1] ~nail ~screws

thumbs ~-down ~-up

thump[1]

thunder[1] ~bolt ~clap ~cloud

thunder ~storm ~struck

thunderous ~ly

thurmal — thermal

thurmodynamics — thermodynamics

thurmometur — thermometer

thurmonuclear — thermonuclear

thurmos — Thermos™[+]

thurmostat — thermostat

Thursday

thus

thwack[1]

thwart[1]

thwort — thwart[1]

thy *[your] — thigh *[leg]

thyme *[herb] — time[2] *[clock][+]

thyroid ~l gland

tiara

tibia

tic *[twitch]

tick[1] *[clock, mark]

tick ~-tock

ticket ~l agency

tickle[2]   ticklish

ticoon — tycoon

tidal ~l wave

tiddler

tiddlywinks

tide *[sea] ~line ~mark — tied *[rope, score]

tidings

tidle — tidal[+]

tidy[4] ~l up

tie *[rope, score]

tie ~d   tying

tie ~break ~-dye ~l pin

tie chee — t'ai chi

tied *[rope, score]

tier *[layer] — tear *[cry],
tire[2] *[sleep][+],
tyre *[wheel]

tiff

tifune — typhoon

tiger ~l lily ~l moth

tight[1] ~ly ~-fisted ~-knit

tight ~-lipped ~ness ~rope

tighten[1] *[firm up] — titan *[person]

tigress

tik — tic *[twitch],
tick[1] *[clock, mark][+]

tike — tyke

tikul — tickle[2+]

tilde

tile[2] *[floor covering]

till *[until, shop]

tilt[1]

timber *[wood]

timbre *[sound]

☞ Can't find your word here? Take off **time** and look
again

---

time[2] *[clock] — thyme *[herb]

time ~l bomb ~l capsule

time ~l card ~-consuming ~frame

time ~-honoured ~keeper ~keeping

time ~-lapse ~less ~l limit

time ~piece ~-saving ~l scale ~table

time ~-warp ~-worn ~l zone

timid ~ly ~ity

KEY TO SUFFIXES AND COMPOUNDS

These rules are explained on pages ix to x.

1 Keep the word the same before adding **ed, er, est, ing**
e.g. cool[1] → cooled, cooler, coolest, cooling

2 Take off final **e** before adding **ed, er, est, ing**
e.g. fine[2] → fined, finer, finest, fining

3 Double final consonant before adding **ed, er, est, ing**
e.g. thin[3] → thinned, thinner, thinnest, thinning

4 Change final **y** to **i** before adding **ed, er, es, est,
ly, ness**
e.g. tidy[4] → tidied, tidier, tidies, tidiest, tidily,
tidiness
Keep final **y** before adding **ing** e.g. tidying

5 Add **es** instead of **s** to the end of the word
e.g. bunch[5] → bunches

6 Change final **f** to **ve** before adding **s**
e.g. calf[6] → calves

timorous ~ly ~ness
tin ~foil ~| opener
tincture
tinder ~box ~-dry
tinge²
tingle²
tinker¹
tinkle²
tinnitus
tinny⁴
tinsel
tint¹
tiny⁴ *[very small]
tip³ *[end, advice] ~-off
tipewriter
tipex
tiphoon
tiphus
tipical
tipify
Tippex™¹ ~| out
tipple²
tipster
tipsy⁴
tiptoe²
tiptop
tirade
tirannical
tirannise
tirannosaurus
tiranny
tirant
tire² *[sleep]
tire ~less ~lessly
tiresome ~ly ~ness
tirn

tishue

tinny⁴ *[metallic]
type² *[sort, write]⁺
typewriter⁺
Tippex™¹⁺
typhoon
typhus⁺
typical⁺
typify⁴

tyrannical⁺
tyrannise²
tyrannosaurus⁺
tyranny⁴
tyrant
tyre *[wheel]

tern *[bird],
turn¹ *[around]
tissue⁺

tissue ~| paper
tit *[bird]
titan ~ic
titanium
titbit
tite
titen

tithe² ~| barn
titillate² titillation
titivate² titivation
title ~d ~| deed ~-holder ~| page
titrate² titration
titter¹
tittle-tattle
titular
tizz ~y
to *[do something]
    ~ and fro
to and fro
to-ing and fro-ing
toad ~stool
toan
toast¹ ~master ~| rack
tobacco ~nist
toberculosis
toboggan¹
today
toddle²
tode

todel
to-dimenshunal
to-do ~| list
toe *[on foot]
toe ~hold ~nail
toem
toffee ~| apple ~-nosed

tight *[firm]⁺

tight *[firm]⁺
tighten¹ *[firm up],
Titan *[person]

too *[also, very],
two *[number]

tone⁺

tuberculosis

toad *[animal]⁺,
towed *[pulled]
toddle²
two-dimensional

tow *[pull]

tome

tofu
toga
together ~ness
toggle ~l switch
toil[1]
toilet ~l paper
toiletries
token ~ism
toksic   toxic[+]
toksin   toxin
told
Tolemaic   Ptolemaic[+]
tolerable   tolerably
tolerait   tolerate[2+]
tolerance   tolerant
tolerate[2]   toleration
toll ~booth ~gate
tolrabul   tolerable[+]
tom ~boy ~cat ~foolery
tomahawk
tomato[5]
tomb *[burial] ~stone
tombola
tome *[large work]
tomorrow
ton *[imperial] ~nage   tonne *[metric ton]
tonal ~ity
tone ~-deaf ~less
toner
tongs
tongue[2] ~-lashing ~-tied ~-twister
tonic
tonight
tonne *[metric]   ton *[imperial][+]
tonsil ~litis
too *[also, very]   to *[do something],
                       two *[number]
tooba   tuba

toocan   toucan
took
tool[1] ~bar ~kit
toom   tomb[+]
toopay   toupée
tooshay   touché
toot[1]
tooth ~less ~y ~ache
tooth ~brush ~comb ~paste ~pick
tootifrooti   tutti frutti
tootle[2]
top[3] ~l brass ~coat ~l dog ~-down
top ~-flight ~l hat ~-heavy

☞ Can't find your word here? Take off **top** and look again

top ~-knot ~-less ~-level ~-most ~-notch
top ~-rated ~sail ~l secret ~soil
top ~-spin ~l table ~-up
topaz
tope   taupe
topic ~al ~ality ~ally
topography   topographer
topple[2]
topsy-turvy
tor *[mountain]   tore *[ripped],
                       tour *[journey]
Torah
torch[1] ~light
torcher   torture[2]
tordry   tawdry[4]
toreador
torid   torrid
torism   tourism
torist   tourist[+]
tork   talk[1]
torment[1] ~or
torn

KEY TO SUFFIXES AND COMPOUNDS

These rules are explained on pages ix to x.

1 Keep the word the same before adding **ed, er, est, ing**
   e.g. cool[1] → cooled, cooler, coolest, cooling
2 Take off final **e** before adding **ed, er, est, ing**
   e.g. fine[2] → fined, finer, finest, fining
3 Double final consonant before adding **ed, er, est, ing**
   e.g. thin[3] → thinned, thinner, thinnest, thinning

4 Change final **y** to **i** before adding **ed, er, es, est, ly, ness**
   e.g. tidy[4] → tidied, tidier, tidies, tidiest, tidily, tidiness
   Keep final **y** before adding **ing** e.g. tidying
5 Add **es** instead of **s** to the end of the word
   e.g. bunch[5] → bunches
6 Change final **f** to **ve** before adding **s**
   e.g. calf[6] → calves

tornado[5]

tornament	tournament
torney	tawny[4]
tornikay	tourniquet
tornt	taunt[1]

torpedo[1] ~es
torpor   torpid
torque
torrent ~ial
torrid

Torrus	Taurus

torso

tort *[law]	taught *[teach]

tortilla
tortoise ~shell

tortology	tautology[+]
tortoys	tortoise[+]

tortuous ~ly ~ness
torture[2]

tortuss	tortoise[+]

Tory[4] ~| Party
toss[1] ~-up

tost	toast[1+]

total[3] ~ity ~ly
totalise[2]
totalitarian ~ism
tote
totem ~| pole
totter[1]
toucan
touch[1] ~-and-go ~down ~line ~-tone
touché *[point taken]
touchy[4] *[irritable]
tough[1] ~ly ~-minded ~ness
toughen[1]
toupée

tour[1] *[journey]	tore *[ripped]
tour ~| operator	tor *[mountain]

tourism

tourist ~y ~| attraction	

tournament
tourniquet
tousle[2]

tow[1] *[pull]	toe *[on foot]

tout[1]
tow ~bar ~line ~path ~truck
toward ~s

to-way	two-way
towed *[pulled]	toad *[animal][+]

towel[3] ~| rail

tower[1] ~| block	
towle	towel[3+]

town ~| centre ~| council ~| councillor
town ~| hall ~house ~| planning

towt	tout[1]

toxic ~ity
toxicology   toxicologist
toxin
toy[1] ~| shop

toylet	toilet[+]
toyletree	toiletry[4]

trace[2] ~able
tracing ~| paper
trachea   tracheotomy
track[1] ~| record ~suit
tracking ~| station
tract
traction
tractor
trade[2] ~| deficit ~-in ~mark
trade ~name ~-off ~| route ~| secret
trade ~sman ~| union ~| wind

tradishun	tradition[+]

tradition ~al ~alist ~ally
traffic
traffic   trafficked   trafficking

KEY TO SPELLING RULES

Red words are wrong. **Black** words are correct.

~   Add the suffix or word directly to the main word, without a space or hyphen
   e.g. ash ~en ~tray → ashen ashtray

~-   Add a hyphen to the main word before adding the next word
   e.g. blow ~-dry → blow-dry

~| Leave a space between the main word and the next word
   e.g. decimal ~| place → decimal place

+   By finding this word in its **correct** alphabetical order, you can find related words
   e.g. about[+] → about-face about-turn

*   Draws attention to words that may be confused

TM   Means the word is a trademark

tragectory	trajectory[4]
tragedy[4]	
tragic ~ally	
tragicomedy	
traid	trade[+]
trail[1] ~blazer ~blazing	
train[1] ~ee ~l line ~spotter	
train ~spotting ~track	
traipse[2]	
trais	trace[2+]
trait	
traitor ~ous	
trajectory[4]	
trajedy	tragedy[4]
trajic	tragic[+]
trajicomedy	tragicomedy
trak	track[1+]
trakia	trachea[+]
trakshun	traction
trakt	tract[+]
trale	trail[1+]
tram ~car ~line	
tramp[1]	
trample[2]	
trampoline trampolining	
trance	
trancept	transept
trane	train[+]
tranquil	
tranquillise[2]	
tranquillity	
transact[1] ~ion	
transatlantic	
transceiver	
transcend[1] ~ence ~ent	
transcendental ~ism	
transcribe[2]	
transcript ~ion	

transducer	
transe	trance
transect[1] ~ion	
transeever	transceiver
transept	
transfer[3] ~able ~ence	
transfigure[2] transfiguration	
transfix[1]	
transform[1] ~ation	
transfuse[2] transfusion	
transgender	
transgress[1] ~ion ~or	
transient	
transishun	transition[+]
transistor	
transit ~ory	
transition ~al	
transitive	
transjender	transgender
transjucer	transducer
transkribe	transcribe[2]
transkript	transcript[+]
translatable	
translate[2] translation	
translucence translucent	
transmishun	transmission
transmission	
transmit[3]	
transparent ~ly transparency[4]	
transpire[2]	
transplant[1] ~ation	
transport[1] ~ation	
transpose[2]	
transseksual	transsexual
transsend	transcend[1+]
transsendental	transcendental[+]
transsexual	
transubstantiation	

KEY TO SUFFIXES AND COMPOUNDS

These rules are explained on pages ix to x.

1 Keep the word the same before adding **ed**, **er**, **est**, **ing**
e.g. cool[1] → cooled, cooler, coolest, cooling
2 Take off final **e** before adding **ed**, **er**, **est**, **ing**
e.g. fine[2] → fined, finer, finest, fining
3 Double final consonant before adding **ed**, **er**, **est**, **ing**
e.g. thin[3] → thinned, thinner, thinnest, thinning

4 Change final **y** to **i** before adding **ed**, **er**, **es**, **est**, **ly**, **ness**
e.g. tidy[4] → tidied, tidier, tidies, tidiest, tidily, tidiness
Keep final **y** before adding **ing** e.g. tidying
5 Add **es** instead of **s** to the end of the word
e.g. bunch[5] → bunches
6 Change final **f** to **ve** before adding **s**
e.g. calf[6] → calves

transverse ~ly
transvestite
trap[3] ~door   trappings
trapeze
trapezium   trapezoid
trash[1] ~y
trattoria
trauma ~tic
travails
travel[3] ~| agency ~| agent
traveller's cheque
traverse[2]
travesty[4]

travler	traveller
travurse	traverse[2]

trawl[1]

tray	
traypse	traipse[2]
trayt	trait
traytor	traitor[+]

treacherous ~ly
treachery[4]
treacle
tread ~ing ~mill
treason ~able
treasure[2] ~| hunt ~| trove
treasury[4]
treat[1] ~able ~ment
treatise
treaty[4]
treble[2] ~| clef

trecherus	treacherous[+]
trechery	treachery[4]
tred	tread[+]

tree ~line ~-lined
tree ~tops ~| trunk

treearj	triage
treeo	trio

treet	treat[1+]
treety	treaty[4]

trefoil
trek[3]
trellis ~work
tremble[2]
tremendous ~ly
tremor
tremulous ~ly
trench[1] ~es ~| coat
trenchant
trend[1] ~setter ~setting
trendy[4]
trepidation

treshere	treasure[2+]
treshery	treasury[4]

trespass[1] ~es
trestle ~| table

trew	true[+]
trewansy	truancy[+]
trewism	truism
trewly	truly[4]
trewthful	truthful[+]

triad
triage
trial[3] ~| run
triangle
triangular ~| number ~| prism
triathlon
tribal   tribalism
tribe
tribes ~men
tribulation
tribunal
tribune
tributary[4]
tribute
triceps

KEY TO SPELLING RULES

Red words are wrong. **Black** words are correct.

~ Add the suffix or word directly to the main word, without a space or hyphen
e.g. ash ~en ~tray → **ashen ashtray**

~- Add a hyphen to the main word before adding the next word
e.g. blow ~-dry → **blow-dry**

~| Leave a space between the main word and the next word
e.g. decimal ~| place → **decimal place**

\+ By finding this word in its **correct** alphabetical order, you can find related words
e.g. about[+] → **about-face about-turn**

* Draws attention to words that may be confused

TM Means the word is a trademark

316

trick[1] ~ery ~ster
trickle[2]
trick-or-treat
tricky[4]
tricuspid
tricycle
trident
tried
triffid
trifle[2]
trigger[1] ~-happy
trigonometry
trik · trick[1+]
trikel · trickle[2+]
trilateral
trile · trial[+]
trill[1]
trillion
trilobite
trilogy[4]
trim[3]
trimaran
trimester
trimmaran · trimaran
trinity *[three in one]
Trinity *[God]
trinket
trio
triode
trip[3] *[fall] ~wire · tripe *[food]
tripartite
tripe
triple[2] ~l jump · triplet
triplicate
tripod
triptych
trise · trice
trisect[1]

triseps · triceps
trist · tryst
trite ~ly ~ness
triumph[1] ~al ~ant ~antly
trivia
trivial ~ly · trivialise[2]
triviality[4]
trod ~den
troff · trough
trofy · trophy[4]
troika
trolee · trolley
troll[1]
trolley
trombone · trombonist
troop[1] *[soldiers] · troupe *[actors]
trophy[4]
tropic ~al ~ally
tropism
troposphere
trorma · trauma[+]
trot[3]
troubadour
trouble[2] ~maker ~shooter ~some
trough *[for animals] · through *[go through]
trounce[2]
troupe *[actors] · troop[1] *[soldiers][+]
trousers
trousseau
trout
trowel
trowns · trounce[2]
trowser · trouser[+]
trowt · trout
troyka · troika
truancy · truant
trubadoor · troubadour
trubbel · trouble[2+]

---

truce		tsetse fly	
truck¹ ~load		T-shirt	
truculence		tsunami	
truculent ~ly		tub³ tubby⁴	
trudge²		tuba *[music]	tuber *[root]
true ~-life ~l north		tube² tubular	
truffle		tuber *[root]	tuba *[music]
truge	trudge²	tuberculosis	
truism		tuch	touch¹⁺
truj	trudge²	tuchy	touchy⁴
trukulence	truculence	tuck¹ ~l shop	
trukulent	truculent⁺	Tudor	
truly		Tuesday	
trump¹ ~ed-up		tuffen	toughen¹⁺
trumpet¹ trumpeteer		tuft¹	
truncate² truncation		tug³ ~of-love ~-of-war	
truncheon		tuishun	tuition
trundel	trundle²	tuition	
trundle²		tuk	took *[take],
trunk ~l road			tuck¹* [in, shop]
trunkate	truncate²⁺	tuksido	tuxedo
trupeez	trapeze	tule	tool¹⁺
trupeezeeyum	trapezium	tulip	
truss¹ ~es		tumble² ~down ~-drier	
trusseau	trousseau⁺	tume	tomb⁺
trust¹ ~ful ~y ~l fund		tumer	tumour
trustee ~ship		tummy⁴	
trustworthy⁴		tumour	
truth ~ful ~fully ~fulness		tumult ~uous ~uously	
try⁴		tuna ~l fish	
		tundra	

☞ Can't find your word here? Look under **tri**

tune² ~ful ~fully ~fulness			
trybunal	tribunal	tung	tongue²⁺
trycycle	tricycle	tungsten	
tryst		tunic	
tryte	trite⁺	tuning ~l fork	
tryumf	triumph¹⁺	tunnel³ ~l vision	
tsar ~ina		Tupawear	Tupperware™

KEY TO SPELLING RULES

Red words are wrong. **Black** words are correct.

~ Add the suffix or word directly to the main word, without a space or hyphen
e.g. ash ~en ~tray → **ashen ashtray**

~- Add a hyphen to the main word before adding the next word
e.g. blow ~-dry → **blow-dry**

~l Leave a space between the main word and the next word
e.g. decimal ~l place → **decimal place**

+ By finding this word in its **correct** alphabetical order, you can find related words
e.g. about⁺ → **about-face about-turn**

* Draws attention to words that may be confused

TM Means the word is a trademark

tupay	toupée	Tutonic	Teutonic
Tupperware™		tutor[1] ~ial	
turban *[head covering] ~ed		tutti frutti	
turbine *[engine]		tut-tut[3]	
turbo *[engine] ~-charge ~jet ~prop		tutu	
turbot *[fish]		tuward	toward[+]
turbulence turbulent		tux ~edo	
turd		TV	
tureen		twaddle	
turf[1] ~l out		twain	
turgid		twang[1]	
turkey *[bird]	Turkey *[country]	twe	twee
Turkish ~l bath ~l delight		tweak[1]	
turkwoise	turquoise	tweazers	tweezers

☞ Can't find your word here? Look under **ter**

		twee	
		tweed ~y	
turm	term[1+]	tweek	tweak[1]
turmite	termite	tweet	
turmoil		tweezers	
turn[1] *[around]	tern *[bird]	twelve twelfth	
turn ~coat ~out ~over		twentieth	
turn ~stile ~table		twenty[4] ~-first ~-twenty	
turning ~l point		twerl	twirl[1]
turnip		twice	
turpentine		twiddle[2]	
turpitude		twig[1]	
turquoise		twilight ~l world ~l zone	
turrain	terrain	twill[1]	
turrestrial	terrestrial	twin[3] *[two] ~l beds ~-bedded	
turret		twin ~-engined ~set ~l town	
turse	terse[+]	twine *[string]	
turtiary	tertiary	twinge[2]	
turtle ~dove ~-neck		twinkle[2]	
tusk		twirl[1]	
tussle[2]		twise	twice
tutelage		twist[1] ~y	
tuter	tutor[1+]	twit[3]	
tuth	tooth[+]	twitch[1] ~es ~y	

KEY TO SUFFIXES AND COMPOUNDS

These rules are explained on pages ix to x.

1 Keep the word the same before adding **ed, er, est, ing**
  e.g. cool[1] → cooled, cooler, coolest, cooling
2 Take off final **e** before adding **ed, er, est, ing**
  e.g. fine[2] → fined, finer, finest, fining
3 Double final consonant before adding **ed, er, est, ing**
  e.g. thin[3] → thinned, thinner, thinnest, thinning

4 Change final **y** to **i** before adding **ed, er, es, est, ly, ness**
  e.g. tidy[4] → tidied, tidier, tidies, tidiest, tidily, tidiness
  Keep final **y** before adding **ing** e.g. tidying
5 Add **es** instead of **s** to the end of the word
  e.g. bunch[5] → bunches
6 Change final **f** to **ve** before adding **s**
  e.g. calf[6] → calves

twitter[1] ~y

two *[number]

two ~-dimensional ~-faced ~fold

two ~-man ~-piece ~-ply

two ~some ~-time ~-way

twoddle	twaddle
twylight	twilight
twyn	twin[3] *[two][+]
	twine *[string]
twynge	twinge[2]
twynkle	twinkle[2]
twyst	twist[1+]
twyster	twister
twyt	twit[3]
ty	tie[+]

☞ Can't find your word here? Look under <u>ti</u>

tyara	tiara
tycket	ticket[+]
tycoon	
tyde	tide[+] *[sea],
	tied *[rope, score]
tyght	tight[+]

tying	
tyke	
tyle	tile[2]
tyme	time *[clock][+],
	thyme *[herb]

type[2] ~cast ~face ~writer

typhoon

typhus   typhoid

typical ~ly

typify[4]

typist

typo

typography[4]	typographer
tyrade	tirade

tyrannical ~ly

tyrannise[2]

tyrannosaurus ~| rex

tyranny[4]

tyrant

tyre *[wheel]	tire[2] *[sleep][+]
tyresome	tiresome[+]
tytan	titan *[giant][+,]
	tighten[1] [firm up]
tytanic	titanic

KEY TO SPELLING RULES

Red words are wrong. **Black** words are correct.

~   Add the suffix or word directly to the main word, without a space or hyphen
     e.g. ash ~en ~tray → ashen ashtray

~-   Add a hyphen to the main word before adding the next word
     e.g. blow ~-dry → blow-dry

~| Leave a space between the main word and the next word
     e.g. decimal ~| place → decimal place

+   By finding this word in its **correct** alphabetical order, you can find related words
     e.g. about[+] → about-face about-turn

*   Draws attention to words that may be confused

TM   Means the word is a trademark

U ~-boat ~-turn	unabridged
ubiquitous ~ly	unacceptable
ucalyptus — eucalyptus	unaccompanied
Ucarist — Eucharist	unaccustomed
Uclid — Euclid	unaided
udder	unanimity unanimous
ufemism — euphemism	unappetising
ufemistic — euphemistic⁺	unashamedly
uforia — euphoria⁺	unassuming
ugenics — eugenics	unauthorised
ugh	unavoidable unavoidably
ugly⁴ ~l duckling	unaware
ukelele	unbearable unbearably
ulcer ~ated ~ous	unbelievable unbelievably
ule — Yule⁺	unblock¹
uliteration — alliteration	uncanny⁴
ulna ~e	unceremonious ~ly
ulogise — eulogise²⁺	uncertain ~ly ~ty
ulogy — eulogy⁴	unchanged
ulser — ulcer⁺	uncharitable uncharitably
ulterior ~l motive	uncivilised
ultimate ~ly	uncle
ultimatum	unconditional ~ly
ultireor — ulterior⁺	unconscious ~ly ~ness
ultrasonic ~ally	uncontrollable uncontrollably
ultrasound	uncontrolled
ultraviolet	unconvincing
ululate ululation	uncouth ~ness
umbilical ~l cord	uncover¹
umbrage	undecided
umbrella	

☞ Can't find your word here? Take off **under** and look again

umpire² *[game] empire *[lands]

umpteen

☞ Can't find your word here? Take off **un** and look again

undeniable undeniably
under ~-age ~-aged ~arm ~carriage
under ~clothes ~cover ~done ~graduate
under ~ground ~growth ~hand ~neath
under ~pants ~pass ~study ~wear

unabated

unable *[not able] enable *[to make able]

KEY TO SUFFIXES AND COMPOUNDS

These rules are explained on pages ix to x.

1 Keep the word the same before adding **ed, er, est, ing**
e.g. cool¹ → cooled, cooler, coolest, cooling

2 Take off final **e** before adding **ed, er, est, ing**
e.g. fine² → fined, finer, finest, fining

3 Double final consonant before adding **ed, er, est, ing**
e.g. thin³ → thinned, thinner, thinnest, thinning

4 Change final **y** to **i** before adding **ed, er, es, est, ly, ness**
e.g. tidy⁴ → tidied, tidier, tidies, tidiest, tidily, tidiness
Keep final **y** before adding **ing** e.g. tidying

5 Add **es** instead of **s** to the end of the word
e.g. bunch⁵ → bunches

6 Change final **f** to **ve** before adding **s**
e.g. calf⁶ → calves

underestimate[2]
undergo ~ing   undergone
underline[2]
undermine[2]
underscore[2]
undersign[1]
understand ~able ~ably ~ing
understood
undertake   undertaken
undertaker
undertaking
undertook

> ☞ Can't find your word here? Take off **un** and look again

undesirable
undew   undue
undignified
undiniabel   undeniable[+]
undo *[take apart] ~ing   undue *[needless]
undone
undoubted ~ly
undrinkable
undue *[needless]   undo *[take apart][+]
unearth[1] ~ly
uneasy[4]
uneatable   uneaten
unecessary   unnecessary[4]
uneconomic ~al
unedifying
uneducated
unekspected   unexpected[+]
unemotional
unemployable
unemployed   unemployment
unenthusiastic
unequal ~led ~ly
unerth   unearth[1]

unethical
uneven ~ly ~ness
unexciting
unexpected ~ly
unfair ~ly ~ness
unfaithful
unfamiliar
unfashionable   unfashionably
unfavourable   unfavourably
unferl   unfurl[1]
unfernished   unfurnished
unfettered
unfinished
unflagging
unflattering
unflinching ~ly
unfocussed
unfold[1]
unforeseeable
unforgettable   unforgettably
unforgivable   unforgivably
unfortunate ~ly
unfounded
unfownded   unfounded
unfrendly   unfriendly
unfriendly[4]
unfulfilled
unfurl[1]
unfurnished
ungainly
ungarded   unguarded
ungodly
ungovernable
ungracious ~ly ~ness
ungrammatical
ungrashus   ungracious[+]
ungrateful ~ly ~ness
unguarded

KEY TO SPELLING RULES

Red words are wrong. **Black** words are correct.

~ Add the suffix or word directly to the main word, without a space or hyphen
   e.g. ash ~en ~tray → ashen ashtray

~- Add a hyphen to the main word before adding the next word
   e.g. blow ~-dry → blow-dry

~| Leave a space between the main word and the next word
   e.g. decimal ~| place → decimal place

+ By finding this word in its **correct** alphabetical order, you can find related words
   e.g. about[+] → about-face about-turn

* Draws attention to words that may be confused

TM Means the word is a trademark

☞ Can't find your word here? Take off __un__ and look
again

unhampered	
unhappy[4]	
unhealthy	
unheard of	
unhesitatingly	
unianise	unionise[2]
unien	union
unicorn	
uniform ~ed ~ly ~ity	
unify[4] unification	
unimaginable unimaginably	
unimportant	
uninhabited	
unintentional ~ly	
union Union Jack	
unionise[2]	
unionist unionism	
unique ~ly ~ness	
unisex	
unison	
unit	
Unitarian	
unitary ~l tax	
unite[2] unity	
universal ~ity ~ly	
universe	
university[4]	
unjust ~ified ~ly	
unkempt	
unkind[1]	
unkle	uncle
unknowing ~ly unknown	
unkouth	uncouth[+]
unkwenchabul	unquenchable
unleaded	
unless	

unlicensed	
unlike ~ly	
unlovable	
unloved	
unlucky[4]	
unmanned ~l spacecraft	
unmarked	
unmenshunabul	unmentionable
unmentionable	
unmistakable unmistakably	
unmoved	
unnatural ~ly	
unnecessary[4]	
unnown	unknown
unobtrusive ~ly	
unpaid	
unpalatable	
unpardonable	
unpleasant ~ly ~ness	
unplug[3]	
unpopular ~ity	
unprejudiced	
unprepared	
unpretentious ~ly ~ness	
unprintable	
unpripared	unprepared
unpritenshus	unpretentious[+]
unprofessional ~ly	
unprompted	
unpronounceable	
unprotected	
unproven	
unprovoked	
unpunished	
unquestionable unquestionably	
unquestioning ~ly	
unraliabul	unreliable
unrap	unwrap[3]

KEY TO SUFFIXES AND COMPOUNDS

These rules are explained on pages ix to x.

1 Keep the word the same before adding **ed, er, est, ing**
e.g. cool[1] → cooled, cooler, coolest, cooling
2 Take off final **e** before adding **ed, er, est, ing**
e.g. fine[2] → fined, finer, finest, fining
3 Double final consonant before adding **ed, er, est, ing**
e.g. thin[3] → thinned, thinner, thinnest, thinning

4 Change final **y** to **i** before adding **ed, er, es, est, ly, ness**
e.g. tidy[4] → tidied, tidier, tidies, tidiest, tidily, tidiness
Keep final **y** before adding **ing** e.g. tidying
5 Add **es** instead of **s** to the end of the word
e.g. bunch[5] → bunches
6 Change final **f** to **ve** before adding **s**
e.g. calf[6] → calves

> ☞ Can't find your word here? Take off **un** and look again

unravel[3]
unreal   unrealistic
unreasonable   unreasonably
unrekwited   unrequited
unrelenting
unreliable
unremitting
unrepentant
unrequited
unresponsive
unritten   unwritten
unruly[4]
unsaid
unscientific ~ally
unscramble[2]
unscrew[1]
unscrupulous ~ly ~ness
unsed   unsaid
unseen
unselfconscious ~ly ~ness
unselfish ~ly ~ness
unsertain   uncertain[+]
unshakeable
unsientific   unscientific[+]
unsightly
unsitely   unsightly
unsivilised   uncivilised
unskilled
unskrambul   unscramble[2]
unskrew   unscrew[1]
unskrupulous   unscrupulous[+]
unsociable
unsofisticated   unsophisticated
unsolved
unsophisticated

unsoshabul   unsociable
unspeakable
unspecified
unspoiled
unspoken
unsporting
unsteady[4]
unsuccessful ~ly
unsuitable   unsuitably   unsuited
untidy[4]
untie   untied   untying
until
unto
untold
untroubled
untrustworthy[4]
untruthful
unuch   eunuch
unusable
unusual ~ly
unwelcome   unwelcoming
unworthy[4]
unwrap[3]
unwritten
unyun   onion *[vegetable],
                              union *[uniting]
unyverse   universe
unzip[3]
up[3] ~beat ~right ~river
upbringing
upgrade[2]
upheaval
uphemism   euphemism
uphemistic   euphemistic[+]
upheval   upheaval
uphold ~ing   upheld
upholster[1]   upholstery
uphoria   euphoria[+]

---

uplands
uplift[1]
upload[1]
upon
upper ~| case ~| class
uprise[2]
uprite   upright
uproar ~ious ~iously
upset ~ting
upshot
upside-down
upskale   upscale
upstairs
upstart
upstream
uptake
uptern   upturn[1]
uptight
uptite   uptight
upturn[1]
upward ~ly ~s
upwood   upward[+]
uranium
Uranus
urban *[city] ~| renewal
urbane *[worldly]
urbanise[2] urbanisation
urchin
Urdu
urea
ureter
urethra
urge[2]
urgency
urgent ~ly
urhythmee   eurhythmy[+]
urinate[2]

urine   urinal   urinary
url   earl *[noble][+]
URL *[uniform resource locator]
urly   early[4+]
urmine   ermine
urn *[vase]   earn[1] *[money]
urnest   earnest[+]
urology   urologist
Uropean   European[+]
urstwile   erstwhile
urth   earth[1+]
urthen   earthen[+]
us
use[2]   usable   usage
useful ~ly ~ness
useless ~ly ~ness
user ~-friendly
userp   usurp[1]
usher[1] ~ette
usual ~ly
usurp[1]
usury
utensil
uterus
uthanasia   euthanasia
utiletarian   utilitarian[+]
utilise[2]   utilisation
utilitarian ~ism
utility[4]
utmost
Utopia ~n
utter[1] ~ance ~ly
uturus   uterus
uver   other
uze   use[2+]
uzery   usury
uzual   usual[+]

KEY TO SUFFIXES AND COMPOUNDS

These rules are explained on pages ix to x.

1 Keep the word the same before adding **ed**, **er**, **est**, **ing**
e.g. cool[1] → cooled, cooler, coolest, cooling
2 Take off final **e** before adding **ed**, **er**, **est**, **ing**
e.g. fine[2] → fined, finer, finest, fining
3 Double final consonant before adding **ed**, **er**, **est**, **ing**
e.g. thin[3] → thinned, thinner, thinnest, thinning

4 Change final **y** to **i** before adding **ed**, **er**, **es**, **est**, **ly**, **ness**
e.g. tidy[4] → tidied, tidier, tidies, tidiest, tidily, tidiness
Keep final **y** before adding **ing** e.g. tidying
5 Add **es** instead of **s** to the end of the word
e.g. bunch[5] → bunches
6 Change final **f** to **ve** before adding **s**
e.g. calf[6] → calves

V ~-neck ~-necked
V ~-shaped ~| sign
vacancy⁴
vacant ~ly
vacate²
vacation *[holiday]   vocation *[job]⁺
vaccinate² vaccination
vaccine
vaceline   Vaseline™
vacillate² vacillation
vacsine   vaccine
vacum   vacuum⁺
vacuous ~ly ~ness
vacuum¹ ~| cleaner
vacuum ~| flask ~-packed
vael   vale *[valley],
                       veil¹ *[cloth]
vagabond
vagary⁴
vage   vague²⁺
vagina
vagrant vagrancy
vague ~ly ~ness
vain *[proud] ~ly   vane *[weather],
                       vein *[blood]
vaiporise   vaporise²
vakansy   vacancy⁺
vakant   vacant⁺
vakate   vacate²
vaksinate   vaccinate²⁺
vaksine   vaccine
vakuous   vacuous⁺
vakuum   vacuum⁺
valance *[cloth]   valence *[elements]⁺
valantine   valentine
valay   valet *[servant],
                       valley *[low land]
vale *[valley]   veil *[cloth]

valediction   valedictory
valence ~| electron
valency
valentine
valer   valour
valet *[servant]   valley *[low land]
valet¹ *[car]
valew   value²⁺
valiant ~ly
valid ~ity
validate² validation
validiction   valediction⁺
valley *[low land]   valet *[servant]
valour *[very brave]   velour *[soft cloth]
valuable
value² ~less   valuation
valuntine   valentine
valve
valyent   valiant⁺
valyu   value²⁺
vamp¹
vampire
van ~guard
vandal ~ism   vandalise²
vane *[weather]   vain *[proud]⁺,
                       vein *[blood]
vanilla
vanish¹
vanity ~| case ~| unit
vanquish¹
vantage ~| point
vaper   vapour
vaporise²
vapour
variable   variability
variant   variance
variation
varicose ~| veins

KEY TO SPELLING RULES

Red words are wrong. **Black** words are correct.

~   Add the suffix or word directly to the main word, without a space or hyphen
    e.g. ash ~en ~tray → ashen ashtray
~- Add a hyphen to the main word before adding the next word
    e.g. blow ~-dry → blow-dry

~| Leave a space between the main word and the next word
    e.g. decimal ~| place → decimal place
+   By finding this word in its **correct** alphabetical order, you can find related words
    e.g. about⁺ → about-face about-turn
*   Draws attention to words that may be confused
TM Means the word is a trademark

varied

varient — variant[+]

variety[4]

varikoze — varicose[+]

various ~ly

varnish[1]

varse — vase

vary[4] *[change] — very *[much][+]

varyabel — variable[+]

vascular

vase

vasectomy[4]

Vaseline™

vasillate — vacillate[2+]

vast ~ly ~ness

vat

Vatican

vault[1] *[jump, place] — volt *[electric]

vaunt[1]

vawnt — vaunt[1]

vaygrent — vagrant[+]

vayn — vain *[proud][+],
vane *[weather],
vein *[blood]

veal

veamence — vehemence

vecs — vex[1+]

vector ~l graphic ~l image

Veda

veer[1]

veermuns — vehemence

veermunt — vehement[+]

veg ~gie

vegan

vegetable

vegetarian ~ism

vegetate[2]

vegetation

vegtable — vegetable

vehemence

vehement ~ly

vehicle   vehicular

veikel — vehicle[+]

veil[1] *[cloth] — vale *[valley]

vein *[blood] ~ed — vain *[proud][+],
vane *[weather]

veiw — view[1+]

vej — veg[+]

vejetable — vegetable

vejetarian — vegetarian[+]

vejetate — vegetate[2]

veks — vex[1+]

vektor — vector[+]

Velcro™

vellum

velocity

velodrome

velour *[soft cloth] — valour *[very brave]

velvet ~een ~y

vena cava

venal

vencher — venture[2+]

vendetta

vending machine

vendor

veneer[1]

venerability * [wisdom] — vulnerability[4] * [weakness]

venerable *[wise] — vulnerable *[weak]

venerate[2]   veneration

venereal disease

venetian blind

venew — venue

vengeance

vengeful

venirial disease — venereal disease

KEY TO SUFFIXES AND COMPOUNDS

These rules are explained on pages ix to x.

1 Keep the word the same before adding ed, er, est, ing
e.g. cool[1] → cooled, cooler, coolest, cooling
2 Take off final e before adding ed, er, est, ing
e.g. fine[2] → fined, finer, finest, fining
3 Double final consonant before adding ed, er, est, ing
e.g. thin[3] → thinned, thinner, thinnest, thinning

4 Change final y to i before adding ed, er, es, est, ly, ness
e.g. tidy[4] → tidied, tidier, tidies, tidiest, tidily, tidiness
Keep final y before adding ing e.g. tidying
5 Add es instead of s to the end of the word
e.g. bunch[5] → bunches
6 Change final f to ve before adding s
e.g. calf[6] → calves

venison	
venjuns	vengeance
Venn diagram	
venom ~ous	
venous *[veins]	Venus *[planet]
venrable	venerable[+]
venrate	venerate[2+]
vent[1]	
ventilate[2] ventilation ventilator	
ventricle	
ventriloquist ventriloquism	
venture[2] ~l capital	
venue	
venum	venom[+]
venurate	venerate[2+]
Venus *[planet]	venous *[veins]
veracity *[truth]	voracity *[greed]
veranda	
verasity	veracity *[truth], voracity *[greed]
verb ~al ~alise ~ally	
verbatim	
verbiage	
verbose ~ly verbosity	
vercabulary	vocabulary[4]
vercimilitude	verisimilitude
verdant	
verdict	
verdigris	
verdure	
verge[2] *[edge]	
verger *[church]	
verginity	virginity
veriashun	variation
veriation	variation
veriety	variety[4]
verify[4] verifiable verification	
verisimilitude	

veritable veritably verity	
verius	various
vermicelli	
vermilion	
vermin	
vermouth	
vernacular	
vernal ~l equinox	
verology	virology[+]
verruca	
versatile versatility	
verse ~d	
verses *[poetry]	versus *[against]
version	
versus *[against]	verses *[poetry]
vertebra vertebrae	
vertebrate	
vertex vertices	
vertical ~ly	
vertigo vertiginous	
vertu	virtue[+]
vertual	virtual[+]
vertuos	virtuous[+]
vertuoso	virtuoso
verve	
very *[much]	vary[4] *[change][+]
vescher	vesture[2]
vespers	
vessel	
vest[1] ~ment ~ure	
vestage	vestige[+]
vestal ~l virgin	
vestibule	
vestige vestigial	
vestry[4]	
vet[3] veterinary	
veteran	
veto[1] ~es	

---

vex¹ ~es ~ation ~atious
vi   vie⁺
via
viable   viability
viaduct
Viagra
vial *[glass]   vile *[awful]⁺
vialens   violence⁺
vibe
vibrant
vibrate² vibration vibrator
vicar ~age
vicarious ~ly
vice ~-chancellor ~-president ~l squad
vice ~l versa
vicinity⁴
vicious ~ly ~ness ~l circle
vicissitude
victim
victimise² victimisation
victor ~ious ~iously
Victorian   Victoriana
victory⁴
victuals
video ¹ ~-conferencing ~disk
video ~l game ~phone ~tape
vidio   video⁺
vie *[compete]   via *[through]
vied   vying
vielence   violence⁺
vier   veer¹
view¹ ~finder ~point
vigger   vigour
vigil
vigilant *[careful] ~ly   vigilance
vigilante *[law keeper]
vignette
vigorous ~ly

vigour
vijil   vigil
vijilantee   vigilante
vikar   vicar⁺
vikarious   vicarious⁺
Viking
vikownt   viscount⁺
viksen   vixen
viktim   victim
viktimise   victimise²⁺
vilage   village
vile² *[awful]   vial *[glass]
vilense   violence⁺
vilify⁴   vilification
villa
village²
villain ~ous ~y
villus   villi
vim ~l and vigour
vinacava   vena cava
vinager   vinegar⁺
vinaigrette
vinal   vinyl *[plastic],
                                      venal *[corrupt]⁺
vindaloo
vindicate² vindication
vindictive ~ly ~ness
vine ~yard
vinegar ~y
vinegrette   vinaigrette
vintage
vinyet   vignette
vinyl *[plastic]   venal *[corrupt]
viola
violate² violation violator
violence violent violently
violet
violin ~ist

---

viper
viralense   virulence⁺
viranda   veranda

☞ Can't find your word here? Look under **ver**

virb   verb⁺
virge   verge²
virgin ~al ~ity
Virgo
virile virility
virjin   virgin⁺
virnackular   vernacular
virology virologist
virsatile   versatile⁺
virse   verse⁺
virtual ~ly ~| reality
virtue virtuosity
virtuoso
virtuous ~ly ~ness
virulence virulent
virus⁵
virve   verve
visa
visage
visaje   visage
vis-à-vis
visceral viscera
viscose *[fabric] viscous *[sticky]
viscosity
viscount ~ess
viscous *[sticky] viscose *[fabric]
vishous   vicious⁺
visible visibility visibly
visinity   vicinity⁺
vision ~ary
visissitude   vicissitude
visit¹ ~ation
visitor

visor
viss   vice⁺
visseral   visceral
vista
visual ~ly
visualise² visualisation
vital ~ity ~ly
vitamin
vito   veto¹⁺
vitreous
vitriol ~ic
vitrius   vitreous
vittle   victual
viue   view¹⁺
viva
vivacious vivacity
vivarium
vivashus   vivacious⁺
vivid ~ly ~ness
vivisect¹ vivisection
vixen
viyul   vial *[glass],
       vile² *[awful]
voat   vote²
vocabulary⁴
vocal ~ist ~ly
vocalise² vocalisation
vocation *[job] ~al vacation *[holiday]
vociferous ~ly ~ness
vodka
voel   vole
vogue
voice² ~-activated ~mail ~-over
void¹
voilà
voile
vokabulary   vocabulary⁴
vokal   vocal⁺

KEY TO SPELLING RULES

Red words are wrong. **Black** words are correct.

~ Add the suffix or word directly to the main word, without a space or hyphen
  e.g. ash ~en ~tray → **ashen ashtray**
~- Add a hyphen to the main word before adding the next word
  e.g. blow ~-dry → **blow-dry**

~| Leave a space between the main word and the next word
  e.g. decimal ~| place → **decimal place**
+ By finding this word in its **correct** alphabetical order, you can find related words
  e.g. about⁺ → **about-face about-turn**
* Draws attention to words that may be confused
TM Means the word is a trademark

vokalise   vocalise[2+]
vokation   vocation
volatile volatility
vol-au-vent
volcanic ~l ash
volcano[5]
vole
voletile   volatile[+]
volition
volkano   volcano[+]
volley[1] ~ball
volluminus   voluminous[+]
volt *[electric] ~age   vault[1] *[jump, place]
voluble volubility volubly
volume voluminous
voluntary voluntarily
volunteer[1]
voluptuous
vomit[1]
voodoo ~ism
voracious ~ly ~ness
voracity *[greed]   veracity *[truth]
vorlt   vault[1]
vornt   vaunt[1]
vortex vortices
vosiferous   vociferous[+]
vote[2]
votive ~l candle
vouch[1]
voucher
vouchsafe[2]
vow[1]
vowel

voyage[2]
voyce   voice[2+]
voyd   void[1]
voyeur
vudu   voodoo[+]
vue   view[1+]
vulcher   vulture
vulgar ~ity
vulgarise[2] vulgarisation
vulnerability[4] *   venerability *
          [weakness]   [wisdom]
vulnerable *[weak]   venerable *[wise]
vulture
vulva
vunrabel   vulnerable
vunrability   vulnerability

☞ Can't find your word here? Look under **ver**

vuranda   veranda
vurb   verb[+]
vurge   verge[2]
vurse   verse[+]
vurtue   virtue[+]
vurtuel   virtual[+]
vurve   verve
vwalla   voilà
vwalle   voile

☞ Can't find your word here? Look under **vi**

vya   via
vye   vie
vyle   vile[2] *[awful],
                   vial *[glass]

KEY TO SUFFIXES AND COMPOUNDS

These rules are explained on pages ix to x.

1 Keep the word the same before adding **ed, er, est, ing**
e.g. cool[1] → cooled, cooler, coolest, cooling
2 Take off final **e** before adding **ed, er, est, ing**
e.g. fine[2] → fined, finer, finest, fining
3 Double final consonant before adding **ed, er, est, ing**
e.g. thin[3] → thinned, thinner, thinnest, thinning

4 Change final **y** to **i** before adding **ed, er, es, est, ly, ness**
e.g. tidy[4] → tidied, tidier, tidies, tidiest, tidily, tidiness
Keep final **y** before adding **ing** e.g. tidying
5 Add **es** instead of **s** to the end of the word
e.g. bunch[5] → bunches
6 Change final **f** to **ve** before adding **s**
e.g. calf[6] → calves

wack	whack[1+]	walkie-talkie	
wacks	wax[1+]	walking ~l frame ~l stick	
wacky[4]		wall[1] ~flower ~paper	
wad *[tight lump]	wade[2] *[water]	wallaby[4]	
wadding		wallet	

> ☞ Can't find your word here? Look under **wo**

waddle[2]		wallop[1]	
wade[2] *[water]	weighed *[how heavy]	wallow[1]	
wadi		walnut	
wafer ~-thin		walrus[5]	
waffle[2] ~l iron		waltz[1]	
waft[1]		wan *[pale] ~ly	wane[2] *[decrease], won *[victory]
wag[3] *[tail] ~tail		wand	
wage[2] *[money] ~l level		wander[1] *[roam] ~lust	wonder[1] *[think, marvel][+]
wager[1]			
waggle[2]		wane[2] *[decrease]	wan *[pale]
wagon ~l train		wangle[2]	
waid	wade *[water], weighed *[how heavy]	want[1] *[desire]	wont *[habit]
		wanton ~ly ~ness	
waif		war[3] *[battle]	wore *[clothes]
waifer	wafer[+]	war ~l crime ~l cry	
wail[1] *[cry]	whale *[mammal][+]	war ~fare ~head ~horse	
wairs	wares	war ~like ~lord ~l paint ~path	
waist *[body]	waste[2] *[misuse][+]	war ~ship ~time ~-torn ~l zone	
waist ~band ~coat ~line		warble[2]	
wait[1] *[delay]	weight *[heaviness][+]	ward[1] ~en	
waiter waitress		wardrobe	
waiting ~l list ~l room		warehouse warehousing	
waive[2] *[give up]	wave[2] *[sea, hand][+]	wares *[goods]	wears *[clothes]
waiver *[surrender]	waver[1] *[unsteady]	warm[1] ~ly ~-blooded ~-hearted	
waj	wage[2+]	warmonger[1]	
wajer	wager[1]	warmth	
wake ~ful ~fulness waking		warn[1] *[alert]	worn *[used, old][+]
waken[1]		warp[1] ~l speed	
waks	wax[1+]	warrant[1]	
walk[1] ~about ~-in		warrantee *[person]	
walk ~-out ~over ~way		warranty *[bond]	
		warren	

---

warrior

wart ~hog

wary⁴

was

wash¹ ~able ~basin ~board

wash ~out ~room ~stand

washing ~l machine ~l soda

wasn't [was not]

wasp ~ish ~-like

wastage

waste² *[misuse]   waist *[body]⁺

waste ~l disposal ~ful ~land ~l paper

wastrel

watch¹ ~es ~ful ~dog ~man ~word

water¹ ~y ~-borne ~colour

water ~cress ~l cycle ~fall

water ~fowl ~front

water ~logged ~mark ~melon

water ~shed ~side ~-ski

water ~tight ~way ~works

waterproof¹

watt *[power] ~age   what *[question]⁺

wave² *[sea, hand]   waive² *[give up]

wave ~band ~length

waver¹ *[unsteady]   waiver *[surrender]

wavy⁴

wax¹ *[candle] ~en ~work whacks *[hits]

way *[direction]   weigh¹ *[how heavy]

way ~side ~ward

waykn   waken¹

waylay ~ing waylaid

wayt   wait¹ *[delay],
                         weight *[heaviness]⁺

we *[us]   wee *[toilet, small]⁺

weak *[not strong]   week *[seven days]⁺

weak ~-kneed ~ling ~ness

weaken¹

weakly *[feebly]   weekly⁴ *[every week]

weal *[mark]   wheel¹ *[car]⁺,
                         we'll *[we will, shall]

wealth   wealthy⁴

wean¹

weapon ~ry

wear *[clothes]   were *[we were late],
                         where *[place],
                         weir *[dam]

weard   weird⁺

wears *[clothes]   wares *[goods]

weary⁴   wearisome

weasel³

weather¹ *[sun, rain]   whether *[if]

weather ~-beaten

weather ~l cock ~l forecast ~l vane

weave² *[fabric]   we've *[we have]

web³ ~l browser ~cam ~cast

web ~-footed ~log ~master

web ~l page ~site ~-toed

we'd *[we had, would]   weed *[plant]⁺

wed³ *[marriage] ~lock

wedding ~l party

Wedensday   Wednesday

wedge²

Wednesday

wee *[toilet, small]   whee *[happy sound]

wee ~d ~ing

weed¹ *[plant] ~killer   we'd *[we had, would]

weedle   wheedle²

weedy⁴

Weeja   Ouija™

week *[seven days] ~end weak *[not strong]⁺

weekly *[every week]   weakly *[feebly]

weel   weal *[mark],
                         wheel¹ *[car]⁺

weep ~ing ~y

weesal   weasal³

weet   wheat⁺

KEY TO SUFFIXES AND COMPOUNDS

These rules are explained on pages ix to x.

1 Keep the word the same before adding **ed, er, est, ing**
e.g. cool¹ → cooled, cooler, coolest, cooling

2 Take off final **e** before adding **ed, er, est, ing**
e.g. fine² → fined, finer, finest, fining

3 Double final consonant before adding **ed, er, est, ing**
e.g. thin³ → thinned, thinner, thinnest, thinning

4 Change final **y** to **i** before adding **ed, er, es, est, ly, ness**
e.g. tidy⁴ → tidied, tidier, tidies, tidiest, tidily, tidiness
Keep final **y** before adding **ing** e.g. tidying

5 Add **es** instead of **s** to the end of the word
e.g. bunch⁵ → bunches

6 Change final **f** to **ve** before adding **s**
e.g. calf⁶ → calves

weeze	wheeze[2]+
weigh[1] *[how heavy]	way *[direction]+
weight[1] *[heaviness]	wait[1] *[delay]+
weight ~less ~lessness	
weight ~lifter ~lifting ~l training	
weighty[4]	
weild	wield[1]
weir *[dam]	wear *[clothes]
weird ~ly ~ness	
wej	wedge[2]
welcome[2]	
weld[1]	
welfare ~l state	
welk	whelk
well[1] *[health, water]	
well ~~-advised ~~-balanced	
well ~~-behaved ~being ~~-bred	
well ~~-disposed ~~-done ~~-founded	
well ~~-groomed ~~-heeled	
well ~~-intentioned ~~-known	
well ~~-mannered ~~-meaning ~~-off	
well ~~-read ~~-rounded ~~-spoken	
well ~~-thought-of ~~-to-do	
we'll *[we shall, will]	
wellington ~l boot	
welly[4]	
welp	whelp[1]
welsh[1] *[cheat]	
Welsh *[from Wales] ~l rarebit	
welt	
welth	wealth+
wen	when+
wench[5]	
wensday	Wednesday
went	
wept	
werd	weird *[strange],
	word *[speech]+

were *[we were late]	whirr[1] *[sound]
we're *[we are]	weir *[dam]
weren't [were not]	
werewolf[6]	
werk	work+
werl	whirl[1] *[turn]+,
	whorl *[pattern]
werld	world+
werr	were *[we were late],
	whirr[1] *[sound]
west ~bound ~erly ~ern ~wards	
westerner	
westernise[2] westernisation	
wet[3] *[soak]	whet[3] *[sharpen]
wet ~land ~ness ~suit	
wether	weather *[sun, rain],
	whether *[if]
we've *[we have]	weave[2] *[fabric]
whack[1]	
whacks *[hits]	wax *[candle]
whale *[mammal]	wail *[cry]+
whaling	
wharf[6]	
what *[question]	watt *[power]+
what ~ever ~soever	

> ☞ Can't find your word here? Look under **we** or **wi**

wheat ~meal	
wheedle[2]	
wheel[1] *[car] ~barrow	weal *[mark]
wheel ~chair ~wright	
wheeze[2] wheezy[4]	
whelk	
whelp[1]	
when ~ever ~soever	
whent	went
where *[place]	wear *[clothes],
	were *[we were late]

KEY TO SPELLING RULES

Red words are wrong. **Black words are correct.**

~ Add the suffix or word directly to the main word, without a space or hyphen
e.g. ash ~en ~tray → ashen ashtray

~- Add a hyphen to the main word before adding the next word
e.g. blow ~-dry → blow-dry

~l Leave a space between the main word and the next word
e.g. decimal ~l place → decimal place

+ By finding this word in its **correct** alphabetical order, you can find related words
e.g. about+ → about-face about-turn

* Draws attention to words that may be confused

TM Means the word is a trademark

where ~abouts ~as ~by

where ~fore ~upon ~withal

wherever

whet³ *[sharpen]   wet³ *[soak]⁺

whether *[if]   weather *[sun, rain]⁺

whey *[milk]   way *[direction]⁺

which *[which one]   witch *[hag]⁺

whichever

whiff¹

Whig *[political]   wig³ *[hair]

while *[when]   wile *[tricks]

whilst

whim ~sical whimsy⁴

whimper¹

whine² *[complain]   wine *[drink]⁺

whined *[complained]   wind *[turn]

whinge ~d ~ing ~r

whinny⁴

whiny *[moaning]   winey *[like wine]

whip³ *[beat] ~cord ~lash wipe² *[clean]

whippersnapper

whippet

whirl¹ *[spin]   whorl *[pattern]

whirl ~pool ~wind

whirr¹ *[sound]   were *[we were late]

whisk¹

whisker ~y

whiskey *[Irish]

whisky⁴ *[Scotch]

whisper¹

whist ~I drive

whistle² ~I blower

whit *[least bit]   wit *[flair, humour]

white² ~ness ~-collar ~I dwarf

white ~-out ~I water

whiten¹

whitewash¹

whither *[where]   wither¹ *[decay]

Whitsun   Whit Sunday

whittle²

whiz³ ~I kid

who *[question] ~ever   hew¹ *[cut]⁺

whoa *[stop]   woe *[grief]⁺

who'd *[who had, would]

whole *[complete]   hole² *[cavity]

whole ~hearted ~meal ~sale ~some

who'll *[who will]

wholly *[fully]   holy⁴ *[sacred],
                          holey *[holes]

whom ~ever

whoop *[shout]   hoop¹ *[circle]

whooping cough

whopper   whopping

who're *[who are]

whore² *[prostitute]   hoar *[frost]

whorl *[pattern]   whirl¹ *[turn]⁺

who's *[who is, has]

whose *[possessive]

who've *[who have]

why

wi   why

wick

wicked¹ ~ly ~ness

wicker ~work

wicket ~I keeper

wide² ~ly ~-angle ~-area network ~-eyed

wide ~I open ~spread widen¹

widow¹

width

☞ Can't find your word here? Look under **we**

wield¹

wier   weir *[dam],
                           we're *[we are]

wierd   weird⁺

wiery   weary⁴⁺

KEY TO SUFFIXES AND COMPOUNDS

These rules are explained on pages ix to x.

1 Keep the word the same before adding **ed, er, est, ing**
  e.g. cool¹ → cooled, cooler, coolest, cooling
2 Take off final **e** before adding **ed, er, est, ing**
  e.g. fine² → fined, finer, finest, fining
3 Double final consonant before adding **ed, er, est, ing**
  e.g. thin³ → thinned, thinner, thinnest, thinning

4 Change final **y** to **i** before adding **ed, er, es, est, ly, ness**
  e.g. tidy⁴ → tidied, tidier, tidies, tidiest, tidily, tidiness
  Keep final **y** before adding **ing** e.g. tidying
5 Add **es** instead of **s** to the end of the word
  e.g. bunch⁵ → bunches
6 Change final **f** to **ve** before adding **s**
  e.g. calf⁶ → calves

wife wives

wig³ *[hair]   Whig *[political]

wiggle² wiggly

wigwam

wild ~ly ~ness ~fire ~l flower ~life

wilderness

wile *[trick] wily⁴   while *[when]⁺

wilful ~ly ~ness

will¹ *[do, power]   while *[when]⁺

will ~-o'-the-wisp ~power

willing ~ly ~ness

willow ~y

willy⁴ ~-nilly

wilt¹

wim   whim⁺

wimen   women

wimper   whimper¹

wimsy   whimsy⁴

win ~ner ~ning

wince²

winch¹ ~es

wind *[turn] ~ing   whined *[complained]

wind¹ *[air]

wind ~bag ~l chill ~fall ~mill ~pipe

wind ~screen ~surfer ~l turbine ~ward

window ~pane ~l sill

windy⁴

wine *[drink]   whine² *[complain]

wine ~l cellar ~l glass

winey *[like wine]   whiny *[moaning]

wing¹ ~less ~span

winge   whinge⁺

wink¹

winkle²

winnow¹

winny   whinny⁴

winter¹ ~time

wintry

wip   whip³ *[beat]⁺,
                               wipe² *[clean]

wippet   whippet

wire² *[metal thread]

wire ~less ~tap

wiry⁴ *[body type]   weary⁴ *[tired]

wisdom ~l teeth ~l tooth

wise² ~ly ~crack

wish¹ ~ful ~fully ~bone

wishy-washy

wisk   whisk¹

wisker   whisker⁺

wiskey   whiskey *[Irish],
                               whisky⁴ *[Scotch]

wisp ~y

wisper   whisper¹

wist   whist

wistful ~ly ~ness

wisell   whistle²

wit *[flair, humour]   whit *[least bit]

witch⁵ *[hag] ~craft   which *[which one]⁺

witch ~l doctor ~l hunt

with ~in ~out

withdraw ~al ~ing ~n   withdrew

wither¹ *[decay]   whither *[where]

withers *[horse]

withhold ~ing withheld

withstand withstood

witness¹ ~es

witticism

witty⁴

wizard ~ry

wizened

wobble² wobbly⁴

woch   watch¹⁺

wod   wad *[tight lump]⁺,
                               word *[speech]

woe ~begone

---

woeful ~ly ~ness
woffel   waffle[2+]
woft   waft[1]
wok *[pan]
woke *[not asleep]   woken
wolf[6] ~ish ~ishly

☞ Can't find your word here? Look under **wa**

woll   wall[1+]
wollaby   wallaby[4]
wollet   wallet
wollop   wallop[1]
wollow   wallow[1]
wolrus   walrus[+]
woltz   waltz[1]
woman ~ly ~ise ~kind
womb
women
won *[victory]   one *[number][+],
                               wan *[pale]
wond   wand[+]
wonder[1] *[think, marvel]   wander[1] *[roam]
wonderful ~ly
wondrous ~ly
wons   once
wont *[habit]   want[1] *[desire]
won't *[will not]
wonten   wanton[+]
woo[1]
wood *[trees]   would *[I would go]
wood ~ed ~cut ~land ~louse
wood ~pecker ~wind
wood ~work ~worm
wooden ~ly ~ness
woody[4]
wool ~len ~liness ~ly
woom   womb[+]
woop   whoop

woozy
wopper   whopper[+]
wor   war[3] *[battle][+],
                               wore *[clothes]

☞ Can't find your word here? Look under **wa** or **we**

worbel   warble[2]
word[1] ~y ~l equation
word ~-processor
wore *[clothes]   war[3] *[battle][+]
worf   wharf[6]
work[1] ~able ~aholic ~bench
work ~book ~force ~horse
work ~load ~man
work ~manship ~-out
work ~sheet ~shop ~station
working ~l class
workitorkie   walkie-talkie
world ~-class ~wide
World War I
World War II
worldly[4]
worm
wormunger   warmonger[1]
worn *[used] ~-out   warn[1] *[alert]
worp   warp[1+]
worrant   warrant[1+]
worrantee   warrantee *[person],
                               warranty *[bond]
worrior   warrior
worry[4]
worse
worsen[1]
worship[3]
worst ~case
wort   wart[+]
worter   water[+]
worth ~less ~while

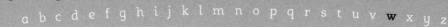

worthy[4]	
wos	was
wosh	wash[+]
wosnt	wasn't
wosp	wasp[+]
wot	watt *[power][+],
	what *[question][+]
wotch	watch[1+]
would *[I would go]	wood *[trees]
wouldn't *[would not]	
wound[1] *[past of wind, hurt]	
wove woven	
wow	

☞ Can't find your word here? Look under **r**

wrap[3] *[pack]	rap[3] *[music, knock]
wrapping ~l paper	
wrath ~ful	
wreak *[havoc] ~ing	reek[1] *[smell]
	wreck[1] *[smash]
wreath *[flowers]	
wreathe *[cover]	
wreck[1] ~age	
wren	
wrench[1]	
wrestle[2] wrestler	
wretch[5] *[person] ~ed	retch[1] *[vomit]
wretched	
wriggle[2] wriggly[4]	
wring *[squeeze] ~er ~ing	ring *[circle, bell][+]
wrinkle[2] wrinkly[4]	
wrist ~watch	
writ *[legal order]	
write *[text] ~-off	right *[correct][+],
	rite *[ceremony]
writer writing	
writhe[2]	
written	

wrong ~ful ~fully ~ly	
wrong[1] ~doer ~doing ~-foot	
wrote *[text]	rote *[learning]
wrought ~l iron	
wrung *[squeezed]	rung *[ladder, bell]
wry *[humour] ~ly	rye *[grain]

☞ Can't find your word here? Look under **wo** or **we**

wu	woo[1]
wud	wood *[trees][+],
	would *[I would go]
wuff	woof
wulf	wolf[6+]
wull	wool[+]
wully	woolly[4]
wuman	woman[+]
wume	womb
wunder	wander[1] *[roam][+],
	wonder[1] *[think, marvel][+]
wundrus	wondrous[+]
wurd	word[+]
wuren't	weren't [were not]
wurk	work[+]
wurl	whirl[1]
wurld	world[+]
wurldwide	worldwide
wurr	were *[we were late],
	whirr[1] *[sound]
wuz	was
wyde	wide[+]

☞ Can't find your word here? Look under **wi**

wyfe	wife[+]
wyle	while *[when][+],
	wile *[trick]
wysiwyg	
wyvern	

X ~-axis
X ~-certificate
X ~-chromosome
X ~-factor
X ~-particle
X ~-rated
X ~-ray

☞ Can't find your word here? Look under **egs** or **ex**

xenofobe   xenophobe[+]
xenofobia   xenophobia

xenon ~l lamp
xenophobe
xenophobia
xenophobic
Xerox™ [1]
xma   eczema
Xmas
xylem
xylometer
xylophone
XYY syndrome

KEY TO SUFFIXES AND COMPOUNDS

These rules are explained on pages ix to x.

1 Keep the word the same before adding **ed, er, est, ing**
  e.g. cool[1] → cooled, cooler, coolest, cooling
2 Take off final **e** before adding **ed, er, est, ing**
  e.g. fine[2] → fined, finer, finest, fining
3 Double final consonant before adding **ed, er, est, ing**
  e.g. thin[3] → thinned, thinner, thinnest, thinning

4 Change final **y** to **i** before adding **ed, er, es, est, ly, ness**
  e.g. tidy[4] → tidied, tidier, tidies, tidiest, tidily, tidiness
  Keep final **y** before adding **ing** e.g. tidying
5 Add **es** instead of **s** to the end of the word
  e.g. bunch[5] → bunches
6 Change final **f** to **ve** before adding **s**
  e.g. calf[6] → calves

Y ~-axis ~l chromosome
Y ~-co-ordinate ~-fronts
yacht ~ing ~sman ~swoman
Yael   Yale[+]
yahoo
Yahweh
yak
Yale ~l key ~l lock
yam
yamuker   yarmulke
yang
yank[1]
Yankee
yap[3]
yard ~age ~stick
yarmulke
yarn
yashmak
yaun   yawn[1]
yaw *[of ship]   you're *[you are]
Yaway   Yahweh
yawn[1]
yeah
year ~ly ~ling ~-round
yearn[1]
yeast ~y ~l extract
yeer   year[+]
yeest   yeast[+]
yeh   yeah
yeild   yield[1]
yel   yell[1]
yelo   yellow[+]
yeld   yield[1] *[give],
                            yelled *[shouted]
yell[1]
yelled *[shouted]   yield[1] *[give]
yellow ~ish ~l fever
yelp[1]

yen
yeoman ~ry
yer   year[+]
yere   year[+]
yern   yearn[1]
yes
yeshiva
yesterday
yet
yeti
yew *[tree]   ewe *[sheep],
                            you *[person]
yews *[evergreen trees   use][2] *[put into service]
Yiddish
yield[1]
yin ~l and yang
yippee
yirt   yurt
yoak   yoke *[round neck][+],
                            yolk *[egg]
yob ~bish
yodel[3]
yoga
yogert   yoghurt
yoghurt
yoke *[round neck]   yolk *[egg]
yokel
yolk *[egg]   yoke *[round neck]
Yom Kippur
yoman   yeoman[+]
yomp[1]
yonder
yoow   you
yore *[years ago]   your *[belonging],
                            you're *[you are]
Yorkshire ~l pudding
yorn   yawn[1]
yors   yours[+]

☞ Can't find your word here? Look under **u**

yorself   yourself[6]
yot   yacht[+]
you *[person]   yew *[tree],
                  ewe *[sheep]

you'd *[you had, would]
youf   youth[+]
you'll *[you will]   Yule *[Christmas]
young ~ish ~ster ~l gun
your *[belonging]   yore *[years ago],
                  you're *[you are]

yours ~l faithfully
yours ~l sincerely
yourself[6]
you'sd   used
youth ~ful ~l club ~l hostel
you've *[you have]
yo-yo

ytterbium
yttrium
yu   yew *[tree],
                  you *[person]

yucca ~l plant
yuck ~y
yud   you'd *[you had,
                        would]
yue   yew *[tree],
                  you *[person],
                  ewe *[sheep]

Yule *[Christmas]   you'll *[you will]
Yule ~l log ~tide
yummy   yum-yum
yung   young[+]
yuppie
yurn   yearn[1]
yurt
yuth   youth[+]

KEY TO SUFFIXES AND COMPOUNDS

These rules are explained on pages ix to x.

1 Keep the word the same before adding **ed, er, est, ing**
e.g. cool[1] → cooled, cooler, coolest, cooling
2 Take off final **e** before adding **ed, er, est, ing**
e.g. fine[2] → fined, finer, finest, fining
3 Double final consonant before adding **ed, er, est, ing**
e.g. thin[3] → thinned, thinner, thinnest, thinning

4 Change final **y** to **i** before adding **ed, er, es, est, ly, ness**
e.g. tidy[4] → tidied, tidier, tidies, tidiest, tidily, tidiness
Keep final **y** before adding **ing** e.g. tidying
5 Add **es** instead of **s** to the end of the word
e.g. bunch[5] → bunches
6 Change final **f** to **ve** before adding **s**
e.g. calf[6] → calves

zany[4]	
zap[3] ~py	
zapper	
zeal	
zealot	
zealous ~ly ~ness	
zebra ~l crossing	
zeel	zeal[+]
zeen	zine
zefer	zephyr
zeitgeist	
zelous	zealous[+]
zelot	zealot
Zen ~l Buddhism	
zenith	
zenofobe	xenophobe[+]
zenofobia	xenophobia
zepelin	zeppelin
zephyr	
zeppelin	
zerconium	zirconium
zero[1] ~l hour ~-rated	
zero ~-sum game	
zero ~l tolerance	
Zerox	Xerox™[1]
zest ~ful ~y	
zigospore	zygospore
zigote	zygote
zigzag[3]	
zilch	
zillion	

zilophone	xylophone
Zimmer™ ~l frame	
zinc	
zine	
zing[1]	
Zionism	
zip[3]	
zirconium	
ziro	zero[+]
zit	
zitegist	zeitgeist
zither	
zoan	zone[2]
zodiac	
zombie	
zone[2]	
zonked	
zoo ~-keeper	
zoological ~ly	
zoologist	
zoology	
Zoolu	Zulu
zoom[1] ~l lens	
Zoroastrian ~ism	
zu	zoo[+]
Zulu	
zuology	zoology
zurconium	zirconium
zygospore	
zygote	
zylofone	xylophone

Key to Spelling Rules

Red words are wrong. **Black words are correct.**

~ Add the suffix or word directly to the main word, without a space or hyphen
   e.g. ash ~en ~tray → ashen ashtray

~- Add a hyphen to the main word before adding the next word
   e.g. blow ~-dry → blow-dry

~l Leave a space between the main word and the next word
   e.g. decimal ~l place → decimal place

+ By finding this word in its **correct** alphabetical order, you can find related words
   e.g. about+ → about-face about-turn

* Draws attention to words that may be confused

TM Means the word is a trademark

Common Abbreviations and their Meanings

A&E	Accident and Emergency (Hospital) Department	B2C	Business-to-customer
AA	Alcoholics Anonymous Automobile Association	BA	Bachelor of Arts British Airways
AAA	Amateur Athletics Association	BBC	British Broadcasting Corporation
ABS	Anti-lock Brake System	BBQ	Barbeque
ABTA	Association of British Travel Agents	B.C.	Before Christ
		BL	Bachelor of Law
ACAS	Advisory, Conciliation & Arbitration Service	BM	Bachelor of Medicine
		BSc	Bachelor of Science
AD	Anno Domini (In the year of our Lord)	BSE	Bovine Spongiform Encephalopathy
ADD	Attention Deficit Disorder	C	Celsius
ADHD	Attention Deficit Hyperactivity Disorder	c	circa (around)
		C of E	Church of England
ADSL	Asymmetric Digital Subscriber Line	c/o	care of
		CAB	Citizens Advice Bureau
AGM	Annual General Meeting	CAD	Computer Aided Design
AI	Artificial Intelligence	cc	cubic centimetres
AIDS	Acquired Immune Deficiency Syndrome	CD-ROM	Compact Disk Read-Only Memory
AM	Ante meridiem (Before noon)	CD-RW	Compact Disk Re-Writable
		CEO	Chief Executive Officer
ANC	African National Congress	CIA	Central Intelligence Agency
Anon	Anonymous	CJD	Creutzfeldt-Jakob Disease
AONB	Area of Outstanding Natural Beauty	cm	centimetre
		CNN	Cable News Network
AS	Autistic Spectrum	COD	Cash on Delivery
ASP	Active Server Pages	CPR	Cardiopulmonary Resuscitation
ATM	Automated Teller Machine		
ATV	All Terrain Vehicle	CSS	Cascading Style Sheet
Ave	Avenue	CV	Curriculum Vitae
AWOL	Absent without leave	DAT	Digital Audio Tape
B&B	Bed and breakfast	DDoS	Distributed Denial- of-Service
B2B	Business-to-business		

DJ	Disk Jockey	HRH	His/Her Royal Highness
	Dinner jacket	HTML	Hypertext markup language
DNA	Deoxyribonucleic Acid	HTTP	Hyper Text Transfer
DNS	Domain Name System		Protocol
DOB	Date of Birth	ie	Id est (that is to say)
Dr	Doctor	ICANN	Internet Corporation for
DVD	Digital Versatile Disc		Assigned Names and
e-	Electronic (prefix)		Numbers
eg	For example	IMAP	Internet Message Access
EFL	English as a Foreign		Protocol
	Language	IMF	International Monetary
e-mail	Electronic Mail, ELM		Fund
ESP	Extrasensory Perception	Inc.	Incorporated
et al.	Et alia (and others)	IOC	International Olympic
ETA	Estimated Time of Arrival		Committee
etc.	Et cetera (and so on)	IOU	I Owe You
ETD	Estimated Time of	IP	Internet Protocol
	Departure		Intellectual Property
EU	European Union	IPA	International Phonetic
F	Fahrenheit		Alphabet
FAQ	Frequently Asked Question	IPO	Initial Public Offering
FBI	Federal Bureau of	IPv6	Internet Protocol version 6
	Investigation	IQ	Intelligence Quotient
FM	Frequency Modulation	IRA	Irish Republican Army
FTP	File Transfer Protocol	IRC	Internet Relay Chat
GATT	General Agreement on	ISBN	International Standard
	Tariffs and Trade		Book Number
GCSE	General Certificate of	ISDN	Integrated Services Digital
	Secondary Education		Network
GDP	Gross Domestic Product	ISP	Internet Service Provider
GIF	Graphic Interchange	IT	Information Technology
	Format	IUD	Intra-uterine device
GM	Genetically Modified	IV	Intravenous
GMT	Greenwich Mean Time	IVF	In vitro fertilisation
GP	General Practitioner	JAR	Java Archive
GUI	Graphical User Interface	JPEG	Joint Photographic Experts
HIV	Human Immunodeficiency		Group [computer file]
	Virus	JSP	Java Server Page
HQ	Headquarters	Kbyte	Kilobyte

LAN	Local Area Network	ODD	Oppositional Defiant Disorder
LCD	Liquid-Crystal Display		
LED	Light Emitting Diode	OPEC	Organisation of Petroleum Exporting Countries
Ltd	Limited Liability Company		
LW	Long Wave	OS	Ordinance Survey Operating System
M&A	Mergers and Acquisitions		
MA	Master of Arts	PM	Post meridiem (After noon)
MB	Megabyte	P2P	Peer-to-Peer Computing
MBE	Member of the Order of the British Empire	PA	Personal Assistant Public Address (system)
MC	Master of Ceremonies	PC	Personal Computer Police Constable Politically Correct
MD	Managing Director		
MEP	Member of the European Parliament	PDF	Portable Document Format
		PE	Physical Education
MIDI	Musical Instrument Digital Interface	PERL	Practical Extraction and Reporting Language
MIME	Multipurpose Internet Mail Extensions	PhD	Doctor of Philosophy
		PIN	Personal Identification Number
MoD	Ministry of Defence		
MOT	Ministry of Transport	plc	Public Limited Company
MP	Member of Parliament	PM	Prime Minister
mpg	Miles per gallon	PMS	Premenstrual Syndrome
mph	Miles per hour	PMT	Premenstrual Tension
MRI	Magnetic Resonance Imaging	PO	Post Office
		POP	Post Office Protocol
MS	Multiple Sclerosis	PoW	Prisoner of War
MS-DOS	Microsoft™ disk operating system	PPP	Point to Point Protocol
		PR	Public Relations
n/a	Not applicable	PTA	Parent Teacher Association
NASA	National Aeronautics and Space Administration	PTO	Please turn over
NATO	North Atlantic Treaty Organisation	Q&A	Question and Answer
		R&D	Research and Development
NHS	National Health Service	RAF	Royal Air Force
OAP	Old age pensioner	RAM	Random Access Memory
OBE	Order of the British Empire	RC	Roman Catholic
OCD	Obsessive Compulsive Disorder	Rd	Road
		RDA	Recommended Daily Allowance
OD	Overdose		

REM	Rapid Eye Movement		UHT	Ultra Heat Treated
Rev	Reverend		UI	User Interface
RIP	Rest In Peace		UK	United Kingdom
RN	Royal Navy		UN	United Nations
ROM	Read-Only Memory		UNESCO	United Nations Educational, Scientific and Cultural Organisation
rpm	Revolutions per minute			
Rt. Hon.	Right Honourable		UNICEF	United Nations Children's Fund
RTF	Rich Text Format			
sae	Self addressed envelope		URL	Uniform Resource Locator
SCSI	Small Computer System Interface		USB	Universal Serial Bus
			UV	Ultra Violet
SEBD	Social, Emotional & Behavioural Disorder		VAT	Value Added Tax
			VC	Victoria Cross
SFO	Serious Fraud Office		VCR	Video Cassette Recorder
SIDS	Sudden Infant Death Syndrome		VD	Venereal Disease
			VHS	Video Home System
SMS	Short Message Service		VIP	Very Important Person
SMTP	Simple Mail Transport Protocol		VP	Vice President
			VRML	Virtual Reality Modelling Language
SOS	Save Our Souls			
SPF	Sun Protection Factor		WAN	Wide Area Network
SQL	Structured Query Language		WAP	Wireless Application Protocol
SSL	Secure Sockets Layer			
St	Saint		WC	Water closet (toilet)
	Street		WC3	World Wide Web Consortium
SUV	Sports Utility Vehicle			
TB	Tuberculosis		WHO	World Health Organisation
tbsp	Tablespoon		WWF	Word Wildlife Fund
TCP	Transmission Control Protocol		WWI	World War One
			WWII	World War Two
TESOL	Teaching of English to Speakers of other Languages		WWW	World Wide Web
			Xmas	Christmas
TNT	Trinitrotoluene (Explosive)		XML	Extensible markup Language
TUC	Trades Union Congress			
TV	Television		XSL	Extensible Stylesheet Language
UFO	Unidentified Flying Object			
UHF	Ultra High Frequency			

Countries, Locations, Cities & Languages of the World[*]

Source: CIA World Factbook 2004 Foreign and Commonwealth Website 2005

*not a complete list

Country name	Capital city	Citizen name	Official languages
Britain, United Kingdom	London	British	English
England	London	English	English
Scotland	Edinburgh	Scottish	English, Gaelic
Northern Ireland	Belfast	Irish	English, Irish
Wales	Cardiff	Welsh	Welsh, English
Ireland (Eire)	Dublin	Irish	Irish, Gaelic, English

Boroughs, counties, cities and districts – England

A–E	E–M	M–S	S–Z
Barking and Dagenham	East Sussex	Medway	Southampton
Barnet	Enfield	Merton	Southend-on-Sea
Barnsley	Essex	Middlesbrough	South Tyneside
Bath and	Gateshead	Milton Keynes	Southwark
North East Somerset	Gloucestershire	Newcastle upon Tyne	St Helens
Bedfordshire	Greenwich	Newham	Staffordshire
Bexley	Hackney	Norfolk	Stockport
Birmingham	Halton	Northamptonshire	Stockton-on-Tees
Blackburn with Darwen	Hammersmith and	North East Lincolnshire	Stoke-on-Trent
Blackpool	Fulham	North Lincolnshire	Suffolk
Bolton	Hampshire	North Somerset	Sunderland
Bournemouth	Haringey	North Tyneside	Surrey
Bracknell Forest	Harrow	Northumberland	Sutton
Bradford	Hartlepool	North Yorkshire	Swindon
Brent	Havering	Nottingham	Tameside
Brighton and Hove	Herefordshire	Nottinghamshire	Telford and Wrekin
Bristol	Hertfordshire	Oldham	Thurrock
Bromley	Hillingdon	Oxfordshire	Torbay
Buckinghamshire	Hounslow	Peterborough	Tower Hamlets
Bury	Isle of Wight	Plymouth	Trafford
Calderdale	Islington	Poole	Wakefield
Cambridgeshire	Kensington and Chelsea	Portsmouth	Walsall
Camden	Kent	Reading	Waltham Forest
Cheshire	Kingston upon Hull	Redbridge	Wandsworth
Cornwall	Kingston upon Thames	Redcar and Cleveland	Warrington
Coventry	London	Richmond upon Thames	Warwickshire
Croydon	Kirklees	Rochdale	West Berkshire
Cumbria	Knowsley	Rotherham	West Sussex
Darlington	Lambeth	Rutland	Westminster
Derby	Lancashire	Salford	Wigan
Derbyshire	Leeds	Sandwell	Wiltshire
Devon	Leicester	Sefton	Windsor and Maidenhead
Doncaster	Leicestershire	Sheffield	Wirral
Dorset	Lewisham	Shropshire	Wokingham
Dudley	Lincolnshire	Slough	Wolverhampton
Durham	Liverpool	Solihull	Worcestershire
Ealing	Luton	Somerset	York
East Riding of Yorkshire	Manchester	South Gloucestershire	

Boroughs, counties, cities and districts – Wales

A–C	C–M	M–R	S–Z
Blaenau Gwent	Conwy	Monmouthshire	Swansea
Bridgend	Denbighshire	Neath Port Talbot	The Vale of Glamorgan
Caerphilly	Flintshire	Newport	Torfaen
Cardiff	Gwynedd	Pembrokeshire	Wrexham
Carmarthenshire	Isle of Anglesey	Powys	
Ceredigion	Merthyr Tydfil	Rhondda Cynon Taff	

Boroughs, counties, cities and districts – Scotland

A–D	E–M	G–R	R–Z
Aberdeen City	East Ayrshire	Inverclyde	Shetland Islands
Aberdeenshire	East Dunbartonshire	Midlothian	South Ayrshire
Angus	East Lothian	Moray	South Lanarkshire
Argyll and Bute	East Renfrewshire	North Ayrshire	Stirling
City of Edinburgh	Falkirk	North Lanarkshire	The Scottish Borders
Clackmannanshire	Fife	Orkney Islands	West Dunbartonshire
Dumfries and Galloway	Glasgow City	Perth and Kinross	West Lothian
Dundee City	Highland	Renfrewshire	Western Isles

Boroughs, counties, cities and districts – Northern Ireland

A–C	C–	C–L	L–Z
Antrim	Castlereagh	County Tyrone	Lisburn
Ards	Coleraine	Craigavon	Magherafelt
Armagh	Cookstown	Derry	Moyle
Ballymena	County Antrim	Down	Newry and Mourne
Ballymoney	County Armagh	Dungannon	Newtownabbey
Banbridge	County Down	Fermanagh	North Down
Belfast	County Fermanagh	Larne	Omagh
Carrickfergus	County Londonderry	Limavady	Strabane

Rest of the world

Country name	Capital city	Citizen name	Official language(s)
Afghanistan	Kabul	Afghan	Dari (Farsi), Pashto
Albania	Tirana	Albanian	Albanian, Greek
Algeria	Algiers	Algerian	Arabic, French, Amazigh
Angola	Luanda	Angolan	Portuguese
Antigua & Barbuda	St John's City	Citizen of ...	English
Argentina	Buenos Aires	Argentine	Spanish
Armenia	Yerevan	Armenian	Armenian, Russian
Australia	Canberra	Australian	English
Austria	Vienna	Austrian	German
Azerbaijan	Baku	Azerbaijani	Azeri, Russian, Armenian
Bahamas	Nassau	Bahamian	English, Creole
Bahrain	Manama	Bahraini	Arabic, English
Bangladesh	Dhaka	Bangladeshi	Bengali (Bangla), English
Barbados	Bridgetown	Barbadian	English
Belarus	Minsk	Belarusian	Belarusian, Russian
Belgium	Brussels	Belgian	Flemish (Dutch), French, German
Belize	Belmopan	Citizen of ...	English, Spanish, Creole
Benin	Porto-Novo	Beninese	French, Fon, Yoruba
Bhutan	Thimphu	Bhutanese	Dzongkha, Tibetan
Bolivia	La Paz	Bolivian	Spanish, Quechua, Aymara
Bosnia & Herzegovina	Sarajevo	Citizen of ...	Bosnian, Croatian, Serbian
Botswana	Gaborone	Citizen of ...	English, Setswana
Brazil	Brasília	Brazilian	Portuguese
Brunei	Bandar Seri Begawan	Citizen of ...	Malay, English, Chinese
Bulgaria	Sofia	Bulgarian	Bulgarian
Burkina Faso	Ouagadougou	Burkinan	French, Sudanic African
Burma (Myanmar)	Rangoon	Burmese	Burmese
Burundi	Bujumbura	Citizen of ...	Kirundi, French, Swahili
Cambodia	Phnom Penh	Cambodian	Khmer/Cambodian
Cameroon	Yaounde	Cameroonian	French, English, Fulfulde, Ewondo
Canada	Ottawa	Canadian	English, French
Central African Republic	Bangui	Citizen of ...	French, Sangho
Chad	N'Djamena	Chadian	French, Arabic
Chile	Santiago de Chile	Chilean	Spanish, English, Mapuche, Aymara, Quecha

Country name	Capital city	Citizen name	Official language(s)
China	Beijing	Chinese	Mandarin (Putonghua),
Colombia	Bogotá	Colombian	Spanish
Comoros	Moroni	Comoran	French, Arabic, Comoran
Congo (Democratic Republic of)	Kinshasa	Citizen of …	French, Lingala, Kingwana, Kikongo, Tshiluba
Congo (Republic of)	Brazzaville	Congolese	French, Lingala, Munukutuba, Kikongo
Costa Rica	San José	Costa Rican	Spanish
Croatia	Zagreb	Croat	Croatian, Serbian, Italian, Slovene, Slovac, German
Cuba	Havana	Cuban	Spanish
Cyprus	Nicosia	Cypriot	Greek, Turkish, English
Czech Republic	Prague	Czech	Czech
Denmark	Copenhagen	Dane	Danish, English, German
Djibouti	Djibouti	Djiboutian	French, Arabic, Somali, Afar
Dominican Republic	Santo Domingo	Citizen of …	Spanish
East Timor	Dila	East Timorese	Tetum, Portugese
Ecuador	Quito	Ecuadorean	Spanish
Egypt	Cairo	Egyptian	Arabic, English, French
El Salvador	San Salvador	Salvadorean	Spanish
Equatorial Guinea	Malabo	Equatorian Guinean	Spanish, French, Fang, Bubi, Ibo
Eritrea	Asmara	Eritrean	Tigrinya, Tigre Arabic, English
Estonia	Tallinn	Estonian	Estonian, Russian
Ethiopia	Addis Ababa	Ethiopian	Amharic, Tigrinya, Oromigna, Somali, Arabic, English, Guaragigna
Fiji	Suva	Fijian	English, Fijian, Hindu
Finland	Helsinki	Finn	Finnish, Swedish, Lapp, Russian
France	Paris	Frenchman/woman	French
Gabon	Libreville	Gabonese	French, Fang, Myene, Bateke, Bapoumon
Gambia	Banjul	Gambian	English, Mandinka, Wolof, Fula
Georgia	Tbilisi	Georgian	Georgian, Russian, Armenian, Abkhaz, Azeri
Germany	Berlin	German	German

Country name	Capital city	Citizen name	Official language(s)
Ghana	Accra	Ghanaian	English, Akan, Moshi-Dagomba, Ewe, Ga
Greece	Athens	Greek	Greek
Grenada	St George's	Grenadian	English
Guatemala	Guatemala City	Guatemalan	Spanish
Guinea	Conakry	Guinean	French
Guinea – Bissau	Bissau	Citizen of ...	Portuguese, Crioulo
Guyana	Georgetown	Guyanese	English, Ameridian Dialects, Creole, Hindi, Urdu
Haiti	Port au Prince	Haitian	French, Creole
Honduras	Tegucigalpa	Honduran	Spanish
Hungary	Budapest	Hungarian	Hungarian
Iceland	Reykjavik	Icelander	Icelandic, English, Danish
India	New Delhi	Indian	Hindi, English, Bengali, Kannada, Kashmiri, Marathi, Oriya, Punjabi, Sindhi, Sanskrit, Tamil, Telugu, Urdu & many others
Indonesia	Jakarta	Indonesian	Bahasa Indonesian, English & many others
Iran	Tehran	Iranian	Persian (Farsi), Azeri, Kurdish Arabic
Iraq	Baghdad	Iraqi	Arabic, Kurdish, Assyrian, Armenian, Turkoman
Ireland	Dublin	Irish Citizen	Irish, English
Israel	Tel Aviv	Israeli	Hebrew, Arabic, Yiddish
Italy	Rome	Italian	Italian
Ivory Coast	Yamoussoukro	Citizen of ...	French, Dioula
Jamaica	Kingston	Jamaican	Patois English
Japan	Tokyo	Japanese	Japanese
Jordan	Amman	Jordanian	Arabic, English
Kazakhstan	Astana	Kazakh	Kazakh, Russian
Kenya	Nairobi	Kenyan	English, Kiswahili
Korea, North	Pyongyang	Citizen of the DPRK	Korean
Korea, South	Seoul	South Korean	Korean
Kuwait	Kuwait	Kuwaiti	Arabic, English
Kyrgyzstan	Bishkek	Kyrgyz / Russian	Kyrgyz, Russian
Laos	Vientiane	Lao	Lao
Latvia	Riga	Latvian	Latvian, Russian
Lebanon	Beirut	Lebanese	Arabic, French, English, Armenian

Country name	Capital city	Citizen name	Official language(s)
Lesotho	Maseru	Citizen of ...	English, Sesotho
Liberia	Monrovia	Liberian	English
Libya	Tripoli	Libyan	Arabic, Italian, English
Liechtenstein	Vaduz	Citizen of ...	German
Lithuania	Vilnius	Lithuanian	Lithuanian
Luxembourg	Luxembourg	Luxembourger	Luxembourgish, German, French
Macedonia	Skopje	Macedonian	Macedonian, Albanian, Turkish, Serbian
Madagascar	Antananarivo	Citizen of ...	Malagasy, French
Malawi	Lilongwe	Malawian	English, Chichewa
Malaysia	Kuala Lumpur	Citizen of ...	Bahasa Malaysian, English, Chinese, Tamil
Maldives	Malé	Maldivian	Dhivehi, English
Mali	Bamako	Malian	French, Bambara
Malta	Valletta	Maltese	Maltese, English
Mauritania	Nouakchott	Mauritanian	Hassaniya Arabic, French
Mauritius	Port Louis	Mauritian	English, French, Creole
Mexico	Mexico City	Mexican	Spanish
Micronesia	Palikir	Micronesian	English
Moldova	Chisinau	Moldovan	Moldovan, Russian, Gagauz, Ukranian
Monaco	Monaco	Monegasque	French, English, Italian, Monegasque
Mongolia	Ulaanbaatar	Mongolian	Khalk, Mongol, Kazakh
Morocco	Rabat	Moroccan	Arabic, Berber
Mozambique	Maputo	Mozambican	Portuguese, Makhuwa, Tsonga, Lomwe, Sena
Namibia	Windhoek	Namibian	English, Afrikaans
Nepal	Kathmandu	Nepalese	Nepali and many others
Netherlands	The Hague	Dutchman / woman	Dutch
New Zealand	Wellington	New Zealander	English, Maori
Nicaragua	Managua	Nicaraguan	Spanish
Niger	Niamey	Citizen of ...	French, Arabic
Nigeria	Abuja	Nigerian	English, Hausa, Yoruba, Igbo (Ibo), Fulani
Norway	Oslo	Norwegian	Bokmål, Nynorsk, Sami
Oman	Muscat	Omani	Arabic, English, Fasi, Baluchi, Urdu
Pakistan	Islamabad	Pakistani	Punjabi, Sindhi, Pashtun, Urdu, English,

Country name	Capital city	Citizen name	Official language(s)
Panama	Panama City	Panamanian	Spanish, English
Papua New Guinea	Port Moresby	Papua New Guinean	Pidgin, Hiri, Motu, English & many others
Paraguay	Asuncion	Paraguayan	Spanish, Guarani
Peru	Lima	Peruvian	Spanish, Quechua, Aymara
Philippines	Metro Manila	Filipino / Filipina	Filipino, English, Tagalog & many others
Poland	Warsaw	Pole	Polish
Portugal	Lisbon	Portuguese	Portuguese
Puerto Rico	San Juan	Puerto Rican	Spanish, English
Qatar	Doha	Qatari	Arabic, English, Urdu
Romania	Bucharest	Romanian	Romanian, English, French, German
Russia	Moscow	Russian	Russian & many others
Rwanda	Kigali	Rwandese	Kinyarwanda, French, English, Kiswahili
Samoa	Apia	Samoan	Samoan, English
Saudi Arabia	Riyadh	Saudi Arabian	Arabic, English
Senegal	Dakar	Senegalese	French, Wolof, Mandinka
Serbia and Montenegro	Belgrade	Citizen of ...	Serbian, Albanian, Hungarian
Seychelles	Victoria	Citizen of ...	English, French, Creole
Sierra Leone	Freetown	Sierra Leonean	English, Mende, Temnel
Singapore	Singapore	Singaporean	Chinese, Malay, Tamil, English
Slovakia	Bratislava	Slovak	Slovak, Hungarian
Slovenia	Ljubljana	Slovene	Slovene, Italian, Hungarian, English
Solomon Islands	Honoria	Solomon Islander	English, Pidgin & many others
Somalia	Mogadishu	Somali	Somali, Arabic
South Africa	Pretoria	South African	Afrikaans, English, Xhosa, Sotho, Swazi, Tsonga, Zulu & many others
Spain	Madrid	Spaniard	Spanish, Catalan, Galician, Basque
Sri Lanka	Colombo	Citizen of ...	Sinhalese, Tamil, English
St Kitts & Nevis	Basseterre	Citizen of ...	English
St Lucia	Castries	St Lucian	English, Patois
St Vincent	Kingstown	Vincentian	English

Country name	Capital city	Citizen name	Official language(s)
Sudan	Khartoum	Sudanese	Arabic, Nubian, Ta Bedawie & many others
Surinam	Paramaribo	Surinamer	Dutch, English, Creole
Swaziland	Mbabane	Swazi	English, siSwati
Sweden	Stockholm	Swede	Swedish, English
Switzerland	Berne	Swiss	Swiss German, French, Italian, Romansch
Syria	Damascus	Syrian	Arabic, Kurdish, Armenian
Tajikistan	Dushanbe	Tajik	Russian
Taiwan	Taipei	Chinese / Taiwanese	Chinese, Taiwanese, Minnanyu, Hakka
Tanzania	Dar es Salaam	Tanzanian	Kiswahili, English, Arabic
Thailand	Bangkok	Thai	Thai, English & others
Togo	Lome	Togolese	French, Kabiye & others
Tonga	Nuku'alofa	Tongan	Tongan, English
Trinidad and Tobago	Port of Spain	Citizen of …	English, Spanish
Turkmenistan	Ashgabat	Turkmen	Russian, Turkmen
Tunisia	Tunis	Tunisian	Arabic, French
Turkey	Ankara	Turk	Turkish, Kurdish, Armenian, Greek
Tuvalu	Funafuti	Citizen of …	Tuvaluan, English
Uganda	Kampala	Ugandan	English, Luganda & others
Ukraine	Kiev	Ukrainian	Ukrainian, Russian, Polish, Romanian, Hungarian
United Arab Emirates	Abu Dhabi	Citizen of …	Arabic, English
United States of America	Washington D.C.	Citizen of …	English, Spanish
Uruguay	Montevideo	Uruguayan	Spanish, Portunol, Brazilero
Uzbekistan	Tashkent	Uzbeki	Uzbek, Russian, Tajik
Vanuatu	Port Villa	Citizen of …	Bislama, English, French & many others
Vatican City (Holy See)	Vatican City	Citizen of …	Italian, Latin, French
Venezuela	Caracas	Venezuelan	Spanish
Vietnam	Hanoi	Vietnamese	Vietnamese, French
Yemen	Sanaá	Yemeni	Arabic
Zambia	Lusaka	Zambian	English, Bemba, Kaonda, Lozi, Lunda & many others
Zimbabwe	Greater Harare	Zimbabwean	English, Shona, Ndebele

Keys

KEY TO SPELLING RULES

Red words are wrong. **Black** words are correct.

~   Add the suffix or word directly to the main word, without a space or hyphen
    e.g. ash ~en ~tray → ashen ashtray

~- Add a hyphen to the main word before adding the next word
    e.g. blow ~-dry → blow-dry

~| Leave a space between the main word and the next word
    e.g. decimal ~| place → decimal place

+   By finding this word in its **correct** alphabetical order, you can find related words
    e.g. about+ → about-face about-turn

*   Draws attention to words that may be confused

TM Means the word is a trademark.

KEY TO SUFFIXES AND COMPOUNDS

These rules are explained on pages ix to x.

1 Keep the word the same before adding **ed, er, est, ing**
    e.g. cool[1] → **cooled, cooler, coolest, cooling**

2 Take off final **e** before adding **ed, er, est, ing**
    e.g. fine[2] → **fined, finer, finest, fining**

3 Double final consonant before adding **ed, er, est, ing**
    e.g. thin[3] → **thinned, thinner, thinnest, thinning**

4 Change final **y** to **i** before adding **ed, er, es, est, ly, ness**
    e.g. tidy[4] → **tidied, tidier, tidies, tidiest, tidily, tidiness**
    Keep final **y** before adding **ing**
    e.g. **tidying**

5 Add **es** instead of **s** to the end of the word
    e.g. bunch[5] → **bunches**

6 Change final **f** to **ve** before adding **s**
    e.g. calf[6] → **calves**